Praise for *Color Blind*

"Very entertaining. . . . Baseball fans will cherish this book."
—*Booklist* (starred review) and a Top Ten Sports Book of the Year

"*Color Blind* is an amazing story of black and white that should be read all over." —John Thorn, official historian for Major League Baseball and author of *Baseball in the Garden of Eden*

"A tale as fantastic as it is true, as American as racism and baseball. . . . Dunkel's extensive research shows—there's enough detail here to satisfy the most rabid fan—and his portraits of Troupe, Paige, and Churchill are lively and warm." —*Boston Globe*

"A terrific book. . . . It is funny, it is sad, it is spellbinding, required reading for anyone who loves baseball, who loves a vivid story well told. . . . *Color Blind* is crammed with characters . . . laced with joy, rocked by sadness, framed by the civil rights struggle." —*Philadelphia Daily News*

"Absorbing. . . . Dunkel writes with a passion and flair that matches the gritty, hardscrabble North Dakota landscape and culture of the Great Depression. His meticulous research and clever writing blows the dust off a forgotten—but important—chapter in baseball history. A fascinating addition to baseball's library." —*Tampa Tribune*

"A captivating recollection of the Bismarck, North Dakota integrated baseball team that won the 1935 semipro national championship. . . . Delivers an important rendering of a too-little-remembered challenge to American society's segregated practices. Strongly recommended."
—*Library Journal* (starred review)

"The colorful yarn of an improbably integrated team's wild days of independent baseball during the Great Depression. . . . A well-told account of a fascinating, and forgotten, chapter in the history of America's national pastime." —*Kirkus Reviews*

"High recommendation. It's a thrilling story. If you love hidden histories, you'll love this book!" —Dave Zirin, Edge of Sports Radio

"Painstakingly researched. . . . [here] is Paige in all his maddening glory . . . against a sepia backdrop of drought, dust storms, and swarms of grasshoppers at the depth of the Depression."
—*Washington Independent Review of Books*

COLOR BLIND

COLOR BLIND

THE FORGOTTEN TEAM
THAT BROKE BASEBALL'S
COLOR LINE

TOM
DUNKEL

Grove Press
New York

"Aren't you done with that book yet?" she would ask, almost weekly. "It must be a long book."

For Mom, who pitched a perfect game into the ninth inning of her life, but missed this Opening Day.

And is there anything that can tell more about
an American summer than, say, the smell of
the wooden bleachers in a small-town baseball park,
the resinous, sultry, and exciting smell of old dry wood.

—Thomas Wolfe

Be an opener of doors for such as come after thee.

—Ralph Waldo Emerson

CONTENTS

PART THREE: TESTED TOGETHER

PREFACE

BEFORE 42

On April 15, 1947, a corner of the earth shook: to be precise, a grimy corner of Flatbush Avenue in the borough of Brooklyn, New York. That chilly afternoon, Jackie Roosevelt Robinson—son of a sharecropper and grandson of a slave; the coal-black ballplayer who, in the words of writer Roger Kahn, "burned with a dark fire"—put on a white wool shirt with *Dodgers* emblazoned across the chest in royal blue. On his back: number 42.

The United States that April was a nation cleaved in half. Segregated restrooms, whites-only restaurants, poll taxes, and voter literacy tests were the law across much of the land. A person of color who wanted to attend a Major League baseball game in Saint Louis had to sit in a designated section of the right field bleachers. It would be another year before President Harry Truman integrated the military, seven years until the Supreme Court drove a stake through the heart of separate-but-equal education. Due to baseball's status as then-undisputed heavyweight champ of all sports, the mere act of Robinson donning the same uniform as twenty-four Caucasian teammates was freighted with significance. Mixed-race baseball represented a prying open of the American Dream, a peek at the prospect of full citizenship for all. Far from New York, people took note. An editorial writer at Wisconsin's unheralded *Manitowoc Herald-Times* felt compelled to sit down at his typewriter and peck away: "It is to baseball's credit that one of the highest walls in the way of real liberation of the Negro has been breached. One of the last and most uncompromising camps of those who adhere to the dogma of white supremacy has been captured. Good Luck, Jackie Robinson."

Not everyone shared those sentiments. Robinson endured innumerable taunts and death threats that season, stoically playing on. By doing so, he and Brooklyn Dodgers General Manager Branch Rickey, the bow-tie-wearing mastermind of this so-called "great experiment," together erased baseball's color line. Robinson's legacy is such that in March 1984 he was posthumously awarded the Presidential Medal of Freedom, putting him in the heady company of Jonas Salk, Martha Graham, General Omar Bradley, Martin Luther King Jr., and the other select few overachievers who've received the nation's highest civilian honor. In a White House ceremony, President Ronald Reagan said Robinson "struck a mighty blow for equality, freedom, and the American way of life." Major League Baseball not only inducted him into the Hall of Fame but took the unprecedented step of retiring number 42 on every team—its way of paying eternal tribute to the shattering of a seemingly impregnable wall of exclusion.

After Robinson crossed the line, obstacles outside baseball soon began to fall as well: in the courts, in the classroom, at the lunch counter. Those barriers had cracks in them prior to 1947, some large enough for men and women to squeeze through, often without fanfare though rarely without some attendant risk. One group of athletes defied the norms of their sport and their society just like Jackie Robinson; but they did it back in the 1930s, when he was still in high school. They played on a color-blind baseball team: half black, half white. They wore the baggy uniforms then considered fashionable. They swung heavy, thick-handled bats perhaps better suited for beating rugs. They fielded with primitive gloves that were just a cut above barbecue mitts. But their team photo could have been taken yesterday.

These were time travelers of a sort, ambassadors from the multiracial future. It might have made more sense for them to have arrived by rocket ship from another planet. Instead, they gravitated one by one to a baseball diamond scratched into the dark soil of the Great Plains, some 1,500 miles from Brooklyn. Out where wheat waves and cornstalks reach for the sky, it was as if a mysterious hand had planted some magic seeds—seeds that would grow to produce a crop of ballplayers the likes of which this country had never seen.

PART ONE

COMING TOGETHER

1

PRAIRIELAND
OF OPPORTUNITY

The theme of the 1933 World's Fair in Chicago was "A Century of Progress" and during its extended run 48 million people poured through the turnstiles. So much to see: that odd rear-engine automobile, pink-cheeked babies snoozing in incubators, a Televisor contraption that—*Honey, can you believe this?*—displayed moving pictures beamed from remote locations. So much to do: walk through a facsimile Belgian village, take a spin in the Sky Ride cable cars, sample Miracle Whip dressing dispensed by Kraft Food's newly patented "emulsifying machine." The World's Fair offered the masses a glimpse of a bright future personified by Westinghouse Electric's Willie the Robot. Bark a command into the telephone receiver by Willie's side and he would obediently shake your hand, stand up, sit down, even smoke a cigarette.

Unfortunately, when the gates closed at day's end too many fairgoers had to leave behind the wondrous, glass-walled "House of Tomorrow" and return home to the wearisome reality of the Great Depression: leftovers again for supper and unpaid bills piling high. One in four Americans had no job in 1933. Large swaths of the country were backsliding from industrial-age splendor into crippled-economy squalor. An editor at the *Chicago Tribune* decided his fellow citizens could use a pick-me-up diversion. He proposed a special sporting event held in conjunction with the Century of

Progress, a midsummer exhibition in which the best baseball players from the American and National leagues would square off and do battle. On July 6, Chicago's Comiskey Park hosted a one-time-only "All-Star Game" and 47,595 people purchased tickets. The American League prevailed, 4–2, thanks in part to a two-run homer swatted by the New York Yankees' irrepressible Babe Ruth. Having surpassed the rosiest of expectations, the All-Star Game became an annual affair. (That home-run ball Ruth deposited in the right field bleachers at Comiskey sold at auction in 2006 for $805,000.)

Three weeks after the All-Star festivities, twenty-year-old Quincy Troupe boarded a Lockheed Orion single-engine airplane at Chicago Municipal Airport. The Orion was a puddle jumper, holding just six passengers plus sacks of mail. Troupe had a man's body, with 210 pounds of muscle drawn tight on his six-foot-three-inch frame, but the lingering boy in him was betrayed by a cherubic baby face. He had never been on a plane before. A friend recommended "a stiff highball" as a cure for his jitters. Troupe had never taken a drink of alcohol before. Anxiety trumped his Christian upbringing and he sipped a preflight cocktail. Around midnight the tiny plane taxied down the runway and angled skyward, bound for a stopover in Minneapolis, then a quick hop to Bismarck, North Dakota. Troupe carried with him a small leather case. It contained his ukulele. His first spare moment in Bismarck he intended to buy sheet music for a new song he'd heard, a melancholy ballad called "Moonglow" that Benny Goodman and Duke Ellington would eventually grab hold of and turn into dueling hit records:

> It must have been moonglow, way up in the blue
> It must have been moonglow that led me straight to you.

Quincy Troupe wasn't a traveling musician. He was a professional baseball player: a *black* professional baseball player, which meant he wasn't going to be appearing in an All-Star Game anytime soon. There were gaping holes in the "Century of Progress" when it came to race relations. To be black in America was to be a second-class citizen at best and, in some corners, viewed as less human than Willie the Robot. Baseball contorted itself like the rest of society, functioning as an agent of unspoken apartheid. The major and minor leagues had been purely white enterprises for nearly fifty years. Up until that morning, Troupe was a switch-hitting backup catcher for the Chicago American Giants of the Negro National League. The book on him was that he had a good head for the game, plus a bazooka arm and lively bat. Raw meat, but grade A. On top of that—sportswriters, beware—he was a Golden Gloves boxer.

In June the Chicago American Giants had gone on the road to face the Pittsburgh Crawfords. The Giants' second baseman was hurt, so Troupe filled in for him and got the nod to play both ends of a Saturday doubleheader. The bad news was that the Crawfords' starting pitcher for game two that afternoon happened to be Satchel Paige. There arguably was no one better in all of baseball, black or white. Paige had a whooping crane's physique and an unortho-dox high-kick delivery, but he threw with supernatural ferocity. A teammate once remarked that trying to catch his fastball "was like catching a bullet."

Satchel Paige was roughly in his mid-twenties, part of the Paige mystique being a missing birth certificate and his uncertain age. Already hailed as king of the Negro Leagues, he was still a legend in the making. Paige brought to the mound a jazz musi-cian's flair for improvisation and showmanship: Louis Armstrong in spikes. He drew upon a dizzying array of pitches, mostly varia-tions on a head-of-the-class fastball and a good-enough-to-get-by curve. He gave them nicknames as if they were old friends, which they were: Be Ball, Jump Ball, Trouble Ball, Nothin' Ball, Wobbly Ball, Hurry-Up Ball, Bat Dodger, and Two-Hoop Blooper, not to mention his signature Hesitation Pitch, in which Paige's body would momentarily freeze mid-motion, confounding hitters. Nearly every batter dreaded having to stand in against "Ol' Satch." Quincy Troupe showed no fear in Pittsburgh. He made an out his first at bat, but the second time up pulverized a knee-high fastball. It cleared the right field fence as if shot from a cannon, ricocheting off the side of Memorial Hospital, more than 400 feet from home plate.

Paige stared in disbelief as the boy catcher circled the bases. Legends are seldom stunned into silence.

That night Troupe dined at the Crawford Grill, a restaurant owned by Gus Greenlee, Pittsburgh's high-profile rogue and highest-profile black man. The Grill was more than a restaurant. It was an all-purpose pleasure palace with a busy bar, a live-entertainment nightclub, and upstairs rooms where love could be discreetly bought and sold. Greenlee also managed a stable of boxers (notably light-heavyweight champion John Henry Lewis) and presided over a thriving numbers racket, all of which had provided him the disposable income to buy the Crawfords baseball team. A big man who puffed big cigars, Gus Greenlee was something of a Robin Hood figure in Pittsburgh's Hill District. A shady character to be sure, but one who employed hundreds of people, ran soup lines, and gave generously to hospitals and the NAACP. Black athletes and fans flocked to his Grill after games. No surprise, then, when Satchel Paige also stopped by for a bite to eat that evening. He broke into a grin upon spotting the youngster who'd cracked the wall-banger home run off him.

"What's your name?" Paige inquired, not that he'd remember. He had total command of his pitches, but people's names flummoxed him. He solved that problem by calling almost everybody Bo'.

"Quincy Troupe," Troupe answered softly, nerves jangling.

"I shouldn't *ever* forget that name after what happened today!" Paige bellowed, playing to the cluster of teammates and hangers-on who, as usual, were cruising in his wake. He cackled, then lowered his voice, turning uncharacteristically avuncular.

"I've got a tip for you, Quincy," said Paige. "You can go a long way in this game if you just listen to what the other players tell you. Don't be a know-it-all, take it easy with the girls, and lay off the liquor."

This was odd counsel coming from Satch, a man with a hard-earned reputation for living large and bending every rule that ever got in his way. He was no stranger to a stiff highball. Troupe, on the other hand, had the demeanor of a lifelong Eagle Scout: diligent, modest, and polite almost to a fault. "I'm more than grateful and thankful for the advice," Troupe replied, swooning inside. The great Satchel Paige had gone out of his way to impart wisdom to a kid opponent. To *him!* Troupe immediately placed the lanky pitcher upon a pedestal from which he would never tumble.

That home run in Pittsburgh proved to be the highlight of Troupe's tenure with the Chicago American Giants. In truth, there weren't many big moments from which to choose. He was glued to the bench, a callow understudy to an older, established catcher who would sit out a game every week or so to rest his achy legs. Limited playing time wasn't Troupe's only frustration. Like a lot of Negro League teams, the Giants had financial difficulties. These were hard times. A couple of Troupe's paychecks had been delayed. As a result, his ears pricked up shortly after that Pittsburgh road trip when someone told him about a baseball opportunity worth investigating. In Nowhere, North Dakota.

Quincy Troupe—the youngest of ten children—was unique in his own way, just as Satchel Paige and Babe Ruth were in theirs. The closest he came to cussing was "doggone," and he wrote letters home to his mother in Saint Louis on a steady basis—almost saintly behavior for a pro ballplayer. Although city bred, there was a touch of hayseed in him and a lot of mama's boy. He'd begun baseball life playing for his hometown heroes, the Negro League's St. Louis Stars. That team also had money troubles. In the waning days of the 1931 season Troupe's teammates on the Stars sent him to inquire about the possibility of getting paid their overdue wages, partly just to see if the rookie would be gullible enough to actually do it. Dick Kent had risen from shoeshine boy to co-owner of the Stars. He also was the sole owner of several cab companies and a black newspaper, the *St. Louis American*. He didn't get that far on personality.

Troupe tapped on Kent's office door. The boss opened up and glared at him. "What you want, boy?"

"Sir, the fellows asked me to come for the balance you owe us," Troupe meekly responded.

Kent calmly walked over to his desk, slid open a drawer, and pulled out a gun. "You young bastard," he growled, waving the pistol for effect. "I'll whip your head flat if you say another word about money!" End of conversation. Also the end of the St. Louis Stars. Within a few days the players walked away and the team ceased operations.

It was now two years later and Quincy Troupe, marginally wiser in the ways of the world, sat gazing out the window of a pipsqueak airplane. Down below the twinkle of Chicago faded to black; stockyards, the Loop, and a whole city of big shoulders were swallowed by the night. He had signed on with a semipro team in Bismarck, in the process swapping office towers for grain silos, trading the glare of neon for the glimmer of a million stars. Team manager Neil Churchill was an automobile dealer with a runaway passion for baseball. And baseball, Troupe would soon learn, provided a welcome outlet for community pride in Depression-battered North Dakota. It was the weapon of choice for grudge matches between rival towns, such an integral part of civic life that Troupe didn't have to pay for his plane ticket. Northwest Airways provided complimentary transportation as a goodwill gesture to Bismarck baseball fans. Keep the faith. Help was on the way.

It's impossible to be half pregnant, but to play semiprofessional baseball was another matter, though almost as oxymoronic. Up until about World War II, the pro-amateur dividing line could be nonsensically blurry. Churchill had visions of building a powerhouse lineup capable of holding its own against the best minor league teams, and maybe a few in the Major Leagues. That kind of quality building material didn't exist in North Dakota. Finding premium ballplayers would require thinking outside the box, outside the state. Outside the northern European, family-farm gene pool. To that end, he'd begun cherry-picking players from the struggling Negro Leagues. This was Neil Churchill's emulsifying machine, if you will: an efficacious blending of black and white, Miracle Whip baseball. God knows what cash cow he was milking. Churchill didn't pinch pennies. He offered Troupe $175 a month, $35 above what he made with the Chicago American Giants. What's more, he guaranteed Troupe the starting catcher's position. Churchill told a *Bismarck Tribune* reporter he'd landed "the black Babe Ruth." That was the car salesman in him talking: no-money-down, zero-percent-financing hyperbole. Troupe knew it, even if *Tribune* readers did not. He had yet to prove himself on a ball field day in, day out. This would be his chance.

The money was good. Yet money alone couldn't lure a twenty-year-old black man to one of the whitest, poorest states in America. It took something more visceral and magnetic: true love. No woman crooked a finger and gave Quincy Troupe that sly, come-hither stare. He was flying west, through the darkness and into the dawn, primarily for the joy of playing baseball, that notorious heartbreaker of a game.

It must have been moonglow, way up in the blue
It must have been moonglow that led me straight to you
I still hear you sayin', "Dear one, hold me fast."
And I keep on prayin', "Oh, Lord, please make this last."

2

GRASSHOPPERS AND
HICKORY STICKS

Bismarck clings to the eastern bank of the Missouri River, positioned just below the midsection of North Dakota, about where a belly button would be if the state had one. It's the capital and, according to the 1930 census, had 11,090 residents: huge by Great Plains standards, but not enough bodies to fill Chicago's Comiskey Park to a quarter of capacity. Mandan sits on the western side of the Missouri, directly across from Bismarck and less than half the size: its blue-collar, tomboy sister city. When John Steinbeck drove across the country in 1960, gathering material for the book that would become *Travels with Charley*, this run of the Missouri River bowled him over. "Here is where the map should fold. Here is the boundary between east and west," he wrote. "On the Bismarck side it is eastern landscape, eastern grass, with the look and smell of eastern America. Across the Missouri on the Mandan side, it is pure west, with brown grass and water scorings and small outcrops. The two sides of the river might well be a thousand miles apart."

Geography played a key role in selection of the government seat. In addition to being centrally located, Bismarck had river and rail access. Geography also played a role in perception. People farther east—residents of Jamestown, Grand Forks, Fargo, and Valley City—felt a kinship with Minneapolis–Saint Paul. They fancied themselves urbane, envisioning the map of North Dakota almost as stages in the evolution of man. The smaller, unrefined burgs sprinkled along the Missouri Slope that ran west of Bismarck—Minot, Dickinson, Williston, Glen Ullin, and other incorporated miseries—figuratively scurried on all fours. Bismarck was a knuckle-dragging hybrid, the gateway to the frontier. Towns nearest Minnesota, so the logic went, walked blessedly upright.

North Dakota entered the union in 1889 as a dry state, an issue that split along the lines of dominant ethnic groups. Those of dour Norwegian ancestry generally favored Prohibition. Those of German or Russian extraction enjoyed lifting the occasional glass. The "dries" were led by Elizabeth Preston Anderson, a whirlwind scold who became a Woman's Christian Temperance Union activist in the 1880s and would stalk the halls of the state legislature for almost fifty years. Mrs. Anderson didn't confine her crusading to demon rum. She successfully lobbied for laws that criminalized prostitution, gambling, and Sunday baseball. Her more liberal side advocated on behalf of child labor laws and women's suffrage. Thus the tightly corseted heart of Elizabeth Preston Anderson harbored some of the dichotomy that animated North Dakota, where progressive prairie populism tried to peacefully coexist with Bible-based conservatism. Praise Jesus! But let us also give thanks for the grain co-op.

The temperance lobby wielded a heavy hammer in North Dakota even after Prohibition ended in December 1933 with passage of the Twenty-First Amendment. Beer made an immediate comeback in the state (though judiciously watered down to the level of 3.2 percent alcohol), but it would take another three years for hard liquor sales to become legal. Some counties stayed dry until 1947, and a few towns lasted into the 1980s. That's not to say drinkers stood idly by, abstaining. Moonshine had a long tradition of flowing as wild and as free as the mighty Missouri. Millions of gallons with syndicate connections seeped out of Minnesota or poured across the Canadian border. Minot, a straight highway shoot from Saskatchewan, got dubbed "Little Chicago." In 1910

an illicit gin mill got busted in Mandan. It was being run by the
police commissioner. Do-it-yourselfers everywhere stoked basement and backyard stills. When Fargo authorities raided one such
loaded home, the local paper poetically remarked it was equipped
to "turn out 30 gallons of bliss and forgetfulness each 24 hours."
North Dakota had enough moonshine action that federal agents
set up shop inside the Bismarck post office.

In the 1930s twin bridges arced over the wide Missouri, con-
necting Bismarck and Mandan. One bridge handled trains; the
other, cars and trucks. Theoretically, that's how traffic moved.
Under cover of darkness, however, the boldest of bootleggers would
let the air out of their car tires, flip off their headlights, and bounce
along the rail ties, praying a locomotive wasn't barreling down the
same track at exactly the same time. Hooch business was especially
good along the Strip, an unincorporated buffer between the river
and Mandan proper. It was chockablock with pool halls, dance
clubs, and "blind pigs," the colorful patois for speakeasies. In those
days the Missouri River served as a demarcation line separating the
Central and Mountain time zones. If you lived in Bismarck, there
always was a bonus hour of late-night fun to be had on the Strip.
The populace took full advantage.

North Dakota had other rough edges. The Heart River fed
into the Missouri on the outskirts of Mandan. Dams had yet to
be built that would control river flow. Long after spring thaw, the
narrow, twisting Heart remained treacherous. Swimmers liked to
ride the currents, but did so at their peril. Drownings were common. Bodies sometimes bloated and then sank before they could
be retrieved. The sheriff's department would attempt to dislodge
those corpses with controlled drops of dynamite. John Sakariassen
grew up in Mandan in the 1930s and never forgot the eerie blasts
that punctuated his childhood. "It would happen a couple of times
a summer," he says. "When you heard that booming, you thought,
'Oh, my gosh, I wonder who drowned?' Because it was a small town
and everybody knew everybody."

Water posed another kind of threat: periodically not enough fell from the sky. Between 1929 and 1939, North Dakota endured nine years of below-average precipitation. In 1936, less than 9 inches of rain was recorded. Crops wilted with numbing regularity. The prolonged drought produced epic dust storms. Drifts of desertlike sand buried barbed-wire fences, allowing livestock to roam at will. Cattle lucky enough to escape dehydration choked on dust.

The Depression hit the Great Plains in the early 1920s, ahead of the rest of the country, which had the luxury of marinating in prosperity a few extra years. North Dakota historian Elwyn Robinson observed that the state had a tragic habit of repeating what he called the "too-much mistake"—perhaps a by-product of its land-grant roots and buoyant pioneer spirit. Whatever its genesis, Robinson detected a pattern of gluttonous growth and raging ambition that frequently lead to a humbling comeuppance. Such was the case in the Depression. Farms expanded too fast, fueled by easy credit. Overproduction eventually caused crop prices to crash, triggering a foreclosure epidemic.

All that played out against the backdrop of a drought-and-dust weather cycle. Then came the kidney punch: a biblical invasion of grasshoppers that flourished in the arid, windy climate. The infiltration began in the spring of 1931 and didn't abate for nearly a decade. At their worst in the mid-1930s, "hoppers" covered more than two-thirds of the state. Bugs as much as four inches deep squirmed over the landscape, nibbling wash hanging on clotheslines, congealing in airborne swarms that blocked the sun and caused streetlights to flick on at midday. Living conditions were every bit as bleak as in Oklahoma, poster child of the Dust Bowl.

Meriwether Lewis and William Clark slept here. In November 1804 the two explorers and their Corps of Discovery mates pushed deep into the Missouri River valley. There they hunkered down for the winter, felling trees and erecting a temporary encampment about forty-five miles north of the spot that would someday be the city of Bismarck. A tribe of Mandan Indians befriended the newcomers, showing them how to secure food and keep warm as temperatures nosedived to forty degrees below zero. Captain Clark noted in his journal, "more Cold than I thought it possible for man to endure." Had the Mandan been able to foresee what complications whites would bring to the virgin West, they might have let Lewis and Clark fumble around till they collapsed in a frostbitten heap. As it was, the Indians provided more than butternut squash and succor. Sakakawea, nineteenth-century go-to girl, went a step further (make that several thousand steps further) and guided the expedition onward to the Pacific Ocean. Others followed in the Corps of Discovery's footprints. Trappers and fur traders materialized, then adventurers such as ornithologist John James Audubon. He wandered up the Missouri in 1843, listening to the hoofbeats of buffalo for miles on end "roaring like the long continued roll of a hundred drums."

The drums were doomed to fall silent. The year 1873 was pivotal. That June the inaugural Northern Pacific Railway train chugged into Edwinton, a scrappy settlement that had taken root along the Missouri River. A month later the town fathers decided to adopt a new name in honor of the German chancellor Otto von Bismarck, who'd never set foot upon the continent. The switch to "Bismarck" was a railroad-engineered marketing ploy. The hope was that von Bismarck would be flattered and, for some inexplicable reason, elect to show his gratitude by funding the continued expansion of train service in North America. The chancellor didn't bite. But the townfolk opted to remain Bismarck even without the benefit of his largesse, and the Northern Pacific executives managed to tap other sources of capital. Navvies laid more track, creeping deeper into Indian land.

The federal government felt obliged to protect railroad crews that were the vanguard of westward migration. In 1872 Fort Abraham Lincoln sprang up five miles south of Bismarck. Lieutenant

Colonel George Armstrong Custer soon arrived with six companies of the dashing Seventh Cavalry. In the summer of 1874 Custer led a large show-of-force reconnaissance mission. They traversed 833 miles of the Black Hills (terrain that lies within present-day Wyoming and South Dakota) in sixty days, ostensibly scouting locations for additional outposts. There was, however, an ulterior motive: to confirm rumors that gold had been discovered. Indeed, it had. Custer sent word back to Fort Lincoln: "I have on my table forty or fifty small particles of pure gold . . . most of it obtained today from one panful of earth."

The fledgling *Bismarck Tribune* breathlessly covered the news. Headline writers seemed to be in competition to outdo one another. "Gold and Silver in Immense Quantities." "Anybody Can Find It. No Former Experience Required." "The Most Beautiful Valleys the Eye of Man Ever Rested Upon." "An Eden and an Eldorado. Held by the Hostile Sioux but Not Occupied." In short order gold was selling for $20 an ounce in Bismarck, which became a popular departure point for manic miners heading to the Hills on their own or by stagecoach. Hotels bulged with guests. The honky-tonk good times rolled at O'Neill's Dance Hall, Jack Champion's Dance Hall, Seventh Cavalry Saloon, and Hole in the Wall Saloon. Bismarck joined the ranks of boomtowns where dreamers, do-gooders, and the depraved tend to converge. The combination of railroad, river, and gold fever made for a rough-and-tumble, transient culture. Before the Presbyterians had a brick-and-mortar church, they held services in a downtown tent that housed a gambling den Monday morning through Saturday night. The collection plate runneth over with poker chips. The intersection of Fourth and Main Streets attracted colorful, questionable characters who could have stepped off the pages of a dime-store western novel. Big Mary. Bejesus Lize. Thums Up. Short and Dirty. Very few pillars of the community frequented that neighborhood, which acquired the disquieting sobriquet "Murderers' Gulch." The fun at O'Neill's Dance Hall alone was disrupted by seven killings.

A physical inventory taken around that time provided a snap-shot of early Bismarck. There were 112 private residences being served by one rail depot, two steamboat offices, three churches, three bathhouses, four blacksmiths, four dance halls, eight hotels, and 36 saloons. Kate Templeton Jewell, whose husband, Marshall, was edi-tor of the *Bismarck Tribune*, decided that security provided by the military amounted to a net loss. It gave comfort to reprobates. "With the advent of the 7th Cavalry at Fort Lincoln," she said, "the char-acter of Bismarck changed materially for the worse." Custer might have concurred. One morning he and two companies of the Seventh Cavalry paid a call on the mayor. They were looking to recover ship-ments of grain stolen from the fort and believed to be stashed in town. The mayor must have known something. Custer returned to Fort Lincoln with the missing supplies and also several suspected thieves, who were tossed into the guardhouse—and promptly escaped.

Gold forever changed frontier dynamics. The U.S. govern-ment abandoned all intent, and ultimately any pretense, of abiding by a treaty that had given the Sioux, the Cheyenne, and scattered other tribes control over vast swaths of the Great Plains. In May 1876 Colonel Custer and 1,200 troops took leave of Fort Lincoln, bound for rolling grasslands several hundred miles away that sur-rounded the Little Big Horn River. They intended to rein in Sit-ting Bull and Crazy Horse, two tribal chiefs who'd lost patience with white interlopers. Well-wishers from Bismarck and Mandan came to bid them godspeed. A regimental band played "The Girl I Left Behind Me" as lines of blue soldiers rode off to oblivion.

Mark Kellogg, a *Bismarck Tribune* reporter doing double duty as a stringer for papers back east, accompanied the Seventh Cavalry. He had the misfortune to be astride a mule, and this may explain why he was among the earliest of the 268 fatalities. The dead in-cluded, most famously, Custer and everyone in the five companies under his immediate command, all of whom trotted into the teeth of Sitting Bull's trap. Kellogg is recognized as the first Associated Press correspondent to die covering a story. There was some benefit to being a civilian. Many of the bodies at the Little Big Horn were horribly mutilated. Kellogg got off comparatively easy. He was found scalped and missing only one ear.

Also killed at the Battle of the Little Big Horn was Private William Davis, third baseman for the Fort Lincoln baseball team.

The players called themselves "Benteen's Base Ball Club," a figurative tip of the hat to Captain Frederick Benteen, a high-ranking officer of the Seventh Cavalry. A soldier who served as recording secretary for the team had written a catty season preview for one of the Dakota Territory newspapers in February 1876. Private Davis didn't impress him: "Fair at the bat, slow runner, and he has the worst fault imaginable, wishing to play 'fancy.' Age 24. In baseball he is scarcely 14." Three other ballplayers deployed on the flanks at Custer's Last Stand were wounded that fateful day: second baseman Private William "Fatty" Williams (prone "to cry for vexation" whenever an umpire called him out on strikes, the team secretary noted, "which was often the case as the bat is Fatty's weak point"); utility man Private Charles Bishop ("heavy hitter with the willow," but "lazy"); and Sergeant Joseph McCurry, ace pitcher ("delivers a swift and correct ball; leaves the army next winter and will no doubt be engaged in some professional or first class amateur nine").

Alas, McCurry never pitched professionally. He did gain notoriety, however, for possibly putting his arm to work in another capacity. A military court of inquiry conducted a postmortem of what went awry at Little Big Horn, focusing on two officers accused of withdrawing their forces prematurely, in effect abandoning Custer. The investigation concluded that Custer and his men had been the victims of bad luck and vengeful Indians. Case closed. Critics cried cover-up, citing examples of what they considered tainted evidence and false testimony. One of the most damning claims was that Sergeant McCurry had forged the signatures of numerous soldiers on a petition submitted in support of the exonerated officers: Major Marcus Reno and the Fort Lincoln baseball club's very own Captain Frederick Benteen.

* * *

Bats and balls (and, later, that magnificent equipment innovation: gloves) got tossed into soldiers' rucksacks. They also were packed into civilians' steamer trunks, saddlebags, valises, and buckboards. The sport spread virally from seaports to the frontier in an increasingly mobile society. There is no big bang theory of baseball. It evolved, like the blues and the miniskirt. Bat-and-ball games were being played in Massachusetts in 1735 and in Pennsylvania in 1831. The New York Knickerbockers put baseball rules down on paper in 1845, but nine innings weren't the norm until 1857 and overhand pitches wouldn't gain acceptance until 1884.

Through every modification, baseball's popularity swelled. By the end of the Civil War, America finally had a pastime with mass appeal; somehow square dancing and rail splitting had never quite captured the public imagination. A pair of milestones marked the transition to commercialism. In 1869 the Cincinnati Red Stockings put ten players on salary, a luxury the team seemingly couldn't afford, since the Stockings unraveled within two years. In 1876 the eight-team National League of Professional Base Ball Clubs began play; this was the first entity with the resources and the leadership to survive over time. (That's the same National League still going strong today.) The 52–14 Chicago White Stockings won the 1876 championship, finishing six games ahead of the spunky Hartford Dark Blues and St. Louis Brown Stockings.

Poet Carl Sandburg grew up in Galesburg, Illinois, in the 1880s on a steady diet of Chicago sports pages, which fed his fantasy that he would someday wake up a big-league outfielder. "What is this fascination about making a hickory stick connect with a thrown ball . . . or running for a fly and leaping in the air for a one-handed catch?" he mused in his memoir *Always the Young Strangers*. "These questions have gone round and round in the heads of millions of American boys for generations." Adulthood didn't necessarily bring definitive answers to such questions.

The professional ranks expanded in 1901 with the spawning of an American League to compete with the National League, but their combined sixteen teams occupied only the top floor of what historian Harold Seymour referred to as the sprawling "House of Baseball." There was plenty of action below and it wasn't confined to schoolyards or playgrounds. Industrial and recreation leagues flourished. Grown men by the tens of thousands laced on spikes and lost themselves in takeout slides and doubles that split the gap. Indian reservations had hardball teams. Employees of coal companies, trolley car manufacturers, police departments, funeral homes, and local Communist parties took to the field together in off-hours. As baseball became the language of leisure, it collided with another cherished American tradition: the will to win. The result was predictable. Dollar bills got stuffed into uniform pockets, usually because a company or a town or some civic-minded pooh-bah had lost patience with losing. This semipro ethos infused the farthest fringes of the sport. Dwight Eisenhower earned spending money patrolling center field for a team in the Kansas State League in 1910, registering under the phony surname "Wilson" in order to protect his amateur status. Young Mr. Eisenhower had his eyes on an appointment to West Point and—who knows?—maybe a career in the military. On a summer day in 1915 an estimated 100,000 fans flooded Cleveland's Brookside Park to watch a game between the White Autos and Omaha Luxers, two regional semipro superpowers.

The *WPA Guide for Alabama* made mention of "a semi pro team in nearly every town." Some of these teams courted a broad audience. When Nashville, Arkansas, hosted Dierks, Arkansas, for a game in 1924, the *Nashville News* reported, "Ladies will be admitted free, as will one-armed and one-legged men and children under 6 years old." Up north in New York, the Brooklyn Bushwicks installed lights on their field in 1930, five years before the Major Leagues took the plunge into night baseball.

Family-owned Bona Allen, Incorporated, of Buford, Georgia, had several thousand employees. It primarily produced shoes but also supplied the raw leather used to make baseball gloves. The semipro Bona Allen Shoemakers crisscrossed the Southeast with players earning a princely $300 to $400 a month. The company mounted a giant shoe on a Chevrolet chassis and an advance man would drive from town to town, handing out leather key chains to drum up interest before ball games. There was a standing offer: every member of an opposing team that beat Bona Allen received a free pair of dress shoes. The company didn't give many away. In 1936, for example, the Shoemakers stomped to a 73–6 record, peeling off a 35–game winning streak. Their ballpark in Buford was a gem. Crowds turned out even when the Shoemakers weren't there. In-progress summaries from important road games were relayed by Teletype to the Bona Allen plant. Somebody would read the updates over a loudspeaker while hundreds of fans sat in the stands outside cheering a deserted field.

Major League baseball held the line at just sixteen teams until 1961, but a crazy quilt of minor leagues got stitched together by independent hands. As far back as 1909 there were 246 minor league teams loosely tied to 35 leagues. These were rogue operators that sold their best players to the highest-bidding big-league club. In 1921 the Major Leagues chose to take more direct control of their destiny and adopted the farm system. American and National league teams were free to own and operate multiple minor-league affiliates that would feed talent up the organizational chain. Branch Rickey, then running the St. Louis Cardinals, was the visionary godfather of this new business model. The New York Yankees followed a few steps behind him. Those two teams set about assembling well-funded farm systems that would give them a competitive advantage for decades to come. Other teams dragged their feet and paid the price as the Yanks and Cards made regular trips to the World Series.

By 1932 the minor leagues had contracted to 102 teams and 14 leagues, but they were still a vibrant enterprise and still predominantly independent. However, the country remained largely rural and provincial. The automobile was duke, not yet king, of the culture. Fans wanted to cheer for a home team that was only a few blocks from home; all the better if they could walk to the ballpark. Since most major and minor league teams were many miles away, local semipro teams bridged that sports gap, although the definition of "semipro" was elastic. At the "light" end of the semipro spectrum, players received a token salary or passed the hat for donations during games. They'd often put in a full day's work before slipping on their uniforms. At the opposite, "heavy," extreme were generously subsidized clubs like the Bona Allen Shoemakers. They charged admission to games, the quality of play was high, the pay was excellent, and work obligations generally minimal. A player's "job" might be to read the newspaper or to hopscotch bars at night chatting up fans. In 1930 the average minor leaguer earned about $65 a month. It was not unheard of for prospects to turn down a pro contract in favor of sticking with their company or town team. The money was likely to be better and there was the added security of year-round employment, no trifling consideration with the economy a shambles.

Players on both the top and the bottom rungs of the semipro ladder—with the exception of those bashful, clean-living Quincy Troupes of the baseball world—would've felt right at home pulling up a bar stool at any of the saloons along Bismarck's "Murderers' Gulch." Most of them were second- or third-generation laborers, miners, and factory hands: men steeped in the notion of hard work and harder play. They loved their liquor, cursed like sailors, caroused at night, smoked between innings, and would rather slide into second base buck naked than read a book. Scores of top major leaguers started—and sometimes finished—in the semipro trenches. Lefty Grove, the soon-to-be-great pitcher for the Philadelphia Athletics and, later, the Boston Red Sox pulled down $490 tossing a single game for a Massachusetts wool mill. The mill team gave him $300 up front, plus $10 for every strikeout he racked up. Not a bad day's wage in 1928, considering that the average worker made less than $30 a week. After eight Chicago White Sox were banned for life by Major League baseball for conspiring to fix the 1919 World Series, several of them lingered on as semipros. Outfielder "Shoeless Joe" Jackson surfaced in Arkansas, shortstop Charles "Swede" Risberg in Montana and later North Dakota.

Johnny Pesky was associated with the Boston Red Sox for more than sixty years. He played shortstop for a decade starting in 1942, then went on to serve as manager, coach, broadcaster, assistant to the general manager and, ultimately, a ceremonial face of the franchise. A native of Portland, Oregon, at sixteen Pesky suited up for the local semipro team. A year later he got recruited by Silver Falls Lumber Company in Silverton, thirty-five miles away. It had an even better semipro team. The pay was $100 a month, plus all the sawdust he could inhale. First day on the job, Pesky took a turn on the power saw. That would be his last turn on the power saw. As his boss explained, "You got valuable fingers, kid." Good shortstops being much harder to find than good lumbermen, Pesky was taken out of harm's way and given other work: grooming the company ball field. Both the lumber company and the lumber team were owned by Tom Yawkey, who also owned the Boston Red Sox. Pesky spent three years essentially auditioning with the semipro Silverton Red Sox, then was offered a Major League contract. "That's old-time baseball, the plantation system," said Pesky. "It was a whole different world."

In Van Meter, Iowa, Bob Feller was busy perfecting his fastball by trying to throw it through the side of a barn on the family farm. He could crank it up to 100 miles per hour, which became his ticket to the Cleveland Indians and, down the road, the Hall of Fame. While in high school during the mid-1930s, Feller pitched for the Farmers Union semipros in Des Moines. He also rented himself out on a per-game basis at tournaments and county fairs. "I used to get $100 and a tank of gas," Feller said years later. "They called it 'spiking up.' Every little jerk town had a team."

There would be no North Dakota without little jerk towns, and, as in Iowa, most of them had a ball team. It was a badge of respectability. If a school, a hospital, and a library were in place, then the time had come to round up a few strapping lads and outfit them with bats, balls, and bases. Then, again, maybe you didn't need to wait for that library to be built. Joe Cutting, a graduate of the University of Minnesota's College of Pharmacy, took a creaking Great Northern Railway train to Williston, North Dakota, in the spring of 1909. He got off with a bag in each hand and a pair of spikes tucked under one arm. He'd been hired to play shortstop for the Williston Orioles, the town team funded by members of the business community's Commercial Club. Williston was wilder and woollier than Cutting expected. "I didn't know for sure if I wanted to stay or not," he said. "The streets were jammed until early morning by rough and ready westerners who would fight anyone who disagreed with them or bet on anything that moved, lived or breathed." (He stayed. Permanently. Cutting married a Williston girl, coached the high school football team, served as police and fire commissioner, and for thirty-five years dispensed prescriptions at Williston Drugs.)

There were hundreds of baseball stories similar to Cutting's. Modest one-horse hamlets managed to rustle up enough spare change to support a club, maybe with a semipro or two anchoring the lineup. Some of those towns were so small and so fragile that they got blown away by the Depression or shriveled to almost nothing in its aftermath. Omemee, Ambrose, Russell, Van Hook, Sanger, Mercer. All future ghost towns. All with teams that would vanish and with ballparks that would revert to underbrush, cleat marks in the dirt replaced by rabbit tracks.

As the state capital, Bismarck was assured of long-term survival, but its baseball fortunes fluctuated with the times. A group of concerned citizens held a meeting at a dry goods store in late June 1881 for the purpose of forming a town team. The second order of business was to challenge Fort Abraham Lincoln to a game on the Fourth of July. Play commenced at the Bismarck fairgrounds after lines of brass bands, firemen, and Sunday school children—preceded by a horse-drawn carriage bearing a woman dressed as the Goddess of Liberty—finished snaking through downtown. Eight years later the Fort Lincoln ball game had been shifted to Memorial Day and Bismarck was clashing with cross-river rival Mandan on July Fourth. The mayor of Mandan stirred the pot, boasting he'd accept any wager on the game between $5 and $50. The *Tribune* reported that "a number of bets were made," which must have delighted the mayor. Final score: Mandan 13, Bismarck 10. One of the celebrants in the pregame parade that day was Sitting Bull, brandishing a banner that read "March of Civilization." He rode a horse alongside his comrade Rain-in-the-Face, the war chief said by some to have cut the heart out of Captain Tom Custer (George's younger brother) at the Battle of the Little Big Horn and eaten it on the spot.

Ironically, the Seventh Cavalry's annihilation signified the beginning of the end of Indian resistance. The government cracked down unmercifully. Within a year, most tribes were corralled on federal land. Sitting Bull fled to Canada, but eventually returned to live on Standing Rock Indian Reservation, some forty miles south of Bismarck. He became a familiar presence in town. Wrapped in a colorful blanket and with his long hair tied in two braids, he'd sit outside the Sheridan House, a combination hotel–train depot, and hawk autographed pictures of himself for a dollar apiece. Other Sioux from Standing Rock were allowed to camp for the summer on the Mandan side of the Missouri River. Trains paused in Mandan to replenish their supply of coal and water and to swap crews. During the changeovers, Indians in ceremonial garb danced by the tracks while passengers tossed coins out the windows.

Those Sioux dancers kept performing till their legs gave out in the 1930s, but the Wild West began to recede as soon as the twentieth century unspooled. North Dakota settled into domesticated contentment, although not without experiencing growing pains. The Bismarck city council decided in 1908 that refinement demanded the smoothing and grading of downtown roads, much to the consternation of one Reuben Stevens. When workers took shovels to North Third Street, he bolted from his house gun in hand, face slathered with shaving cream, and shooed them away. A more temperate, unarmed response would seem to have been in order, since Stevens was an attorney who'd served two terms in the state legislature and, more to the point, had accidentally shot and killed his first wife while duck hunting. But there's only so much progress a man can take.

A year earlier the *Bismarck Tribune* had pondered whether common sense was evaporating everywhere in the rush toward modernization, observing that the town of Rugby "is paying $1,800 per month for a baseball team and has no sewer system. It appears that the baseball teams are draining the towns of the state." At that same time, representatives from eight North Dakota and Minnesota towns held talks about ways to control the spiraling cost of baseball. They contemplated forming a "Prairie League" and instituting a salary cap of $600 per team. After those discussions fizzled, Bismarck responded by going cold turkey and pulling the plug on baseball. The local diamond was quiet until 1911, when the team came back from the dead as part of a low-key league confined to the state's Missouri Slope. A patron made available a ball field that he owned near the statehouse. The business community launched a Bismarck Baseball Association and contributed $1,000 in seed money. Part of that grubstake (so much for old lessons learned) was used to pay for a hotshot pitcher from Saint Paul. By 1916 Bismarck had gone completely semipro, with the managerial reins turned over to Chick Kirk, a former minor leaguer from Iowa. He lured players throughout the Midwest and northern Plains. "Kirk's Koltz" had a korny name, but they collectively hit .311 and won the Missouri Slope League. They repeated as champs in 1917, but there would be no "three-peat." World War I drove town ball into hibernation.

When the soldiers came back from Europe, Bismarck fans again revived their team for the 1920 season, albeit on a semi semi-pro basis. Thirteen businessmen pledged $100 apiece, which was only enough to buy the services of seven players. The war hiatus had whetted the appetite for baseball. There were now twenty town teams active on the Missouri Slope, plus a flock of independents. Even the state prison in Bismarck had a team; it was surprisingly strong and included a couple of non-incarcerated paid semipros. The warden let the "Grove All-Stars" (a name derived from a stand of trees that once shaded the penitentiary grounds) make road trips. At least, he did so until two convict players bolted during a game in Hebron, North Dakota. Thereafter, the All-Stars enjoyed perpetual home-field advantage.

That spring of 1920 four special initiatives were put to a statewide referendum. Supporters sought exemptions from the prevailing Sunday blue laws for cigarette sales, movie theaters, boxing matches, and baseball games. Voters approved only Sunday baseball, providing that no activity took place within 500 feet of a church. It quickly became a Sunday afternoon ritual to stop by the ballpark and root, root, root for the home team. Spectators would park along the foul lines or deep in the outfield grass and watch from the comfort of their cars, tooting horns when somebody made a circus catch or stroked an extra-base hit. It was a different era. Hits were "bingles," batters were "stickers," and outfielders defended "the garden." Pitchers paid no heed to *game* counts, much less pitch counts. Lefty Needham—one of Bismarck's salaried players—tossed eighteen innings of scoreless ball, all in the course of a solitary Sunday's work that saw him win the first two games of a triple-header.

In order to afford someone like Lefty Needham, town teams depended upon the generosity of business leaders and groups such as the Elks for core support, which was augmented by ticket sales, fund-raisers, and small contributions. Although money was a constant concern, the Bismarck Baseball Association got giddy after World War I. It bought a plot of land on the south side of town and built a ball field. It also got into the bad habit of rolling over operating-expense debt. Come May 1922 about fifty stalwart fans gathered at the American Legion hall in search of ideas on how to close a budget gap of nearly $5,000. A boxing exhibition pulled in less money than expected. Plans were made for a booster dance and possibly a summer high school football game. Blackface entertainment being a nationwide craze, the Elks promised to donate a portion of the proceeds from their annual minstrel show. Performances were held on two nights in June at Bismarck Auditorium. The *Tribune* hailed the show as a "foot-stomping, rip-roaring mélange" of banjo music, dance, and "razzy jazzy deck-hand songs." Professional actors and a large cast of volunteers took the stage in burnt-cork makeup, dressed as "Negro mammies" and "old darkies." All for naught. Red ink continued to flow and the baseball team had to seriously tighten its belt. The number of paid players shrank steadily over the next few years. Blue-chip pitcher Charlie Boardman survived the purge and led the Bismarck staff in 1925. He was one of those rare North Dakotans with Major League experience, though his had been more than a decade ago and consisted of seven games with the Philadelphia Athletics and St. Louis Cardinals. Boardman's arm had some mileage on it, but his temper was as good as new. When an umpire blew a call he wasn't averse to expressing his displeasure by heaving the game ball over the outfield fence.

A touring team from Scobey, Montana, took on Bismarck that summer of 1925. The Scobey management had gone on a spending spree, attracting players by dangling paychecks as fat as $600 a month in front of them. The team's big guns were center fielder Oscar "Happy" Felsch and shortstop "Swede" Risberg, pariahs from the World Series–throwing Chicago White Sox. They set the tone for a rowdy collection of Scobey boozers and bullies who played stone-cold-sober baseball and dropped only about one of every ten games. Scobey had the press clippings, but Charlie Boardman had his changeup working to perfection. He gave up only seven hits in a 9–5 win. Boardman was sharp during most games, averaging 14 strikeouts. Bismarck finished atop a five-team league in 1925, manhandling the towns of Hazen, Dickinson, Hebron, and New

Salem. But it was a tarnished crown. The product had been diluted and the schedule pared back. Interest flagged. Boardman jumped ship toward the close of the season, signing with those moneybags from Scobey. The starting shortstop skipped some games to go golfing, a sacrilegious act that prompted the *Bismarck Capital*—a newsweekly—to wonder whether "he could be prevailed upon to believe that the national game needs him worse than the game that came to us from abroad." The *Capital* posed a painful question: "Is Bismarck a baseball town?"

The team had skidded into a deep ditch. Perhaps it was only fitting that an automobile man would try to pull it out.

3

BIRTH OF A SALESMAN

Cataclysmic change can be imperceptible. Ice age glaciers bulldozed North America in fraction-of-an-inch bites, the slow-motion grind carving the serpentine Saint Croix River that aeons later served to keep Minnesota from bumping into Wisconsin. The resulting lumpy terrain was packed with pocket lakes and forests. The latter provided timber for Victorian-era homes in Minneapolis and Saint Paul, with sawmills whining until the grand tracts of pine were buzz-cut bald.

Neil Orr Churchill was born in February 1891, when snow cloaked the gritty river town of Saint Croix Falls, Wisconsin. He was the last of Rebecca Orr Churchill's five children, of whom two died in infancy and one didn't make it through adolescence. Rebecca had married at seventeen. Her husband, George, worked as a lumberman. The winter after Neil's birth, George fell during a shift in the woods and complained of lingering headaches. A case of "la grippe," the arcane euphemism for influenza, complicated his recovery. More than a month passed and George showed little improvement. His wife took him to Saint Paul for medical treatment. Too late. He died before doctors could operate to relieve the pressure on his brain. After that devastating blow, Rebecca Churchill's finances were always a juggling act. She took in boarders. She took in laundry. She sold cakes and pies out of her kitchen. Neil Churchill liked to say of his hardscrabble boyhood, "If there was another side of the tracks, that's where I was born." He was speaking not of the wrong side, but of some woebegone place beyond; a no-man's-land where people were worse than poor—they were peripheral.

Sports provided an escape. Despite his girth, Churchill was surprisingly agile and light on his feet, nimble enough to be a decent tap dancer. Baseball suited him best. One summer he played on sixteen teams. Before graduating from Saint Croix Falls High School, he already had two years of semipro catching experience under his belt. He hooked on with an interstate league and briefly caught Burleigh Grimes, a pitcher who was so cantankerous he'd throw at a batter's head even when issuing an intentional walk. Grimes went on to become the last legal spitballer in the Major Leagues.

Success eluded Churchill away from the diamond. He had a restless, rebellious streak. After high school he moved to Minneapolis and landed a $35-a-month, dead-end job clerking at a dry goods store, then returned to the Saint Croix Falls area and opened his own retail shop. It failed. He and his uncle started a contracting business. They went broke. In July 1915 he eloped with Estelle Tuttle, a schoolteacher who had beguiling electric-blue eyes. They roared off on his motorcycle. A year later they welcomed a daughter, Becky, into the world. Neil Churchill now had a family, but no steady means of supporting them. The Churchills relocated to a town just south of Minneapolis. Neil borrowed $800 from a relative and became proprietor of a luncheonette. He stuck with that a few years and sold the business for no profit. It was 1919. Churchill, closing in on thirty, had yet to find his niche.

He took a road trip to clear his head and to search for employment. While he was passing through Bismarck, North Dakota, a case of food poisoning knocked him flat for a few days. His somersaulting stomach turned out to be a blessing in disguise. He liked the ambience of the town: friendly but not cloying, small but not claustrophobic. Churchill could picture himself living there and, as fate would have it, Lahr Motor Company was looking for a salesman. He was hired on a six-week trial basis. Within nine months he leapfrogged to sales manager. Bismarckers, being of pragmatic, agrarian stock, embraced the automobile with caution. A *Bismarck Tribune* editorial fretted about the emergence of reckless drivers who were courting disaster at speeds up to forty-five miles per hour. But the promise of easy transport across the yawning expanses of the prairie proved irresistible. In 1913 there were 13,000 cars in the state. That number spiked more than thirteenfold by 1930. North Dakotans gobbled up motor vehicles at a rate 50 percent higher than the national average. And Neil Churchill was only too happy to put them behind the wheel of a shiny Willys-Knight or Overland coupe.

He and his wife, daughter, and mother settled into a downtown apartment. Life was good. Suddenly—shades of star-crossed George Churchill—disaster struck. Estelle got sick. A devout Christian Scientist, she put her trust in the Lord and the recuperative powers of fresh air. Sitting on the porch waiting for her fever to break probably did more harm than good. In June 1920 Estelle Tuttle Churchill, age twenty-six, became another victim of the flu epidemic. Exactly what happened next is subject to conjecture. Families prefer to bury some secrets with the dead. It could be that Neil Churchill was driven to his knees by grief. He also might have come to the clearheaded conclusion that single parenthood would torpedo his nascent career and, therefore, he needed temporary relief. What's certain is that he found another home for his daughter and didn't have to look far. His mother took custody of four-year-old Becky. Not only that; the two of them moved back to Wisconsin, where Rebecca Churchill resumed barely making ends meet by running a boardinghouse and baking her pies.

Could a father make a more wrenching decision? Whether that one unfolded according to plan or not, it proved to be permanent. Neil Churchill never again lived under the same roof as Becky. For all intents and purposes, in the summer of 1920 his young daughter became his kid sister.

* * *

North Dakota farms and factories staggered through the 1920s. Cars being the disruptive technology of their day, the automobile business held a steadier line until the whole economy imploded. While workers in other industries were losing jobs, Churchill had no trouble finding them. He left Lahr Motors for a different Bismarck dealership, then in late 1923 left the state to become Minneapolis zone manager for upstart Chrysler Corporation. Around that time he became romantically involved with another schoolteacher. Helen Center was a college graduate from Mandan and the descendant of a pioneer ranching family. They married in September 1924 and on their honeymoon traveled by car to Wisconsin and Washington, D.C. Helen wandered through the Smithsonian museums in Washington, enraptured. She had about forty-five minutes to drink everything in; then Neil dragged her to a baseball game at Griffith Stadium. She was happily highbrow. He was contentedly lowbrow. However, the newlyweds had in common a burning desire to leave Minnesota and get back to North Dakota. Walter Chrysler unknowingly made that possible through a triangulation of fate.

Chrysler had learned engineering from correspondence-school courses but quickly proved himself to be a wizard at applied mechanics. In 1912, when he was just thirty-six, he was tapped to be the head of production at Buick's Flint, Michigan, plant. Five years later he became company president. Three years after that, Chrysler retired prematurely from Buick and quickly regretted it. He took troubleshooting jobs salvaging two money-losing car manufacturers, but was bitten by the bug to build something from scratch. He created Chrysler Corporation and, in the winter of 1924, went to New York City for the annual auto show. He rented the lobby of the Commodore Hotel and put on display a revolutionary six-cylinder-engine sedan that was capable of cruising at an astonishing seventy miles per hour. Samuel Wickham "Wick"

Corwin attended that auto show and was so impressed he signed on as a charter Chrysler dealer. Corwin had been selling cars in Bismarck since 1914. Buicks were his mainstay and were how he'd originally met Walter Chrysler. The man gave abysmal business presentations (Chrysler would get so nervous his shirts became soaked with perspiration, as if his armpits were cooled by a sprinkler system), but Wick Corwin regarded him as a genius. When he decided to jump onto the Chrysler bandwagon, Corwin set about finding a partner who already knew that line of cars and could credibly woo customers. Churchill fit that bill to a T. "The best retail salesman I've ever seen," Corwin said; plus, he had frontline Chrysler experience.

In June 1925 Corwin offered Neil Churchill a piece of his Bismarck dealership, providing him and Helen with their ticket home. Corwin Motors officially became Corwin-Churchill Motors. The two partners meshed perfectly. Corwin had been polished to a high sheen at an elite New Jersey prep school and Princeton University. He looked like an Ivy Leaguer supplied by central casting: tweedy, reserved, square-jawed, and handsome with a shock of wavy hair. He was the rock-steady, back-office numbers cruncher. Churchill complemented him well as an up-from-the-streets, joke-telling front man. He wasn't a natural salesman, insisting that he'd worked hard at mastering the subtleties of persuasion and cultivating an attention to detail. Churchill didn't tolerate dust on fenders or so much as a scrap of paper on the showroom floor. When closing a sale he'd pull a notepad and pencil out of his suit pocket—he always wore a three-piece suit and always had his necktie knotted firmly in place—and do basic math with prospective buyers.

"You smoke, don't you? Ever think how much that costs you a month?" Churchill would ask, scribbling the dollar amount on his pad. "You drink? Don't tell me where you get the booze, but how much do you spend a month?" He'd write down that number, mutter a bit, scribble a bit . . . then render a verdict. "Cut back 10 percent on smoking and drinking and you can afford the monthly payments. I could put you in a Chrysler coach today for $1,670. Great car."

During the winter of 1925 Neil Churchill got reacquainted with his adopted town by assuming control of the Bismarck Phantoms, a municipal basketball team made up of recently graduated college players with nifty two-hand set shots. His involvement was strictly off-court. He purchased the uniforms and equipment, booked opponents, and handled ticket sales. Scheduling Phantom games would soon bring him into contact with another salesman extraordinaire. Abe Saperstein had been born in London but was a product of North Side Chicago's public schools and playgrounds. He stood five-foot-three on tiptoes, but got hired in 1926 by the city's Welles Park recreation center, where part of his duties entailed coaching basketball. Saperstein was twenty-four, a tailor's son with no direction in life beyond not wanting to grow old mending shirts and altering suits. At Welles he met Walter Ball, a former Negro League pitcher who fronted a black baseball team that wanted to do some barnstorming in greater Illinois. Saperstein talked his way into becoming Ball's booking agent. A few years later he also took on a black Chicago basketball team called Tommy Brookins' Globe Trotters. They split up after one winter of hustling games. By then Saperstein had appropriated the name and the concept of a black team with crossover appeal, starting his own New York Harlem Globe Trotters despite having no connection to either New York or Harlem.

It was shoestring-and-a-prayer basketball. Five young black guys and little Abe (driver, promoter, publicity flack, and emergency sixth man) cruised Illinois, Iowa, and Michigan in a Model T Ford, scrounging exhibition games with whoever was curious enough to play them and split the proceeds. Seven days a week on the road. Tiny tank town after tiny tank town. One auditorium, church basement, Grange hall, and unheated armory after another. They posted jaw-dropping seasonal records of 101–6, 145–13, and 151–13 against less than stellar competition. The name evolved

into the Harlem Globetrotters and the spurts of straight basketball became increasingly leavened with slapstick comedy and trick
shots. Squeals of audience laughter drowned out the squeak of
sneakers sliding across hardwood floors. Newspapers declared Abe
Saperstein "The Great White Father of Negro Basketball." The
Globetrotters became a regional draw and over time rode that wave
to international stardom. Saperstein never forgot that the core of his
business depended upon packing arenas in entertainment-starved
flyover states like North Dakota, with his team often lining up
against hotshot local quintets like the Bismarck Phantoms. In negotiations, he threw his weight around to maximum advantage like
a martial arts sensei. But so did Neil Churchill, who weighed more
and knew Saperstein since the Trotters' earliest scuffling days. Gil
Olson, a forward on the Phantoms, happened to be in Churchill's
office at the car dealership one day when the phone rang.

"Abe, how are you?" Churchill answered cheerily. "OK . . . we
have open dates that weekend." The Globetrotters were making a
California swing and Saperstein wanted to break up the trip with a
Bismarck stop. He offered Churchill 40 percent of the ticket gross.

"No," Churchill declared. "*You'll* get 40 percent. We get 60
percent." With that, he hung up the phone. Olson looked aghast.
"Just wait a second," Churchill assured him. "He'll call back."

A few minutes later the phone rang again. Saperstein again.
"Yeah, Abe. Oh, you've *reconsidered*! . . . No, I won't go for that either." Saperstein had countered with a 50–50 offer and Churchill
hung up on him a second time. Olson thought he was crazy not to
take the deal. "Gil," Churchill explained, "they can't go anyplace
between Minneapolis and the West Coast but *here*."

The telephone rang one last time. Saperstein surrendered. He
accepted the short end of a 60–40 split.

Churchill drove hard bargains more to benefit his players
than himself. The Phantoms subsisted on ticket revenues that they
divvied up like waiters pooling tips. The Globetrotters were an
established business. Saperstein paid his players a salary, though he

by no means pampered them. They came through North Dakota on another road swing and ran smack into a below-zero blizzard. Saperstein traveled alone by car that trip. His team piled into an army surplus truck. Churchill peeked inside the truck that snowy day and saw Harlem Globetrotters swaddled in blankets, shivering. The heater didn't work. Churchill gave the truck driver directions to Corwin-Churchill Motors and had his mechanics install a new heater on the fly. No charge. The Globetrotters rejoiced. Saperstein probably did, too. Neil Churchill may have spared him the indignity of becoming the first sports promoter to ever cancel a basketball game because of frostbite.

Bismarck's business leaders—the engine that powered the town baseball team—convened their annual booster meeting in the spring of 1926 and found the manager of the Phantoms amenable to taking on more athletic responsibilities. The weekly *Capital* newspaper revealed, "Neil O. Churchill has taken a leading interest in the organization."

Everybody called him "Church" and he knew virtually everybody in Bismarck. He was by then a respected member of the corporate gentry and looked the part: thirty-five years old with wire-rimmed glasses and slicked-back dark hair. Church didn't smoke or drink, but did indulge with wild abandon at the dinner table. At five-foot-eight with a department-store-Santa-Claus belly, he made an inviting target for the local press. Reporters delighted in poking fun at his "avoirdupois" and characterizing him as "imposing," "portly," and "elephantine." Appearances can be deceiving. In addition to his semipro experience in Wisconsin, back in the early 1920s Churchill had played some ball for Bismarck. He volunteered to return as player-manager for the 1926 season, astutely limiting his role to that of pinch hitter and substitute first baseman.

After studying the team's broken balance sheet, Churchill and the Bismarck Baseball Association faced fiscal reality and dumped all the semipros. They would make do with free, homegrown talent: a strategy that assumed a ready supply of printers, painters, and interior decorators who had exceptional hand-eye coordination. A couple of semipros elected to stay on without pay because they'd forged close ties to the community and, in addition, were past their prime. First baseman–accountant Ed Tobin was thirty-three years old. Infielder–laundry foreman Floyd Fuller was thirty-five and had three children. ("One a girl," Fuller always said, "and the other two ballplayers.") Catcher Kelly Simonson had come from Wisconsin purely to play ball for money, but had married a Bismarck girl and landed a full-time job selling shoes. The *Bismarck Tribune* looked on the bright side of diminished expectations, reporting that "the city has had rather disappointing experiences in past seasons when several semiprofessional players were engaged who got all the money and nothing was left for the home players."

Luck shone upon rookie manager Churchill in the person of Harold "Doc" Love, a diminutive chiropractor with a big-time curveball. He'd grown up in Mandan and declined a minor league contract in favor of pitching for Palmer School of Chiropractic in Davenport, Iowa. In 1926 Doc Love struck out 137 batters in 127 innings. His most impressive outing came against the town of Turtle Lake. He tossed a complete-game 2–1 victory, but took two weeks to do it. Because of a 6 p.m. baseball curfew, play kicked over to a second Sunday. Bismarck bunted home the winning run in the bottom of the twenty-seventh inning, much to the relief of 1,000 drained supporters. Churchill got so excited he couldn't contain himself in the coach's box. According to the *Capital*, "One fan said that Church looked like a trained walrus while he was Charleston-ing out near third base, but Church takes his baseball seriously."

That applied off the field as well. Churchill, the consummate salesman, persuaded fourteen businesses to contribute money for new uniforms. Each player wore on his back the name of a different sponsor: Grand Pacific Billiard Parlor, Frank's Place, Richmond's Bootery, Corwin-Churchill Motors. Churchill cut the price of grandstand tickets from 75 to 50 cents and had the bleachers removed so more people could pull cars up close to the field and enjoy baseball at their convenience. Practice was held Tuesday, Thursday, and Friday nights. Players who didn't show up didn't start the next game. Church was the second-best hitter, going 9 for 31 off the bench. More important, he guided the team to a 14-3-1 finish, capped off by a Missouri Slope championship. The Bismarck papers praised him for saving baseball, which he accomplished while upgrading the schedule with the addition of some tough out-of-state opponents.

A season-high crowd of 1,500 fans came out for a game with the House of David, a semipro team unlike any other. The Davids lived on a Benton Harbor, Michigan, commune established by broom maker–preacher Benjamin Purnell. He claimed to be God's point man for the impending kingdom on earth. More than 1,000 followers bought into that prophecy and at least half of them flocked to Michigan, turning all their worldly possessions over to Brother Purnell. Men obeyed his decree and did not trim their hair and beards. Everybody adhered to a vegetarian diet and abstained from sex. They were as devoted as worker bees to the queen of a hive. The Israelite House of David colony became a tourist attraction and shrine to Holy Roller industriousness, with its own amusement park, jazz band, hotels, restaurants, greenhouse, timber operation, miniature-car racetrack, and wildly popular baseball team. House of David players performed sleight-of-hand pantomime with baseballs and supposedly invented the "Pepper" warm-up drill, fan-friendly antics that probably inspired Abe Saperstein and his Harlem Globetrotters to lighten up.

Cracks developed in utopia when state attorneys prosecuted Benjamin Purnell for fraud and having sex with thirteen underage women. By 1926 he was in failing health, his case heading to court, and the House of David community on the verge of splitting into pro- and anti-Purnell factions. The baseball team soldiered on through the scandal, touring extensively and playing at its

customary high level. Bismarck fought House of David tooth and
nail in a 3–2 loss, which had to put Neil Churchill in the mood for
doing another Charleston. His determination to raise expectations
and shake things up was especially evident the last weekend in June.
He booked two games with the McCoy-Nolan Colored Giants, a
black barnstorming team from Milwaukee. That Saturday the Ku
Klux Klan held its first rally in Bismarck. The Klansmen donned
silk hoods, held a parade, and gathered around a large electric cross.
A Klan band supplied live music. The Klan Fireworks Company
stood ready to light up the sky once darkness fell.

A few blocks away Churchill's team whipped the Colored
Giants 7–3. Only 150 fans showed up. The temperature flirted
with 100 degrees. Maybe the heat kept people away. Then, too,
maybe they were uncomfortable with blacks and whites sharing
the same ball field. The *Capital* seemed unnerved by the idea. Its
game-day story crowed about how the home team held the visitors to four hits "and literally made monkeys of them, something
a great many people maintain is an impossibility as far as colored
folks are concerned."

Monkeys? Colored folks? That was the kind of language normally associated with a Klan march, not a Bismarck newspaper. Yet
there it was, captured in print: the worst of the Deep South rising
up in the far North.

"Shoulders will be looser fitting this year, giving the wearer freer
swinging action. There is very little change in the caps; the buttons
and the peak remaining. Gloves will be worn on one hand only."

In mid-April 1928 Neil Churchill invited the press—what
little there was of it in Bismarck and Mandan—and curious fans to a
mock fashion show at a downtown hotel. Tongue planted in cheek,
he unveiled the team's redesigned baseball uniforms: matching
black hat and stockings, gray pants accented by a dark blue stripe
on each leg, and gray shirt with "Bismarck" on the front. Doc Love

and eight teammates suited up as runway models, some brandishing baseball-bat walking sticks. "Belts will be worn, showing a greater tendency toward *belting* than last year," Churchill continued, a pun on his players' lack of power at the plate.

The team had played small ball in 1927 (going two months without hitting a home run), but played it superbly. In late August Bismarck hosted a tournament for a half dozen of the best teams in central North Dakota. The grandstand overflowed. The Elks band revved up the crowd. William Kontos, proprietor of the Olympia café, didn't need much revving, not having missed a home game since 1919. His foghorn voice kept exhorting Love to throw his killer curve. "Give 'im the dark one! Give 'im the dark one!" Bismarck edged Jamestown 5–4 in the championship game. In the tenth inning right fielder Charlie Boardman—the prodigal player who'd come back from Scobey, Montana, and taken a job in town as a biscuit salesman—doubled to deep center, then took third base on a wild pitch. Doc Love drove him in with a sacrifice fly. Churchill shimmied and shook with glee in his coach's box.

The *Tribune* couldn't resist commenting that "the most startling feat" of the tournament occurred when Churchill visited the press box and sat on a metal folding chair, flattening it as if it were made of matchsticks. Apparently that was enough embarrassment for one day, as Church failed to appear that afternoon for the "Heavyweight Sprint Championship of Central North Dakota," a publicity stunt arranged by radio station KFYR. He was supposed to race Arthur Ziegenhagel, a supersize outfielder from the town of Lehr. KFYR awarded the title to Churchill in absentia. He was the butt of jokes at the tournament, but a week later got showered with praise during a baseball banquet at the Grand Pacific Hotel. His team presented him with a thank-you check for $100, suggesting he blow it on a trip to the Yankees-Pirates World Series. Former governor Joe Devine, a second baseman for the Pittsburgh Pirates before entering politics, gave a laudatory toast, declaring that Churchill's ball club "developed civic pride and waked the masses to the realization that they are living in a *real* city!"

Churchill endured a lot of ribbing for his hyper attention to details, which in the extreme had him advising players on how many sandwiches to eat before games. He had no intention of easing up. Besides new uniforms for 1928, other changes included a new roof on the grandstand, a new outfield scoreboard, and a new press box. (No mention was made of new, sturdier chairs.) The Bismarck Grays—as they came to be called during this incarnation—went on to compile a 17–12 record that year and were runners-up in the Central North Dakota tournament. Churchill continued ratcheting up the schedule and caught flak for not having enough patsies on his calendar. Fans like good baseball, but, given their druthers, prefer a juicy win.

Gilkerson's Union Giants, a classy black traveling team out of Chicago, rolled into town one July weekend. They trounced the prison all-stars 25–2 on Saturday, then clubbed the Grays 7–2 and 10–2 on Sunday. In the course of that doubleheader drubbing, catcalls rained down on manager Churchill. It's not known if those jeers were racially tinged, but the newspapers rose to his defense with unusual vigor. A *Bismarck Capital* editorial lambasted "the filthy, insulting fan element in the grandstand. . . . Thank God there are only a few of them." The *Tribune* issued this pointed reminder: "No one in Bismarck has done more for baseball than Mr. Churchill. Few men have done more to promote clean sport of any kind."

The pressure of trying to stay competitive with a lineup of moonlighting ballplayers weighed on Churchill. He and Helen had started a family: their son Neil C. was just two years old. Add to that the demands of running a car dealership. Over the winter Churchill reflected on the time commitment that baseball demanded. Something had to give. He resigned as manager. His players and the Association of Commerce wouldn't hear of it. They lobbied hard for him to reconsider. He did. In April the *Tribune* splashed a banner headline across the sports page: "Neil O. Churchill Named Manager of the 1929 City Baseball Nine." That was genuinely big news. Bismarck existed in a bubble, as self-contained as a space colony. The closest town of any significance was a hundred miles away, that being the distance railroad barons chose between train stops when they were busy slicing and dicing the state. As for the centers of American politics, culture, and sports, they seemed beyond the moon. Just three years earlier Corwin-Churchill Motors had set a long-distance record for North Dakota radio reception. Shortly before dawn one morning an employee fiddled with the dials on an Atwater Kent console that was for sale at the dealership along with all those gleaming Chryslers. Spits of static subsided and for half an hour the showroom swelled with the sounds of orchestral music broadcast from New York City.

On the Great Plains, Yankee Stadium and Wrigley Field were temples of the imagination. A two-minute walk from Corwin-Churchill Motors, where the Northern Pacific railroad tracks crossed Washington Street, ballplayers cavorted in the flesh at the city ballpark. They tipped their hats to customers at the Olympia café and stood in line at the butcher shop. Outfielder Louis Lenaburg? "Could've made the bigs if he hadn't injured that left shoulder during the war." "Floyd Fuller still covers ground going toward the hole, doncha think?" About noontime Doc Love might be spotted walking down Main Street. "Hey, Doc, throw your best bender tonight, will ya? Those mugs can't hit."

Riding the town-team roller coaster from May through September was infinitely more compelling than watching forty acres of wheat grow. Neil Churchill's return to managing in 1929 should have been the prelude to a Hollywood-ending undefeated season, but his mind clearly was on other things. He canceled six games and for two others had to borrow players from Mandan. The Grays lost more than they won and mercifully shut down in August, letting more than a month of good baseball weather go to waste. Their last game was against Minot, a hotbed of moonshining that could still afford to keep all but three of its players on salary. Bismarck committed ten errors that day and got thumped 15–5.

The sting of that dreadful season lasted all winter. It didn't begin to ease until the friends of Bismarck baseball held their annual organizational meeting. That was a rite of spring, the time to rally the faithful and argue anew the pluses and minuses of hiring semipros. The 1930 meeting generated an abnormal amount of buzz. Neil Churchill had again submitted his resignation, this time nonnegotiable. He would help promote the team, but his dugout days were over. The Association of Commerce now was acting as the collective voice of Bismarck business and, therefore, the driving force behind town ball. It scrambled to come up with a post-Churchill plan. One idea under serious consideration involved paying stipends to "eastern college boys" who would form a combined Bismarck-Mandan team while also serving as baseball tutors for scores of youngsters. A *Tribune* editorial heartily endorsed the program, equating it with the Boy Scouts: "The sport is to be conducted on the plane of welfare work for the young, to be made the means of training for healthy manly boys and future good citizens."

Bold talk, but not much follow-through. In the end, the Association of Commerce let those future citizens fend for themselves and chose a lazybones solution: outsourcing. It cut a deal with Gilkerson's Union Giants, the black semipros from Chicago. The Giants were paid $350 a month in exchange for making Bismarck their summer home. Ominously, opening day was canceled because of a dust storm. Things slid downhill from there. Overloaded with prior schedule commitments, the Union Giants packed up and left Bismarck in July. The baseball void got filled by a pickup group of players who sponsored themselves: Doc Love, Kelly Simonson, and the rest of the old guard who'd been shunted aside by the rent-a-team experiment.

Outsourcing proved such a spectacular flop that the Elks stepped forward and took command of the team in 1931. They overorganized to the point of dysfunction. A steering committee appointed a manager. A bizarre compensation plan was implemented in the unlikely event ticket sales turned a profit. Position players earned a point for every practice and game attended. Pitchers received 1½ points for every game they pitched. The Elks' business manager and superintendent earned points for every game they *watched*. Welcome to bureaucracyball. The team excelled at accumulating bonus points but couldn't score many runs. It was another miserable summer filled with losses and embarrassment. In a game against the town of Beulah, Bismarck's second baseman got into a fight with the opponents' shortstop. Fans rushed onto the field and disrupted play for twenty minutes. In another game Bismarck made ten errors. On Labor Day, usually reserved for a big-name rival, they played the staff of the state training school for delinquents. Warhorse Doc Love symbolized the team's sagging fortunes. Plagued by a sore arm, he started only one game. He lasted a third of an inning, walked three batters, hit another, and trudged off the mound, never to pitch again. The Elks had their fill of baseball and went back to organizing charity raffles.

The Lions Club picked up the sponsorship baton in 1932. If failure is infectious, Bismarck had a 105-degree fever. A junior high school math teacher took over as manager. The team responded by losing its first five games. One time the players flat-out quit in the first inning when an umpire's call didn't go their way. On July 13 Bismarck played a ball game unlike any other in its history. That Wednesday night they traveled thirty miles north to Wilton. In the top of the second inning, with the field bathed in twilight, Bismarck left fielder Balzer Klein dug in at the plate.

Wilton's pitcher lost control of a fastball. It tailed inside. At the last fraction of a second, Klein turned toward the pitch, exactly the wrong thing to do. The ball struck him above his left ear. He crumpled to the ground as teammates gasped. Dazed and shaken, Klein took himself out of the lineup and sat on the bench for the remainder of the game, watching Bismarck lose yet again, 7–5. He smoked a cigarette. He drank some water and popped a few aspirins. A Bismarck fan who was in the stands offered to drive him home, proceeding straight to St. Alexius Hospital once they hit town. By then Klein had lost consciousness. He died at 5:30 the next morning of a brain hemorrhage caused by a fractured skull. The Good Samaritan fan who checked him into the hospital was Neil Churchill. Two days later he was among seven witnesses called to testify at a coroner's hearing. Churchill said it looked as if Klein got caught "flatfooted" and momentarily froze on that deadly pitch.

Balzer Klein was twenty-six years old and drove a bread truck for Bismarck Bakery Company. His wife and family laid him to rest at St. Mary's Cemetery the following Monday. Three hundred mourners attended the funeral service; his casket engulfed by floral arrangements sent by town baseball teams throughout North Dakota. Klein spent his last hours in the company of Neil Churchill, the two of them speeding down country roads in a Chrysler Airflow. After that winter's snows receded and the coffin-lid of ice melted on the Missouri River and the landscape turned green again with the promise of new life and boys began pulling baseball gloves out of bedroom closets, Churchill made an unexpected decision: he wanted to manage again.

He had a change of philosophy along with his change of heart. No more pitcher-chiropractors. No more left fielder–truck drivers. This time his preference was pure ballplayers, the best he could find, the kind unlikely to get caught flatfooted by an errant fastball. This time Neil Churchill would open his wallet to get those players, if need be. Baseball teams, he'd come to realize, were like cars: you get what you pay for.

4

WORLDS APART

Quincy Troupe had never seen a Major League game in person. He'd listened to a few on the radio, but Babe Ruth, Lou Gehrig, Ty Cobb, Rogers Hornsby? Those were disembodied names, floating above him like clouds. "The great white baseball players of my childhood days," said Troupe, "moved in a world I did not know."

The world he knew, and traversed, was stratified and color-coded. The Tuskegee Institute in Alabama, a bedrock of black higher education, had taken to issuing an annual report on the number of confirmed lynchings in the United States. There would be twenty-six in 1933, the year Troupe decided to roll the baseball dice and fly to Bismarck. Twenty-four of the victims were black. Troupe lived in Saint Louis, and one of those lynchings hit close to home. A nineteen-year-old black man from Saint Joseph, Missouri, reportedly confessed to kicking and beating a white woman. A mob of seven thousand enraged citizens descended on the city jail, easily overwhelming the guards. They dragged the suspect outside and hanged him from an elm tree on the courthouse lawn, then for good measure doused his body with gasoline and set it afire. Onlookers cut off pieces of the dead man's clothes for souvenirs. When told about the gruesome killing, the governor of Missouri came up spectacularly short in terms of summoning righteous indignation. "I have no comment to make," he said.

The country as a whole was picking its way through the briar patch of racism, at times unsure which way to turn. President

Franklin Roosevelt, aware of other recent lynchings in Maryland, Texas, California, and Tennessee, publicly condemned the violence as "collective murder" and a vestige of "pagan ethics." Congress, which had been trying to pass antilynching legislation since 1922, redoubled its efforts to move a bill forward. On a more intellectual level, the *New York Times* editorialized against the burgeoning fascination with eugenics, denouncing research under way to find a link between ethnicity and achievement and to prove the existence of a "pure race."

Troupe's personal journey was indicative of how millions of blacks tried to navigate a hostile environment. He was born on Christmas day 1912 in a cabin outside Dublin, Georgia. Known for being one of the last places where Confederate president Jefferson Davis took refuge before his capture by Union soldiers, Dublin looked much as it had in May 1865: a nondescript farming community tucked halfway between Atlanta and Savannah. Quincy walked four miles to and from school. His father, Charles, earned a living sharecropping, just scraping by. He and Mary Troupe taught their ten children—six of them still living at home—to fear God as proper Baptists should and to keep their cool among whites as prudent blacks must. However, the Troupes had grown weary of Georgia's racial hierarchy and the effect it was having on family members. One son verbally clashed with the farm overseer, whom he refused to address as "sir." Another son, who'd lost a leg from a childhood infection, sometimes carried a gun for protection.

When Quincy was ten years old, his father received a letter with a Saint Louis postmark. Milking the moment, he placed the envelope on the dinner table and wouldn't open it until the family finished saying grace. Good news was inside. He'd recently written to a friend seeking help and the friend had delivered. "I have a job in Saint Louis," Charles announced upon reading the letter. American Car and Foundry, a maker of railroad cars, had a factory opening. It was his for the asking. Charles and two older sons soon left for Missouri. They would work and save some money, then send for everyone else to join them. Mary and the others stayed behind, making do for the time being as laborers on a turpentine farm, tapping pine trees to release the gooey resin. Even Quincy pitched in. Tearful farewells were exchanged at the Dublin train station, and then Mary took her four remaining children to get something to eat. This would be Quincy's first meal at a restaurant. A hush fell over the room. A waitress hustled over to the entrance and hissed, "Get out of here! We don't serve no niggers!" The Troupes backpedaled. They purchased bread and cheese at a grocery store and ate in their horse-drawn wagon.

A few months later Quincy was again in tears. He had to give away his puppy "Wallace" to friends because the family was heading to Saint Louis. The Troupes reunited in close quarters, cramming into a rented flat that had no indoor plumbing. They fetched water from a nearby lumberyard. None too soon Charles found a three-room house in the working-class neighborhood of Compton Hill in central Saint Louis. Life resumed its usual sweet, uneventful rhythm. Quincy was big for his age, but painfully shy. He loved the movies and as often as possible disappeared into the darkness of the theater, taking a seat in the back rows by the whirring projector, a section derisively known as "nigger heaven." In order to have money to spend on movies, he got a paper route. It wound through a white area of town, and fighting his way back home after deliveries became routine. Troupe took up boxing as a matter of survival, but baseball stole his heart. The matchmaker responsible was Miss Harmon, an elementary-school teacher who had a keen eye for the game. She noticed Quincy's strong arm and encouraged him to be a catcher. Over the years he would flirt with other positions but never abandon catching for long.

Troupe ate, slept, and dreamed baseball. A favorite pastime was bottle-cap ball, the poor man's stickball. If you could hit something as small as a swerving soda-bottle cap, maybe you had the batting eye to someday make it as a pro. A role model was tantalizingly close at hand. James "Cool Papa" Bell lived in Compton Hill and played

center field for the St. Louis Stars. He was said to be the fastest
man in the Negro Leagues, and also one of the best-dressed. Boys
in the neighborhood tagged after Bell as if he were the pied piper.
Troupe was no exception, although he was apt to be hiding at the
back of any pack of admirers. He began hanging around Stars Park,
eager to catch a glimpse of Bell and Bell's teammates. The club had
a policy that any youngster who returned a fair or foul ball hit out
of the stadium could come in and watch the rest of the game, free.
Stars Park was a ball hawk's paradise. The left field wall, which
had to be built around an existing trolley car barn, measured just
269 feet from home plate. Quincy Troupe saw a lot of free games.

The stadium stood across the street from Vashon High School,
where Troupe developed into a dual-threat catcher and pitcher. In
his senior year the team vied for the city championship, an honor
somewhat compromised by the fact that segregated Saint Louis
had only two black public high schools. Regardless, it made for a
nice role reversal. The championship game was played at Stars Park
and "Cool Papa" Bell sat in the stands for once watching Quincy
play ball as Vashon coasted to the title. That was a year of personal
upheaval. Charles Troupe died of heart failure. All of Quincy's siblings had moved on to start their adult lives, so he and his mother
had the once raucous house to themselves. Baseball became the
reliable constant in his life.

The Stars made Troupe their batboy. Bell, George "Mule"
Suttles, and Ted Radcliffe—three of the best and brightest stars—
took him under their wing. Radcliffe had the biggest impact. Tem-
peramentally, he and Troupe were cut from different cloth. Radcliffe
was a motormouth and, by his own admission (and embellishment),
a Hall of Fame skirt chaser. But he prided himself on being a devoted student of the game and a dual threat. Primarily a catcher,
he also pitched well enough to take a regular turn in the rotation.
Only a handful of professional players have ever trafficked back
and forth between those two disparate positions. Troupe got tutored in all aspects of baseball, but especially soaked up Radcliffe's

tips on catching. He learned to distract a batter with seemingly innocent chatter, and to fake the batter out by setting a target on the outside corner of the plate and then signaling the pitcher to throw an inside fastball. He matured quickly as a player. After Troupe graduated from high school, the St. Louis Stars manager asked if he'd be interested in joining the team as a backup pitcher. Quincy was shy. Quincy was deferential. Quincy also was stubborn. He hated pitching. He declined the offer and played amateur ball that summer in Springfield, Illinois. The following spring he tried out for the Stars. As a catcher. The Stars signed him in 1931 to an $80-a-month contract.

Black baseball and steady employment did not go hand in hand. Club owners were not men of vast wealth. Sometimes the books wouldn't balance. Some checks bounced. Players' contracts were more promises to pay than ironclad obligations. Nobody lawyered up. The league's decentralized structure almost encouraged freewheeling behavior. After Dick Kent's pistol-waving theatrics and the subsequent demise of the St. Louis Stars, Troupe endured a bouncing-ball 1932, playing for the Detroit Wolves and New Jersey's Newark Browns. Those teams both folded and he latched onto the Homestead Grays in Pittsburgh. The Grays were slow payers, so he quickly moved on to the Kansas City Monarchs. In 1933 the Chicago American Giants came courting. They, too, had money issues. At twenty, Troupe was no stranger to Negro League frustration. Budgets didn't allow for much bus or train travel. Players wedged themselves into seven-seater sedans and gutted out epic, butt-numbing car rides. Restaurants turned them away. Days could pass between hot showers. Hotels that catered to groups of black men were hard to find. Those that did take blacks usually offered complimentary bedbugs. Equally disheartening, baseball's segregation policy showed no signs of weakening. During Troupe's time with the Newark Browns, a scout asked if he'd ever given thought to playing in the big leagues. Of course, he had, but it seemed a pipe dream. The scout next said something

Troupe dismissed as a joke. He suggested living in South America or Mexico just long enough to become fluent in Spanish, then returning home and trying to pass as a Latino ballplayer. The scout wasn't kidding. The only possible entry point to the Major Leagues for the likes of Quincy Troupe was through the back door.

Baseball wasn't born monochromatic. During the sport's prolonged shakeout period—from the early days of town ball and general disorganization to the foundation laid in 1901 for the dual American and National leagues—at least fifty-five blacks got paid to play alongside white teammates. Bud Fowler is credited with breaking that ground. In 1878 he joined the Lynn Live Oaks, a minor league team in Massachusetts. He kept going for twenty-six winding-road years that coursed through twenty-two states and thirteen amateur, semipro, and Negro leagues; he also had his own barnstorming team. Fowler mostly was a second baseman, and his position made him easy prey for opponents who resorted to the spikes-high slide, one of the dirtiest and most effective forms of intimidation. He got sliced by so many base runners he finally lashed short wooden staves to his legs. Some say Fowler deserves credit for inventing the shin guard.

Inevitably, baseball, like every other social institution, bowed to the prevailing pressure of prejudice. Two protagonists dominated the narrative. Moses Fleetwood Walker technically was not the first black man to go pro (in 1879 William White, who wasn't white, filled in for a game with the now-forgotten Providence Grays), but he is considered baseball's de facto integrator. Most players of that era were rough-hewn and rough-spoken, callous of hand and, oftentimes, of mind. "Fleet" Walker attended Oberlin College, studied law at the University of Michigan, and was polished, articulate, and athletic; his tragic flaw was pigmentation. A steady-hitting catcher, Walker played his way onto the minor league Toledo Blue Stockings in 1883. That August Toledo hosted an exhibition game

with the National League's Chicago White Stockings. Teams would
schedule those extra mid-season clashes in order to pump up dwin-
dling cash reserves. Enter protagonist number two: Adrian "Cap"
Anson, Chicago's pugnacious player-manager.

Anson was everything Walker was not: crude, impatient,
bullying—and a superstar, the nineteenth century's Mr. Baseball.
He would go on to bat over .300 for twenty consecutive seasons
and become the first player to reach the glorious 3,000-hit plateau.
Excellence is a megaphone. Whatever Cap Anson said carried disproportionate weight with his peers, even when the words veered
toward bigotry. That day in Toledo, Anson caught sight of Fleetwood Walker and threw a fit. His performance was lacking in shock
value, Anson having acted out so often in front of so many umpires
that he'd been dubbed the "King of Kickers." This time, however,
he had a new beef. A black man was on the field. *Black! My God, who
could stand for that? Let them steal bases and pretty soon they'll be taking
our women.* Somebody spoke up, reminding Anson that if the White
Stockings refused to play, the fans would demand ticket refunds,
and there would be no pot of money for the two teams to share.

The White Stockings took the field, but Anson didn't change
his mind or hold his tongue. The heresy of blacks infiltrating baseball set his blood boiling. This was a man thoroughly calcified in
his ways. Baseball gloves came into vogue in the early 1880s, but
Anson wouldn't wear one. To do so was cheating, girlish. He thus
owns the distinction of being the last Major League first baseman
to play bare-handed, though he finally relented and slipped on a
glove in 1892. Fleetwood Walker could be equally firm in his resolve. Despite the obvious discomfort he caused within the clubby
confines of baseball, Walker refused to give in and go away. In 1884
the Blue Stockings moved up to the American Association, which
was one of the three major leagues then in existence. By accident,
Walker earned a place in sports history: he became the first black
person to make it to the mountaintop of professional ball on a
full-time basis. A few months later his younger brother Welday,

an outfielder, signed with Toledo. He was the second black player in the major leagues.

There would be no more.

Welday Walker appeared in only five games in 1884. Fleetwood played in forty-two and batted .263, one of the highest averages on his team. Still, the Blue Stockings declined to bring back either of the Walker brothers in 1885. Baseball gradually purged itself of people of color. Discrimination sank to the level of satire. That summer the management of the exclusive Argyle Hotel in Babylon, Long Island, wanted to offer guests a unique diversion, something to relieve the tedium of too much boating and ballroom dancing. Somebody proposed having the hotel's black waiters stage demonstration baseball games. Swell! The only problem, from a customer-relations perspective, was that guests would be likely to feel uncomfortable watching a black man do anything besides shine shoes or bus a dinner table. The solution? Call those waiter-ballplayers the "Cuban Giants" and instruct them to speak heavily accented gibberish that sounded reasonably like Spanish. The ruse worked, too well. Not only were the mock Cuban Giants a hit at the hotel; they played such high-caliber baseball they began touring the country in off-peak months and evolved into a premier semipro team.

Ornery John McGraw pulled a variation of that con in the Major Leagues. In more than forty turbulent years as a player and manager, he took a backseat to no one as a competitor. Tripping opposing runners or grabbing them by the belt didn't cause McGraw to lose any sleep. In 1901 he was piloting the Baltimore Orioles and decided to sign black second baseman Charles Grant under the pseudonym "Charlie Tokohoma," claiming he was a Cherokee Indian (though, oddly, one with a Japanese surname). The charade worked for a few spring training games, until Chicago White Sox owner Charles Comiskey ratted out Grant. That sort of subterfuge wasn't Fleet Walker's style. After being dumped by the Blue Stockings, he returned to the minor leagues and kept plugging away as

an openly black catcher. He was not done with baseball or with Cap
Anson. By 1887 Walker had migrated from Ohio to New Jersey,
landing with the Newark Little Giants of the International League.
The tide was running against him. On July 14 the *Sporting News*,
the esteemed "Bible of Baseball," sounded the alarm about minor
league teams providing a safe haven for black athletes, who at that
time probably numbered less than two dozen. "A new trouble has
just arisen in the affairs of certain baseball associations [which]
have done more damage to the International League than to any
other we know of," a *Sporting News* editorial snorted. "We refer
to the importation of colored players into the ranks of that body."

Three days later the Newark Little Giants made the big mistake of scheduling a summer exhibition game with, of all teams,
Cap Anson's Chicago White Stockings. The Little Giants not only
had Fleet Walker on their roster as a catcher, but also George
Stovey as a pitcher. They constituted the first all-black battery in
professional baseball. Anson tossed a double tantrum. This time
he didn't flinch. He announced that his team would stay put on
the bench unless somebody did something. Fast. "Get that nigger
off the field!" he barked at the umpire, referring to Stovey. Hasty
negotiations ensued. The game proceeded as scheduled with Stovey
and Walker remaining in the dugout in order to keep peace. That
same day directors of the International League met in Buffalo and
adopted a policy, as one newspaper reported, "of no more contracts
with colored men." Many baseball watchers believed, but could not
prove, that the International League took this step at the behest
of Major League owners, who secretly had forged a gentlemen's
agreement to keep the game whites-only.

With his sour demeanor and curlicue mustache, Cap Anson
made a perfect villain, the Snidely Whiplash of baseball segregation. But the problem wasn't his speaking out repeatedly against
blacks as much as it was so many others repeatedly keeping silent.
An ill wind blew unchallenged. The last black man drummed out of
organized ball in America was pitcher Bert Jones, banished in late

July 1898 from the same semipro Kansas State League that later
would welcome outfielder Dwight Eisenhower with open arms. By
then, the Walkers were long gone. Welday couldn't find a baseball
job in 1888. His brother hung on till 1889, when the minor league
Syracuse Stars cut him loose. Fleetwood was only thirty-two, but
his life never regained traction. He married twice; managed a hotel
and a movie theater in Ohio; served a year in prison for mail theft;
was attacked by a group of white men and ultimately acquitted of
stabbing one of them to death in self-defense.

For a time he and Welday edited a black newspaper. In 1908
Fleetwood published *Our Home Colony*, a treatise supporting Marcus
Garvey's back-to-Africa movement. Ironically, he wound up on the
same wavelength as his nemesis, Cap Anson. Rejecting the prospect of racial comity, Fleetwood Walker wrote that it was "almost
criminal to attempt to harmonize these two diverse peoples while
living under the same government."

Baseball formed two parallel universes. Blacks developed their own
school, town, semipro, and professional teams. Whites had theirs.
Commingling on the field was possible only on the lowest tiers
of organized ball and even then it was rare to behold, like an orchid blooming in December's chill. When Quincy Troupe's plane
touched down at Bismarck Municipal Airport about noon on July
26, 1933, he stepped into an alien environment of tumbleweed,
yowling coyotes, cowboy-movie panoramas, and restaurants serving lutefisk. Yet he immediately spotted a familiar face, an orchid
growing in North Dakota. Roosevelt Davis, a pitcher for the St.
Louis Stars when Troupe was batboy, met his flight.

Davis had been in town a month. He was the first knight-errant
ballplayer to answer Neil Churchill's call. At thirty, Davis had lost
some zip on his fastball, but he compensated with guile, a suitable
curve, and applied physics, also known as cheating. He was well
schooled in the practice of doctoring a baseball. Nick it with a belt

buckle. Scratch it with a sliver of sandpaper. Furtively apply a gob of saliva or a dab of grease. Whatever was required to make a pitch misbehave on the way to home plate, Davis could and would do it without hesitation. In June the *Tribune* had trumpeted his arrival in town with a headline at the top of the sports page: "Bismarck Drubs Fort Lincoln 16–0 as Negro Hurler Makes Debut." Davis struck out sixteen that game; in another he fanned an astonishing twenty-three. Although North Dakota batters showed signs of wising up to his junk balls, he'd won four of six starts.

Davis helped Troupe load his luggage into a loaner car provided by Neil Churchill, and together they drove downtown to the Princess Hotel, where accommodations were anything but regal. The Princess had been built as a crash pad for workers on the Minneapolis, St. Paul, and Sault Ste. Marie Railway. It was first called the "Soo" Hotel. After a name change to the Princess in the 1920s, it embarked on a second life as no-frills public lodging: four-floor walk-up, communal baths, concrete-and-cement-block construction. With elegance a nonfactor, newspaper ads for the Princess extolled it as being "the most nearly fireproof hotel in the state." It also was the only hotel in Bismarck that accepted black guests. Troupe checked in, unpacked his bags, then went to visit with Davis, who had a room down the hall. He opened the door and found the pitcher standing in front of a mirror, rubbing lotion onto the top of his head. It smelled god-awful. "This is mange medicine," Davis explained matter-of-factly. "My hair's falling out. I'm using this stuff to stop it."

Mange medicine? Troupe had to wonder what he'd gotten himself into. Chicago suddenly seemed very, very far away: a lush planet with great, thick steaks somewhere on the other side of the universe. "How do you like it, Roosevelt? How strong is the baseball out here?" asked Troupe, eager to talk about something other than male-pattern baldness.

"I'm doing okay," Davis said. "These people don't know a thing about baseball, except that they want you to *win*."

Troupe was young enough to think of baseball in familial terms. He described it as a mother, father, and best friend "all rolled into one." He still had his idealism and all his hair, but he and Rosie Davis—who'd put mange medicine on a baseball if that would make it unhittable—were a matched pair in one regard. Neil Churchill had brought them both to North Dakota for the same reason: to win.

Troupe left Davis to his scalp massage and took a walk. He was in the mood for a movie, but already had seen the feature playing around the corner at the Capitol Theatre: Irene Dunne as a scheming, deranged mother-in-law in *The Silver Cord*. He decided instead to go shopping for the sheet music to "Moonglow." He found it. A few heads no doubt turned at the sight of a tall, well-dressed black man ambling down the street. Troupe was making history in a prairie town that hadn't yet shaken off the dust of its wild and woolly past. He and Davis were the first blacks ever to play ball on the local team, discounting Gilkerson's Union Giants, who were outside contractors (and, furthermore, not integrated). There were only forty-six blacks living in Bismarck, mostly confined to the blue-collar south side near the river. One of those residents, Nancy Millett, harked back to pioneer days. She had come west sixty years before as a domestic servant. The master of the house died unexpectedly and his distraught wife moved to New York City. Millett married and stayed in Bismarck. Imagine that. The black woman who cooked and cleaned for Colonel George Armstrong Custer was ninety-one and going strong. And she lived only a few blocks from the baseball field. The whisper in town was that long ago there'd been a dalliance with a white soldier at Fort Lincoln and Nancy Millett had borne a child out of wedlock. That son was grown now, a tinsmith living on the white, east side of town.

He and Mrs. Millett did not speak.

5

OVER THE COLOR LINE

Quincy Troupe had come to the bull's-eye of North America. The Atlantic, Pacific, and Arctic oceans and the Gulf of Mexico were equidistant from Bismarck. He knew what it must have felt like to serve in the Seventh Cavalry under Custer. Bismarck was an outpost on the baseball frontier. His hometown St. Louis Cardinals and the Chicago Cubs—the Major League teams closest to North Dakota—were both about 750 miles away. Fans of pro ball tended to follow the Minneapolis Millers, a AA minor league franchise that was *only* a 370-mile drive east.

Troupe arrived in town on the heels of unusual tumult. In late May 1933 North Dakota's governor, William "Wild Bill" Langer, whose party ties were to the populist, borderline-socialist Nonpartisan League, imposed martial law for several uneasy days. The Depression seemed to have everybody on edge. A new eighteen-story art deco statehouse was under construction in Bismarck, the old neoclassical one having burned to a crisp in 1930 when a pile of oily rags in a utility closet caught fire. In early May unskilled laborers on the project called a wildcat strike, seeking a raise from 30 to 50 cents an hour. Tempers flared, work ground to a halt, some conservative legislators smelled a communist conspiracy, and five people were arrested. In a clumsy attempt to resolve the dispute, Governor Langer summoned the National Guard, weapons drawn. The strikers quickly accepted a 10-cent-an-hour pay increase.

The statehouse fire had a subplot that further strained relations between Bismarck and Jamestown. They were sworn baseball
enemies, but the fight now took a political turn. Since the poor
yokels in Bismarck didn't know how to properly dispose of dirty
rags, community leaders in Jamestown pushed to have the capital
moved to their fair city for safekeeping. The tug-of-war had to be
settled at the ballot box. In March 1932, North Dakotans decided
overwhelmingly to do nothing: 11,686 voters favored relocating
the capital; 68,895 disapproved. The attempted hijacking did not
sit well with Bismarckers, but did add spice to a baseball rivalry
already hotter than five-alarm chili.

With the capital cemented firmly in place and martial law
lifted, Bismarck returned to its sleepy ways. Quincy Troupe and
Roosevelt Davis needed only a few days to get the lay of their
new surroundings. With the exception of a few modest hills, the
landscape looked flat and freshly carpeted in green. Francis Jaszkowiak had a small farm and repair shop on the western fringe of
town, tucked in a coulee near a makeshift hobo camp. Residents of
the sparsely developed but upscale west end could walk less than
a hundred yards from their front doors and hunt pheasant. Main
Street, which ran perpendicular to the Missouri River, was the
central artery. The bottomlands south of Main, where the baseball
field was located, flooded every spring. Blue-collar families and
Bismarck's handful of blacks inhabited those soggy neighborhoods.

A grid of streets three-quarter-mile by one-quarter-mile north
of Main Street constituted the downtown core. The architecture,
like the people, was purposeful and unpretentious. Everything and
everyone who counted was within walking distance. The spinster
sisters Bonnie and Catherine Morris lived on North Sixth Street.
They harvested fresh gossip, especially anything related to the
latest death and funeral. A guilty-pleasure landmark occupied the
shoebox storefront at 515 Broadway. Jack Lyons' Ideal Irish Lunch
Stand specialized in greasy hamburgers topped with greasy grilled

onions that slid smoothly down delighted throats. Lyons was a
former riverboat captain whose father had survived the Battle of
the Little Big Horn. His burgers cost 10 cents and their enduring
popularity was believed owed to the fact that nobody washed Jack's
grill. Ever. A courageous soul once tried to clean the exhaust fan,
but quickly excused himself so he could go puke.

Norman Rockwell would have found plenty of Middle America
inspiration in Bismarck. Finney's drugstore at Fourth and Broadway
had a soda fountain and its Baby Buffalo sundae gave patrons reason
enough to live. One block away the city's elite (all male and heavily
Protestant) gathered to get a trim and schmooze at John Dolan's barbershop in the basement of the First National Bank. The biggest em-
ployer other than the government was Oscar H. Will Company. Will
was friendly with Indians and developed scores of durable hybrids
of their crops, distributed under his label "Pioneer Seed." Mandan
squash, the great northern bean, and Pride of Dakota corn sprouted
worldwide. Will's son George extended the brand by jerry-rigging
a coffee roaster to accept sunflower seeds. You could spot Bismarck
natives by how well they'd mastered the oral gymnastics of cracking
and spitting sunflower shells. The focal point of downtown was the
intersection of Fifth and Main streets. The Northern Pacific train
station dominated the south side of Main. The Patterson Hotel,
where politicos dined and conspired, presided over the northeast
corner. It was the tallest building in North Dakota when it opened
in 1911, soaring all of seven stories.

Corwin-Churchill Motors was at North Second Street and
Main, less than a five-minute walk from the Patterson Hotel. It was
"Bismarck's pioneer garage," so advertisements boasted, and the
oldest in North Dakota. Wick Corwin opened for business before
World War I but never purchased the property. He and Churchill
remained tenants of Ed Hughes, arguably the richest, crankiest man
in town. Hughes's empire encompassed large chunks of real estate
and Hughes Electric, the power company that kept Bismarck and
Mandan humming. As a rule, manufacturers at that time shipped

autos by train only half assembled. Since Corwin and Churchill had to keep a crew of mechanics on staff to put together incoming Chryslers and their lower-priced Plymouth spinoffs, why not do general repairs on all types of vehicles? Come to think of it, why not wash cars and pump gas? Why not provide winter storage? The dealership operated around the clock, six days a week, closing only on Sunday because of the almighty blue laws. Corwin-Churchill Motors even provided ambulance service for the city. During the Depression it ventured beyond cars and sold shortwave radios, Goodyear tires, golf balls, shotgun shells, refrigerators, movie cameras, fishing tackle, and live bait.

There was another incentive for keeping extended hours. Corwin-Churchill, and several other Bismarck car dealers, catered to a tiny segment of special clients. They wanted quick tune-ups on supercharged engines. They were interested in short-term storage, just a few days at most. They mostly drove dusty automobiles with Canadian license plates. Other than perhaps the nosy Morris sisters, nobody spoke openly about those transient customers or asked many questions. Running moonshine? Unequivocally an illegal activity. There was, however, no law against providing garage space for cars that reeked of whiskey and beer.

Corwin-Churchill Motors looked like a country store with a Napoleon complex. The low-slung, two-story building had expanded over time, gobbling up most of the block between First and Second streets. A canopy covered two gas pumps standing vigil out front. The showroom was like a fishbowl. Floor-to-ceiling windows on the Main Street and Second Street sides gave passersby unobstructed views of Walter Chrysler's latest dreamboats. Neil Churchill's office was behind the showroom. Its decor leaned toward Mid-Twentieth-Century Bank President. Three leather-covered chairs faced a large, blocky wooden desk. The walls were finished in faux-leather wainscoting. Instead of fine art, Churchill displayed trophies won by the town baseball and basketball teams. He and Helen moved into a house just a few blocks from the dealership along with their infant son and Helen's widowed mother and sister. The Churchills were riding high: proud owners of one of the first electric dryers in town, a new Chrysler parked in their driveway every few months, and a live-in maid to handle the cooking and cleaning. They shared a happy, but typically bifurcated, marriage.

Bismarck, like every other city in the 1930s, was a grand men's club. Feminist notions would have been as warmly received as an outbreak of hoof-and-mouth disease. Helen busied herself with corporate-wife diversions such as the Presbyterian Ladies Aid Society and Tuesday Bridge Club. At night, she read novels or researched papers on Scandinavia and essayist Thomas Carlyle for her Wednesday Study Club. But Helen was the pragmatic one, the glue holding the family together; much as Wick Corwin was the bonding agent at Corwin-Churchill Motors. Neil dashed home for supper promptly at six o'clock, wolfed down a meal (he always was served last because he ate so fast), and bolted back out the door. Churchill belonged to the Masons, the Shriners, Rotary, and the Bismarck Horse Club. In summer he coached baseball. In winter he was preoccupied with Phantoms basketball. At other times, he could surface anywhere. Churchill would drive to South Dakota to catch Bismarck High School's football team in action. He and Ford dealer Fred Copelin acted as ringside judges for boxing nights at Fort Lincoln. The *Tribune* spotted him dressed as a flapper playing a "somewhat plump member of the chorus" in a musical produced by the Business and Professional Women's Club. The Elks staged a "Minstrel Frolic," and there he was belting out a comic ditty, "If You Can't Land Her on the Old Veranda."

Churchill and Wick Corwin rarely socialized with each other. They were friends, but had no mutual interests. Church palled around a lot with John Fleck, who owned the Buick-Cadillac dealership. Both closely followed and supported high school sports.

Bismarck cheerleaders, in a fit of perkiness, would acknowledge their attendance at basketball games with cries of "Churchill, Churchill, he's our man. If he can't do it . . . *Fleck* can!" Every year Fleck and Churchill each informally sponsored a child from a disadvantaged family. They tried to outdo each other picking up the tab for books, clothes, and toys, part of the satisfaction coming from competitive gloating: "I just bought my kid a Roadmaster bike. Why's yours still riding a cheap Huffy?" Nothing brought the two of them as much pleasure as cards. Churchill played tournament-level bridge with Helen, but he never turned his back on a hand of gin rummy or poker with his buddies. In a pinch, he and Fleck would play a card game called "Shadow" over the phone. A group of serious card sharks periodically rented a suite at the Patterson Hotel and held all-night poker sessions fueled by alcohol and cigars. To be offered a seat at the table was a badge of social distinction. Fleck and Churchill were regulars. Churchill said of those poker marathons, "I don't have any reason to smoke. I inhale all the smoke I need playin' cards."

Ed Patterson, who owned the hotel, had at one time or another been mayor, councilman, and county commissioner. He knew the going rate for buying a judge and which ones liked to have their palms greased. Patterson personified the combination of toughness, resiliency, and shrewdness that had won the frontier. Around 1923 he discovered a delightful loophole in state law: any commercial building undergoing renovation automatically received a waiver from paying property taxes. It became terribly important to add an eighth, ninth, and tenth story to his hotel, but not terribly important to finish the job. He turned loose a skeleton crew of two masons with a creaky, wooden cement mixer powered by a swayback mule.

Time generally goes slowly in prairie towns, but it all but stopped on the upper floors of the Patterson Hotel, which remained a tax break in progress for more than thirteen years. However, "construction" had no effect on late-night poker. The games continued behind closed doors without interruption.

*   *   *

North Dakota winters can get so cold that faces feel like death masks. Winds whip with such fury people sometimes walk backward into a gale. The months-long endurance test makes each spring a much-anticipated event. In Bismarck, Gafney-Shipley stationery store liked to celebrate by giving a free typewriter to whoever correctly predicted the date when the ice broke up on the Missouri River. The Wachters, a ranching family who also owned the ice house that supplied every icebox in the vicinity, soon would begin trucking cattle from winter holding pens on South Seventh Street to pastures outside the city limits, taking with them the bovine stench that had fouled the air since fall.

Many owners babied their cars, storing them during the winter on blocks as if they were boats in need of dry-docking. Once March thawed out, hundreds of vehicles got taken out of mothballs and reintroduced to the road. Birds sang. Tulips bloomed. Thoughts turned to baseball. The 1933 season differed from previous years in that Neil Churchill had five volunteer assistants to lighten his load, handling the grunt work of field maintenance, scheduling, and ticket sales. Unfortunately, they couldn't do much about the disorganized scrapheap of players he inherited. Churchill called an early-spring practice. A high school student was among the first-base candidates. The two best pitchers on hand were a state employee nicknamed "Honey Boy" and a teacher nicknamed "Smiley"; men unlikely to turn into tigers on the mound. None of the opening-day starters would be in the lineup by September. The dugout had a revolving door. More than twenty replacement players flitted in and out as Churchill tried to cobble together the perfect dozen or so for his roster. He remained popular, thanks to his good-hearted nature, but now that he was prepared to pay for high-quality performance, accountability entered into the bargain. In car-dealer parlance, he wouldn't be keeping clunkers on his lot.

The recruiter in him never rested. In late June the team was a disappointing 6 and 6. Ralph Sears, a student at Columbia University in New York, passed through town on his way home to Oakland, California. Churchill talked him into trying out for shortstop, liked what he saw, and persuaded Sears to stay for the summer. A week later Churchill reeled in Roosevelt Davis, who was pitching for the Columbus Blue Birds of the Negro National League. The Blue Birds were in last place, losing money, and on the verge of moving to Cleveland. Churchill sold Davis on the idea of making the much longer move to North Dakota. No doubt the price was right, probably about $200 a month.

Neither Churchill nor Davis was blazing a new trail—not at this point, anyway. Individual black ballplayers had been pushing west since the advent of the railroad, some latching onto white teams. Bud Fowler—the groundbreaking, shin-guard-wearing Massachusetts infielder—drifted to Minnesota in the 1880s. Pitchers tended to be most in demand, since they can be great equalizers on a ball field. So it was that black pitcher Walter Ball found a home with the Grand Forks, North Dakota, town team in 1899. Black pitcher Brick Jones was imported from Minnesota by the Dickinson, North Dakota, team for the express purpose of facing Bismarck on July 4, 1904. (A *Tribune* reporter was there to see Jones get summarily knocked out of the box: "The Bismarck team bumped him for fifteen safe hits, sending him to the tall timbers.") Peripatetic black pitcher John Donaldson got scooped up by Scobey, Montana, in 1925; the same summer, that team wooed pitcher Charlie Boardman away from Bismarck.

Of immediate concern to Churchill were the goings-on in Jamestown, the perpetual thorn in Bismarck's side. Having failed to kidnap the capital, Jamestowners seemed intent on asserting their athletic superiority. They'd quietly tapped into the Negro Leagues for several players in 1932, Kansas City Monarchs pitcher Wilber "Bullet" Rogan being one of them. Jamestown roared to a 32–7 record, with Rogan winning 22 of 25 starts. He went back to the Monarchs in 1933, but Jamestown shored up its starting rotation with three black pitchers, raising the semipro stakes significantly in North Dakota. By snatching Roosevelt Davis from the Columbus Blue Birds, Churchill anteed up, sending a message that he was preparing to beat the Jamestown team at its own elevated game. Conventional wisdom held that mixed-race baseball met with minimal opposition on the northern Plains because of a regional tradition of tolerance. Minnesota enacted antidiscrimination laws in 1899. Twelve states granted women the right to vote before Congress got around to passing the Nineteenth Amendment in 1920; eleven of them were west of the Mississippi River. On the other hand, racial comity can be a product of indifference rather than open-mindedness. Blacks were in short supply in states such as North Dakota and, therefore, not intruding on anybody's comfort zone. Native Americans were more prevalent and paid the price, as scapegoated minorities often do. The epithet "prairie nigger" became entrenched in the western lexicon.

The social and political ripple effects of integrated baseball were lost on Neil Churchill. He never consulted with anyone or articulated any altruistic motives for signing black players. His agenda—forward-thinking in its own right—was to pump up the win column by putting the best possible team on the field. In July the *Tribune* reported, "Bismarck's biggest weakness so far this season, Manager Neil O. Churchill said Tuesday, is inability to hit in pinches to produce much-needed runs." Three regulars were hitting under .220. Securing the services of Quincy Troupe (whom the *Tribune* habitually referred to as the "giant Negro catcher") became imperative. Churchill coupled that pickup with the signing of Paul Schaefer, a white pitcher-outfielder with Minnesota's East Grand Forks Colts of the independent Class D Northern League. The day after Troupe flew from Chicago to Bismarck, he and Schaefer made their debuts against the Cleveland All-Nations, a gimmick team featuring players of different ethnic backgrounds at every position. Churchill's old promoter friend Abe Saperstein

was the All-Nations' booking agent. Schaefer played right field and
had two singles in four at-bats. Troupe went hitless, but showed
off his arm by picking a runner off second base. The game was
called because of darkness after nine innings with the score knotted 2–2. A moral victory for Bismarck. All-Nations had won 52
of its last 57 games.

Churchill felt relieved having Troupe and Schaefer in the fold
prior to a home game against Jamestown on August 2. In June they'd
slapped Bismarck around 14–8. That was before the retooling, and
Churchill had still more moves in mind. Just in time for the rematch
he nabbed Lester Moore, an infielder hitting a hair under .300
for the Fargo-Moorehead Twins of the Northern League. Moore
stepped right into the lineup at third base. Roosevelt Davis battled
Jamestown left-hander Barney Brown, a fellow Negro Leagues
exile, pitch for pitch. Each got nicked for just four hits. Brown
notched eleven strikeouts to Davis's nine. They worked briskly,
like two men with cabs waiting outside the ballpark, meters running. The game ended in a lightning-quick 1 hour and 23 minutes.
Davis lost focus for a fateful moment, serving up a solo home run
in the top of the seventh inning that accounted for all the scoring.
A reporter deemed the pitching duel "one of the niftiest baseball
games staged here in many a moon."

Four days after being shut out by Jamestown, Churchill
brought aboard some left-handed-swinging punch in the person
of infielder Granville Haley. He was thirty-two and had made the
rounds of semipro and Negro League ball. He spent three seasons
with Gilkerson's Union Giants, including 1930, when they were
Bismarck's hired-hands team. Churchill plucked Haley from the
Cuban Stars. Born in Missouri, he didn't have a drop of Cuban
blood in him, but looked the part. His mother was so fair everyone
called her "Blondie." He followed suit, so light-complexioned he
went by the name "Red" instead of Granville. Only five-feet-nine,
Haley had deceptive strength and a tendency to golf low pitches
over the right-field fence. One year with the Union Giants he

bashed 41 homers. Churchill penciled him in at shortstop, bumping Ivy Leaguer Ralph Sears to second base and sending a Bismarck townie to the bench. Haley quickly made his presence felt. His second game was against a semipro team from Gary, Minnesota, that had a respectable 22–6 record. Bismarck mauled them 20-1. Haley batted third in the order and lashed five hits, including a home run in the first inning. Troupe, in the cleanup spot, also had five hits and also had a home run. Schaefer tossed a six-hitter, and the only run Gary scored was unearned.

It's not often that a team explodes for twenty runs and nobody pays attention. But the slugfest proved anticlimactic, eclipsed by other events of the day. A third blood-feud game with Jamestown was on tap for the coming weekend, and all of North Dakota suddenly regarded it as Christmas in August. The reason was a breaking-news item that appeared in the *Tribune* without warning. Readers would have been less surprised to learn that grain prices had quadrupled overnight: "Satchel Paige leading right-handed flinger of the national colored league will pitch for Bismarck against Jamestown here Sunday afternoon it was announced Thursday by Manager Neil O. Churchill of the Capitol City Club."

The only player who could come close to matching Babe Ruth feat for feat and quip for quip and thrill for thrill was about to get on a westbound sleeper train and ride it to where the buffalo roamed. Neil Churchill, poker-playing car dealer, had pulled an ace out of his sleeve and stunned the sports world. Satchel Paige, considered by many the greatest baseball show on earth, was North Dakota–bound.

6

THROWING FIRE

Jimmie Crutchfield, a college-educated outfielder who played with Satchel Paige on the Pittsburgh Crawfords, had this to say: "When Satchel got to the ballpark it was like the sun just came out."

Some people naturally shine. They can brighten a lecture hall or a Broadway stage or a pitcher's mound. The light emanates from within, some unfathomable fusion of charisma, passion, and prodigious talent. Paige had star-power wattage. He could be vain and infuriatingly irresponsible, but never dull. Henry David Thoreau said that some people step to the beat of a different drummer. Ol' Satch, even when he was young Satch, marched to a ten-piece band jamming inside his head. He was terminally unpredictable, the prize inside the Cracker Jack box of baseball. The dog didn't eat Satchel's homework. That could happen to any schmo. No, a goat had gobbled the birth certificate that his mother kept inside the family Bible. He hated clocks and loved to break speed limits. He carried a gun (a habit more than one black ballplayer acquired as a result of making too many road trips through the back hollows of the Jim Crow South), but also a harmonica. He often signed autographs "Satchell" because why stop at one "l"? He jitterbugged and he waltzed. He canoodled on the piano in smoky bars and swore that shooting pool built more leg strength than running. He liked to soak his precious right arm twice a day in scalding-hot bathwater and, when boarding a train at the last possible second en route to his next baseball stop, was known to theatrically wave at the conductors and chirp, "All right, brothers, let us ramble!"

Colorful quotes gushed out of him like quarters from a Vegas slot machine stuck on three red cherries. Certain Satchelisms ("Don't look back, something might be gaining on you" and "Age is a question of mind over matter. If you don't mind, it doesn't matter.") would enter the annals of folk wisdom. Lesser-known comments had their charms, too. Paige felt that baseball executive Branch Rickey was something less than a straight shooter, prompting his aside that "Mr. Rickey, as the Bible says, sometimes spake in diverse tongues." A frustrated hitter lamented that Paige's fastball "looks like a marble" leaving his hand. Paige caught wind of that and sniffed, "He must be talkin' about my slowball. My fastball looks like a fish egg."

A clever ad-lib attracts attention, but it doesn't win ball games. Satchel was much more than the sum of his quirky parts. "He threw fire," said Buck Leonard, who terrorized most Negro League pitchers but insisted he never got a hit off Paige. Multiple witnesses testified to remarkable things they'd seen him do with a baseball. A favorite trick was to place a matchbox or gum wrapper on home plate, then shuffle back to the mound and pound strike after strike after strike at that precise spot. He could prop up a sheet of plywood that had some nails driven halfway into its surface and finish hammering the heads into place . . . with fastballs. Like many artistes, Paige had legions of friends, but few intimates. A person who made it into the inner circle was onetime teammate Buck O'Neil, among the Negro League's finest gentlemen. He knew the nooks and crannies of Paige's personality. "Satchel was a comedian. Satchel was a preacher. Satchel was just about everything," O'Neil said. "We had a good baseball team, but when Satchel pitched, a *great* baseball team. The amazing part about it was that he brought the best out in the opposition, too."

* * *

Like Quincy Troupe and Neil Churchill, Leroy Paige came from humble surroundings. It didn't take long for him to overcome any residual humbleness. Ditching the surroundings would take more time. He was the seventh of eleven children, all packed tight into a weather-beaten shack on the south side of Mobile, Alabama, in an empty-pockets neighborhood called Down the Bay. His father was a part-time gardener and full-time ne'er-do-well who soon skipped off. His mother, Lula, the rock of the family, was illiterate. She washed and cleaned for white folk, getting 50 cents a day.

Gangly and paper thin, Leroy hustled spare change by toting luggage at the Louisville and Nashville train depot. Along with tips he earned a new name. A friend thought Leroy loaded himself up with so many bags he looked like a "satchel tree." That's one explanation. Another is that somebody noticed Leroy's shoes were as big as those damn bags he lugged around. Hence, he became "Satchelfoot." A third version holds that he got the name from occasionally pilfering the bags that passengers had entrusted to his care. (If that's true, what a shame they didn't dub him "Snatchel.") A fourth theory is that as a boy he once borrowed his father's satchel. Take your pick. All that matters is that early on Leroy figuratively got left by the wayside and Satchel took his place.

Mobile had been a center of the slave trade. By the early 1900s —when that hungry goat munched Leroy Paige's birth certificate— it remained rigidly segregated. The Ku Klux Klan had yet to be declawed. Mobile, however, had one aberrant burst of liberalism. Unlike every other city in Alabama, it did not prohibit Sunday baseball. Pickup games broke out in parks, alleys, and side streets every day of the week. Beanpole Satchel Paige could be spotted in the middle of many of them. He talked as well as he played. It's not unusual for adolescents to bend facts, but Satchel turned them into a taffy pull and never outgrew the urge to stretch to the limit. Did he really develop his laser-like control as a kid by pelting birds with rocks and butterflies with clamshells? Did he stumble upon the mechanics of his hesitation pitch while tossing bricks? Only Satchel knew for sure.

"He'd rather play baseball than eat," Lula Paige sighed. That caused her some measure of anxiety, since she dismissed the sport as foolishness; an instrument of the devil that paved the way to serious sinning. Lula refused to watch her son play ball, but it had absolutely zero deterrent effect on him. The only activities that competed for Satchel's attention were fishing and petty theft, bicycles being a special temptation. He took his flirtation with crime too far in the summer of 1918. He was walking home from a sandlot game and ducked into a general store without a penny in his pocket. Pieces of costume jewelry beckoned, glittering like gold. "Unless you've gone around with nothing, you don't know how powerful a lure some new, shiny stuff is," Satchel explained, looking back upon that pivotal day from the perspective of adulthood.

He impulsively grabbed a handful of cheap rings and dashed out the door. The store manager gave chase, collaring him about a block away. Satchel stuffed the rings into his mouth, but quickly coughed up the evidence. Alabama judges didn't bother with wrist slaps. Not then. Not with black defendants. The full weight of the law came crashing down upon his slim shoulders. He had a history of cutting school. He had sticky fingers. He needed to be taught a lesson. That July Leroy Paige—as best the authorities could determine, a few weeks past his twelfth birthday—was remanded to the Alabama Reform School for Juvenile Negro Law-Breakers. It was a junior prison farm situated a dozen miles from Montgomery, the state capital, and 200 miles from his home. Hundreds of boys were fenced in there, forced to attend school, milk cows, and harvest corn by way of paying their debt to society. Young Mr. Paige owed the state of Alabama six years.

The Reform School for Juvenile Negro Law-Breakers sounds Dickensian. In actuality, it had redeeming social value. Satchel missed, but didn't pine for, his family. Reform school provided structure and discipline he sorely needed. He (begrudgingly) went to class, toiled in the fields, sang with the choir, and drummed in the drum and bugle corps. He also played baseball under the tutelage of coach Edward Byrd, a stickler for fundamentals who taught him what would become his signature high-kick, windmill-arm delivery. Satchel was six-foot-three, 140 pounds, and seemingly blessed with an extra complement of joints. He looked like a lounge chair unfolding when he threw a baseball, but his right arm was packed with gunpowder. Coach Byrd showed him how to harness it and throw fire.

Satchel walked the straight and narrow in reform school. He was released—because of good behavior—six months early, on New Year's eve 1923; a spindly eighteen-year-old with some accumulated maturity and not an ounce of bitterness. "If I'd been left on the streets of Mobile, I'd of ended up as a big bum, a crook," he said after establishing himself as a household-name ballplayer. "You might say I traded five years of freedom to learn how to pitch."

He never had a job other than baseball, never needed one, and wasn't qualified for much else. According to Satchel, it all began in the spring of 1924 when he went to watch the semipro Mobile Tigers. His older brother Wilson was a pitcher-catcher for them. Satchel, unable to sit quietly in the stands, talked the Tigers' manager into giving him an impromptu look-see and unleashed ten unhittable pitches. As Satchel recalled, the dumbfounded manager inquired, "Do you throw that fast consistently?" To which Satchel purportedly answered, "No, sir. I do it all the time."

Apocryphal anecdote or not, the Mobile Tigers inked him to a nominal contract of $1 a game, payable only when there was enough spare cash in the team's cookie jar. Undaunted, Paige pitched like a million bucks, going 30–1 that season. He stayed with the Tigers for the better part of three summers, rarely losing. An intriguing footnote to his pitching biography occurred in 1926. With two outs in the bottom of the ninth inning of a 1–0 game that Paige ached to win, his infielders muffed three plays in a row. Satchel had a meltdown. He invited the outfielders to come sit behind the pitcher's mound. It was his way of saying, "If we're going to give away a ball game, I'd rather do it myself." Paige reared back and struck out the next batter on three fastballs. That stunt didn't originate with him—a couple of pitchers on black barnstorming teams would yank their fielders to jazz a crowd—but this marked Paige's foray into showmanship. He loved it. Playing shorthanded became part of his repertoire.

The Mobile Tigers could not hold Paige for long. Both parties realized that. The Chattanooga Black Lookouts of the Negro Southern League heard of his exploits and dangled a $250-a-month contract. Lula Paige fretted about turning her son loose in the world, but Satchel eased those fears by promising to keep only $50 a month for himself. He pitched most of 1926 for the Lookouts but finished with the New Orleans Pelicans. A pattern was emerging. By his own admission, money didn't talk. It screamed a high-decibel siren song that he couldn't resist. His primary allegiance would always be to his bank account, not his team.

New Orleans was a pit stop. The Birmingham, Alabama, Black Barons of the Negro National League grabbed him in 1927 and held tight for three years. In 1929 Paige set the league record for strikeouts with 184. Rather than rest his arm that winter, he migrated for a month to Cuba, where a team threw $110 a game at him. Black baseball was part Wild West. Everybody wheeled and dealed. Some cards were marked. Some people got stabbed in the back. Paige was under contract to the Black Barons, but in 1930 the management sublet him to the Baltimore Black Sox and the Chicago American Giants. Meanwhile, the Pittsburgh Crawfords' Gus Greenlee sent a mash note: "The Crawfords might possibly be interested in having you pitch for them next season." Paige, well aware of his escalating box-office appeal, sent a coquettish reply: "I might possibly be interested in pitching for the Crawfords sometime."

Satchel, however, began the next baseball season with the Nashville Elite Giants, who soon pulled up stakes for Cleveland. The city grated on his nerves. League Park, then home of the Major League's Cleveland Indians, was a constant visual reminder of baseball's intransigence regarding race. Whether Paige would have been content in the regimented Major Leagues is an open question. Free spirits of any color were not encouraged to apply. Still, every ballplayer yearns to test his mettle against the best of the best. League Park symbolized a dream denied. "It burned me," Paige admitted, "playing there in the shadow of that stadium."

He escaped that shadow at the tail end of 1931. Greenlee succeeded in lassoing him, for a price that may have been as low as $250 a month (said Satchel) or as high as $550 (said a Chicago sports editor), especially if Greenlee was icing the cake with performance bonuses. The transition to Pittsburgh went smoothly. Why not? The Crawfords of 1931–1932 were one of the strongest clubs ever assembled. Paige was a star among stars. The cast included mythic catcher Josh Gibson, outfielders "Cool Papa" Bell, Oscar Charleston (the "black Ty Cobb"), and pitcher-catcher Ted "Double Duty" Radcliffe, who'd mentored Quincy Troupe with the St. Louis Stars in 1930 but long before that had grown up in Mobile playing ball with Paige. Sportswriter Damon Runyon slapped the moniker "Double Duty" on Radcliffe after taking in a Crawfords doubleheader. Radcliffe was Paige's catcher for game one, in which he hit a grand-slam home run to seal the victory. In the nightcap he changed gloves and threw a shutout.

The Crawfords were the talk of the Negro Leagues. Beyond that, Paige had become smitten with Janet Howard, a petite waitress at Greenlee's Crawford Grill. Cupid sneaked up on him in the most unromantic fashion. "From the minute she first set a plate of asparagus down in front of me," Satchel said, "I began to feel paralyzed." Not even love's paralysis could still his restless feet, however. Paige pitched regularly for the Crawfords, but Greenlee also rented out his ace to traveling and semipro teams for $500 a pop. That struck Paige as double dipping; in effect Big Gus was asking him to work overtime for nothing. Greenlee would say Satchel had a good deal compared with the average Negro League player, who in the 1930s made about $170 a month (down about 30 percent from the 1920s). That's not how Satchel looked at it. Babe Ruth commanded $80,000 from the Yankees in 1932. Maybe no team would toss that kind of money at Paige, but the average major leaguer got paid the equivalent of $1,100 a month. Wasn't Ol' Satch worth more? He wasn't "average" by any standard he'd ever encountered. Increasingly, Paige felt underpaid and underappreciated in Pittsburgh. It showed on the field. In August 1933, his record stood at a lackluster 5–7. The bloom was off the Crawfords rose. As if on cue, another suitor appeared. Neil Churchill could not abide Bismarck playing second baseball fiddle to Jamestown. In search of heavy artillery, he called Abe Saperstein, whose tentacles reached deep into the black athletic community.

"We want the greatest colored pitcher in· baseball today," Churchill declared. "Tell me who rates as tops now."

"Your man is Satchel Paige, but I don't think you can land him," Saperstein said. "Paige is pitching for the Pittsburgh Craw-fords and they need him too bad to let him go." By the way, he added, Paige wasn't just the best colored pitcher. He probably was the best pitcher, *period*.

Undeterred, Churchill asked Saperstein for a contact number. He may have been emboldened by having Red Haley and Quincy Troupe, both of whom Paige knew, in his pocket. Churchill reached Satchel that night and made the sales pitch of his life. It worked. For somewhere between $300 and $400 a month—with a used Chrysler tossed in as sweetener—he convinced baseball's fastest gun to head west. Paige once bragged that he "wouldn't throw ice cubes" for $400 a month, but that was before this latest in his long line of blowouts with Greenlee. He wanted out of Pittsburgh, the sooner the better. In some ways North Dakota suited him, given its abundance of fiercely independent farmers and ranchers, its stubborn cusses and sagebrush eccentrics. Paige had thoroughbred ability, but the heart of a wild stallion. Yet the significance of what he was about to do didn't sink in immediately.

"It wasn't until after I signed up with Mr. Churchill that I found out I was going to be playing with white boys," he said. "For the first time since I'd started throwing, I was going to have some of them on my side. It looked like they couldn't hold out against me all the way after all."

7

SHOWTIME

Neil Churchill didn't just play cards. He played cards for money. He played frequently and at times recklessly. When a game couldn't be found, he'd wager on something, somewhere, with someone, or maybe shoot up to Winnipeg and drop a few dollars on the ponies. Neil Churchill had the fever. "He'd gamble on what time the sun would come up," chuckles Lyle Porter, who as a boy fetched balls at Bismarck games and practices.

Old-timers still talk about some of those bets. There was the day Churchill raced Harry Potter (who didn't do anything more supernatural than manage Bismarck's municipal airport) to Fargo, 186 miles. Winner take all. They left from the Patterson Hotel, Churchill going the distance in his Chrysler Airflow sedan, Potter driving to the airport and jumping into his single-engine yellow Stinson. Churchill, whose lead foot was well known to the police, smoked Potter. Another time he raced sprinter Jesse Owens head-to-head across the outfield grass of the ballpark; actually, head-to-two-heads: Churchill was on horseback. Nobody alive today can recall who ate whose dust, but money surely was riding on the outcome.

Churchill played bridge for 10 cents a point but preferred poker for appreciably higher stakes. He lost an apartment building he owned when the cards didn't fall in his favor one night at the Patterson Hotel; on another occasion he had to surrender the keys to a new Chrysler. Word travels fast through back channels in small towns. Compulsive gambling may not have been a recognized addiction in the 1930s, but people were aware Neil Churchill carried that monkey on his back. Some Bismarckers took umbrage at the thought of fat cats tossing cars into a poker pot while so many families were subsisting on relief checks and scrambling to pay mortgages. A more empathetic Wick Corwin told his partner that he worried about him. Churchill didn't want to hear it. He had his extracurricular activities under control, thank you very much. In one respect, he functioned at a higher level *because* of them. Like other businesses, Corwin-Churchill Motors limped through the Depression. How, then, did Neil Churchill find the wherewithal to rejuvenate a semipro team or go on a shopping spree to get Satchel Paige? Simple: the magic of symbiotic vices. His gambling addiction supported his baseball addiction. As long as Churchill's luck held away from the ball field, he could afford to keep putting a new and improved team on it. Sometimes he enjoyed the best of both worlds and bet on his ball team.

Gambling was a wink-and-a-nod crime thoroughly ingrained in the culture of the northern Plains, where daily existence qualified as a roll of the dice. Farmers' fortunes are tethered to weather, the ultimate fickle finger of fate. Recreational gambling was so popular that newspapers felt comfortable making public mention of the action. In 1926 a basketball game between Churchill's Phantoms and a team from the town of Glen Ullin had to be moved to a neutral site because of a scheduling conflict at World War Memorial Hall, the Phantoms' home court. Permission was secured to play at the reform school's gymnasium in Bismarck, with the *Tribune* noting, "The state board of administration stipulated, however, that the $500 side bet between the two teams be called off and that no other betting of any kind be permitted. Representatives of the two teams agreed to the terms."

Seven years later—on Saturday, August 12, 1933—the *Tribune* splashed a bold headline across the full width of its sports page: "Baseball Spirit Grips City as Bismarck–Jamestown Game Nears."

Satchel Paige's arrival was imminent and preparations were under way. Extra bleachers had been erected in anticipation of a beyond-capacity crowd that might top 2,500. Northern Pacific added a special baseball train that would leave Jamestown at 8:30 Sunday morning and chug into downtown Bismarck at precisely 11:03. The Bismarck Association of Commerce was organizing a volunteer car caravan to meet the train and take all curious Jamestown fans on a one-hour tour of the capital, guaranteed to finish in plenty of time for the scheduled first pitch at 3:00.

The *Tribune* story reiterated the roster changes Churchill had made since the teams last met ten days earlier, with "Red Haley, Cuban, heavy-hitting and spectacular-fielding shortstop" and "Quincy Troupe, giant Negro" augmenting the signing of Paige. A possibly epic confrontation loomed. Baseball junkies were having heart palpitations. Pete Zappas, owner of the Palace Café in James-town, sent a telegram to Neil Churchill on Friday before the big game: Some Jamestowners were prepared to bet $500 that they'd be riding the return train on Sunday night wearing victory smiles. Any takers? As the *Tribune* reported, Churchill and Bismarck fan Fred Thimmesch "in their reply offered to raise the ante to $1,000." That was not chump change. It is the equivalent of nearly $17,000 today, evidence that North Dakotans took their baseball almost as seriously as they did their corn and wheat.

Gus Greenlee took baseball seriously, too, and didn't see the humor in his marquee pitcher breaking a contract and bolting for Bismarck. He pulled some strings and had Paige briefly detained by the Pittsburgh police. But as Paige once said of himself, "I'm Satchel. I do as I do." And so he did. Like wood smoke, he shifted direction and was gone. His sleeper train pulled into Bismarck late Saturday afternoon. Troupe, Haley, and Churchill were standing on the station platform.

"Hey, Troupe!" Paige called out. "Man, that train picked up horses, chickens, everything. And a few miles down the track they waited for a cattle roundup!" A porter trailed behind, toting three bulging suitcases. Despite his penchant for pulling up stakes as regularly as a Gypsy caravan, Paige disdained traveling light.

Troupe handled the introductions. "Satch, this is Mr. Churchill, owner of the team. And you know Haley."

"We're glad to have you with us," Churchill said, beaming with delight. "I hope you'll like our little town."

Haley shook Paige's hand. Five years ago in Alabama they'd been teammates with the Birmingham Barons. "As I live and breathe," said Paige, "what are you doing here?"

"Playing ball, Satch, but I never thought I'd see you out here doing the same."

Churchill drove his three prized players to the 200 block of South Seventh Street, on the working-class side of town. Troupe and Haley were renting rooms in the home of Louis and Edith White, a black couple in their fifties. Louis worked as a porter and car washer at Copelin Motors. Owner Fred Copelin and Churchill were friends. It was the ideal living situation for young Quincy Troupe: a family atmosphere with Haley able to fill the role of baseball big brother. Paige would be staying with the Whites for a few days, then go his own way, most likely ending up at the spartan but always accommodating Princess Hotel. For now, however, Churchill could take comfort in knowing that his mischievous pitcher would at least get one good night's sleep. Indeed, the next afternoon Paige was on the job early, taking infield practice at the ballpark with his new teammates. Churchill sidled up to him. "Satch, are you ready to pitch today?"

"Oh, yeah. Ready as I'll ever be."

Paige sensed that Jamestown wasn't showing proper respect for a worthy opponent, "givin' Bismarck the hee-haw," as he put it. He intended to bring them down a peg. Maybe someone had shown him a copy of the *Jamestown Sun*. People couldn't seem to believe the Northern Pacific Railway was charging only $1 for a round-trip to Bismarck. A *Sun* reporter wrote in his pregame story, " 'It is so cheap that we can't afford to stay at home and wait in suspense to hear how badly we beat them' is the sentiment expressed on the street today."

Nobody on the streets of Jamestown apparently had heard about the signing of Satchel Paige.

Bismarck's ballpark was of classic small-town design. A horseshoe-shaped grandstand—painted dark green—curled from first base to third base. A roof shielded those fortunate ticket holders from the sun and rain. A chicken-wire screen spared them the pain and indignity of getting bonked by foul balls. They had their choice of about ten rows of rump-busting wooden planks on which to sit, like church pews for masochists. Beyond the confines of the grandstand were the lower-priced, exposed bleachers with the same hardwood seating. Directly behind and above home plate, a tiny bunker of a press box clung to the grandstand roof. Appended to the back of the grandstand was a cinder-block locker room (sans showers) shared by both teams. There was no home-run fence. Bleacher bums could opt to stand or park their cars deep in the outfield, providing they didn't mind dodging any extra-base hits that came bouncing by.

The field was two blocks from Corwin-Churchill Motors, just south of where West Main Street crossed Washington Street. Railroad tracks ran along the eastbound shoulder of Main Street, which was elevated in that part of town, creating a grassy berm that paralleled the right-field foul line of the ball field. Fans who couldn't afford to buy a ticket or who didn't have time to stay for an entire game could watch free from the hillside. That's also where the spillover crowd congregated in the event of a sellout. For Sunday's game against Jamestown, the hill was packed as tight as anyone had ever seen it. In all, an estimated 3,000 people came to see the Satchel show.

Left-hander Barney Brown, who'd bested Roosevelt Davis 1–0 when the teams last met two weeks earlier, took the mound again for Jamestown. He was terrific again. But Paige was Paige. He got touched for one hit through five innings and robbed two batters with fielding gems, leaping to snare a line drive up the middle and later spearing a hard one-hop comebacker—which he milked for maximum effect, pausing to dry his right hand on the resin bag before flinging the ball to first base just in time to nip the runner. In the top of the sixth, Paige faltered. He gave up a pair of hard singles and a double, sandwiched around a one-out walk. Jamestown jumped to a 2–0 lead and looked to be on the verge of busting the game open. Paige responded by turning up the heat, impressing a *Jamestown Sun* scribe by fanning the next two hitters "with balls that were so fast one could hardly see them."

Meanwhile, Barney Brown glided on cruise control as Bismarck eked out just two hits over seven and two-thirds innings. Then it was his turn to stumble. He walked Haley. Troupe—who'd previously struck out with the bases loaded—laced a triple to left field, driving in Haley. Paul Schaefer followed with a triple to center, scoring Troupe. Game tied, 2–2. A pumped-up Satchel Paige strode onto the field for the top of the ninth inning. "They don't get no mo' runs!" he barked. Better yet, they didn't get no more base runners. Paige struck out the side on ten pitches. Brown answered in the bottom of the ninth by recording two quick outs before plunking second baseman Ralph Sears on the arm with a pitch. Next up was Bismarck's leadoff batter, Bill Morlan, one of Churchill's pickups, out of Iowa. After taking a strike, he slashed a hard, sinking line drive. Jamestown's left fielder dived for the ball, but it squirted under his glove. Sears tore around second base and didn't stop at third. He kicked into high gear and slid across home plate, sending up a spray of dust as the relay throw nestled into the catcher's glove. The umpire signaled . . . *safe!*

The crowd erupted as one. Bismarck wins 3–2! Paige had struck out an astonishing eighteen batters. Jamestown fans, some of whom ended up on the wrong end of a $1,000 bet, scowled on the train ride home, but they could appreciate the sentiment expressed in the next day's edition of the *Sun*: "The two teams played a brand of baseball that is not any better any place in the country, no matter where the players are from or the diamond is located. The game was a masterpiece."

Neil Churchill couldn't have agreed more. A memorable ball game. And he had a wad of cash in his pocket to prove it.

While the Bismarck ball game dominated the *Jamestown Sun* sports section that Monday, the front page of the paper contained a grim Associated Press wire story. Three black men in Tuscaloosa, Alabama (Satchel Paige's home state), had been "spirited away by a lynching party." Two bodies later were found "riddled by bullets." The other man was missing. All three had been in police custody after being indicted for the killing of a white woman. That kind of hate crime was largely unknown in North Dakota. Discrimination took the form of segregated housing, inequitable job opportunities, restaurants that refused to serve minorities, and the knee-slapping popularity of minstrel shows. Those prejudices were the product of a cloistered homogeneity that hasn't changed much over time. Thus an elderly man in contemporary Bismarck can look back upon the 1930s and decry how "darkies who were well-dressed and educated" had difficulty finding hotel rooms in town. He can look back without a trace of rancor in his voice, as if "darkies" were textbook-English terminology for inhabitants of the small African country of Darkonia.

Neil Churchill often told a story about a farmer who walked into the Corwin-Churchill showroom wearing a sweat-stained shirt and dirty overalls. The sales staff dismissed him as a gawker. Churchill finally asked the man what he wanted and discovered that those dirty overalls were stuffed with money, which the farmer used to pay in full for a brand-new Chrysler. Moral of the story: things aren't always what they seem. So it was with race relations in Bismarck. The last person publicly hanged in North Dakota was a black man, but no frenzied mob strung up Jim Cole on the morning of March 24, 1899. Cole, a talented amateur musician, worked as a domestic servant in the home of an upper-class Bismarck family. He'd become obsessed with Saphronia Ford, a fourteen-year-old black girl. After she spurned his clumsy advances, he shot her dead in the street one afternoon and immediately ran over to the jail and turned himself in. The *Tribune* covered the murder extensively. The paper and the town showed remarkable respect and sympathy for Cole, though it's uncertain that would've been the case had he killed a young white girl. The sheriff permitted about a dozen friends to visit him in jail one day. He strummed a guitar and sang for them. He smoked a cigar on his march to the gallows and somebody donated a new black suit for him to wear. When the rope was placed around his neck, Cole expressed sorrow for his actions and thanked his guards, especially Deputy Sheriff Edward Patterson (future rascal and owner of the Patterson Hotel) for being "a good friend in time of need." The *Tribune* reported he "was brave to the last" and Sheriff Horace Bogue remarked that the prisoner "in every way conducted himself as a gentleman." Just after dawn, Cole said "Let her go, boys!" and the trapdoor sprang open. That wasn't quite the end of him, however. In the weeks leading up to the hanging a collector's-item phonograph record went on sale in Bismarck. It was a rendition of the gospel song "Oh, Happy Day" sung by doomed vocalist Jim Cole.

Some forty years later Satchel Paige hit town and encountered racial dynamics more layered and nuanced than what he had known growing up in Alabama. Some things struck a familiar chord. Bismarck's ragman was known to everyone in the white community as "Nigger Baker," just as Paige rented a room from a woman colloquially called "Nigger Betty." The American Legion ladies' auxiliary had put on two spring minstrel shows, with a blackface mammy chorus dressed in calico performing such showstoppers as "That's Why Darkies Were Born" and "Mammy's Little Coal Black Rose." Other things never could have occurred in the South.

A black student, Ed Spriggs, starred in three sports at Bismarck High School in the 1930s and went on to attend the state teachers' college in Valley City, where he was elected class president. Neil Churchill asked his semipro baseball and basketball players to help out at the dealership by cleaning cars and running errands (rest assured Satchel Paige wiggled around that rule). When a white Corwin-Churchill employee balked at working alongside blacks, Wick Corwin fired him.

Paige pitched four and a half weeks for Neil Churchill during the last gasps of summer 1933. He said there was a tense moment early on, but never specified the game in which it occurred. Paige contended that his outfielders butchered a few fly balls and he got on them between innings. "If you did that in the league I play in you'd get booted out," he groused. Somebody in the dugout mumbled what sounded to him like "dirty nigger." Paige shot back, "I'm sure clean enough to be playing with your kind. Where would you high and mighty boys be without me?"

When it came time to take the field again, Paige finished his warm-up tosses, pivoted on the mound, and noticed he had no outfielders behind him. They defiantly remained in the dugout. Paige let them stay there and, still fuming, pitched the next half inning shorthanded, striking out the side in spite. He returned to the dugout, reconsidered the situation, and apologized for losing his cool. That cleared the air. Paige said that going forward he and his Bismarck teammates were a band of brothers. Opponents were a different matter. In Paige's second start he eviscerated the Beulah Miners and their number one pitcher, Frank Stewart. The Miners were Central North Dakota baseball champions in 1931 and 1932. Paige struck out twenty of them while notching a three-hit shutout. That whipping triggered a little trash talk. Beulah demanded a rematch and dared Churchill to pitch Roosevelt Davis. Churchill complied. Using his spitball to full advantage, Davis humbled Beulah 6–2, handing Stewart another loss. In the course of those two games some ugly comments were directed at certain Bismarck players. Paige confided to teammate Bob McCarney that he'd get even with Stewart in particular for running his mouth. A few days later, Churchill geared up for a round-three game with Jamestown by signing Dan Oberholzer, an infielder from Minneapolis with six years of minor league experience. In a second move that must have caught Paige by surprise, Churchill pinched an insurance pitcher from the Beulah Miners: Frank Stewart.

Bismarck and Jamestown were becoming a league of their own. Each team now had four blacks in the starting lineup. This level of play was a cut above anything else on display in North Dakota. Curious fans were coming from all over the state to see for themselves. Game four of the season series (their second meeting since Paige arrived on the scene) was played in Jamestown. Once again, extra bleachers were added. The Northern Pacific Railway again fired up its game-day passenger train and eight hundred Bismarckers climbed aboard, entertained by the "Little German" oompah band decked out in their lederhosen and alpine hats. To get prime seats, people started streaming into the ballpark three hours before the game. Jamestown's pep band battled Bismarck's Little Germans note for note. Jamestown's mayor, Oscar Zimmerman, making use of a newly installed public-address system, welcomed everyone, but Elmer Marrell stole the pregame ceremony. He'd pitched for Jamestown in 1883 and was showered with applause as he slowly walked onto the field, in uniform. Some 3,200 ticket holders squeezed into the grandstand and bleachers. The hundreds who couldn't get in stood seven deep beyond the outfield fence. The *Jamestown Sun* pronounced it the biggest crowd to ever attend a ball game in North Dakota.

Paige and Lefty Brown rose to the occasion. Bismarck drew first blood. In the top of the first inning Red Haley doubled to center and Quincy Troupe—batting right behind him as usual—scorched a double to right, sending Haley scampering home. With one out in the bottom of the fourth inning Troupe walked to the mound to confer with Paige. Shortstop Art Hancock, Jamestown's cleanup hitter (and a Negro League alumnus), was due

up. Paige had thrown a sidearm fastball in Hancock's previous
at bat and he flied out to deep right field. Since Hancock had
an uppercut swing, Troupe suggested Paige mix things up and
throw overhand. Satchel took the twenty-year-old catcher's advice under consideration—and threw another sidearm fastball.
Hancock jacked it high over the right field fence. The next two
batters singled. Paige was on the ropes, but recovered and got
out of trouble with two quick ground-ball outs.

The 1–1 score held through six innings, then through nine
innings. Paige and Brown wriggled out of minor jams, but mostly
breezed through the batting order. The score remained dead-
locked through twelve innings. Bismarck had seven hits, Jamestown eight. Satchel Paige had nineteen strikeouts, Barney Brown
eleven. With darkness falling, the umpires stopped play. No one
asked for their money back. "The ball game was declared to be
equal to any big league game ever played by fans who have seen
games coast to coast," said the *Jamestown Sun*.

People begged for an encore, and the managers hastily arranged
a three-game series to be played in Bismarck over Labor Day weekend. Oddly, the most interesting play in the twelve-inning suspended
game didn't appear in the box score. It escaped the attention of everyone but Bob McCarney and Paige. McCarney, a Corwin-Churchill
car salesman and bon vivant, showed up that day nursing a hangover.
Churchill benched him and asked pitcher Frank Stewart, the race
baiter who had gotten under Satchel Paige's skin, to fill in at first base.
In the second inning a Jamestown batter hit a dribbler toward the
pitcher's mound. Paige pounced on the ball and "threw wide" to first
base, according to the *Bismarck Tribune*. The throw pulled Stewart
off the bag and smack into the path of the oncoming runner. They
collided. Only the Jamestown player got up. Stewart was carted off
to the hospital with a season-ending dislocated elbow.

An unusual play and a tough break for Stewart. But a wide
throw? Anybody who ever played with Satchel Paige would swear

he never threw a baseball in his life without knowing exactly where it was going.

Paige lived up to his reputation on and off the field. He was not the type to sit in his room writing letters home to mama. He had a Chrysler at his disposal and found his way to the Dome, hippest of the speakeasies on the dark side of Mandan. He made a connection with a cabdriver who delivered moonshine. Paige enjoyed a good time, preferably in mixed company. Neil Churchill caught wind of this and raised the awkward topic, not with Paige, but with his straight-arrow catcher. "Quincy, uhm, I don't know how to put what I'm going to say to you, but, uh, it's about Satchel. The fans really are wild about his performance and so am I, but there's one thing I'd like you to talk to him about," Churchill stammered. "I understand that a man has to go out with a woman. But, uhm, there's a way to do it in any walk of life."

Churchill eventually got to the point: "Just tell him to be careful about riding white girls around in broad daylight."

Good luck to Troupe getting Ol' Satch to toe the line, *any* line, especially one that involved the conquest of either batters or lady friends. It says something about Churchill's high opinion of Troupe—and about Troupe's maturity—that he turned to him as an intermediary rather than to Red Haley or Roosevelt Davis. All of Bismarck had taken to Troupe and vice versa. Kids would come to team practices and the "giant Negro" would chat with them and help break in their new gloves. He got involved with youth baseball programs. The town showed its appreciation on a Wednesday night in late August by holding Quincy Troupe Night at the ballpark. He was presented with a travel bag before the game, that the *Tribune* noted "he bashfully accepted with a grin." Bismarck and the Cleveland All-Nations battled to a 4–4 tie, but it was more a good-natured exhibition than serious baseball. Troupe pitched four innings, and after being relieved by Paige, played every infield position for one inning apiece.

Bismarck had not suffered a loss since, in the parlance of the local newspapers, the "elongated Negro hurler" pulled on a uniform. The team was steamrolling through its schedule. In a home-and-away series with the town of Dickinson, Bismarck took both games by a combined score of 19–3. Paige pitched the home game, which the *Tribune* deemed "something of a farce." In the late innings Bismarck's runners began "clowning" on the bases and Paige unveiled some "freak" pitching motions. Their game faces were back in place for the three Labor Day weekend games with Jamestown. October stood waiting in the wings and Churchill was still tweaking his roster, recruiting three players from the Cleveland All-Nations and an outfielder from Minneapolis. The big addition was Walter "Beef" Ringhofer, the All-Nations' big-bopper first baseman. Bismarck canceled its traditional Labor Day boxing matches because all eyes were focused on the baseball field. Saturday night's game ended in a 7–7 tie due to darkness, and on Monday Bismarck would mash Jamestown 11–3. Sunday afternoon was the heavyweight bout. Jamestown's manager, Oscar Butts, threw Churchill a curve by renting a pitcher from the Chicago American Giants, Quincy Troupe's old team. Willie Foster traveled to North Dakota just to duel Satchel Paige. By now the script was familiar: emergency bleacher seats in place and fans pouring into the park several hours early. Total attendance approached 4,000, maybe more; "probably the largest turnout in North Dakota's history," according to the *Tribune*. A new twist was the deployment of four umpires, double the usual number and a sign of heavy betting action.

In a way, this was a coming-attractions matchup. Paige and Foster had been tapped as starting pitchers for the first Negro League all-star game, set for mid-September in Chicago. As expected, their Labor Day meeting turned into a typical Bismarck-Jamestown catfight, with Bismarck coming out on top 3-2 in extra innings. What wasn't expected was Paige driving in all three runs

in addition to piling up 15 strikeouts. His crucial at bat came in
the bottom of the tenth inning. Oberholzer doubled; then Paige
slashed a single that delivered the game-winning run. After this
Labor Day series, it was widely acknowledged that Bismarck had
the best team in and around North Dakota. By far. The bandwagon
was rolling and Paige didn't want to get off. He shocked Negro
League executives by opting out of the all-star game in Chicago
and instead sticking by Neil Churchill's side. Yet another game was
scheduled with Jamestown and Paige outdueled Barney Brown a
third time, 3–1. Bismarck finished with 38 wins, 12 losses, and 5 ties.
The team never lost a game after picking up Paige, going 14–0–3
from mid-August to mid-September. He pitched in twelve of those
seventeen games, winning six of seven starts and wrestling Brown
to that show-stopper twelve-inning tie. His last victory came on
the last day of the 1933 season against an amalgam of minor league
all-stars from the American Association. They challenged Bismarck,
perhaps feeling their oats because seven members of the team had
just signed Major League contracts. Furthermore, they demanded
Bismark raise ticket prices just for that game. The *Tribune* remained
skeptical about the elongated Negro's talents, opining, "It will be
interesting to see what Paige can do with players of this caliber."

What he did was take those cocky minor leaguers to school.
The All-Stars got hammered 15 to 2. Bismarck cranked out nineteen
hits, Ringhofer leading the charge by going five for five. Paige struck
out fourteen and limited the stars to four hits. Their two gimme runs
came in the top of the ninth inning when Satchel's mind must have
wandered to his plans for a postgame night on the town. He committed two errors and blew his own shutout. Still, Paige was in total
command. How good a performance? The *Bismarck Capital* didn't
stop at "sensational" and "untouchable." It anointed him, "'Mahatma'
Satchell [sic] Paige," quite a compliment from a newspaper that once
unfavorably compared "colored folks" to monkeys.

The next afternoon Neil Churchill was honored at a Rotary
Club luncheon and that night the Grand Pacific Hotel threw a

celebratory steak dinner for the team. A number of players missed taking bows because they were already headed home. Paige drove to Pittsburgh to pick up his girlfriend before flying to California for a fall barnstorming tour. He dropped Quincy Troupe in Chicago. "Well, Troupe, keep in touch," Paige said as they parted company— no easy task, since Satchel was famously impossible to reach. "I kinda like Bismarck. Maybe I'll go back out there next year."

Troupe was feeling pleased, having led the team in batting with a .432 average. He caught a bus from Chicago home to Saint Louis and availed himself of the opportunity to do something he'd never done: watch white men play Major League baseball. He bought a ticket to Sportsman Park and sat through a Cardinals game. It was a shock to the system, like that moment when a son realizes his father has flaws and may not be the Perfect Man. "I was never so let down," Troupe said. "I had grown up accepting the idea that white baseball was superior to black."

Not true. His eyes told him so. He belonged down on that field, which from his seat in the colored section of the grandstand looked to be about a million miles away.

8

NAMELESS DREAD

For weeks on end in 1933, *Bismarck Capital* readers devoured the syndicated serial romance "Lady in Flight." Fictional Tom Ridley, handsome unemployed college graduate, was traveling the country in his tricked-out van in search of cosmic truth and adventure when, as fate would have it, he offered rides to gentleman hobo Bitter Waters and then Naida, a "pretty girl of mystery" who soon revealed that she was, in fact, missing heiress Isabel Haydon, reported to have been kidnapped, but who actually fled on her wedding night from James Marbury, the cad she belatedly discovered was a swindler and to whom she would never, ever return—which meant that for the time being the three serendipitous companions had to continue to duck the police who were searching for Isabel while, close behind, danger lurked: "Driving at night to evade detection, the van is followed by Red Clegg, a tough character."

To be continued . . .

Men and women of Bismarck lost themselves in the real-life exploits of Neil Churchill and his players for the same reason they plowed through thirty-six installments of "Lady in Flight" and, after that, "Blind Alley," the multipart saga of a nightclub singer-dancer whose life gets upturned by a "mysteriously rich, mysteriously powerful" stranger. The allure was sweet escapism. The *Bismarck Capital* said in an editorial lauding Churchill's baseball team, "The games this past summer have taken our minds off business troubles, have provided excellent entertainment and have given incentive to many out of the city fans to make regular calls in the Capital City."

"Business troubles" was a gracious euphemism for the Great Depression, which by then had fully bared its teeth. Personal dramas by the thousands played out across North Dakota, but in these, unlike newspaper serials, happy endings weren't ensured. Rufus Lumry, a descendent of Oscar Will, the seed company impresario, was a Boy Scout in those dreary days. The Scouts delivered holiday turkeys and food packages to Bismarck's down-and-out citizens. Some were reduced to living in cardboard–and–tar paper hovels, heating them with chunks of coal that fell off the tenders of passing trains. "It was pretty tragic," says Lumry. "The fathers couldn't hack it, those poor bastards. They couldn't feed their families."

It's understandable that people might gravitate to a ball game for a few hours of relaxation, bringing with them buckets of bootleg beer and a few wrinkled dollar bills to wager. Why not? Everywhere else they looked or went, misery seemed to follow. The despair had a stench so strong it attracted a "mysteriously powerful" visitor. Lorena Hickok was a former reporter with the *New York Daily Mirror* and Associated Press, and a close friend (some mused *romatically* close) of Eleanor Roosevelt. She joined the federal government during the early days of Franklin Roosevelt's presidency, working as chief investigator for the Federal Emergency Relief Administration. As part of her job, Hickok wandered afar from Washington, D.C., and filed boots-on-the-ground reports documenting how the Depression was affecting ordinary Americans. The fall of 1933 found her in North Dakota, traveling more than two thousand miles by car in a week. What Hickok encountered at times brought her to tears.

A couple of county commissioners from Mandan took her to a rural church to meet with beleaguered farmers. Wheat had sold for 30 cents a bushel a year ago, but cost 77 cents to grow. This year's crop had been wiped out by the drought and two summer hailstorms. Asked how he was faring, one man replied, "Everything

I own I have on my back." He was wearing two pairs of overalls because he had no underwear. When Hickok and her chaperones left the church and returned to their car, they found it occupied by half a dozen scruffy strangers. "They apologized and said they had crawled in there to keep warm," Hickok related in a letter to her boss, Harry Hopkins, Roosevelt's social welfare czar in charge of the Federal Emergency Relief Administration, Civil Works Administration, and Works Progress Administration. "I am quite sure that anything that could be done in the way of getting clothing out to these people *immediately*—shoes, overshoes, warm underwear, overcoats—would do quite a bit toward clearing up unrest among North Dakota farmers!"

In Bismarck Hickok brushed up against a sluggish bureaucracy that infuriated her. Officials of the state relief committee complained about "the bums" and "the undeserving" seeking government assistance. Red Cross representatives conceded they were holding clothes and other provisions in reserve so as not to get caught short during future "emergencies." Hickok dashed off a blistering note to Hopkins, declaring that the issue of relief eligibility should have been resolved long ago and wondering "what constitutes an emergency in the eyes of the little old ladies who seem to be running the Red Cross." Sorrow dogged her every step. She saw starving horses with ribs poking through loose skin and heard about women giving birth on beds covered with topcoats because sheets had become luxury items. In the town of Williston 95 percent of the farmers had gone bankrupt. In Minot a man said his seven children didn't attend school during the winter because he had no warm clothes for them. The man had on a worn suit and worn sweater that he and his eldest son took turns wearing, depending on who needed to look spiffier. Bottineau was an especially beaten-down town. Hickok stopped to chat with one of the "better-off" families. She noticed newspapers stuffed into the cracks of the porous house. The kitchen floor was made of crushed tin cans and discarded license plates. Two small boys scampered about dressed in nothing but

tattered dungarees. They had no shoes or socks. Their feet were
purple from the cold. The husband, wife, and two children slept in
the same bed. "We have to, to keep warm," the woman explained.
She was pregnant and due in January.

On October 31, Hickok wrote a personal letter to Eleanor
Roosevelt, uncorking bottled-up emotions. "These plains are beautiful. But, oh, the terrible, crushing drabness of life," she confided.
"If I had to live here, I think I'd just quietly call it a day and commit
suicide. The people up here—farmers, people on relief, and those
administering relief—are in a daze. A sort of nameless dread hangs
over the place."

The purpose of the Civil Works Administration (CWA) and its
more ambitious successor, the Works Progress Administration
(WPA), was to jump-start the economy by artificially inducing
employment, utilizing federal funds to underwrite such sundry
activities as building bridges and writing state histories. The Bismarck baseball committee—which counted Neil Churchill among
its six members—was more than willing to do its part. The team
had soared to rarefied heights. Attendance surged. Expectations
were sky-high for 1934 and beyond. A little federal government
largesse could help fulfill those lofty aspirations while putting
shovels, paintbrushes, and—equally important—paychecks into
idle hands. The committee proposed a $5,000 renovation of the
town ballpark. The CWA contributed nearly $2,700 in materials
and labor, assigning nineteen subsidized workers to the project.
The baseball committee picked up the rest of the rehabilitation
costs. There was a long to-do list: new dugouts, new concession
stand, and construction of a seven-foot-high outfield fence. The
playing surface was graded and 140 feet of permanent bleachers
were added, boosting capacity to 3,000 and making possible a
"knothole gang" seating section where kids under sixteen could
watch games free.

While the ballpark was getting a makeover, the team pursued off-season interests. Churchill sold cars, presided over his Phantoms basketball domain, and assisted the Rotary Club with its Community Chest fund-raising campaign. Pitcher Roosevelt Davis went home to Philadelphia. Outfielder Bill Morlan played and refereed basketball in Jefferson, Iowa. Infielder Dan Oberholzer studied engineering at the University of Minnesota. Quincy Troupe took courses at Lincoln University in Jefferson City, Missouri, and kept in shape boxing and dribbling a basketball. Red Haley stayed in baseball mode, joining Satchel Paige's Royal Giants for a barnstorming tour of California. Knowing its readers had a bottomless appetite for all things Paige-related, the *Tribune* ran a story in late November describing how "the elongated Negro Hurler who pitched for Bismarck last summer" had captivated West Coast fans. Los Angelenos celebrated Satchel Paige Day between games of a doubleheader between the Royal Giants and Joe Pirrone's All Stars. Satch laid it on thick in a *Los Angeles Times* interview, claiming to have developed his pinpoint control by throwing baseballs at stuffed animals on carnival midways, winning more cigars and kewpie dolls than any human being had a right to win.

North Dakota's most avid baseball towns didn't go into hibernation for the winter. New Rockford stole Roosevelt Davis away from Churchill, offering contracts to him and a catcher from the Negro Leagues' Kansas City Monarchs. Valley City enticed brothers Art and Charlie Hancock to leave Jamestown and hired ex–St. Louis Cardinal outfielder George "Showboat" Fisher as player-manager. Jamestown also raided Churchill's till, robbing him of Oberholzer, the engineering student-infielder, and landing several Negro Leaguers to replace the departed Hancock brothers. One of those pickups was Double Duty Radcliffe, the well-traveled catcher-pitcher who had been a teammate of both Paige and Troupe, as well as almost everyone else in black baseball. In January Churchill drove to Jamestown to talk with Abe Saperstein, whose Harlem Globetrotters were in town for a basketball exhibition. He let Saperstein know he was in the market for a left-hander with good off-speed stuff, somebody whose pitching style would contrast nicely with Paige's flamethrowing. Bismarck had lost a few pieces of its arsenal, but none that were irreplaceable. Churchill still had the ultimate weapon in Paige. On January 26 the *Tribune* said the mercurial pitcher was "returning to the Capital City next week to prepare for the next baseball season."

Next week came and went. No sign of Paige in Bismarck.

Next month came and went. Still no Paige. In late March, Paige phoned Churchill from somewhere on the road to say that he'd won twenty-three games in California, felt fully rested, and would be in Bismarck the first week of April. No problem. April came. Satch did not. Neil Churchill and the baseball committee had stuck their necks out: $5,000 worth of credibility was on the line. A remodeled 3,000-seat ballpark was soon to be christened and the player most capable of selling tickets to fill all those seats had yet to show his face in town.

It was a nail-biting melodrama worthy of a *Bismarck Capital* thirty-six-part serial: "Hope Diamond," the roller-coaster story of a small-town car dealer with a gambling habit who builds the baseball team of his dreams, placing bets for fame and fortune on a mysterious pitcher from down South who has no birth certificate but does have an affinity for fastballs, fast cars, and faster women and who, for the moment, is gone with the wind. Will Satchel take the mound again in Bismarck? Does his baby-face catcher hold the key? Will Neil Churchill hit the baseball jackpot?

To be continued . . .

PART TWO

PLAYING TOGETHER

9

COME AND GONE

Satchel Paige didn't think in straight lines. Nor did he drive in them. Come early May 1934 he was still en route to North Dakota from California, via Pittsburgh and Nashville. The upside to the detour and to the delay was that he had talked left-hander Leroy Matlock, another independent-minded Crawfords pitcher, into joining him in leaving Gus Greenlee's fold. Maybe. An alternative rumor had Sug Cornelius, a pitcher with the Chicago American Giants, riding shotgun, not Matlock. Either way, Neil Churchill would soon have the matched set of starters he so desired.

Red Haley covered for his teammate, telling pesky Bismarck reporters that Paige took to the road in the signing-bonus Chrysler Churchill had given him the previous fall. He said the odometer read about "a million miles," so Satch, wisely, was puttering along, for once experiencing the joys of driving below the speed limit. The newspapers said Paige was "expected momentarily" and then, when a week went by without any sign of him, hedged their bets, promising a sighting "later" the next week. By May 21 the prognosticating had degenerated to "The exact whereabouts of Paige is still unknown." Wherever Satchel was, he no longer had his Chrysler pointed toward the Dakotas. Greenlee had laid down the law to him and Matlock, explaining in no uncertain terms that they were under contract to the Pittsburgh Crawfords and only the Crawfords and, therefore, should consider themselves professionally grounded. The manager of the American Giants—having lost Quincy Troupe to

Bismarck in July 1933—took a harder line with Cornelius. He got a court injunction barring him from leaving Chicago, effectively clipping his wings.

Churchill made the mistake of waiting too long for Paige to blow back into town. He should have known better. Tornadoes followed more predictable paths. Suddenly Satchless and also without the reliable number two starter he'd been expecting, Churchill had to quickly duct-tape together a staff. He rummaged through the scrap heap to find an opening day starter: "Smiley" Simle, the schoolteacher who'd pitched himself off the team the year before. Smiley had shed thirty-two pounds over the winter. His pants fitted better, but he lost the opening day ballgame to the Beulah Miners, 7–6. Churchill wasted no time trolling for reinforcements. Nearly a dozen men would take the mound through the spring and summer. He wooed four pitchers away from the Negro Leagues. Spoon Carter and Jerry Henderson fizzled; Irving "Lefty" Vincent and Barney Morris, while not true aces in the Paige mold, developed into a pair of dependable stoppers. Frank Stewart, his arm healed after that wicked collision at first base in Jamestown the preceding August, came back and pitched solidly for a month; as did Jimmy Dodge, acquired from Devils Lake. Dodge was a curiosity: an "Indian hurler" who'd cracked white baseball. Bill Lanier threw a no-hitter for the University of North Dakota and soon found himself in a Bismarck uniform, Churchill having outbid a minor league team for his services. Lanier wasn't the youngest hole-plugger, though. Tommy Lee, teenage sensation of Bismarck's American Legion baseball team, got pressed into action, too.

The duct tape held. Following that season-opening loss to Beulah, Bismarck reeled off a dozen wins before suffering an eleven-inning 8–7 defeat on Memorial Day, a defeat made all the more insufferable because it came at the hands of those devils from Jamestown. The game drew 2,000 fans, normally a fine crowd but half the number who likely would have come take a peek at Satchel Paige. Even in his absence the usual Bismarck-Jamestown drama unfolded. Jamestown was up 7 to 5 entering the top of the ninth inning, with its wayward Negro Leagues first baseman Walter "Steel Arm" Davis cracking two home runs. Bismarck answered twice to tie the game and, down to its final out, strung a few hits together for what appeared to be the go-ahead score only to have the home plate umpire flag the runner for drifting beyond the baseline. Every great rivalry needs good rhubarbs. One immediately broke out. Amid the huffing and puffing, the umpire consulted his rule book and changed his mind: the run counted. Jamestown responded by ruling the ump out of bounds and threatening to quit play unless he reversed the call. Pride was at stake. So, too, were a lot of grandstand bets. The standoff ended when Churchill—whose pulse seemed to quicken only at the dinner table—restored calm by telling the umpire to stick with the original decision and void the run. He then ordered his players to stop arguing and take the field. They did. Two innings later Jamestown rallied for the win.

Bismarck's record now stood at 12–2, and the team had been playing for just two weeks. Churchill had a roster half the size of a Major League club, but a ramped-up schedule every bit as demanding. The grind included nine road games in eight days in late May, and another nine games over six days in late June. They also were venturing farther afield with greater frequency, committed to traveling to Winnipeg (a ten-hour drive north) eight times during the season for exhibition games or tournaments. Yet the team showed no evidence of burnout, steadily winning about three of every four games. Churchill's patchwork pitching staff performed admirably, but, in contrast to past years, Bismarck's defining strength was its offense. The bats crackled. In a five-game series at Winnipeg's Wesley Park just before Memorial Day, the team swept perennially tough Gilkerson's Union Giants by a cumulative score of 47–20. The series began on Thursday with a doubleheader in which Bismarck sprayed thirty-seven hits. Haley put up the best numbers, going 6 for 9 with four doubles and a home run.

The next morning's *Winnipeg Free Press* called Bismarck "the most powerful hitting club" to barnstorm in western Canada. The paper's sports columnist observed, "It's a long time since ball fans have seen anything to equal the batting punch uncovered by Red Haley. The lumbering second-sacker enjoys putting that 'apple' out of sight. Troupe and Ringhofer of the Bismarck club dig themselves in, too. Extra base hits are right down their alley."

But how long would those hits keep falling in? Long enough to erase the memory of dear departed Satchel Paige?

Abe Saperstein acted as matchmaker for Bismarck's 1934 team, a role made possible by the tangled fraternity of baseball. He'd had a falling-out with the Cleveland All-Nations, severed ties, and begun doing promotional work for the Negro League's Chicago American Giants. Three white players from the All-Nations lived in Chicago and remained loyal to Saperstein. He steered them toward Churchill, who was able to sign the trio and instantly catapult Bismarck's infield to another level. First baseman Walter "Beef" Ringhofer and shortstop Harold Massmann had appeared in a few games for Bismarck in September 1933. Third baseman Joe Desiderato was new to the team. All three were being tracked by pro scouts.

Ringhofer resembled a side of beef and hit with Angus-like power. He was paired on the right side of the infield with Haley, the sole holdover from 1933. Massmann and Desiderato were baseball twins: both in their early twenties, both a wiry five-foot-ten, both reserved in temperament, both with excellent arms, and both given to digging out grounders with the tenacity of truffle-hunting pigs. Saperstein used to hit Massmann 100 practice balls a day. It showed. According to conflicting newspaper stories, Massmann had been an All-American basketball player at either Villanova or St. John's, although neither university had a record of him matriculating. (Embroidering wasn't confined to Satchel Paige; Abe Saperstein loved to dress up players' biographies by making them graduates of impressive-sounding East Coast colleges, like Villanova or St. John's.) Desiderato indisputably came from an Italian immigrant family and had dropped out of school in eighth grade. His father, Giuseppe Desiderato, worked in the stockyards and as an elevator operator, patiently squirreling away enough money to buy a house in the largely undeveloped North Side of Chicago. Joe, the eldest son, didn't care for the ambience of Wrightwood Avenue. Too boring. Against his father's wishes, Joe kept sneaking back to their former rowdy Irish-Italian neighborhood to play ball and visit friends. That irked the old man no end. One night Giuseppe hid under the basement steps and whacked his son with a two-by-four when he came tiptoeing home from another crosstown pilgrimage. That didn't knock a lick of sense into Joe, who soon left the new neighborhood *and* the old one. He was considered the city's top semipro third baseman. The White Sox were eyeing him, but Desiderato married at nineteen and, despite never having moved out of his parents' house, had responsibilities. When Neil Churchill offered him $140 a month to play ball, he bought a train ticket to Bismarck.

As victories piled up, Churchill lectured his team about the dangers of overconfidence. That very day Lefty Vincent tossed a one-hitter and shut out Valley City, which remained well stocked with salaried players. Just as Churchill hoped, Bismarck showed signs of outgrowing the North Dakota competition. Mandan no longer had a spot on the schedule; nor did the towns of Glen Ullin, Turtle Lake, and Williston. The prison team offered only token resistance, so Churchill shook off the dust and played first base against them while the team batboy romped in right field.

In early June 1934 Bismarck dedicated its renovated ballpark, a source of much chest-thumping pride. Bismarckers contended that nothing compared favorably anywhere on the northern plains, grandly referring to their home field as "the Big League park." Certainly no rinky-dink home runs were being hit. It was 332 feet down the left field line, 340 feet to the right field corner, and nearly 400 feet to straightaway center. Churchill bragged that of the sixteen Major League stadiums only Philadelphia's Shibe Park had a larger footprint. An indication of Bismarck's desire to run with bigger dogs was the selection of House of David as its opponent for the ballpark dedication. The Davids' story had taken some odd twists. The religious colony bifurcated after the legal ordeal of founder Benjamin Purnell and his subsequent death in 1927. Half the community remained loyal to Purnell's teachings and kept the name Israelite House of David or simply House of David. The other half followed his wife, calling themselves the Israelite House of David as Re-Organized by Mary Purnell, or the City of David. Adding to the confusion, imposter baseball teams popped up and co-opted the brand. Spring Valley House of David and the Colored House of David had no connection to the religious communes, but they adopted the same bearded look. If that wasn't complication enough, the original House of David ball team sought to maximize its success by splitting into East, West, and Central travel squads. To flesh out those rosters, the team enlisted nonbelievers, some of whom sustained the illusion by wearing false bushy beards. The adjuncts included pitching retreads Grover Cleveland Alexander and Mordecai "Three Finger" Brown, who between them had won 612 Major League games.

The House of David players who toured North Dakota in 1934 clearly supposed they were playing a Bismarck team with more bark than bite. They pitched a female in the opening game of their doubleheader. Not just any female, however. Twenty-three-year-old Texan Babe Didrikson had won two gold medals (javelin and 80-meter hurdles) and a silver (long jump) at the 1932 Summer Olympics in Los Angeles. She also excelled at swimming, diving, bowling, and billiards; had once scored 104 points in a high school basketball game; and had recently discovered golf, embarking on a path that would soon lead to her decade-long domination of the LPGA. House of David management knew the value of hype and Didrikson generated plenty. Syndicated sports columnist Grantland

Rice stoked the fire at the 1932 Olympics by anointing her "without any question the athletic phenomenon of all time, man or woman."

But those medals and accolades were won in sports other than baseball. Babe had a good curve, but mediocre heat. Bismarck showed her "little respect," said the *Tribune*, teeing off for five hits and five runs in the first inning, inducing Didrikson to call it an early day. Bismarck hung on for a 7–5 win but lost the nightcap 6–5 in ten innings. Those close games with House of David weren't flukes. Other touring teams had a rougher go of it against Bismarck. The Kansas City Monarchs, genuine royalty of black baseball, got humbled 7–0. Barney Morris fired a three-hitter. Ringhofer mashed two home runs and Troupe added a third, an inside-the-park ricochet shot. The Detroit Colored Giants, who were an otherworldly 107–18 in 1933, quietly rolled over 8–0. Massmann homered. Desiderato, Haley, and Troupe—batting second, third, and fourth in the order—had two hits apiece. It was a football atmosphere that night. The musicians of KFYR radio's thirty-one-piece Lone Scout Band wedged themselves into the grandstand, energizing fans with brassy blasts from the horn section.

Only a couple of Bismarck residents remained on the souped-up roster, and they were bench players. Neil Churchill was building a "town team" powered by mercenaries. Some egos inevitably got bruised. Floyd Fuller, for one, had been a staple of the infield for eleven years before Churchill returned as manager. He was forty years old. He understood the situation. Fuller quietly walked away, but never attended another Bismarck ball game as long as he lived. The town as a whole embraced the change, winning being the universal solvent for ruffled feathers. The business community stepped up in force. The Prince Hotel—owned by grumpy Ed Hughes, the electric company baron—paid for new uniforms: white with black trim, a stylized "B" on the front, "Prince Hotel" splashed across the back, and players' numbers bumped to their sleeves. Bergeson's clothiers gave Harold Massmann a straw hat for hitting the first home run in the remodeled ballpark. Massmann also hit the second home run and earned free haircuts for the rest of the season courtesy of Murphy's barbershop. Lefty Vincent got his straw hat from Alex Rosen and Brother clothing store for poking a home run that helped beat Gilkerson's Union Giants. Quincy Troupe and Bill Morlan received complimentary shaving kits from French and Welch Hardware for going deep in the same inning of a game.

The one constant of baseball life was Jamestown. No foe, in or out of state, caused more recurring headaches. The teams met again in Bismarck over the July Fourth holiday. A newspaper ad promised no letdown in the post-Paige era: "All the old color will be there, all the pageantry, all the bombast, all the heart throbs, all the carnival atmosphere." Indeed, they split two tight games, Bismarck winning 3–2 and losing 4–2. That series was the swan song of burly Beef Ringhofer, who got picked up by the minor league Louisville Colonels. No matter how short or how long their stay, out-of-state semipros like Ringhofer revolutionized North Dakota baseball. Blacks, however, had a disproportionate impact. They were game changers. Negro League refugees brought with them speed, big-time experience, and often charisma: a combination of qualities seldom found in farmboy ballplayers. Quincy Troupe pegged out runners from his knees during games and at practices amazed wide-eyed kids by chucking baseballs over the left field fence while standing at home plate. Double Duty Radcliffe, who was catching (as well as pitching and playing outfield) for Jamestown, would bet batters $1 they couldn't steal a base off him. After leaving Bismarck to pitch for the town of New Rockford, Roosevelt Davis paid homage to Paige when he faced his former team. He deliberately walked the bases loaded twice just to see if he could squirm his way out of those innings without giving up any runs. Side bets on his chances of succeeding were probably being taken in the grandstand. Davis escaped both jams unscathed, but Bismarck got the last laugh by cuffing him 13–3.

Many spectators at a Jamestown, Valley City, New Rockford, or Bismarck ball game had never before seen anyone who looked like Roosevelt Davis or Quincy Troupe. They were as rare a sight as winter rainbows. The population of North Dakota in 1930 was 680,845. The census listed 377 "Negro." Jamestown had two blacks adrift in a sea of 8,187 inhabitants. The towns of Beulah, Valley City, Washburn, and Turtle Lake were 100 percent white. Bismarck seemed wildly multicultural with 11,000 people, of whom 46 were black. Era Bell Thompson graduated from Bismarck High School in 1924, then went to college and became an editor at *Ebony* magazine in Chicago. Growing up, she felt like an exotic species. White classmates marveled at her pale palms, asked to touch her hair. Whenever the topic of slavery was slated for discussion in history class, Thompson cut school.

Bismarck in the 1930s was not much different from the Bismarck of the 1920s—Era Bell Thompson's time. Black ballplayers moved freely about town, but they were advised to confine their socializing to the lower-class South Side. You couldn't safely assume that every proprietor on the North Side would be as ecumenical as Jack Lyons, who even allowed Indians to patronize his hamburger stand. If Troupe, Haley, Paige, and Davis wanted to eat at a restaurant, they knew how the game was played: find one that didn't mind selling black customers takeout meals at the back door. Beyond the orbit of the state capital, the racial climate tended to be more unstable. During the Depression, Moose Kay, a black drifter, wandered through McLeod, an unincorporated village in the sparsely settled southeast corner of North Dakota. He liked baseball and stopped to watch a game between McLeod and the town of Milnor. Afterward, he offered his services on a barter basis: in exchange for meals and a place to stay, he'd be willing to coach McLeod's team for the rest of the summer. Moose knew his baseball. Things went swimmingly until the Fourth of July, when a white man, who'd likely done too much celebrating, verbally attacked Kay, who'd also been celebrating. Kay floored him. That punch instantly ended his coaching gig and put his life at risk, as was duly recorded years later in McLeod's official centennial history: "Moose got scared and crawled on a night freight train. The ball team felt pretty bad over this."

The veneer of civility could crack under even the slightest stress. Third baseman Joe Desiderato cringed at the way hecklers hounded his black teammates during road games. "I saw the kind of abuse that those guys took," he told relatives back in Chicago. "Way beyond what people should tolerate." When the team crossed the border into Canada, the hostility didn't necessarily diminish. At times, it got worse. Whatever city they were in, Churchill had an all-or-nothing policy. If a hotel or restaurant turned away or disrespected a single Bismarck player, everybody turned on their heels and left together. Said Desiderato, "We always stayed as a family."

Dakotans groped their way along the racial divide. Newspapers in Beulah and Bismarck made habitual use of the adjectives "dusky," "dark," and "Ethiopian" in their local baseball coverage, perhaps as an aid to readers whose idea of keeping score was to count the number of black and white players appearing in a ball game. The *Jamestown Sun* kept its writing color-blind. Al Breitbach owned the Jamestown radio station and the finest hotel. On the side, he managed the baseball team, and it was he who made the decision to tap into the Negro Leagues. As in Bismarck, black players stayed at the town flophouse. They were accepted by white teammates, but shunned in most larger social circles. Gradually, their prowess on the field generated wider acceptance within the community. Up to a point. "One big problem was that one or two of them started fooling around with white gals. That went over like a lead balloon," recalls Al Wiest, who lived in Jamestown but hired on to play semipro ball for Crystal Springs, North Dakota. Double Duty Radcliffe, horndog supreme, was one of those black players who crossed the color line both off and on the field.

Miscegenation was a taboo of the times. Its shadow reached as far as Quincy Troupe's G-rated love life. In 1932 he briefly played for the Negro Leagues' Detroit Wolves. A cute waitress named Jackie worked at a restaurant frequented by the team. Troupe eventually screwed up the courage to make a move, telling Jackie he had been thinking of her during that day's game and got four hits in four at bats "all for you." Only Quincy could get away with a line that hokey. Jackie let him walk her home. As they sat talking inside her apartment, someone knocked on the door. Jackie opened up and found two Detroit plainclothes policemen standing there. They wanted to know where she worked, where she had grown up. They also wanted to know if she was white. Once she convinced them she was a light-skinned black woman, the officers bade her good night.

Bismarck had no plainclothes cops monitoring social decorum. One afternoon Troupe sat at the dining room table of his rooming house, writing a letter to his mother. Mrs. White paid a neighborhood girl to help with the cleaning and cooking. She was about sixteen, with red hair and blue eyes. Quincy gazed up from his letter and noticed the red-haired girl lying on the living room couch, her skirt hiked up thigh-high. The temperature suddenly soared in the dining room. Quincy put down his pen and walked over to the couch. He knelt down. He bent over and kissed her square on the lips. She kissed back.

"Quincy, don't," she whispered. "Mrs. White will see us." They kissed again.

Quincy stood up, flustered. "Be more careful," he said. "You shouldn't do this to *any* man!" With that, she smiled demurely, straightened her dress, and disappeared into the kitchen. Quincy returned to the dining room and resumed writing the letter to his mother. He told her Bismarck was playing great baseball and that he was leading the team in hitting. He sent his love.

Quincy made no mention in his letter that he'd just kissed a white girl. There were some things Mama didn't need to know.

10

FEELING THE HEAT

Bismarck had a born-again ballpark, but the same gone-mad weather. The grandstand glistened with fresh green paint. The desiccated outfield grass looked leprous. An unforgiving sun baked the infield dirt into concrete. Land can die of thirst, and North Dakota teetered on the brink: tongue swollen, eyes glazed. On May 9, 1934, the dust storm that became "Black Sunday" touched down. It had gathered force in Montana, rose to a frenzy in the Dakotas, and didn't dissipate until reaching the Atlantic Ocean. In between an estimated 12 million tons of powdered northern plains got dumped onto the great doughnut of Chicago alone. A North Dakota county official wired a grim message to Senator Gerald Nye, who was out of harm's way in Washington, D.C.: "Drought situation critical. No moisture in ground. Dust storms almost daily. Soil drifting like snow."

Morris Markey, a freelance writer for the *Saturday Evening Post*, drove to Montana, Minnesota, and the Dakotas with notebook in hand, eager to confront hard times face-to-face. He got off to a promising start by getting trapped in a blinding dust storm. The "curtain of flying earth" lasted nearly an hour. Markey's three-part article on the collapse of the multistate economy hit newsstands in late July. He botched some elementary facts (notably stating that 99 percent of North Dakota's banks had failed to reopen after President Roosevelt declared a five-day national "bank holiday" in March 1933; the state banking examiner said the correct figure was 3 percent), and he made the more egregious mistake of coming off as smugly elitist. He questioned the logic of government aid to farmers and slammed North Dakota politics as "confused to the point of almost complete eccentricity." The *Saturday Evening Post* was bombarded with so many complaints that editor George Horace Lorimer went beyond issuing an apology. He ordered a staff reporter who was "western born and reared" to retrace Markey's route. Nothing short of making it rain for a week could have placated the aggrieved natives. Newspaper editorials took turns pummeling the *Post* and urging state officials to file a libel suit. The *Valley City Times-Record* got especially lathered up, alleging that "eastern publications" had a history of maliciously twisting the truth for nefarious purposes: "The result is that North Dakota seems to be regarded as a state which is populated by people who are a sort of half devil and half child and who are in a chronic condition of beggary. We are a sort of national joke as a state, supposed to live in a kind of barbarism with no real values to speak of and being the happy hunting ground for all kinds of foolish experiment."

Markey wasn't the only easterner to pass through during that hot, dry summer. Eleanor Roosevelt may have shared with her husband some of those impassioned field reports Lorena Hickok had compiled for the Federal Emergency Relief Administration. In August Franklin Roosevelt and the first lady made a whistle-stop train trip through the Great Plains. They spent a broiling Tuesday in North Dakota. The president departed from the town of Devils Lake on a choreographed motor tour. He stopped at Fort Totten Indian Reservation and then took an hour-long ride around the perimeter of Devils Lake itself, the largest body of water in the state but evaporating at the alarming rate of half a foot a year. A dusty but ecstatic welcoming committee of 35,000 people swamped the train depot in Devils Lake. When Roosevelt's motorcade returned, he was hoisted onto the caboose of his waiting train. He told the crowd he'd spotted someone along the roadside holding a sign that read, "You gave us beer, now give us water." Roosevelt let loose a horse laugh. "Well, that part was easy," he said. His toothy grin faded. "My friends, I can't say my heart is happy today because I have been seeing with my own eyes what I have been reading about for so long."

There was one subject on everyone's mind, and Roosevelt lost no time addressing it. He announced he hadn't yet decided whether to support the damming of the Missouri River. Patience was required, the president cautioned. (How much? It would take Congress until 1944 to pass comprehensive flood-control legislation and nine years beyond that to get a damn dam built in North Dakota.) He closed his impromptu pep talk by praising Americans' bottomless reservoir of courage and optimism. "We hope that nature will provide better for you. I'm not going to give up in an attempt to solve the problem of North Dakota!"

Those words of empathy elicited thunderous applause. With a wave of hands and a flutter of flags and puffs of dark smoke, the presidential train chugged off to Minnesota. The drought lingered. The year 1934, the driest on record, would see only 9.5 inches of rain sprinkled on North Dakota: just slightly more than half the 17-inch average. Lives wilted. A frustrated farmer sent a letter to the Federal Land Bank in Saint Paul, perhaps because he'd grown tired of cursing and praying. It was a litany of rancid luck. Hordes of grasshoppers had appeared, and he poisoned them. The sun had scorched a round of crops, so the farmer and his family replanted. Their reward was a stunted, pathetic second harvest. In desperation he sold eighty-six head of cattle for a meager profit. But he'd managed to keep his farm. He was still a North Dakotan and proud of it.

"We have lived here 28 years on this place but have never seen such a season when everything a man does goes wrong," he wrote. "We have faith that we will soon enter a cycle of more wet years again. We seem to have battled with conditions unsuccessfully, but our motto still is: 'We stick, we win.' "

Nobody from the Bismarck baseball team cheered President Roosevelt in Devils Lake. They were traveling to Jamestown for another game in their operatic Bismarck-Jamestown rivalry. This one would be a mini skirmish. Play was halted after four and a half innings (with Jamestown ahead 4–3) because of impending darkness and a threat of rain. Neil Churchill may have leaned on the umpires to stop the game. He had to get on the road as quickly as possible to make the long drive to Winnipeg. He was taking with him a dozen players from Bismarck and Jamestown. Starting the next night, Churchill would manage that combined squad in a five-game exhibition series against the Chicago American Giants.

Canadians hungered for high-quality baseball. The Winnipeg games were sure to pull nearly 3,000 fans apiece, and they bore the fingerprints of a joint promotion by Saperstein and Churchill. The Negro Leagues had reached the midpoint of their season and gone into a hiatus. The American Giants had won the Negro League World Series in 1933 and currently occupied first place. Saperstein wanted to use the downtime to make a few extra bucks showcasing the Giants across the border. Churchill, in need of money to meet his ballooning semipro payroll, was the logical choice to assemble a team of worthy foils. Led by shortstop Willie Wells (Negro League batting champion in 1930 with a .403 average) and left fielder George "Mule" Suttles (a six-foot-six, 260-pound home run machine), the Giants qualified as heavy favorites. However, they failed to take care of business on the field. The boys from North Dakota outhit, outpitched, and outdefended them, taking four of five games.

It attested to Churchill's shifting priorities that he chose to go on vacation immediately after the Saturday doubleheader that finished off the American Giants. He'd acquired a lakefront house in Minnesota from a customer who'd defaulted on a car loan. The six Bismarck players who'd accompanied him to Winnipeg dashed home for the Missouri Slope tournament, which was being held that Sunday. In the past those were considered must-win games that decided baseball bragging rights for the western half of the state. But the tournament had dwindled to just Bismarck, Dickinson, and Beulah, the only Slope towns that still had subsidized teams. As it turned out, the Winnipeg contingent arrived late. Bismarck had to forfeit its opening game, along with any realistic chance of winning the tournament. That didn't seem to bother Churchill's players much.

Some smaller towns felt Bismarck was getting too big for its baseball britches. A July editorial in the *Beulah Independent* called Neil Churchill "yellow" for not scheduling more games with the Beulah Miners. A columnist for the paper politely disagreed, writing, "'Church' is too much of a gentleman and good sportsman" to put on airs. Be careful what you wish for. Whether or not that editorial spurred him to action, Churchill arranged an end-of-season round-robin tournament in Bismarck over the Labor Day weekend. Only Dickinson and Beulah were invited. Bismarck took the tournament and beat Beulah twice along the way, providing Churchill with a convenient yardstick to measure his team's progress. Back in May Bismarck had dropped its first game of 1934 to Beulah, 7–6. The last game of the season, played on Labor Day, more than made amends. In what amounted to a technical knockout, play was stopped after seven innings with Bismarck administering a 21–0 whipping. The game wasn't even as close as that lopsided score implied. Beulah committed eleven errors, Bismarck pounded out eighteen hits, and a *Tribune* reporter hyperextended his metaphor while crafting the lead to his story: "Singing its swan song to the machine gun staccato of a base hit symphony, Bismarck's grand baseball team established itself as the outstanding nine of western North Dakota."

Beulahns saw things differently. The *Independent* said the town's ballplayers were "no cream puffs." They'd take their Labor Day pasting like men and regroup with a vengeance come spring. Meanwhile, most of them would be busy sweating in the coal mines, unlike Bismarck's carpetbaggers who'd be fast retreating to "other climes." Churchill's players did disperse far and wide, with smiles of satisfaction on their faces. Their 1934 record of 61 wins, 19 losses, and 3 ties qualified as a job very well done. Despite some critical defections—first, Beef Ringhofer jumping to the minor leagues; then in late July Desiderato returning to Chicago, followed by Lefty Vincent hastily leaving North Dakota when his mother died—Bismarck made a regional name for itself. The team played, and won, more games than ever before. Neil Churchill learned to overcome the loss of a megastar pitcher by jigsaw-puzzling together a balanced ball club. But success had a price. The Bismarck Baseball Association was back in debt, still short $600 on the cost of construction materials used to renovate the field. In addition, players' salaries were eating up a minimum of $1,700 a month, which had Churchill digging deep into his pocket and his poker winnings.

Because of that cash crunch Bismarck baseball didn't cease on Labor Day. Three bonus games were added in early October, brushing up against duck-hunting season. A group of American League players had decided to barnstorm in the frost belt. Jimmie Foxx, the Philadelphia Athletics' strong-as-a-bull first baseman; and Heinie Manush, a steady-hitting outfielder for the Washington Senators, were the main attractions. Bismarck, Jamestown, and Valley City—the towns with the biggest semipro investments—pooled their resources to form a North Dakota all-star team. Each town would host the major leaguers for one game and keep the net revenue. The show would then go on the road for a wrap-up doubleheader in Winnipeg. Churchill did everything he could to goose Bismarck ticket sales, publicly expressing hope that the game would "wipe out the remaining deficit" on the city ballpark. The baseball year poetically ended the way it began: with Bismarckers anxiously awaiting the arrival of Satchel Paige. Churchill contracted with the mercurial one to come pitch against Jimmie Foxx and company. Paige sent a letter to Red Haley, confirming that he would soon be back in North Dakota for an encore performance.

Local papers had been running sporadic updates on his exploits. Nineteen thirty-four was a good year for legend-building. Paige's Negro Leagues statistics sparkled: 14 wins, 2 losses, 144 strikeouts,

and a paltry 26 walks. He erected a drawbridge at home plate, allowing a miserly 2.16 runs per game. On July Fourth Satchel put on a
show, no-hitting the Homestead Grays and chalking up seventeen
strikeouts. His pitches that day had gravity-defying movement. The
Grays' first baseman Buck Leonard, certain that Paige was up to dirty
tricks, repeatedly asked the umpire to examine the baseballs for scuff
marks or gashes. The ump finally tossed one ball out of play. Paige
felt insulted. "You're gonna have to toss all of 'em out," he hollered
from the mound, "'cause they *all* gonna jump!"

In his next start, four days later, the balls were still misbehav-
ing. Paige fired a ten-inning shutout against the Chicago American Giants. On September 9 he pitched a charity game at Yankee
Stadium in front of nearly 30,000 people. It was billed as a shoot-
out between young guns and instantly became a classic in Negro
Leagues lore. Gazing across the diamond, Paige saw his mirror
image. Left-hander Stuart "Slim" Jones of the Philadelphia Stars
stood six-feet-six and was pencil-thin at 185 pounds. He was twenty-
one years old, with mesmerizing stuff and coming off a 21–7 season. The teams scrapped to a 1–1 tie, the Stars scoring in the first
inning and the Crawfords answering in the seventh. In the ninth
inning the Stars backed Paige into a corner, loading the bases with
only one out. He responded in high style by striking out the next
two batters. The sun faded before either Satch or Slim did. Yankee
Stadium had no lights. As darkness closed in, the game ended with
Paige strutting back to the dugout after the ninth inning. There
would be no winner, no loser; just a pitching duel frozen in time.

Chester Washington was at Yankee Stadium for the *Pittsburgh
Courier*. "The House of Satchell [sic] had scored another signal tri-
umph," he wrote. "Fans gave him a real ovation for his never-say-die
spirit." Those fans might have showered Paige with more applause
had they known where he'd spent the previous night. Satch liked to
travel alone. He'd driven straight through from Pittsburgh to New
York for the game, arriving so late that he had no choice but to park
on 157th Street and sleep in his car. The Crawfords batboy roused

him the next day by tapping on the window. "I got into my uniform just in time to get that first pitch over the plate," Paige said.

Such heroic tales relayed from afar kept the love light burning in North Dakota. If anything, absence made the heart grow fonder. Bismarck had a schoolgirl crush on its "elongated Negro hurler." Cupid's arrow was all the more keenly felt because Ol' Satch could be such a rascal, Mister Sweet Talk with his crocodile smile, his killer kiss, and one foot perpetually out the door. A week before the American League barnstormers hit town, the *Tribune* pumped the showdown with a panting, five-part banner headline that Neil Churchill could have written:

Bismarck Will Be Mecca
for Slope Baseball Fans Next Sunday

WILL SWARM HERE TO WATCH
SATCHEL AGAINST ALL-STARS

Faithful Have Been Waiting Many a Day
for Just Such an Opportunity

PAIGE WILL GET ACID TEST

American Leaguers Will Have Bludgeons
Primed for Negro's Fast Ones

Sadly, there were no fast ones to behold and no acid test, only heartbreak. Sports history repeated itself. Paige left Bismarck in the lurch. He was . . . who knows where? Pinning him down could be as maddening as trying to catch a butterfly with tweezers. "I'm Satchel. I do as I do." And he had done it again.

The American League visitors—tired after a long season, unfamiliar with one another as teammates, and sometimes playing out of position—weren't a lock to win those barnstorm games.

The North Dakota all-stars had motivation on their side and a lineup packed with Negro Leagues alumni: Red Haley, Double Duty Radcliffe, Steel Arm Davis, Lefty Brown, and Art Hancock. Quincy Troupe preferred to go home to Saint Louis and have a tearful reunion with his mother's cooking. North Dakota edged the American League 6–5 in Valley City, turned up the gas 11–3 in Bismarck (with Radcliffe subbing for Paige on the mound), and spanked the big shots 11–0 in Jamestown. The pros saved face by winning both games in Winnipeg.

Walking off the field after the Bismarck game, one major leaguer muttered, "I knew there were a lot of good Negroes in baseball. I just didn't know they were all in Bismarck."

A few months later, many of those "good Negroes" were gone. Without warning, Jamestown dumped all its black semipros. Dickinson and Devils Lake followed suit. In the case of Jamestown, poor performance couldn't be blamed. The team had recently completed a 38–15 season. Nor were finances an issue, since the Jamestown Baseball Association promptly pulled out its checkbook and began hiring experienced replacement players, albeit players of a different color. Were the Baseball Association and manager Al Breitbach pressured into doing an about-face? The *Jamestown Sun* didn't see it that way. The paper put a happy face on the sudden change in policy. This wasn't turn-back-the-clock racism. This was "Jamestown's latest diamond venture—an all white baseball club."

Yes, indeed. Made perfect sense. Although, by the same token, some states considered the poll tax democracy's latest venture: all-white voting.

11

MARRIAGES AND SEPARATIONS

Satchel Paige failed to make his triumphant return to Bismarck that autumn because he was otherwise engaged. He'd purchased a ring to slip on Janet Howard's finger and, while none of his scheduled appearances was ever guaranteed, he did in fact present himself at the altar on October 26 in Pittsburgh. Howard was nearly a foot and a half shorter than her husband and some years younger, but had no reservations about standing up to him. She was confident, practical, and assertive: just what Paige probably needed in a partner and probably couldn't abide. He had two less than flattering pet names for Janet: "Trouble" (as in, "Uh-oh, here comes Trouble") and "Toadalo" (her big, brown eyes reminded him of a frog). Yet no one else had ever stirred within him the urge to settle down.

They'd been dating for three years and decided to marry on relatively short notice. Finding a reception venue was a breeze. Gus Greenlee made the Crawford Grill available free of charge and paid the lion's share of the catering bill, sparing little expense. The party lasted into the wee hours, propelled by three live bands and an eight-course meal. Paige picked a best man with a similarly infectious personality and impressive scrapbook: Bill "Bojangles" Robinson, the dapper tap dancer of Broadway and Hollywood renown who taught Fred Astaire's feet to fly and who knew his way around a pool hall to boot. The laughs and the liquor flowed in such abundance that Greenlee managed to sneak a fastball by wily

Satchel Paige. They'd been privately discussing a contract exten-
sion, possibly for the same penurious monthly salary of $250 plus
presumed bonuses that Greenlee had been paying his franchise
player for several years. It was not a done deal, however. At the
reception Paige indulged in a few too many celebratory toasts.
Whoosh. Greenlee whipped out a pen and some legal papers.

"Satchel won't be leaving us, don't worry about that! I've got
a new contract here for him!" he told the startled guests, who
were about to witness the Crawfords' owner and the Crawfords'
top pitcher renew their vows in public. Paige dutifully signed on
the dotted line as his wife and Bojangles Robinson peered over his
shoulder. Then everybody went back to the dance floor. The groom
didn't fully grasp the significance of what had happened until the
champagne fog lifted the next day.

There would be no romantic toes-in-the-sand honeymoon
for Mr. and Mrs. Paige. They immediately flew to the West Coast
for a working vacation. The California Winter League was in full
swing. From late October to February, it functioned as baseball's
after-hours lounge. A few major leaguers always showed up along
with a mishmash of minor leaguers, semipros, and precocious ama-
teurs. The Pasadena Merchants, MGM Studio, White King Soap
Makers, and Pirrone's All Stars were regular sponsors. For more
than ten years black teams had been invited to join in the laid-back
California fun. Paige agreed to pitch the 1934–1935 mini season for
a group of mostly Negro League players organized by Tom Wilson,
owner of the Nashville Elite Giants. Red Haley, who was not quite
ready to shut things down after leaving Bismarck, headed west with
Paige. Satchel spent those sun-dappled few months torturing batters (winning 10 games while amassing 104 strikeouts in only 69
innings) and trying to adjust to the demands of being married. He
would end up comparing life with Janet to the existential dilemma
of having to face slugger Josh Gibson with a full count and the
bases loaded: "Knowing how good he could hit, you don't want to
let go of the ball, but you had to."

Just as sharks must move constantly through water in order to breathe, Paige had to keep pitching to feel completely alive. His right arm was a biomechanical wonder. If he rested, it apparently rusted. The week of his wedding he had shoehorned in three exhibition games with the Crawfords in Cleveland and Columbus, Ohio; and in Pittsburgh. Paige was pitted against the man who quickly became his baseball soul mate: Jay Hanna "Dizzy" Dean, the ebullient pitcher for the St. Louis Cardinals. Dean had just finished a fantasy season, going 30–7 and being named the National League's Most Valuable Player. He'd also won two World Series games, including an 11–0 shellacking of the Detroit Tigers in the decisive seventh game.

Dizzy and his younger brother Paul (aka "Daffy," also a Cardinals pitcher) set off on a countrywide tour to cash in on their World Series celebrity. Dizzy was the alpha brother, an Arkansas-born, Oklahoma-cured country ham who knew how to turn homespun charm into gold. His barnstorming shtick was white-versus-black pseudo all-star games. He pulled crowds as big as 20,000 and cleared as much as $5,000 an appearance. On October 21 the Deans' traveling team played the Pittsburgh Crawfords in Cleveland. For the first time ever: Ol' Satch against Ol' Dizz. Paige got the better of Dizzy, pitching six innings and striking out thirteen batters as the Crawfords won 4–1. A columnist for the *Cleveland Plain Dealer* wrote that fans were left in awe of "da'k Mistah Satchel Paige's speed trap." It was the start of a beautiful, mutually beneficial friendship. Leroy Paige and Jay Hanna Dean were two loquacious sons of the South, both of them funny, crazy-like-a-fox, unschooled, unpredictable, and unhittable. The only glaring differences were their skin color and bank accounts. Baseball salaries had been beaten down by the Depression, but Dean said he made $14,000 barnstorming that autumn, after which he signed a new Cardinals contract paying him about $20,000 for 1935. This pained Paige to the bone. "They were saying Diz and me were about as alike as two tadpoles. But Diz was in the majors and I was bouncing around the peanut circuit."

In August Paige experienced one of his more unusual baseball bounces. It came on the peanut circuit. Greenlee rented him
to the hairy House of David touring team for about a week. The
Denver Post had been running a regional semipro tournament since
1915, and executives at the paper finally decided to let black teams
participate. The Davids interpreted that rule to their advantage by
adding two black players to their otherwise lily-white ranks. The
two players were Satchel Paige and Cy Perkins, his trusty Pittsburgh Crawfords catcher. In a giant step forward for racial diver-
sity, the two teams that advanced to the finals of that 1934 *Denver
Post* Tournament were the Kansas City Monarchs and the House
of David. Nothing could have been better for business. A record
crowd of 11,120 poured into Merchants Park, which was crammed
so tight that people roosted on top of the outfield fence like crows
on a telephone wire. Thousands of others never made it inside.

Paige entertained everybody by throwing his pregame warm-
up pitches while seated in a chair. When the time came to get serious, he stood up and tamed the Monarchs 2–1, scattering eight hits
and striking out twelve. The *Denver Post*'s Leonard Cahn wrote,
"The Bearded Beauties banked everything on Satchel, and the colored Whizbang did not disappoint." Not at all. It was his third win
in five days, enabling the House of David to claim the first-place
prize of $5,964. (As Paige came to know only too well, that was a
pittance compared with the $5,389 bonus Dizzy Dean and each
of his Cardinal teammates would receive for winning the World
Series a few months later.)

Paige thrilled Denverites with his crisp pitching. And he
shocked them by infiltrating the House of David. Although the
tournament was an enormous athletic and financial success, the
rules committee soon issued a clarification. Henceforth, black teams
were welcome at the *Denver Post* Tournament, but only one such
team per year. In addition, beginning in 1935, teams had to be
either all-black or all-white. No more mixing of the races. Despite

the splendid show he'd put on in Colorado, the colored Whizbang would have to go elsewhere to play integrated baseball.

Satchel Paige struggled through his rookie year of marriage. Janet's profligate spending had an immediate, unsettling effect on his wallet. "After that honeymoon, I started noticing a powerful lightness in my hip pocket," Paige quipped. Neil Churchill had already learned how to take domesticity in stride without breaking a sweat. He owned a vine-covered three-bedroom Tudor on the west side of Bismarck within easy walking distance of Corwin-Churchill Motors and the ballpark, but he drove everywhere. Physical exertion held no appeal, and he couldn't spare the time away. This was a fat man stretched precariously thin with work, his sports teams, community meetings, card games, and a full household. The Churchills now had two children: seven-year-old Neil C. and one-year-old Diane. Helen's sister and mother—who'd lost her home and savings in the Depression—moved in with them, as did a teenage housekeeper.

Helen Churchill didn't pay much attention to the fortunes of her husband's ball teams. Aside from being manager of the family, she'd become a staple of the *Tribune*'s Society and Clubs page, usually mentioned in conjunction with meetings of her weekly study group, which continued to delve into topics unlikely to be discussed at any length in the Bismarck dugout. The ladies tackled the Civil War during the winter of 1934. By spring they were immersing themselves in books and lectures devoted to the theme "The Search for a Philosophy of Life." Neil Churchill had less weighty matters on his mind. He'd been appointed to the entertainment committee of the Association of Commerce and served as program chair for the Rotarians. The businessmen of Bismarck didn't get overly cerebral when they gathered in their convivial haze of cigar and cigarette smoke. They listened to a talk about provisions of the National

Recovery Act, discussed deploying the Boy Scouts to help thwart any Halloween mischief brewing in the streets, and pondered ways to increase ticket sales for the annual Booster Day baseball game.

Churchill's summer baseball success carried over to basketball. He integrated the Phantoms team with the addition of reserve forward Johnny Spriggs, a Bismarck High School graduate whose grandmother was Nancy Millett, Colonel Custer's onetime servant girl. He persuaded Harold Massmann, his Chicago-based shortstop, to remain in town for the winter and play guard on the basketball team. The Phantoms lost twice to the silky-smooth Harlem Globe-trotters, but won the state tournament by crushing Grand Forks YMCA 38–18 in a battle of the two-hand set shots. Churchill's amateur show business career rolled along, too. The American Legion's Thanksgiving carnival and minstrel show filled World War Memorial auditorium for two nights. "Hambones" Churchill, his face smeared with burnt cork, played one of the comics whose job was to kill time during set changes. He sang "Liza Jane." He and Bill McDonald, a Scout leader and sales manager at the gas company, did a bit in which they took turns gazing through a telescope, trading ad-libs about members of the audience, and pretending they could spy on people in faraway places.

Had Hambones Churchill trained his telescope on Saint Louis he might have spotted something that wasn't so funny: the impending loss of his catcher and favorite player. Quincy Troupe spent the off-season playing pickup basketball and taking a few college courses. For the second year in a row, he'd led Bismarck in hitting, this time with a .395 average. (Red Haley was a distant second at .353.) On Christmas day Troupe turned twenty-two. His best baseball years stretched ahead of him like an open road paved with gold. No offense to Bismarck, but he hoped to spend those years somewhere more exciting and more centrally located than North Dakota. Talented catchers are cherished commodities and Troupe's market value had increased appreciably. His phone rang a lot that winter. The Chicago American Giants wanted him back and he tentatively agreed to return. Then the Kansas City Monarchs called. They wanted him too. The Monarchs locked him up when principal owner James Leslie "J. L." Wilkinson upped his offer with a signing bonus: a brand-new Ford sedan. Troupe would soon pack his equipment bag and head to Marshall, Texas, for spring training.

First Neil Churchill's mad-genius pitcher had flown the coop; now his model-citizen catcher took flight. Each of them was gone in a flash, without warning, as if borne away by a dust storm. If Churchill felt discouraged, he didn't show it. He couldn't afford to. Part of his job as manager was to play drum major and whip up enthusiasm. Without strong fan support the remodeled Bismarck ballpark could become a white elephant. Only 1,500 tickets had been sold for the Major League all-star game in October that Paige skipped—not nearly enough to lighten the ball and chain of the team's debt.

In early March a downtown department store made a show of buying the first season ticket for 1935 and giving it to longtime employee Alma Sundquist as a birthday gift. Churchill attended the presentation. Someone asked him about the team's prospects. The airtight fielding couldn't get much better, he said. Meanwhile, the ability to hit for power should be improved and the pitching looked "greater than ever." Five holdover players already had been signed, in addition to four new ones. "We'll have the finest team in this part of the country," Churchill declared, "providing all the players report."

He declined to reveal the name of anybody under contract. What about that caveat "providing all the players report"? Was Churchill hinting at something big in the works? Did he imply that Bismarck fans had a surprise coming? Hmm. Satchel Paige had returned to Pittsburgh after the conclusion of California winter ball. And there was talk among baseball insiders that he and Gus Greenlee were feuding again.

12

CAT AND MOOSE

Lynching doesn't seem the stuff of vigorous debate. As with cannibalism or pedophilia, what's to argue? Congress, however, engaged in just such a surreal war of words in 1935. When all was said and *not* done, lawmakers again failed to pass an antilynching bill. Senator Hugo Black of Alabama and Senator James Byrnes of South Carolina—both future U.S. Supreme Court justices—led the filibustering opposition. Black warned that taking action might have the unintended consequence of inciting even more mobs to violence. Byrnes argued that government intervention threatened to undo the "fine progress" being made in race relations in the South. By all accounts, none of the twenty victims destined to be lynched that year got to express an opinion.

While Washington fiddled, Harlem blew its top. On March 19 New York police arrested a sixteen-year-old Puerto Rican boy for shoplifting a pocketknife on West 125th Street. Witnesses alleged that the suspect got roughed up as he was being taken into custody. False rumors swirled that he'd been killed, and the loose talk brought to a boil percolating discontent with segregation, job discrimination, and city police tactics. Legitimate protesters and mischief-minded instigators took to the streets, some hurling rocks and some looting white-owned businesses. Before order could be restored 4 people were dead, 130 had been arrested, and an estimated $2 million in property damage done. Sociologists later identified mass frustration with public institutions as a root cause of the uprising, and characterized the episode as America's first "modern" race riot.

As sanitation workers swept up the broken glass in Harlem, Satchel Paige fired up his Chrysler and fled Pittsburgh. He had come home from winter ball in California stewing about the terms of his Crawfords contract and Gus Greenlee's wedding-day shenanigans. He lobbied hard for a raise. Greenlee, who claimed to have lost $30,000 on his ball team in the last three years, turned a deaf ear. Paige responded by telephoning an old pal in North Dakota. Neil Churchill met his boomeranging pitcher's demands without hesitation. Between straight salary and a snazzy red Chrysler convertible that Churchill threw in, the pay package was worth at least $700 a month. Paige hopped into his car and this time drove directly to Bismarck.

Greenlee's crowd-magnet pitcher had dissed him and gone AWOL for the second time in less than two years. Enraged, he placed a long-distance call of his own. Sounding like a B-movie gangster, Greenlee warned Neil Churchill that he'd carve him to pieces if he ever got within knife-slashing distance, a threat that had to make Churchill grateful for every inch of the 1,124 miles between Pittsburgh, Pennsylvania, and Bismarck, North Dakota. Greenlee didn't let Paige off the hook, though. In addition to owning the Crawfords, he served as president of the Negro National League. He put his power to use by conspiring to have Paige banned from the Negro Leagues for a year. Chester Washington, the *Pittsburgh Courier* sportswriter who was Gus Greenlee's head cheerleader, penned a column excoriating Paige for "his 'galivantin'' tactics" and rejoicing that he'd been cut down to size. "Heroes come and heroes go," Washington clucked. "The league helped to make him and now the League may be the medium to break him. Satchell [sic] apparently made the mistake of regarding his contract as a 'scrap of paper' and now he must pay the penalty."

Paige didn't brood about any penalties that might have to be paid and never looked back after he hit the gas on his way out of

Pittsburgh. Very little fazed him. If Greenlee banned him from planet Earth, he'd go find a team to play for on Mars. There was peace of mind to be found in an immutable law of the baseball universe: somebody somewhere always has need of a pitcher who can throw knee-high strikes at will. In the spring of 1935, Neil Churchill once again happened to be that someone. Paige made it to Bismarck on March 24. Depending on how you look at it he was either one month early for the first practice of 1935 or ten months late for opening day 1934. This was a big story in a town where big stories were so rare that newspapers found room to print the names of all 399 youngsters who passed their municipal swimming-pool test (congratulations, Ruben Wedlet, Wallace Rorcepp, and Jackie Schierbeck) and all 678 elementary school students who had perfect attendance for the month of January (bravo, sixth graders Vera DeGroot, Arzella Ode, and Jonah Goehner). The second coming of baseball's foremost vagabond pitcher merited a prominent headline in the *Tribune*: "Satchel Paige Arrives in Bismarck Fresh from 17 Wins on Pacific Coast. Dusky Mound Veteran Is Ready for Big Season with Capital City Club." A few weeks later the stakes were raised. "Biggest Baseball Season in History Is Predicted for Bismarck. Sensational Paige Tops Off Veteran Returning Lineup."

That supporting cast of veterans was led by Red Haley, who had slid comfortably into the role of on-field captain and also opened up a shoeshine parlor in town. As usual, there were some turnover holes in the lineup that needed patching. Harold Massmann, the basketball-playing shortstop, accepted an invitation to the Boston Braves minor league training camp. Churchill replaced him with Axel "Al" Leary, an infielder from Great Falls, Montana, who had a bit more home run pop. To fill the void left by Quincy Troupe, Churchill raided the minor league Sioux City Cowboys. Their catcher, Floyd Anderson, had formerly played for the town of Beulah, and Churchill made an offer lucrative enough to entice him back to North Dakota. Beyond that, eight prospects were fighting for an outfield spot and 1934's spare-parts pitching staff had to be retooled with Paige as its core.

Joe Desiderato came back to hold down third base. They called him "The Cat": his reflexes were that keen, his glovework that fluid. This was a perpetually cool cat. Cast from the same genteel mold as Troupe, Desiderato never showed emotion on the field, never let an obscenity escape his lips, got along with everybody, and shrank from the spotlight. His sister Virginia always chided him: "Joe, you've got to speak up for yourself!" It wasn't his nature. He was an indispensable member of the chorus, not a lead singer. Part of that winter of 1934–1935 Desiderato drove the Harlem Globetrotters team bus for Abe Saperstein. The novelty quickly wore off. Like Paige, he reported to Bismarck a few weeks early, itching for the new season to get under way.

Paige had trouble finding a place to live in Bismarck. His flamboyance and dalliances with white women made him a hot-potato tenant. Churchill intervened, but it's unclear which of two South Side rentals he procured. Paige either moved into a converted boxcar once used to house Soo Line Railroad work crews or a cabin owned by Wick Corwin that had been property of the Northern Pacific Railway. It's possible Paige lived in one location and kept the other as a backup bachelor pad. Regardless of the address, the accommodations were rudimentary. Since discomfort loves company, Paige asked Desiderato to be his roommate. It was a package deal. Janet Paige would be splitting time between Pittsburgh and Bismarck. Marie Desiderato accompanied her husband to North Dakota, as did their five-year-old daughter, also named Marie. Together the Paiges and the Desideratos made one happy, diverse, bathroom-sharing extended family. Little Marie not only got to sit in the dugout during baseball practices but became the first white child to ever gaze up at a certain stringbean pitcher and coo "Uncle Satchel."

* * *

In the grand scheme of things, Bismarck hadn't changed in the eighteen months since Paige was last there. Just as before, he could stand on the edge of town and let his eyes wander over wide-angle vistas capable of absorbing a city the size of Pittsburgh without spoiling the view. Wheat was still the king of crops and, though Prohibition had been repealed, moonshine was still being bottled in stubbornly dry North Dakota. Business deals still got sealed with a handshake. Farmers' wives still had faces like worn linoleum, their girlish looks scuffed away by years of back-bending chores and prairie winds. Their husbands still felt more comfortable in faded overalls than fine suits, still preferred to pay cash, still loved their Bismarck baseball team, and, as Paige said, still "came to town with hats full of money to bet on us."

There were some differences, however. Thousands more North Dakotans had gotten chewed up by the Depression. A third of the state was on government relief. In a few counties, the welfare rolls approached 70 percent. March 1935 brought a spell of soggy weather; although the drought had just stepped outside for a smoke: dry conditions and blast-furnace temperatures made a comeback by summertime. Semipro baseball culture had undergone changes, too. Dollars to spend on municipal baseball were drying up. Valley City and Bismarck were the only integrated teams left standing. Jamestown not only went all-white but shed payroll by limiting the roster to fourteen players. Devils Lake entered into a partnership with the Cleveland Indians, which supplied the town with all the low-level minor leaguers it wanted and subsidized half their salaries. Beulah made do with a sixteen-year-old second baseman and a seventeen-year-old first baseman, having aligned itself with a new Western Slope League that forbade paying ballplayers.

In April 1935, Helen gave birth to the Churchills' third child, Randy. Papa Neil savored the moment, but doted on his other baby: the ball club. Bismarck was on the verge of outgrowing North Dakota, despite the American Legion's having withdrawn its modest financial support. That left Churchill on his own. Energized by the thought of a full season enlivened by Satchel Paige's fastballs, he saw a window of opportunity to build a regional power team. He booked his heaviest schedule yet: nearly eighty games from mid-May to mid-August, two thirds of them on the road. His team was an army on the move. During one stretch it played only 3 of 21 games at home; during another, only 2 of 17.

The bandwagon rolled down Main Street, banners flying and horns honking. More businesses stepped aboard. Mandan Creamery and Produce Company had boys hawking ice cream cones and chocolate bars in the grandstand to keep fans "pepped up and enthusiastic." The first Bismarck player to hit a double would enjoy a tenderloin steak on the house at Grand Pacific Hotel; the first home run was good for a case of Gluek's beer from Nash-Finch wholesalers. Even the first player to strike out got to ease his pain with a six-month gratis subscription to the *Bismarck Capital*. There was no gift for the first player to get injured, but catcher Floyd Anderson earned that dubious distinction on opening day as Bismarck lost a 2–1 heartbreaker in Jamestown. Although Paige gave up only five hits, his teammates could muster just three. It didn't take long for Troupe's absence behind the plate to be felt. The winning run scored in the eighth inning on a passed ball that squirted through Anderson. He had a good excuse for the miscue: one of his legs had been fractured earlier in the game, bringing his season to an end.

The *Jamestown Sun* didn't downplay what it considered a significant victory. A headline cut to the chase ("White Baseball Team Successful as It Takes Opener"), and the article hammered home that point: "The all white Jamestown baseball team proved their ability to play a fast brand of ball as they defeated the powerful Bismarck aggregation. . . . This Jamestown team is as good or better than any colored combination ever to appear here." A wave of euphoria washed over the town. Warren Covert was visiting from Kearney, Nebraska. The win over Bismarck so impressed him that the next evening he took the entire Jamestown team to dinner and afterward hosted a party at the opera house. "I have never seen

Satchel Paige defeated before, although I have seen him win a good many ball games," Covert said, explaining his festive mood. "Any team that can beat him is playing baseball."

For the next week the sky spit rain. Churchill held practices indoors at the World War Memorial building, preparing for a rematch with Jamestown in Bismarck. He surveyed the roiling clouds and professed not to be worried: "All the club needs is a dry diamond and then watch them go." All the club needed, actually, was for Satchel Paige not to get struck by lightning. He didn't, and he limited Jamestown to three hits, striking out four of the first six batters and fifteen in all. Newcomer shortstop Al Leary went two for three, and Haley contributed a two-run double. Bismarck won 4–0. The only sour note was the crowd. There were 800 fans scattered throughout the stands, several thousand short of a sellout. True, it was a cold, damp Sunday in May, but it also was the home opener. Those vacant seats were a harbinger of what might lie ahead if the moribund economy didn't begin to revive. Even Satchel Paige's drawing power had limits. People with empty pockets don't buy tickets to ballgames, especially not if they can stand on a hill outside the fence and watch for nothing.

Bismarck stumbled out of the gate with a 3–2 record. Paige pitched in four of those initial five games, winning two and allowing only 12 total hits in his three starts. He was razor sharp, as evidenced by 40 strikeouts in 26 innings. The rest of the team performed about as well as a set of dull steak knives. Churchill had yet to find another quality pitcher to ease the burden on Paige. Offensively, Bismarck averaged 3½ runs and 6 hits in its first four games, tepid results for a lineup that supposedly had rectified a power shortage. In game five the team mugged the town of Williston 14–5, but it was a painful mismatch. Paige clowned his way through four innings, tossing one pitch underhand. Churchill responded with two quick player signings. He resurrected Lefty Vincent, who had pitched for him in 1934 but moved on to the Pittsburgh Crawfords. Churchill again stuck his hand into Gus Greenlee's cookie jar, but this time

Greenlee didn't cry foul or threaten to take an ax to him. Maybe that should have been a tip-off. Vincent imploded in his Bismarck pitching debut, in one inning of work getting battered for five runs and issuing five walks. He was nursing a sore shoulder that rapidly deteriorated. Churchill had bought a lame horse.

His other addition to the roster addressed a long-term weakness. Bismarck desperately needed a middle-of-the-order intimidator who could make a pitcher's knees knock. Churchill planned to groom Walter "Beef" Ringhofer for that role, but Ringhofer ran off to the minor leagues before paying any long-term dividend. Back to square one. Churchill went hunting for another home run hitting stud and got lucky. He traded up from "Beef." He stalked bigger game and managed to bag a "Moose."

Nobody outside Michigan's Upper Peninsula paid much attention to the village of Crystal Falls unless something extraordinary happened. September 30, 1893, was that kind of day. Shortly after 9 p.m. the Mansfield iron mine collapsed, setting in motion one of the worst disasters in the state's history. The break occurred in a honeycomb of tunnels directly underneath the Michigamme River, which flooded the affected mine shafts in a matter of minutes. Sixty men worked the night shift. Twenty-seven died: "drowned like rats," as a newspaper bluntly reported. The next-to-last person who made it out alive—Victor Johnson—emerged in his stocking feet, having jettisoned a pair of waterlogged boots while madly scrambling and swimming to safety. Johnson had come to Crystal Falls from Finland, shedding the surname Isotalo in hopes of boosting his chances of employment. Jobs in the mines were controlled by Swedish immigrants who looked down on Finns as vodka-swilling bumpkins.

Johnson and his wife returned to Finland a few years after the Mansfield tragedy, but in the early 1900s they resettled in Crystal Falls to raise their three children. Hilma was trained as a midwife in Europe and, over time, delivered more babies in Iron County, Michigan, than most doctors. Victor had an artistic side, the odd miner who played the violin to unwind after swinging a pickax all day. Their daughter Lempi studied piano and aspired to be an opera singer. Victor understandably discouraged his two sons from following him into the mines. The oldest son, Tauner (anglicized as "Donald") eventually enlisted in the army. Vaino ("Vernon") would make his living belting baseballs. They were both hell-raisers as kids, bursting with the raw kinetic energy that courses through booze-and-brawl mining towns, growing up in a company-owned A-frame near the railroad tracks where alcohol always was within easy reach. A number of Italian families in that Odgers Mine neighborhood operated private "tippling houses." Misters Benacarri, Dalmossa, Penatti, and Alpernini all were purveyors of homemade wine and spirits. Whiskey sold for 35 cents a pint, a price the Johnson boys could readily afford. People learned to steer clear of Donald, an ugly drunk who once punched out a horse. Vern was a life-of-the-party scamp, although once the party got going it usually ended with him on the floor in a daze. "He was a binge drinker. He'd drink till it came out his ears," recalled his nephew, Duane Johnson.

Vern acquired the sobriquet "Sock." No mystery where that came from. Balls flew off his bat with the speed and trajectory of clay pigeons at a skeet shoot. He was an outstanding student, but quit school after eighth grade to concentrate on baseball. He married the girl next door—Milma Vetetenen, daughter of another Finnish iron miner—but loved his independence more than her. Sock seemed at war with himself, a jumble of conflicting aptitudes and interests. A crack pool player who chafed at authority, he loved reading and was a whiz at math. His long fingers could deftly roll smokes (preferably Velvet brand tobacco) and also caress a piano keyboard despite never having had the benefit of music lessons. Sock never talked about his exploits, but folks in Crystal Falls did. They rehashed that Herculean home run he hit at the town ball field. It sailed over the right field fence and over the school beyond the fence, and came to rest in Jack Paro's front yard. Had to travel at least 500 feet. Then there was the story that began with Sock and Donald asking their father if they could take his Buick for a spin around town—and ended with them running out of gas and money in Oklahoma. Sock scraped together the dough to get home by playing a few ball games for an Okie semipro team.

In 1925 he agreed to suit up for Crystal Falls, the quid pro quo being a small salary plus a job with the county public works department throwing the occasional spadeful of dirt. At six-foot-three and 210 pounds, with hands as big as skillets, Sock Johnson cut as daunting a figure as Quincy Troupe, but he had angular Nordic features accentuated by a swoop of blond hair and ice-blue eyes. He had a picture-book left-hand swing. His foot speed and outfield skills were average, but offset by a throwing arm that struck fear in the heart of base runners. Teammate Frosty Ferzacca commented that Sock had "a million-dollar arm and a ten-cent brain." Manager Jack Shemky took precautions with that unpredictable brain: he had the Crystal Falls police force take Sock into quasi-protective custody on Saturday nights as a public service, a way of ensuring that Sock wouldn't bring a hangover with him to the ball field on Sunday.

That plan didn't always work to perfection. One Sunday afternoon Crystal Falls played a black touring team and Shemky benched Sock for disciplinary reasons. It apparently had been a very good Saturday night, but he refused to take his punishment sitting down. Johnson walked across the diamond and asked the visitors if they could use an extra player. Sure. How'd you like to pitch? Sock gave that a shot and Crystal Fallers had something new to talk about. He threw a shutout against his own team and scored the game's only run, lofting a fly ball deep over the center field fence in the top of the ninth inning. He celebrated by running the bases backward while thumbing his nose at Jack Shemky.

Upper Peninsula pitchers dealt with him for several years— pirouetting on the mound to watch Sock's home run balls grow small against bright blue skies—before professional scouts took serious note. The *Ironwood Daily Globe* reported in March 1929 that the Milwaukee Brewers would be giving a spring tryout to the man "who emulated Babe Ruth last summer while playing for the Crystal Falls team." The Brewers at that time were part of the Class AA American Association, one tantalizing step below the Major Leagues. They decided to take a pass on Johnson. Two years later he finally went pro, beginning the season with the Grand Island Islanders of the baseball-basement Class D Nebraska State League, then getting snatched up by the Oklahoma City Indians of the Class A Western League, two steps below the Major Leagues. He hit a combined .356 in 1931. Nonetheless, his coaches considered him an unfinished product. The Indians re-signed Sock with the intent of dialing back his home run swing so that he'd have less difficulty handling curveballs and changeups. The pupil got the message. *Tulsa Tribune* sportswriter Jack Charvat couldn't get over how much the "swatting Swede" (who, in reality, was a phenomenal Finn) improved in 1932.

"Scouts are already wondering how high the bidding will go for his services at the end of the season," Charvat wrote. "Many a nice, new baseball has been propelled from his bat beyond the confines of Western League parks. Today there isn't a more dangerous hitter in the minor leagues."

Sock didn't lack confidence. He felt invincible at the plate, almost pitying pitchers who had to face him. "They can't throw fastballs by me," he said. "I don't mind murdering a curve and a change of pace is just my dish." Knuckleballs, anyone? His average climbed to .373 that year. Oklahoma City ditched the Western League and joined a newly formed Texas League in 1933. The *Galveston Daily News* dragged out the B-word in urging fans to keep an eye on this kid Johnson: "an embryonic Babe Ruth."

Little did anyone know that Sock performed under the pressure of harboring a few dark secrets. He wasn't quite the precocious talent he seemed. He was born in 1903, not 1909, as he'd been telling scouts and team owners. Moreover, he didn't have his drinking under control, and that demon can stay in the closet only so long. In 1933 Johnson started falling off the wagon. He appeared in fifty-six games for Oklahoma City, his batting average free falling to .202. That summer the Indians peddled him to the St. Joseph Saints of the Western League. Johnson found his batting eye again with the Saints, but lost his nickname. Suddenly "Sock" was out and "Moose" was in. That was about as far as it went in terms of turning over a new leaf. In August Moose wouldn't get out of bed to accompany the team on a road trip. He had a bad case of hangover flu. The Saints slapped him with a $100 fine and an indefinite suspension, saying he'd "broken training" several times. Moose happened to be leading the league in hitting, but also in irresponsibility. He'd worn out his welcome. The Saints cut their losses and traded him to the Muskogee Oilers, doormats of the Western League.

In 1934 the Oklahoma City Indians decided to give him another chance. The Indians quickly had second thoughts and again turned the Moose loose. He resurfaced with the Sioux City Cowboys, his third Western League team in less than a year. Something clicked. Or maybe he simply dried out in the Iowa summer sun. Playing just half a season, Johnson led the league with 24 home runs. He also hit .340. Those were eye-catching numbers. Bird dogs for the Boston Red Sox and Cincinnati Reds came sniffing around, but they got a whiff of the boozehound and backed off. The Cowboys brought him back for 1935, and Johnson quickly reverted to his rambunctious ways, running afoul of management during preseason practice. He was between baseball jobs when Neil Churchill called. Bismarck catcher Floyd Anderson, who'd briefly played for the Sioux City Cowboys, had told Churchill about Johnson.

Joining a semipro team would be a humiliating comedown. On the plus side, the pay was several notches above the Western League; he'd be playing alongside Satchel Paige; and Johnson's wife, Milma, was willing to come to North Dakota to help keep the demons at bay. His baseball career had collapsed like the Mansfield iron mine. Why not go to Bismarck? It was the only light at the end of his tunnel. Moose Johnson needed Neil Churchill as much as Neil Churchill needed him.

On the evening of May 24, 1935, President Franklin Roosevelt sat at his desk inside the White House and pressed a gold telegraph key, sending a signal from Washington, D.C., to Crosley Field in Cincinnati. Someone there flipped a switch, and the stadium became bathed in the brilliance of incandescent light. Major League baseball's first night game commenced and the Reds nipped the Philadelphia Phillies 2–1 before 22,422 amazed fans. A new era in sports had begun.

The day before, cleanup hitter Moose Johnson stepped into the batter's box at Bismarck's ballpark for the first time. That sweet swing uncoiled and he lined a sharp single, driving in Joe Desiderato. Satchel Paige took over from there and tamed Valley City 5–1. Bismarck went on to win three of its next four games. On back-to-back days they beat Devils Lake, the town team that was a holding pen for the Cleveland Indians' minor leaguers. Paige silenced Devils Lake 3–0 on 1 hit, and then Bismarck batters exploded for 18 hits in a 10–7 win, with Johnson crushing one of the longest home runs ever seen in the city. For Neil Churchill the highlight of that second game came when he sat down in the dugout and wrote his lineup in the scorebook. He'd found a permanent replacement for Floyd Anderson, the bad-luck catcher who broke his leg. Without question the new man would be a perfect fit for this team and offer some protection in the batting order for Moose Johnson. He was a young, strong, highly touted black ballplayer. By the name of Quincy Troupe.

13

LONG RIFLE RIDES AGAIN

Quincy Troupe once more became a bona fide, wholly professional ballplayer in March 1935. He packed his signing-bonus Ford sedan and drove to Wiley College in the flatlands of East Texas. There he hunkered down—a ukulele man in cactus country—with the Kansas City Monarchs for a month of spring training. This was one of the glamour franchises of black baseball. Between 1923 and 1929 the Monarchs won four Negro League championships. They were the first team to crack the code of night baseball, driving from game to game in 1930 with a small convoy of trucks equipped with generators and portable lighting stanchions. Owner J. L. Wilkinson decided to pull out of the Negro Leagues the next season and barnstorm full-time. Crowds still turned out. By 1935 the leaders of the Monarchs were "Bullet" Rogan, at age forty-two winding down an illustrious career as a pitcher-outfielder; slick second baseman Newt Allen; and stud pitcher Chet Brewer, who had a curveball that swooped like a hungry gull and who was said to be the highest-paid professional black player now that Satchel Paige had retreated to semipro purgatory in North Dakota. Despite Troupe's two stellar years in Bismarck, manager Sam Crawford penciled him in as a backup catcher and platoon outfielder.

Wiley was a tiny, predominantly black college without much of a sports program. While the Monarchs were in residence, it was the school's debating team that caused a sensation by upsetting the University of Southern California, reigning national champions.

Troupe and Crawford must have gotten caught up in forensic fever. They soon found themselves in a running argument over lines of authority on the field. Sam Crawford spent most of his time in the Negro Leagues as a pitcher, retiring as a player in 1922. Troupe had a catcher's mind-set. Matters came to a head a few weeks after training camp broke, when Brewer took the mound against the ubiquitous House of David. The second batter of the game jumped on a curveball that the Monarchs left fielder hauled in while pinned to the fence. Troupe made a mental note. That same batter came up a few innings later, by which time Brewer had given way to a relief pitcher with comparatively lifeless stuff. The count was two and two. *Throw heat*, Troupe thought. *This guy will kill a hanging curve.* Crawford yelled from the bench, giving the signal for a curveball. *No, no. Fastball's best in this situation.* Crawford kept signaling: Curve, curve, curve. Troupe ignored him and flashed a sign to his pitcher: index finger pointing down, denoting a fastball. The result was a weak infield pop. Inning over.

As Troupe took a seat in the dugout, Crawford asked a question to which he probably already knew the answer: What kind of pitch did that batter just hit? "Fastball," Troupe replied. Crawford blew his top at the act of insubordination. They exchanged words, some of them heated. The debate continued for several days, with Crawford sticking to his guns. Presented with what amounted to a my-way-or-the-highway ultimatum, Troupe chose the highway: Route 71, the road to North Dakota. To do his job properly, he needed the freedom to call his own pitches. Neil Churchill, catcher turned car dealer turned baseball manager, understood. It was a Monday in May. If Troupe whipped that Ford hard, he might be able to make it to Bismarck in time for Wednesday night's ball game.

That morning he quit the Monarchs and got into his car.

He made it by Wednesday. With pleasure, Churchill inserted him into the starting lineup at catcher. Troupe didn't miss a beat. He got two hits in the Devils Lake game in which Moose Johnson connected on his tape-measure home run. He also moved back into Louis and Edith White's house, again bunking down the hall from Red Haley. The next afternoon the House of David arrived in Bismarck for a Memorial Day doubleheader. In the past that would have been the prescription for a downbeat holiday. Not this year. The Davids put on their usual pregame show. Outfielder Bob Zeller wowed fans by stuffing a baseball inside his mouth, as if he were an olive and the ball a pimiento. That could have been an omen for what was about to happen to his team.

In game one, Churchill turned to grab-bag starter Charlie Bates, whom he'd just bird-dogged from the Devils Lake team. Bates took a 7–4 lead into the eighth inning, Bismarck having roughed up grizzled Grover Cleveland Alexander. With two outs in the eighth, Bates tired. He gave up a walk and two singles, capped by a bases-clearing triple that tied the game. Exit Charlie Bates. Enter bum-armed Lefty Vincent, who proceeded to uncork a wild pitch. The runner on third took off. Troupe rooted in the dirt for the ball and flipped it to Vincent. He missed the tag, but the umpire called the runner out for failing to touch home plate. The Davids blew their Christian cool. Nobody took the Lord's name in vain, but umpire Tom Cayou was fair game. A *Mandan Pioneer* reporter said "a riot" ensued. Spectators rose to their feet, screaming. Policemen trotted onto the field "to quell the shouting of the full visiting team gathered around Cayou." When play resumed Churchill tapped Satchel Paige to pitch the ninth inning. He quieted the House of David by inducing a harmless dribbler to first and fanning the next two batters.

In the bottom of the ninth, Joe Desiderato led off with a lazy fly and Al Leary grounded out. That brought up Troupe. He singled. So did Haley. Moose Johnson drew an intentional walk, loading the bases. Churchill plucked reserve first baseman Leroy Drengberg off the bench to pinch-hit. Drengberg ran the count to one ball and two strikes. The pitcher went into his windup . . . and

Troupe caught everybody in the stadium by surprise: he bolted from third like a Number 9 train comin' down the track, and slid safely into home. End of game. Bismarck won 8–7 on a rare walk-off stolen base.

Paige was the winning pitcher of record. He rested about half an hour and then threw a full nine innings, subduing the House of David 7–0 on three hits. Troupe, Haley, and Johnson rapped home runs. The back-to-back victories spoke loud and clear: Bismarck could play with anybody. The top five slots in the order (Desiderato, Leary, Troupe, Haley, and Johnson) accounted for 20 of the team's 21 hits in the doubleheader; against one of the most storied independent clubs. The *Tribune* got carried away and began referring to Bismarck's batting quintet as "Murderers' Row," an appellation originally applied to Babe Ruth's and Lou Gehrig's 1927 New York Yankees. Immediately after burying the House of David, the team left for Canada. Bismarck and the Kansas City Monarchs had been invited to serve as the opening attraction at remodeled Osborne Stadium in Winnipeg. Chet Brewer locked horns with Satchel Paige. It was a pitching rematch of the 1934 *Denver Post* Tournament, when the House of David hired Paige as a ringer and he beat Brewer and the Monarchs 2–1 in a standing-room-only championship game. This time the two foes fought to a nine-inning 0–0 tie before it got too cold to continue. Paige struck out seventeen, Brewer thirteen. The *Winnipeg Free Press*, which said Paige produced "more smoke than a burning oil well," loved every scoreless minute: "The finest mound duel ever unfolded in Winnipeg." Afterward, Brewer needled his counterpart, bragging that he would beat Paige not just the next time they met, but *every* time they faced each other from there on out.

Satchel Paige couldn't conceive of such a possibility. Another pitcher own him? Brewer might as well have said he could heave a baseball into the air and stop it from falling back to earth. "It just can't be done," muttered Paige.

* * *

Gopher Days were popular events on the northern plains calendar, even though they amounted to glorified community pest control. No one dressed in furry costumes. Children didn't amuse their parents by impersonating bucktoothed rodents. People simply had great fun cutting the tails off all the gophers they could catch and kill—live gophers being the bane of every farmer's and rancher's existence—and competing for medals and cash prizes. Towns planned street festivals to coincide with the purges, amassing piles of as many as 100,000 gopher tails. On June 14, 1935, the ball teams from Bismarck and Devils Lake played a doubleheader in Brinsmade, North Dakota, as part of its Gopher Day celebration. (Back in Bismarck, state and federal agents were busy chasing bootleggers. They seized 3,397 bottles of moonshine in two raids.) Paige rested in Brinsmade. Bismarck still won both games. Desiderato and Troupe handled the pitching. Neil Churchill had his own cause for celebration, which had nothing to do with gophers or beating Devils Lake. Determined to ease the strain on Paige, he'd put out feelers for additional pitchers. Double Duty Radcliffe—who had landed with the Brooklyn Eagles after Jamestown jettisoned its black players—was willing to return to North Dakota, but couldn't get released from his Brooklyn contract. On Gopher Day Churchill succeeded in coming to terms with Barney Morris, who'd gone back to Louisiana after the 1934 season. When Bismarck hosted the Kansas City Monarchs the following weekend, Morris was on the mound for the first game of a Sunday doubleheader. He got saddled with a hard-luck 2–1 defeat, but his fastball, curve, and changeup were in fine form. Churchill saw enough to be convinced he had a solid backup to Paige.

As for Paige, he pitched the second game that afternoon and made a liar and a 2–0 loser out of mouthy Chet Brewer. Moose Johnson inflicted the major damage with a home run and an RBI single. Paige gave up five harmless hits, and only two runners got as far as second base, in part because Troupe threw out three Monarchs trying to steal.

In general, however, June was considered another disappointing month. Bismarck played .500 ball for three weeks, then had a late spurt to end with 17 wins, 12 losses, and a tie. Injuries were taking their toll. The *Tribune* speculated about a "jinx." Anderson had fractured his leg. Vincent's sore shoulder wouldn't heal. Outfielder Bill Morlan broke his arm. Morris couldn't shake flu-like symptoms and had to be hospitalized for a few days. Troupe hobbled around on a spiked foot and Desiderato banged up a hand. More worrisomely, Johnson missed a game in late June because of "stomach trouble," which had to give Churchill a headache. The ball club depended heavily on its star pitcher's right arm and its star left fielder's continued sobriety.

The funk didn't dampen Paige's spirits. He remained his inimitable, impenetrable, leg-pulling self, especially in dealing with the press. A Canadian journalist got so snookered that he described Paige as "shy and reserved." Satchel took some liberties during that interview in revealing that he'd turned pro in 1922 (actually, 1926) while out west in Phoenix (make that down south in Chattanooga), once struck out eighteen batters in a row (eighteen, yes; consecutively, no), and battled Willie Jones (real name, *Stuart* Jones) at Yankee Stadium before 49,000 fans (more like 30,000, but who's counting?). The Canadian became so enamored of Paige that he concluded his story with the exclamation "No wonder white men draw color lines!"

The *Bismarck Capital* assigned cub reporter Gaylord Conrad, the publisher's son, to do a column on "probably the best known semi-professional ball twirler in America." He got taken for a ride too. Paige told him he was born in New Mexico and that fried chicken and baking powder biscuits were staples of his training table. Having observed a certain red Chrysler convertible flying down the streets of Bismarck, Conrad wrote that Paige enjoyed driving around town "at a fast clip." That was partially true. Satchel did love speeding, but he ventured way beyond city limits.

*   *   *

They'd heard about this warrior from afar, the one who showed no fear and stirred the hearts of comrades. The Sioux called him *Mila Mazawakan*, "Long Rifle." They were not referring to George Armstrong Custer. Long Rifle was the name that the Sioux of Standing Rock Indian Reservation bestowed on, of all people, Satchel Paige. That crossing of paths seemed preposterous, as if pages had been ripped from wildly disparate novels—say, *Huckleberry Finn* and *The Last of the Mohicans*—and shuffled like cards. The wandering prince of black baseball consorting with descendants of Sitting Bull? Strange but absolutely true. On his truncated first tour of duty in Bismarck during August and September 1933, Page stuck close to the capital. During this second, full-season stint, he ranged far and wide, usually free of spousal responsibilities because Janet Paige more often than not remained in Pittsburgh.

As with every team he'd ever played on, Paige was a workhorse: the staff Clydesdale. As with every team he'd ever played on, there were times when he inexplicably didn't show up for work. Statistics for anything other than Major League baseball were suspect. Teams kept their own scorebooks. Newspapers didn't cover some games and reported others sketchily. Box scores contained mistakes. That being said, records for June 1935 indicate that Bismarck had 29 games. Paige pitched in at least 13 of them. Sometimes he might be called upon to pinch-hit or take a turn in the outfield, but in 8 of those 29 games, including 5 of the last 6 games played that month, he didn't appear at all. Where was he? Here, there, and anywhere. Neil Churchill *sometimes* knew of his whereabouts. Satchel had what amounted to a permanent hall pass. He'd accept one-game freelance pitching assignments in flyspeck towns like Heaton. Why not give the farm boys a thrill and earn a few bucks on the side? Catchers on those teams would get $5 combat pay, compensation for the pounding their glove hand took from being subjected to nine innings of blistering fastballs.

Paige loved to fish almost as much as he loved to pitch. Fishing was something he'd done as a kid in Alabama to help put food on the table. He dropped lines into many of North Dakota's finest fishing holes and rivers. That may have been what inspired him to make the drive to Standing Rock Indian Reservation. It straddled the North Dakota–South Dakota border some forty miles from Bismarck: 2,200 acres of undulating hills, woodlands, and lakes fat with walleyes. Of course, there's a more colorful alternative explanation of how he came to know the Sioux. Satchel, married but not as precise with self-control as he was with his pitches, claimed to have struck up a friendship with Dorothy Running-Deer, a staunch baseball fan. He said Dorothy brought him to the reservation to meet her father, who, Paige also claimed, "raised rattlesnakes in a deep pit in the back of his hut."

Rattlesnake breeders are, themselves, a rare breed. Paige asked the father if he'd ever been bitten by a rattler. "Lots of times," he replied. Enough times that he kept a supply of homemade snake-oil remedy inside the house. Paige asked a follow-up question that might have occurred only to a hypochondriac pitcher: what would that goop feel like if you rubbed it on your arm? Very, very hot, said Running-Deer. He didn't recommend using it for anything other than neutralizing snake venom. For whatever reason, though, he gave Satchel a jug, as well as the secret Sioux recipe. It took just a few days for Paige's curiosity to get the better of him. He rubbed a few drops onto his right biceps. Nerve endings that he didn't know he had screamed for relief. "It's a wonder my arm didn't fly outta the room!" Paige said. By trial and error he learned how to dilute Running-Deer's concoction, and it became part of his postgame, muscle massage ritual. Whatever was in that jug apparently worked. Churchill couldn't wear him out. Paige threw more than twice as many innings as most pitchers. He might miss a game now and then because fish were biting somewhere, but he never missed one because of a sore arm.

That snakebite elixir traveled everywhere with him. He refused to divulge the ingredients. Teammates and reporters guessed that his precious jug contained a mix of kerosene and olive oil. Or could it be wolfsbane and wild cherry stems? Satchel was as tight-lipped as a prisoner of war. He took to calling the mystery lotion "Deer oil." Beyond that, he wouldn't say a word.

June sizzled on its way out the door, leaving thermometers stuck in the upper nineties. The heat wave somehow ignited the Bismarck players. They swept three games from the Colored House of David knockoff team, which breezed into town with a 43–5 record and left with its confidence shaken. Moose Johnson bounced back from his stomach ailment, spanking two home runs in one of those games. Utility man Bob McCarney went 5 for 5 in another. On July 3 the temperature crept to 100 degrees: a high for the year, exacerbated by forty-mile-per-hour winds that raised a dust devil lasting fifteen minutes.

Just past the halfway point of the schedule, Johnson was Bismarck's best hitter, with a .444 average. Paige lapped the rest of the pitching staff with 16 wins and 2 losses. Yet Churchill kept opening his wallet. He acquired Hilton Smith from the Monroe Monarchs, the team Churchill had raided earlier to get Barney Morris. Smith, like Paige, was long and lean, but his body language didn't say "athlete." He carried himself with all the swagger of a librarian, although this librarian could bust a curveball that turned batters' knees to jelly. He was twenty-seven years old and from Giddings, Texas. His schoolteacher father had gotten him interested in baseball, and they had played together on the town team. Smith went to Prairie View A&M College, blossomed as a pitcher, and after his sophomore year turned semipro in Austin. The Monroe Monarchs discovered him in 1932 and the laconic Texan made an indelible impression: He went 31–0 that season. He had six quality pitches, including a slider and screwball, and threw them from several arm angles. He also could hit and play the outfield. There were no behavioral issues. Hilton Smith, the teacher's son, tutored illiterate teammates on road trips. He would fit right in with Churchill's no-smoking, no-drinking choirboys like Troupe and Desiderato. His wife, Louise, characterized Smith as "someone who just took life as it comes." Life, and Neil Churchill's $150 a month, told him it was time to go to North Dakota.

He debuted on a Friday night, playing center field against an all-star team from La Junta, Mexico. They'd won 56 out of 69 games on a marathon American tour. "The greatest ball team on the road bar none," said House of David first baseman John Tucker. Bismarck stopped La Junta cold, 8–1. Smith doubled and scored the first run. Paige struck out 13 and scattered 3 hits. Moose Johnson tomahawked two home runs and rang up 5 RBI. The next day Paige and Barney Morris split the pitching and the Mexicans lost again, 6–3.

On Sunday Hilton Smith stepped into the rotation. He defused Devils Lake 7–2 with a five-hitter. He'd kept his poise in a bases-loaded situation, wriggling free thanks to a strikeout and a key double play. His biggest cheerleader was Satchel Paige, who whooped and hollered encouragement from left field. Paige had been a last-minute substitute. He was back in the outfield Monday night. Not good. It looked as if Moose Johnson couldn't hide in the driest state in the country. His demons had found him.

The second-youngest member of the team (after Quincy Troupe) was its bridge between the old and new eras. Bob McCarney hopped a freight into Bismarck as a teenager with 50 cents in his pocket. He sold pencils on the street until his athletic prowess helped him get hired for a menial job at Corwin-Churchill Motors. Just twenty in 1932, he ran the town baseball team for part of that summer after Neil Churchill had stepped away. A tall, barrel-chested, whiskey-soaked Irishman with a carnival barker's voice, McCarney quickly clawed his way from broom pusher to car salesman. Soft sell was not his style. The classic "Mac" story involved a schoolteacher in the western Badlands who'd come into some money. He drove a Chrysler convertible out to her house, hoping to talk the woman into buying it. He succeeded, but was gone most of the week. "What took you so long?" Wick Corwin inquired upon his return. "Well," McCarney drawled, "it took me a day just to get her britches off."

The other ballplayers did oddball chores for Churchill at the dealership. McCarney was the only legitimate full-time employee, so he had to beg off long road trips. That in itself made his relationship with Churchill different. McCarney also had a touch of Moose Johnson in him, further muddying the situation. After one stretch of away games, Churchill stopped by the showroom on his way home. It happened to be a day when McCarney, who didn't accompany the team, had enjoyed a liquid lunch. Churchill, a soda sipper, bounded into Wick Corwin's office. Gotta fire Mac, he huffed. Alcohol on his breath: customers were sure to be offended.

Corwin, who exhibited a priestly tolerance of his partner's gambling and baseball obsessions, looked up from his desk and laughed. Priorities! Priorities! "While you were off chasin' that goddamn little, white ball around, he sold two automobiles," he said in McCarney's defense. "That's more than some of our other men have sold all month."

Mac remained on the Corwin-Churchill payroll. And kept drinking. He kept playing ball, too. He was the ideal utility man, a good hitter off the bench and able to fill in at any position, even as an emergency pitcher or catcher. McCarney was especially thrilled to share the field with Paige and Troupe, knowing that in a perfect world they'd both be major leaguers. Stars can easily corrupt team chemistry. Ball games can be won or lost away from the park: over coffee at late-night diners, in a hotel room where players are shooting the breeze, inside a car making a butt-numbing ride to Winnipeg.

Fortunately for Churchill, he had more low-maintenance players like Desiderato, Smith, Morris, Leary, and Troupe (who willed himself to stay out of kissing range of his landlord's frisky cleaning girl) than he did live-wire characters such as Johnson and Paige. They all got along. Somebody sent a bogus telegram to McCarney that said the Valley City team was about to offer him a lucrative contract. Haley, an inveterate practical joker, was the prime suspect but never confessed. When Paige had a diva moment, teammates would gleefully remind him of his execrable outing with the Birmingham Barons, in which he hit eight batters in a row, one of whom chased him from the mound waving a bat. When not playing ball, they played pinochle and poker. Troupe, Haley, and Paige also liked Conquin, or "Coon Can," a variant of rummy popular in the South. Johnson, Haley, and Paige shot pool, and there were half a dozen billiard parlors in Bismarck to keep them occupied. Moose, easily bored by Eight Ball, would break out his trick shots. "Come down to the palace of broken hearts," he'd chortle while chalking his stick, "and listen to the click of the ivories." When things got too quiet, they'd make music. Troupe strummed his ukulele. Johnson banged on the piano. Paige might pull out a guitar, harmonica, or mouth harp, but his forte was sing-alongs. The Mills Brothers were friends of his. When in the mood, he'd lead the harmonizing on one of their hits: *Pack up all my care and woe, here I go, singing low. Bye, bye blackbird.*

For Churchill to minimize his cares and woes as manager, he needed Paige to be content in and out of uniform. So far, so good. Paige enjoyed a period of relative baseball bliss and was grateful for it. "I will always do anything I can for Mr. Churchill," he said. Gus Greenlee couldn't solve the Paige riddle. Churchill came close. Incentives held Satchel's attention. Call it the carrot-and-shtick approach. In the Corwin-Churchill showroom, a rearview mirror with an embedded clock caught his eye. It's yours, said Churchill, if you win our next big game. Done. He became infatuated with a .22 rifle, and Churchill made the same pledge. Paige won that game too.

Deep down, Long Rifle was a man alone in a crowd. He felt most comfortable with Troupe and Haley, although he had a habit of pulling rank on his young catcher. The three of them went hunting on the outskirts of town one morning. Paige told Louis White that he was "going to give Quincy and Haley their first lesson in shooting rabbits." Troupe explained that he'd grown up in Georgia hunting and fishing. Nice to know, but Satchel claimed dibs on the first rabbit they flushed. When it sprang into view, he aimed, fired . . . and missed. Troupe shouldered his gun, took a single shot, and nailed it. Paige's eyes widened as if he'd just served up a game-winning home run. "Say, Haley," he murmured, "this youngster ain't foolin', is he?"

Paige fancied himself a boxer as well as a marksman. He'd corner the "youngster" before games and goad him into sparring. Troupe, a Golden Glover, put up with Satchel's ridiculous bobbing and weaving, and discovered something unexpected: Ol' Satch packed a decent punch. Troupe formulated a theory. In addition to a wide wingspan, Paige had long, strong fingers that imparted abnormal backspin on his fastball, causing it to rise—or appear to rise—several inches. Troupe believed that this explained why so many batters insisted his pitches looked pea-size compared with everybody else's. Drawing a bead on Paige the person could be equally difficult. He was his own rising fastball. "He could clown one moment and become deadly serious the next," said Troupe. "His complex personality made him immensely interesting."

Good catchers are amateur psychologists. Troupe learned to go with the flow of those pendulum swings. They were driving back to Bismarck once from a tournament in Canada when Paige started to rag Troupe about owning a Ford: *Cheaply built pieces of junk . . . Mule wagons . . . Why don't you step it up and buy a classy Chrysler like mine?* Troupe took the ribbing in stride, but got so distracted by Paige's monologue that he failed to slow down for a tight turn. The Ford skidded off the road, tires screeching. Paige disappeared from view in the front passenger's seat. Haley, Morris, and Smith got tossed like dice in the back. Troupe regained control of the car and slammed on the brakes, skidding to a stop on the lip of a ditch. Barney Morris popped open a rear door, clutched his stomach, and fell onto the ground, writhing. "Oh! Oh, Lord!" he gasped.

Troupe rushed over to him in a panic. "What's wrong?"

Morris struggled to speak, but couldn't. He was laughing too hard. "Whooo! Hooo! I've never seen anything like that!" he howled, eyes welling with tears. "The big man down on the floor rolled into a ball. Man, what a sight!"

Red Haley stumbled out of the car. "See if Satch is all right!" Morris told him, still holding his stomach. Paige emerged from the shadows, feeling no pain, just acute embarrassment. When the car went into its spin, he'd tucked into a fetal position and dived under the dashboard. "It ain't funny!" he croaked. "Looka heah, Troupe, if you can't drive this jalopy no better than this, let me take over."

Troupe was staring at the front grille, assessing the damage. The Ford had come through without a scratch. "I admit I missed the curve sign," he snapped. "But whose fault was *that*?"

"OK," Paige replied. "Promise not to miss another sign and I won't say another word to you between here and Bismarck."

Long Rifle looked frazzled. Not wanting to risk further upsetting his pitcher, Troupe took himself out of the game. "I'll let Haley drive."

Everybody piled back into the car. Haley pulled out the choke and turned the key. The engine growled back to life. He drove for hours through the Dakota gloom in silence, serenaded by the harmonious snores of his teammates: *Make my bed and light the light, I'll be home late tonight. Blackbird, bye bye. . . .*

14

"A Riotous Opera of Extra-Base Hits..."

Some North Dakotans wrestled with the question of how an automobile should properly fit into their daily life. Owning a vehicle that didn't earn its keep, like a tractor or threshing machine, made no practical sense. Yet newspaper ads and radio commercials kept reassuring them that every American wanted—no, *needed*—the latest model Ford, Chevy, DeSoto, or Chrysler. Consider the conflicted farmer who ambled into Corwin-Churchill Motors (in his work clothes) and purchased a gleaming Chrysler Imperial sedan. Eight-cylinder engine. Eight-passenger seating. Fat whitewall tires. Fender skirts as big as hoop dresses. "The car of tomorrow is here today." That was the marketing slogan, but it didn't stop this farmer from driving his luxurious Imperial off the lot and straight to Texas to pick up a prizewinning hog he'd bought. Oh, my. Several hundred pounds of squealing pig sprawled in style across the rear seat. The "car of tomorrow" deserved better treatment, but what could the poor man do? There was work to be done.

Neil Churchill was in much the same fix as that farmer with his flashy Chrysler Imperial. He'd paid handsomely to assemble a ball team that arguably was too luxurious for the task at hand; a town team so good that very few towns wanted to play them anymore. Had Churchill contracted the semipro equivalent of gold fever? Was he repeating the "too-much mistake" that, historically, tripped up so many North Dakotans? Nearly half of Bismarck's games in 1935 were against Devils Lake, Valley City, and Jamestown, and Bismarck had comfortable winning records against all three. Other towns chose to keep their dignity and their distance. Churchill was forced to bolster the schedule with out-of-state tournaments and traveling teams such as the tireless House of David.

In mid-July Bismarck knocked heads with Jamestown six times in five days, taking all but one game. Three of those wins were neutral-site exhibitions in Winnipeg, where Moose Johnson blasted three home runs, two of them bombs that landed in an amphitheater beyond the right field wall. The last of those six games was the most intriguing. It took place back in Bismarck with Satchel Paige pitching. Jamestown turned to its new manager, Ray Starr, a twenty-nine-year-old right-hander who'd thrown forty innings in the Major Leagues in 1933 and since then had bounced around the International League. The *Jamestown Sun* characterized the decision by the Jamestown Baseball Association to hire Starr as "another step in their great experiment of producing an all white baseball team which could turn out consistently good baseball." By then somebody at the *Sun* or at the Jamestown Baseball Association should have realized that this wasn't exactly cutting-edge change, that the Major Leagues had been producing nothing but white teams for nearly half a century.

Paige wasn't keen on seeing the "great experiment" succeed. He asked his teammates to get him one run. That's all he wanted: *one run*. Red Haley complied leading off the bottom of the fourth inning. He sent a Ray Starr fastball zooming over the right field fence for a solo homer. Other than that gopher ball, Starr gave up only six hits. Paige, however, put on a clinic. His Two-Hoop Blooper was spectacularly bloopy. His Nothin' Ball was nothin' but invisible. He held the visitors hitless through five innings, striking out eight of the first twelve men who faced him. Jamestown couldn't land a punch. They scratched out three singles while going down swinging fifteen times. One runner got as far as second base. On an error. That was it for scoring threats. Paige delivered a coolly efficient 1–0 shutout. The testiest moment came when the home plate umpire refused to call a strike on a Bismarck batter because he felt Starr had quick-pitched him. Both benches partially emptied. These spats were getting to be old hat. A reporter for the *Mandan Pioneer* wrote that this disruption occurred in the sixth inning, "instead of the seventh, as usual."

During that Jamestown series Churchill made another chess move, signing first baseman Ed Hendee off the roster of the Wilkes-Barre Barons in the New York–Pennsylvania League. He was a minor league lifer, but baseball smart and a proven .300 hitter. Almost certainly Moose Johnson told Churchill to grab him. They'd been teammates on the Sioux City Cowboys. At thirty-four, Hendee was several years older than any Bismarck player. What to make of that graybeard addition, especially coming in July? Churchill wanted to stabilize his infield. Bob McCarney played a good first base; but he couldn't be relied on to make road trips, and there were a lot still on tap. Hendee—who left the coal mines of his native Iowa at age sixteen to turn pro—could smoothly step into that role. Heck, he could run the team. In 1934 Ed Hendee wore the mantle of player-manager for the minor league Richmond Colts, where he achieved some notoriety by getting arrested for violating Virginia's blue laws. The Colts had organized a Sunday benefit game on behalf of the local Crippled Children's Hospital. Good cause, wrong day of the week. Richmond police swooped in and hustled Hendee off to jail. He was fined $5 and released on $1,000 bond. Prosecutors dropped the charges later that summer. By then the defendant had kissed Richmond good-bye and joined the Sioux City Cowboys.

There were practical reasons for Churchill preferring someone with Hendee's consistency and experience. Seating capacity at the Bismarck ballpark had been expanded to 2,500, but the record attendance projected for 1935 hadn't panned out. Crowds topped 2,000 only a few times. Every remaining game, therefore, had pocketbook implications. Churchill was caught in a vicious cycle. To make money and dig the team out of debt (plus justify that stadium expansion), attendance needed to go up; to generate the excitement that would put more people in the stands, he had to improve the product by spending more money on players, thus further widening the budget gap. Churchill accumulated more debt for the anticipated greater good of increasing revenue.

Bismarck's operating expenses exceeded those of most Negro League and some minor league teams. Churchill footed the bill largely by himself, but his poker and bridge winnings weren't sufficient. Nor were the bets he placed on his ball team—and there were plenty of them. He would even leave the dugout during games and hustle side wagers in the grandstand. *Two bucks says Satch doesn't give up another run. . . . Anybody want to bet me Moose can't hit a homer today? How about a double? . . . How many runs you think your team'll score this inning if I pull an outfielder?* Churchill didn't let many opportunities slip by. A Chrysler executive came to Bismarck on Corwin-Churchill business and stopped by practice, seriously overdressed in a seersucker suit and panama hat. He and Neil Churchill got to talking and that quickly led to a friendly bet. Churchill asked ball boy Bobby Myhre to bring him a baseball. Mr. Seersucker signed it; then Churchill summoned Myhre again. "Give this to Quincy," he instructed, "and say Mr. Churchill wants him to throw it over the fence."

Little Bobby did as he was told. So did Troupe. He walked over and stood by home plate, shook his right arm to loosen up, reared back, and launched that ball over the left field wall, some 330 feet away. Churchill told Bobby to go find the ball. Off he went on his bicycle, soon to return with the baseball bearing the visitor's signature. "I'll be damned!" exclaimed Mr. Seersucker. He took out his wallet, counted off some bills, and handed them to Churchill. Easiest $100 he ever made.

Churchill's machinations and hustles weren't nearly enough to push the team into the black. It wasn't because he enjoyed the scenic drive that he booked so many exhibitions and tournaments in Winnipeg. Canada had generous appearance fees and cash prizes. Every extra dollar helped the cause. In July 1935 Churchill received a telegram from a sports promoter in Wichita, Kansas, notifying him that Bismarck had been awarded a berth in the first nationwide semipro baseball tournament. Thirty-two of the best amateur teams in the country would slug it out starting August 13. The last team standing would get a cut of the gate receipts, perhaps netting as much as $5,000.

Wichita! That was the main reason Churchill snagged Ed Hendee. There were more names on his wish list. After Paige finished handcuffing Jamestown, the team hit the road to South Dakota for three days. When they returned to Bismarck a new player was there, waiting to join them. That new player was not so new to Paige, Troupe, and Haley. They considered him an old friend. They couldn't help it. Sooner or later everybody in black baseball seemed to make the acquaintance of Theodore Roosevelt Radcliffe.

He laid claim to being Satchel Paige's first catcher. They'd met on the sandlots of Mobile, Alabama, as teenagers. "Satchel was wild as a March hare when he started playing," Radcliffe said. "He had me running all over the place to catch his pitches."

They lived only five blocks apart, but those five blocks made a world of difference. Radcliffe had a birth certificate and the benefit of a stable family: His father was a home builder. Both boys were born on July 7, Ted in 1902, Satchel some fuzzy number of years later. Physically, they were nothing alike: the young pitcher slim as a foul pole; the young catcher stocky and as roundly contoured as a gingerbread boy. When it came to personality, however, there was significant overlap. Something in the air or the water or the chalk used to line Mobile ball fields hyperstimulated their imaginations. Satchel had few peers as an athlete, but Ted Radcliffe posed a serious threat in terms of outtalking him. The things that came out of their mouths! Embellishments, exaggerations, poppycock, balderdash, fish stories, whoppers, bald-faced lies, and any combination thereof. Hear Radcliffe yapping in peak form: "We used to make a rag ball, tie it up with tape, and soak it in kerosene, then light it and play night ball with it." Picture that: fifteen-year-old Satchel Paige, right hand smoldering and blistered with second-degree burns, blowing fireball after fireball past neighborhood batters, whose infrequent base hits sparked brushfires in the outfield grass. Those were the days. They never happened, but what a joy to relive 'em.

Those halcyon days ended for Radcliffe in 1919, when he and his younger brother Alex hopped a train to Chicago. Their oldest brother lived there, and the big city beckoned. The rest of the family soon joined the exodus from Alabama. The Radcliffe clan moved into an apartment on the South Side near Comiskey Park. The White Sox called Comiskey home, but the Negro League's Chicago American Giants were tenants. Ted swore he saw Rube Foster, the Giants' pipe-puffing manager, use wisps of smoke to communicate with his players on the field. Radcliffe by then was five-feet-ten and a blocky 220 pounds, adept at both pitching and catching. He broke in with the semipro Illinois Giants making $3.50 a game, but eventually caught on with the more prestigious Gilkerson's Union Giants. In 1928, at the relatively advanced age of twenty-six, he turned pro with the Negro League's Detroit Stars. From there, he fashioned a familiar ballplayer biography: early marriage, early divorce, second marriage, and a movie montage of fleabag hotels, kidney-crunching road trips, and battered suitcases. Fade out, Detroit Stars. Fade in, Homestead Grays. Quick cuts to the Pittsburgh Crawfords . . . Columbus Blue Birds . . . New York Black Yankees . . . Jamestown, North Dakota . . . Brooklyn Eagles—and a telegram from Neil Churchill.

When Damon Runyon dubbed him "Double Duty" in 1932, Radcliffe posted career numbers with the Crawfords: a 19–8 pitching record and .325 batting average. Those were hard statistics, not his own inflated figures: he'd played over the moon that year.

Radcliffe's reputation was more down-to-earth: excellent defensive catcher, good pitcher (thanks to his mastery of the shady emoryball and spitter), average hitter, and all-star self-promoter. Churchill had seen Radcliffe up close in Jamestown and knew exactly what he was getting. Double Duty's unusual versatility made him a two-for-the-price-of-one addition. Bismarck now had a fourth frontline pitcher and more outfield depth: on days when Radcliffe caught, Churchill could use Quincy Troupe in center field.

Radcliffe brought energy that was good for more than livening up road trips. To the surprise of teammates, he seldom smiled on the field. He was all in-your-face business, as evidenced by "Thou Shalt Not Steal," printed in block letters on the front of his chest protector. Smiling may have been out, but talking was in. When pitching, Duty would rag hitters the way Paige did. "Here it is! Here comes my fastball!" (Although he might lie and serve up a curve.) When he was catching, he'd buzz in a hitter's ear. *Why insult my pitcher by bringing that bat with you? If you somehow get on base, better not try stealin' on me.* There was a bonus: Radcliffe had an old folk remedy that he used to quickly sober up Moose Johnson after beer binges: wrap a towel around some crushed ice and stick it between his legs. Sure to clear the cobwebs out of any addled brain.

Joe Desiderato was familiar with Radcliffe from Chicago baseball circles, but had never met him. Blacks and whites went their separate ways in the Windy City and nearly everywhere else. Desiderato came to regard that as a pity. "The two best talkers you ever want to hear are Double Duty and Satchel," he said of his teammates. "They'd hold [the attention of] a whole room full of people and you'd be in awe at the way they would come out with their conversation."

On or off the field, a gag was required to keep Double Duty quiet. The challenge was filtering out the nonsense. Satchel Paige deftly twisted and shaped the truth into balloon animals. Radcliffe made messy mud pies. Did the Ku Klux Klan really tell Neil Churchill to stop integrating his ball team? Did Duty really carry a

.32 pistol in case the Klan came calling? Did Satchel really take time off to travel to the Mayo Clinic in Minnesota and get treated for gonorrhea? What about those perks Radcliffe supposedly enjoyed in Jamestown? "A different girl every day," he babbled. "There was a girl, seventeen, and her daddy owned the biggest store in Jamestown. She'd get me anything out of the store; suits, whatever. She had her daddy's car and we had some sex right by the car. Oh, that girl was pretty!"

Two days after Radcliffe showed up, Churchill struck again. He stole good-hit-good-glove infielder Dan Oberholzer away from Jamestown, which had stolen him from Bismarck during the prior off-season. Oberholzer, thirty, had spent five years in the minor leagues before going semipro. By reinserting him at second base, Churchill freed up Red Haley for deployment in a new-look outfield: Johnson in left; Haley in center; and Hilton Smith, Barney Morris, and Troupe rotating in right. Oberholzer announced his return to the Bismarck lineup with a home run. It came in the opening game of a doubleheader against a Canadian-American all-star team. Bismarck blew them away, 13–0 and 8–1. Smith and Paige pitched matching three-hitters. The team was on a tear. They'd won nine of their last ten games. Neil Churchill had the pieces he wanted nailed in place for Wichita.

The next day a freelance photographer came to the ballpark. He herded everyone together for a team photo, infielders kneeling in the front row with Churchill, outfielders and pitchers lined up neatly behind. Six black men. Six white men. With the exception of Churchill, each of them wore a uniform with "Bismarck" emblazoned on the front and a dark baseball cap with a white "B" set inside a diamond insignia. Moose Johnson rested his huge right paw on Paige's shoulder, as if reminding him to stand still. Troupe, to Johnson's left, seemed on the verge of cracking a smile.

Click.

That evening they coasted to a 6–1 win over a mill team from Grand Forks. Most players eased off the throttle. Not Ed Hendee. He slashed a double in the third inning, slid hard into second base, and instantly regretted it. His lead foot got caught under the bag, generating enough violent torque to dislocate his right knee.

Only two weeks till Wichita. What was that about an injury jinx?

Bismarck went nocturnal. The July heat wave became so oppressive that downtown was more lively at 10 o'clock at night than at 10 o'clock in the morning. Popcorn vendors worked the streets. Diners stayed open late, windows aglow as in an Edward Hopper painting. About the only thing that had cooled off was the baseball war with Jamestown. The Northern Pacific Railway stopped running special trains. Nobody plunked down thousand-dollar bets. The teams closed out the month of July with two games at Bismarck's field. It was Double Duty Radcliffe's turn to make his pitching debut, which came on a steamy Tuesday night. He was as nasty as the weather. In keeping with the towns' history of bickering, there was disagreement over how many hits Radcliffe allowed. The *Jamestown Sun* said two. The *Bismarck Tribune* counted only one. The papers concurred on the final score: 2–0, which rankled Jamestown manager Ray Starr, once again the losing pitcher.

"You son of a bitch," he hissed at Radcliffe as they walked off the field. "You out-niggered us!"

"No, cracker," Radcliffe barked back. "We out*played* you!"

The next night Hilton Smith tamed Jamestown by firing a cool, calm, and collected three-hitter. Tempers flared again. In the sixth inning Radcliffe, who was catching Smith, got beaned at the plate; probably payback for having pitched so well the day before. In the seventh inning (which the *Mandan Pioneer* had said was prone to fireworks), Smith whacked a disputed home run. Trailing 9–0, Jamestown's players threw a hissy fit. They quit, got into their cars, and drove off in a huff. A few days later they canceled an end-of-season game scheduled for mid-August. The sore point, of course, really wasn't that controversial home run. It was the widening chasm between the two teams. Bismarck kept getting better, and Jamestown couldn't keep pace. The great all-white experiment had failed. Al Wiest, the catcher who lived in Jamestown but signed a contract with another North Dakota semipro team, said, "The balance was thrown catawampus when Bismarck started loading up with the black players." But, he added, those players were something to see.

Baseball wasn't the only thing out of balance. North Dakota had turned upside down. William Langer got elected governor in 1932 by not sugarcoating his speeches. "Shoot the banker if he comes on your farm," he thundered on the campaign trail. "Treat him like a chicken thief." Langer issued a moratorium on farm foreclosure sales shortly after taking office. That helped some, but by 1940 one third of family-owned farms would go under. Dark clouds kept gathering. Per capita personal income in North Dakota was $145 in 1933, less than half the national average of $375. Agriculture had one of its worst years in 1935; the relief rolls rose to nearly 40 percent and kept climbing. People weren't just forced out of their homes. They were forced out of their state. During the 1930s, almost 6 percent of North Dakota's population left, most choosing to wipe the slate clean and start anew in Minnesota, Washington state, or California. It was, in other words, no time to be selling season tickets to Bismarck baseball games.

Weather became a protagonist, the embodiment of misfortune stalking the land. It zigzagged in 1935 from drought to sloshy spring to frying-pan summer to completely catawampus. Late on the afternoon of August 6 winter paid a visit. The storm and chinook winds lasted half an hour, tracking just north of Bismarck. Hailstones as plump as baseballs dented car roofs, bombarded livestock, killed 100 chickens, and destroyed crops on the cusp of being harvested.

Young Lawrence Legler tended what was expected to be a prizewinning 4-H corn crop in Kidder County. The storm reduced it to two acres of mush. In Pierce County a man died after being kicked in the head by a hail-spooked horse. The Bismarck team was safe and sound in Canada, dealing with real baseballs. In the space of four days they won tournaments in the towns of Portage la Prairie and Virden. Both had $1,000 purses. Hilton Smith and Satchel Paige topped themselves. In Portage la Prairie they turned in matching two-hitters on the same day.

The Canadian swing extended Bismarck's streak to 19–1, the sole blemish a 6–5 loss to Devils Lake, now loaded with Cleveland Indian farmhands. The team drove home to close out the schedule with a Friday-Saturday-Sunday three-pack of games against the Twin City Colored Giants. The Giants were a second-tier traveling club. Players had nine-to-five jobs that limited them mostly to weekend jaunts. Their budget was so crimped that they sometimes stayed at campsites or slept in the visitors' dugout. Right fielder Maceo Breedlove, by far the Giants' best player, once pawned his watch on a road trip to buy enough gas to get the team back to Minneapolis–Saint Paul.

Neil Churchill wanted a weak opponent to push around on the eve of the Wichita tournament. It would be like chugging a can of Confidence Builder. But token opposition wasn't conducive to big crowds. Two days after Satchel Paige's 1–0 vivisection of Jamestown in July, the Association of Commerce had issued a statement declaring that the last game of the season, on August 11, would be a fund-raising "booster game." Fans were encouraged, if not begged, to show up in force and make the turnstiles sing. "All hail the good work of Mr. Churchill," the Association said. Jamestown had originally been scheduled to play that booster game, but backed out after the dispute over Hilton Smith's home run. The Colored Giants took their place and the Association of Commerce quickly swung into action. Ticket sellers canvassed the city. The Lions,

Rotary Club, and Kiwanis heavily promoted the big game—against a team that had to pawn a watch to pay for gasoline.

Tickets cost 50 cents for reserved grandstand seats and 25 cents for general admission. The goal was to sell 3,000. The *Bismarck Capital* did its part with a pom-pom-waving editorial that said Bismarck would have been saddled with a team "fit only to engage in play of the alley and pasture league type" if Churchill and a small coterie of patrons had not breathed life back into town baseball. "If there should be a sudden slacking of support, the backers of the team would not only be out their time and energy," the *Capital* cautioned, "but also might be placed in an embarrassing situation financially. Bismarck has done something in its baseball team that is worthy of support."

Yes, but pay good money to see the Twin City Colored Giants? On Friday night Bismarck scored four times in the bottom of the first inning off the Giants' pitcher-manager. The big blow was an unquestionable home run by Hilton Smith with Quincy Troupe and Moose Johnson aboard that cleared the left field wall with plenty to spare. Barney Morris pitched for Bismarck. Sensing a laugher in the making, he waltzed through the second inning and gave up three sloppy runs. Troupe was behind the plate and gave his pitcher an earful for slacking off. Morris buckled down. So did his teammates. Shortstop Al Leary bopped two home runs in what became a semi-competitive 8–5 win.

That morning the Association of Commerce had rattled the cup one last time for Sunday's booster game, issuing another statement in praise of the team's 68–14–3 record. (Semipro statistics being unreliably soft, the *Tribune* said Bismarck entered the weekend at 63–14–4.) The Association reminded the public that Satchel Paige was deserving of a large audience "before which to do his stuff." Then it got down on bended knee. "So it is earnestly requested that a record crowd shall attend and give a proper start to the 'on to Wichita' movement. Mr. Churchill and his associates are entitled to this."

Despite the financial pinch he was feeling, Churchill remained a buyer. On Saturday he signed Art Hancock as extra Wichita insurance. Hancock was one of the black players who'd been cut adrift by Jamestown. He swung a heavy, 38.5-ounce bat with authority and took over in center field for Bismarck, allowing Haley to move back to the infield and man first base in Ed Hendee's absence. That night Hancock homered against the Colored Giants. So did Haley. So did Johnson: twice. Bismarck won 9–5 behind Hilton Smith, but graciously kept the score down. The *Tribune*'s beat writer said the team seemed to be "belting base hits almost at will." They stopped at seventeen.

They were just warming up for booster day.

The Sunday afternoon pitching honors went, naturally, to Paige. A stiff wind prevailed, and the only realistic chance the Colored Giants had of winning was for Paige to get blown off the mound. He stood fast. One young Colored Giant asked out of the lineup when he heard who was pitching. As with Custer at Little Big Horn, it was over the moment it began. The *Tribune* soared to new heights of purple prose in chronicling the onslaught. "With an overture of five home runs in the first inning opening a riotous opera of extra-base hits and a profusion of singles, Bismarck's mightiest baseball team sang its swan song for the season."

Paige didn't bear down too hard, what with the Wichita tournament fast approaching. In the top of the first inning Maceo Breedlove took him deep for a two-run homer. Bismarck answered in the most declarative of ways with five solo home runs: Oberholzer, Leary, Hancock, Johnson, and Desiderato. Boom, boom, boom, boom, boom. The game was a thing of beauty but only for sadists who admire the well-oiled, ruthless precision that makes possible abject domination. The scoreboard read 21–6. With a little extra effort it might have read 210–6. Bismarck hammered out 22 hits, then stopped even pretending to try. In the eighth inning Churchill told his players to bat from their unnatural side of the plate: lefties hitting from the right, righties hitting from the left. It was an act of grace; done, in the tortured wording of the *Tribune*, "to quell the staccato-like explosions emanating from Bismarck bludgeons, which were becoming monotonous."

In the ninth inning, Bismarck rewarded those stalwarts who stayed to the bitter end. Just before the first Giants batter stepped in, Paige dipped into his old barnstorming bag of tricks and called in the outfield. Johnson, Hancock, and Smith took seats in the dugout. Paige wasn't finished. He told his infielders to go sit down too. Desiderato, Leary, Oberholzer, and Haley walked off. That left Paige and Barney Morris, who was subbing at catcher so Troupe and Radcliffe could enjoy a day off. Right about then, Churchill may have bounded into the grandstand to scare up a few last-second bets. *Anybody think the Giants can score? How many runs? How much cash ya willing to put up?*

The score at that time was 21–4. Paige had complete faith in his fastball and a 17-run lead. He struck out the first two Colored Giants before giving up a dink single. Breedlove, who'd stung him for a home run and pair of doubles, fouled off a series of fastballs. Paige switched to his curve and watched a line drive disappear into the open-prairie outfield for a sympathy home run and two runs batted in. "I hit it into left field and nobody was out there," Breedlove said afterward. He felt ridiculous, but did what a player is supposed to do: "I ran around the bases."

Paige struck out the next batter, officially closing the book on the regular season. Moose Johnson finished on a rampage, going 11 for 14 with three home runs against the shell-shocked Colored Giants. He and Paige may not have gotten their hands dirty very often at Corwin-Churchill Motors (however, it would have been worth any price of admission to watch Satchel try to do a valve job on a Chrysler Imperial), but they earned their keep as ballplayers, laying waste to the semipro competition. Johnson jacked 26 home runs. Nobody else on the Bismarck team reached double figures. His batting average hovered around .440 all summer, comfortably ahead of everyone else's. Hitters up north didn't have any more success against Paige than hitters had back east or down south or out west. Paige lost two one-run games (on opening day to Jamestown and late in June to Devils Lake) while posting between 25 and 29 wins, some box scores being incomplete.

Factoring in Canadian exhibitions and tournaments, Bismarck had a best-guess record of 68 wins, 23 losses, and 4 ties. Churchill still refused to stand pat. He negotiated a deal with J. L. Wilkinson, owner of the Kansas City Monarchs, to let Chet Brewer—Satchel Paige's doppelgänger—spike up for the Wichita tournament. In poker jargon, Neil Churchill was "all in." Maybe he should've thought twice about that. Bismarck squashed the Twin City Colored Giants on booster day, but in a larger sense was the losing team. The hoped-for stampede of fans didn't materialize, whether because of hard times, a pushover opponent, or the annual Bismarck air show held that same day. The Association of Commerce missed its 3,000-ticket target by such a wide margin, attendance figures were never released.

On Sunday night after the game Churchill left for Kansas. He took eleven players, plus walking-wounded Ed Hendee and Bill Morlan as bench coaches. Roy McLeod, the athletic director at Bismarck High School, came along as team trainer. Brewer would meet up with them in Wichita. A few members of the entourage traveled by train with the heavy equipment and luggage. (Everyone who didn't live in Bismarck brought all their belongings because they'd be going separate ways after the tournament.) Paige and Troupe drove their own cars. The rest of them wedged into two Corwin-Churchill sedans.

The disappointing booster day crowd didn't faze Churchill. Baseball finances could wait. He focused on only one thing: winning in Wichita. He liked the cards he was holding, this town team bulging with out-of-towners. Thirty-one managers also on the way to Kansas probably felt the same about their teams. They soon would meet face-to-face and call each other's bluffs. Who had a lowly pair of eights? Who was sitting pretty on three aces?

PART THREE

TESTED TOGETHER

15

LITTLE MAN, BIG IDEA

In Wichita, as in many spurs-jingling western towns, some familiar names put their stamp on local history. Half-Scotsman, half-Cherokee Jesse Chisholm opened a trading post near the banks of the Arkansas River during the Civil War, before there was a defined "Wichita." A route he mapped out for long-distance wagon travel and trade—the eponymous Chisholm Trail—later became a dusty highway for punching cattle between Texas and Abilene. When Wichita incorporated in 1870, 124 people signed the petition setting those wheels in motion. The only woman in the group was Catherine McCarty, whose son would grow up to be Billy the Kid. Soon Wyatt Earp blew into town and found a job as a police officer. After just a year on the force, he got canned for engaging in a fistfight with a candidate for county sheriff and beating the daylights out of him. Earp decided to move on to greener pastures: Dodge City.

In 1874 an editorial in the *Wichita Beacon* newspaper grumbled, half in jest, about trouble brewing in the river city: "Our callow youths have inaugurated the 'National Game' in the midst of us. What shall we do to circumvent their initiations?" Nothing, of course. Not even gun-toting Wyatt Earp could have done much to arrest the spread of baseball. When some of those callow youths got older they formed a town team, thereby offending certain righteous citizens who were intent on banning Sunday games. The city council voted 7–4 in favor of leaving the ballplayers alone, but resisted the temptation to impose a ban on righteous citizens.

Satchel Paige said Wichita was "baseball crazy." He probably didn't realize how crazy. On June 21, 1925, the town hosted a sporting event that sounded like an outrageous put-on, but was anything but. That morning the *Beacon* published an unusual reader advisory: "Strangleholds, razors, horsewhips and other violent implements of argument will be barred at the baseball game at Loland Park this afternoon when the baseball club of Wichita Klan Number 6 goes up against the Wichita Monrovians, Wichita's crack colored team. The colored boys are asking all their supporters to be on hand to watch the contest, which besides its peculiar attraction due to the wide differences of the two organizations, should be a well played amateur test."

A Ku Klux Klan team taking the field against black opponents? Lions laying down bunts with lambs? Calling that a bizarre tableau would be an understatement, especially since the Klan was more than a rumored specter in Wichita. It had an estimated 6,000 members, representing a sizeable chunk of the city's approximately 75,000 residents. Yet there were no incidents of violence at that game, no injuries suffered other than wounded pride. The "colored boys" laid a 10–8 humiliation on the white supremacists, who wore baseball uniforms and, therefore, couldn't lodge a protest claiming they'd been unfairly encumbered by robes and hoods.

Raymond Harry Dumont had been born into that milieu (a word no self-respecting Wichitan would employ) of cowtown raunch and back-of-beyond sports in December 1904. He did not exude true grit. His manner was so relentlessly sunny-side-up that by the time he was six, friends were calling him "Happy," soon shortened to "Hap," a name he would never shake. Hap Dumont seemed to pole-vault over adolescence and land square in adulthood. He was diminutive, squirrel-cheeked, prematurely stoop-shouldered, and soft as a week-old peach where muscles should be, and he wore his hair slicked back like a big-band leader; a teenager blessed with all the physical attributes of a baseball fan, not a baseball player. But the kid had pluck. Dumont was an only child and still in school when his salesman father died. He helped his mother carry on

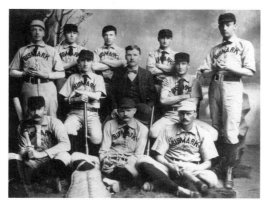

Deputy county treasurer William Falconer (center), managed the poker-faced 1889 town team called the Bismarck Reserves, playing with misspelled uniforms. On May 24 the *Bismarck Weekly Tribune* reported, partly in jest, "there will be a base ball game or two on the Fourth of July and it has already been suggested that Sitting Bull should umpire. He will be fair and impartial." STATE HISTORICAL SOCIETY OF NORTH DAKOTA 435-6

New England, North Dakota, was founded in 1887. Most residents hailed from Vermont or Massachusetts and they brought with them a reminder of life back east: baseball. STATE HISTORICAL SOCIETY OF NORTH DAKOTA 0175-024

The 1914 city amateur baseball championship drew an estimated 100,000 fans to Cleveland's Brookside Park to watch Telling's Stollers battle Hanna's Cleaners. The Stollers won the deciding third game, 8-3. COURTESY OF THE LIBRARY OF CONGRESS

Bismarck's state penitentiary team, known as the "Grove Giants" or "Grove All-Stars," was comprised of inmates and a few non-incarcerated ringers. They played only home games. STATE HISTORICAL SOCIETY OF NORTH DAKOTA D0344B

The House of David religious commune in Michigan fielded one of the most popular and accomplished semipro touring teams. In 1934 they signed a big-name guest pitcher: Olympian Babe Didrikson. COURTESY OF CHRIS SIRIANO, FOUNDER-DIRECTOR OF HOUSE OF DAVID BASEBALL MUSEUM

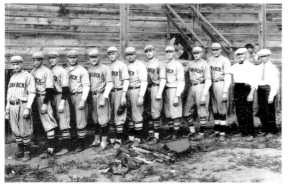

A younger, thinner, bespectacled Neil Churchill (seventh from left) played catcher for the 1926 Bismarck town team. COURTESY OF CHURCHILL FAMILY

The only known photograph of the 1935 Bismarck town team, taken two weeks before they left for Wichita. Kneeling, left to right: third baseman Joe Desiderato, shortstop Axel "Al" Leary, manager Neil Churchill, second baseman Dan Oberholzer, first baseman Ed Hendee. Standing, left to right: pitcher Hilton Smith, infielder-outfielder Red Haley, pitcher Barney Morris, pitcher Satchel Paige, left fielder Vernon "Moose" Johnson, catcher-outfielder Quincy Troupe, pitcher-catcher Ted "Double Duty" Radcliffe. Courtesy of Hake's Americana & Collectibles

The inimitable Leroy "Satchel" Paige (left) joined the Kansas City Monarchs for a fall barnstorming tour shortly after the 1935 National Baseball Congress semipro tournament, still wearing his Bismarck cap. Quiet Hilton Smith (center) spent much of his career pitching in the shadow of Paige, but outshined him in career statistics. Youthful but no longer baby-faced, Quincy Troupe (right) was still catching at age 39. All photos courtesy National Baseball Hall of Fame Library, Cooperstown, New York

Dapper car dealer Neil Orr Churchill (left) on the streets of downtown Bismarck, North Dakota. Courtesy of the Churchill family

WNS CRUSH TULSA OILERS 18-
It Was Rock and Sock at Tech Field Yesterday

Well-traveled Moose Johnson took his sweet swing to the minor league Tulsa Oilers in 1938, one of four teams he played for that season. *San Antonio Express-News* / Zumapress.com

Erle P. Halliburton's mighty Cementers team from Duncan, Oklahoma, circa 1936, in their eye-catching, tomato-red uniforms. Courtesy of Halliburton

Promoter Raymond "Hap" Dumont, in hat, used boundless, sometimes misdirected, energy to build a semipro baseball empire. One of his dumber ideas was the pneumatic home plate duster. Special Collections and University Archives, Wichita State University Libraries

When the town team was at its peak, the Bismarck business community jumped on the bandwagon and showered players with free gifts: from a dress shirt for smacking the first home run of the season to a case of Schlitz "Vitamin D" beer for making the first error.

Prolonged drought and an invasion of grasshoppers devastated North Dakota's wheat and corn crops. Relief rolls swelled and farm families fled the state for literally greener pastures. COURTESY OF THE LIBRARY OF CONGRESS

President Franklin Roosevelt's "Dustbowl Special" train chugged into Bismarck in early August 1936. He borrowed a car at Corwin-Churchill Motors and toured the countryside with a pack of reporters, stopping to chat with beleaguered farmer Mike Hellman and his son, John. COURTESY OF THE LIBRARY OF CONGRESS

One of the novelty acts of semipro baseball was the Stanzak brothers team from Waukegan, Illinois. They were among thirty-two teams Hap Dumont invited to the 1935 National Baseball Congress tournament in Wichita. NATIONAL BASEBALL HALL OF FAME LIBRARY, COOPERSTOWN, NEW YORK

More than a dozen Major League scouts attended the 1935 NBC tournament. They came to watch all the top semipro players, but were only interested in signing the best white ones.
COURTESY OF *THE WICHITA EAGLE*

A syndicated drawing of Satchel Paige, its origins now unknown, touched all the racial-stereotyping bases. It appeared in newspapers at the time of the NBC tournament. Those papers included *The Wichita Eagle, Bismarck Tribune,* and *Kansas City Call,* a black-owned weekly.

Players Tangle in Semipro Baseball Tourney Game

HERE is a hot action photo by The Eagle photographer, Harold Lyle of the fist fight between Franklin and Phoenix players in the afternoon game Thursday. For a time it looked like a free for all between the two opposing clubs with fans joining in but order was restored after two players had been banished from the game.

Tempers erupted between the all-white Franklin (Massachusetts) Clarmacs and all-black Phoenix (Arizona) Broncos during Hap Dumont's 1936 semipro tournament. *The Wichita Eagle* described it as "a free for all between the two opposing clubs with fans joining in."
COURTESY OF *THE WICHITA EAGLE*

Satchel Paige was one of a kind. So, too, this baseball autographed by him at the 1935 Wichita tournament. It's the earliest known ball bearing his sole signature and sold at auction in 2008 for $6,000.
COURTESY OF HERITAGE AUCTIONS

Neil and Helen Churchill about to indulge in one of his favorite pastimes: eating. She was refined and college educated. He was a meat-and-potatoes guy in every way. COURTESY OF THE CHURCHILL FAMILY

An unidentified Bismarck player wore this jersey at the 1936 National Baseball Congress tournament in Wichita. It's one of the few surviving pieces of memorabilia from Neil Churchill's semipro dream team. COURTESY OF HAKE'S AMERICANA & COLLECTIBLES

Semipro baseball may be dead, but Hap Dumont and his ever-present cigar live on outside Lawrence-Dumont Stadium in Wichita. PHOTO COURTESY OF KEITH WONDRA

by becoming her junior breadwinner. In summer he worked the manual scoreboard for the Class A Western League team, known at different times as the Wichita Jobbers, Wichita Wolves, Wichita Witches, Wichita Izzies, Wichita Larks, and Wichita Aviators. All year long he delivered the *Wichita Eagle* in the early morning and at night answered telephones for the paper's sports department.

Despite those distractions, Dumont finished at the top of his class at Wichita High School in 1923. Graduation day was not a joyous occasion for young Hap. As soon as he took the stage to give the valedictorian address, his mind went blank. That was bad enough, but then he started to cry. He managed to collect himself and deliver the speech, but the panic attack didn't bode well for his postgraduation plans. Hap Dumont had decided to bid a quick, fond farewell to Wichita and seek his fortune as a stand-up comedian, or "monologist" as they were known on the vaudeville boards. He plugged away at that brutal craft for about a year, going places but getting nowhere. Rock bottom came in Chicago. He didn't bomb in front of an audience; he failed to even detonate. An agent had booked him into a Greek theater packed with native Greeks, none of whom spoke English. Standing alone on that stage and staring out at row after row of unresponsive, blank faces was like facing a firing squad that used silencers. Show business seemed to be showing Hap Dumont the door. He wisely exited stage right.

Returning to Wichita with his tail between his legs would have been an admission of failure. A friend who promoted boxing and wrestling matches in Missouri encouraged Dumont to do the same in Kansas. He decided to give that a try. It was not an outlandish transition. Dumont had flopped as a comic, but generally fared well in one-on-one situations. People liked Hap. He could be glib, pleasantly persistent, and persuasive. He also looked the part of a sports promoter, partial as he was to rumpled suits, fedoras, and cigars. In his twenties Hap Dumont possessed the absentminded, ditzy charm of a much older man. He ate ice cream for breakfast, was afraid to fly, had a habit of sitting on his hats, and wore shirts speckled with tobacco slobber. He would breeze through stop signs in a daze while driving and habitually left clothes behind in hotel rooms. However, his brain was capable of focusing clearly and completely on business, which he chose to conduct in the town of Hutchinson, not far beyond the northern reaches of Wichita. From there he arranged to bring the Swedish national wrestling champion to Topeka for his first American bout. Nobody ever got rich booking Swedish wrestlers. When the economy began to falter, Dumont joined the *Hutchinson News* as a reporter and did sports promoting in off-hours. His love life heated up. He met Gladys Dodd, a Wichitan eight years his junior who was a basketball fan and not at all put off by a man who chain-smoked cigars and sat on his hat. They married in 1927.

Financial security became more of a priority and Dumont found a modicum of it back in Wichita. A few months before the 1929 stock market crash, the *Eagle* offered him part-time employment as a night sports editor. A columnist at the paper helped get him a day job stocking shelves at Goldsmith Book and Stationery Company for $25 a week. Goldsmith's was a high-end retailer of long standing. In addition to stationery supplies and books (hardcover only, no lowly paperbacks), the store sold Hummel figurines, Spanish porcelain, and office furniture. Ike Goldsmith wanted to branch out into sporting goods. From a desk in a far corner of the second floor, Dumont set up a one-man command post. Nearly every school, recreation department, and company team in the Midwest that purchased athletic equipment made it onto his mailing list. Hap pestered newspaper editors for contacts. He served as a volunteer business manager for Wichita's amateur basketball team.

In the spring of 1931 the circus came to town and, in a way, joined *him*. An advance man stopped by the *Eagle* newsroom to inquire about arranging a ball game for the performers and roustabouts. The circus had to shut down on Sunday because of blue laws, but baseball was a legal activity on the Sabbath in Wichita. The advance man was hoping his circus team could scare up a game and maybe make a little money on its day off. Dumont happened to be on night-desk duty and overheard that conversation about a possible ball game. "Hell," he said, offering to help, "I'll put it on myself." After only a few phone calls, he'd lined up some firemen to play the circus troupe. People actually paid to see them go at it. How many chances do you get to see a clown in oversize shoes run down a fly ball? The game grossed $1,600 and Dumont cleared $35. He'd accidentally fallen back into the promotion business. An idea percolated in his head. Why not hold a tournament at the end of the summer for the state's semipro baseball teams? Dumont managed to pull everything together by August, though it wasn't an easy sell. "I had to comb the state to find sixteen teams," he later told a reporter.

He rented Island Park, the creaky wooden stadium that was then home to the Wichita Aviators. In the finals of his test-model tournament, the semipro Abilene Bakers beat Wichita Water Company. This was during the depths of the Depression. The Bakers earned $190 in prize money and had need of every penny. The players had worn spikes for the tournament, but none of them could afford socks. Dumont broke even packaging the event; his employer made a nice chunk of change. All the baseballs and equipment were purchased from Goldsmith's. Dumont thus had a dual vested interest in keeping the state tournament going and growing, which he did in part by throwing the doors wide open to all comers. The Arkansas City Colored Beavers and other Kansas black teams eagerly participated. The tournament did well enough that Dumont dropped his part-time job as an *Eagle* sports editor. By 1933, 5,000 tickets were sold for the championship game, this time won by Wichita Water Company. A day later Island Park burned to the ground. Someone had carelessly tossed a cigarette and the grandstand burst into flames like fireplace kindling.

Hap Dumont saw an opportunity to play the same public-service construction card that Neil Churchill did in Bismarck. The

Civil Works Administration was actively priming the employment pump in Wichita. Day laborers on government relief stood knee-deep in mud, using shovels and wheelbarrows to fill in sections of the Arkansas River as part of a flood control project. Other jobs-program workers soon would be busy planting trees and paving roads. Dumont met with city manager Bert Wells and discussed building a new baseball stadium about a mile downriver from the charred remains of Island Park. He asked about freeing up some CWA manpower and money. Dumont already had a site in mind: an industrial tract on the west side of the river called "Payne's pasture," terminus of the old Chisholm cattle trail. He got so enthusiastic that his mouth ran ahead of his brain. "If the city'll put up a good baseball park to accommodate a national tournament of non-pro baseball," Dumont told Wells, "I'll get it here."

Wells thought about that proposition for a few days and responded favorably. Some $60,000 in federal Civil Works Administration funds was made available. He may not have been swayed exclusively by Dumont. Ike Goldsmith, a respected elder of the business community, had access to Wells and reason to buttonhole him. His company would sell a lot of sporting goods if a new ball field got built and if Hap Dumont delivered on his promise of a national semipro tournament. By January 1934 blueprints were being finalized. Steam shovels and bulldozers stood poised to begin chewing up Payne's pasture. Plans called for a $125,000 concrete stadium to rise at the corner of Maple and Sycamore streets. That ballpark and that tournament would come to mean more to Dumont than he ever imagined.

On Saturday morning, January 27, 1934, Hap Dumont said good-bye to his wife and children—eight-week-old Nancy and four-year-old Ray—and headed to Chicago for a sporting goods manufacturers convention. Because of Dumont's aversion to flying, he and a colleague at Goldsmith's drove the 500-plus miles.

Because of Dumont's notoriously bad driving, he was the designated passenger. There had been some discussion about canceling the trip. That Wednesday Gladys Dumont had woken and found a small pimple on her nose. It became mildly infected. As a precaution, her doctor sent her to the hospital that Friday. The doctor told Gladys and Hap there was "one chance in a thousand" that something so benign could become problematic. Reassured, Hap went to Chicago. By Sunday those odds were no longer so favorable. The skin infection—belatedly diagnosed as erysipelas, caused by an acute strain of streptococcus bacteria—had turned lethal. Gladys developed blood poisoning. Her condition was quickly downgraded to critical; just how critical was evident in the measures taken to contact her husband, who was somewhere on the road between Kansas and Illinois. Phone calls were placed and telegrams sent; KFH radio in Wichita broadcast emergency messages intended solely for Raymond Dumont, as did stations in Saint Louis and Chicago. He received word only on arriving at his convention hotel. A heavy weekend snowstorm had immobilized the Midwest. Airports were closed and many highways impassable. Dumont caught a train from Chicago to Kansas City, where the Atchison, Topeka and Santa Fe Railway took the extraordinary step of delaying the Number 15 train to Wichita for nearly an hour so he could make his connection.

Hap Dumont sat on that train and watched the clock, with nothing much to do but listen to the rumble of steel wheels on steel tracks, thumping as steadily as a heartbeat. Smoke a few cigars . . . try to sleep . . . think of the first time he met Gladys and the last thing he said to her before going to Chicago . . . worry about the kids missing Mommy . . . check the clock again . . . slurp some coffee . . . read the bulldog edition of Monday's *Kansas City Star* . . .

It struck him like a bullet.

At the very bottom of the left-hand column of the *Star*'s sports page—below the update on Babe Ruth's battle with flu and the announcement that a benefit hockey game would be held for Ace

Bailey of the Toronto Maple Leafs, who'd recently had his skull fractured in an on-ice collision—a six-line Associated Press news brief screamed for his attention: "*Wichita, Jan. 29.* Infection from a small pimple on her nose caused the death here today of Mrs. Gladys Dumont, 26, wife of Raymond Dumont."

The burial took place at Wichita Park Cemetery. Honorary pallbearers included Ike Goldsmith and Pete Lightner, longtime *Wichita Eagle* editor and sportswriter. Lightner had ended his Tuesday column with a mention of Hap Dumont's ill-fated "race" to get from snowy Chicago to his wife's bedside, concluding—as only a sportswriter would—that "decisions of the Great Referee can't be questioned, strange as they may seem."

Reeling from the loss of his wife, Dumont sought shelter in the arms of his other true love: work. He threw himself into helping make the new baseball stadium a reality and into organizing a semipro tournament worthy of it. Construction began in March 1934 on a 3,600-seat facility. The dimensions were pitcher-friendly: 336 feet down the left field line, 320 feet to the right field foul pole, and 360 feet to dead center. The work progressed in stages, with more seats being added as more federal funds got channeled into the project. By July capacity had increased to 4,300. By September to 5,700. By November it was up to 8,500. City officials gave the ballpark a name: Lawrence Stadium, in memory of Robert Lawrence, a businessman and state legislator during the pioneer days. Dumont meanwhile called his largely phantom organization the National Semi-Pro Baseball Congress, soon trimmed to National Baseball Congress. He installed himself as president. It was important to *sound* important. "National Baseball Congress" conveyed gravitas. It evoked footsteps striding purposefully down marble hallways inside a building where men sat at long, polished conference tables having weighty discussions about seeding brackets. It connoted dozens of employees in spacious, well-appointed offices.

In actuality, the National Baseball Congress consisted of Hap Dumont hunched over a cluttered desk inside a glorified stationery store. Just him and his telephone. Previous attempts had been made to create a national semipro tournament, but they lacked either reach or staying power. The National Association of Independent Baseball Clubs and the National Amateur Baseball Association of America both crashed shortly after takeoff and were gone by World War I. The healthier National Baseball Federation began holding championships in 1915, but it stuck close to its roots in Cleveland. The 1935 NBF tournament attracted twenty teams from only five states, thirteen of them representing Ohio or Pennsylvania. Entries from Cleveland had won three of the last four titles.

Dumont thought he could succeed where others had failed because he had a logistic advantage—Wichita's mid-America location—and because of his own marketing savvy. He certainly seemed to be doing something right with his Kansas state tournament. Fifty-four teams registered in the summer of 1934, playing at the nearly complete Lawrence Stadium. Total attendance mushroomed to 35,000. But that was kiddie-pool sports promotion compared with what he was trying now. His template was the *Denver Post*'s highly successful regional tournament. Two employees in the *Post*'s circulation department had organized a state amateur baseball playoff in 1915 with a $400 prize. It was done for community relations purposes, like the paper's summer opera series and trout fishing contest. After five years, out-of-state teams started coming. The tournament stretched to ten days. In 1930 a sports editor was put in charge. He added night games and travel teams such as the House of David and the American-Canadian Clowns. Attendance surpassed 50,000. Prize money grew to $13,000. The *Denver Post* tournament acquired a subtitle: "The Little World Series of the West." In 1934 the Kansas City Monarchs became the first black team granted admission; a *Pittsburgh Courier* sports columnist called this "the most significant announcement in a decade" for black baseball. The Monarchs and the House of David shared the same booking agent. It was the owners of the Monarchs who helped the Davids land Satchel Paige as a guest pitcher for the 1934 Denver tournament. Why aid the enemy? To boost attendance, which would in turn boost the prize money. The Paige tactic worked. A record 62,232 fans turned out. The prize purse jumped to $16,700.

Dumont intended to outdo the *Denver Post* tourney in terms of both size and sizzle. He decided on thirty-two teams with a double-elimination format: each team had to lose twice before packing up and going home. That might make the long road trip to Wichita more palatable and also ensured about two weeks of almost nonstop baseball. The eligibility requirements were deliberately kept lax. Basically, any player not on a professional roster could take the field. The collective standards were stricter: Dumont wanted to capitalize on town loyalties and, therefore, wanted nothing to do with unaffiliated touring teams like the House of David or the Kansas City Monarchs. He made a point of being generous with prize money, tying it directly to ticket sales. Forty-five percent of the gross would go into a pot and be divided on a sliding scale among the top eight finishers. In addition, teams would receive $25 for every game they won. He publicly predicted that the payout for the inaugural NBC tournament—casually referred to as the "Little World Series" or simply "the National"—would be between $10,000 and $20,000.

As a former newspaperman, Dumont knew the value of media exposure, either paid or planted. He lobbied crusty Taylor Spink hard. Spink was the publisher of the *Sporting News* in Saint Louis, the unofficial house organ of amateur and professional baseball. Dumont all but begged for an extended grace period on advertising buys. "Mr. Spink, if you carry me," he said, "I won't spend a nickel on myself until I pay you." The old man cut him some slack on centerfold ads and also came through with a few short articles pumping the National. Dumont took a stab at stirring up free publicity by offering Edwin "Alabama" Pitts the lavish sum of $1,000 to be an umpire at the tournament. Newswires gobbled up that human-interest story. Pitts didn't have an inning of umpiring experience. He'd spent the past five years in New York's Sing Sing Prison becoming a cause célèbre. Jailed at nineteen for armed robbery, he took up baseball and football as part of his rehabilitation. Pitts was a natural. "The most promising jailbird athlete in America," declared the *Los Angeles Times*.

Two professional football teams gave him tryouts while he was still behind bars; but just a few weeks ahead of his scheduled release in early June 1935, Pitts signed with the Albany Senators of the International League. The governing body of minor league baseball made national headlines by nixing the contract because of his criminal record. Pitts appealed that edict to Kenesaw Mountain Landis, commissioner of Major League baseball. Public opinion swung heavily in his favor. While stuck in limbo awaiting Landis's decision, Pitts heard from a variety of suitors besides Hap Dumont. The House of David promised to sign him to a contract if the Albany Senators backed out. So did the New York football Giants. So did Hal Roach, the Hollywood producer who churned out the "Our Gang" comedy shorts. Commissioner Landis brought the courting to an abrupt end by overturning minor league officials and ruling in favor of Pitts. He reported to the Albany Senators as planned (embarking on what proved to be a disappointing four-year minor league career), and Hap Dumont had to make do with conventional umpires who had no press clippings.

Come July 1935 Dumont fared better in his pursuit of another big name. He got a media boost when Honus Wagner—the beak-nosed retired Pittsburgh Pirates shortstop and one of baseball's living legends—agreed to be part of the opening ceremonies in Wichita in mid-August. Wagner also consented to serve on the rules committee with two other all-time greats: regal Walter Johnson and irascible Ty Cobb. Tournament applications began piling up on Dumont's desk. More than 300 teams wanted in. The publicity committee (Hap Dumont) and the selection committee (Dumont) sorted through the stack of papers, searching for the most deserving clubs. Won-lost records alone wouldn't carry the day. Dumont fretted over his invitation list as if he were a lion of high society tossing a grand dinner party. Success depended on having just the right mix of accomplished people. After ample reflection, refinement, and rejiggering, he settled on thirty-two teams from sixteen states. The draw just barely passed muster as "national." Only two teams hailed from the East and five from the South. The rest came out of the Midwest and far West.

Despite the western tilt, it was an eclectic field, featuring an all-Japanese team from Stockton, California; an all-Indian team from Wewoka, Oklahoma; and four all-black teams: the Austin (Texas) Centennials, San Angelo (Texas) Sheepherders, Monroe (Louisiana) Monarchs, and Memphis Red Sox. There was an all-siblings team: the Stanczak brothers of Waukegan, Illinois. Dumont considered holding a mini tournament within a tournament, having received inquiries from ten brothers' teams, including the Marlatts of Caspar, Wyoming, the Simones of Topeka, Kansas, and the Deike boys from Hye, Texas. He ultimately decided to admit only the Stanczaks, who somehow convinced him they were the one true "world championship family team."

Distance and duration had their own winnowing effect. This wasn't a tournament that teams could enter on a whim. Two weeks of travel and hotel expenses would eat up at least $1,000. New York City's Union Circulators chartered a bus to Wichita. The Buffalo Blue Coals of Buffalo, New York, chartered an airplane, while the Halliburton Cementers of Duncan, Oklahoma, were transported in company president Erle P. Halliburton's private plane. The majority drove. Since there was no interstate highway system, the overland routes tended to be long, winding, and punishing. Ten teams traveled more than 1,000 miles by car. The team from Lompoc, California, just north of Santa Barbara, journeyed farthest, logging 1,978 miles getting to Kansas.

With more than five hundred players and coaches converging on Wichita for the National, there were plenty of colorful baseball names rolling off tongues: Porky Takata, Swede Carlson, Jigger Smith, Monk Pryor, Earl "Pie" Huckleberry, Bebee Twitchell, Tarzan Long, Shorty Guinotte, Hardy "Three Finger" Ware, Highpockets Johnson. The Memphis Red Sox had a one-armed pinch hitter named "Ball." The ace pitcher of the Japanese team was four-foot-eleven, 115-pound, thirty-four-year-old Kenso Nushida, nicknamed "Boy Wonder"; he was the first Japanese American to play in the minor leagues. A host of left-handed pitchers answered to "Lefty," among them Lefty McClure, Lefty Walbridge, Lefty McClendon, Lefty Denton, Lefty Chambers, Lefty Stone, and Lefty Johns. No pitchers named "Righty" were anywhere to be found.

This was a rare powwow, a meeting of baseball's Best of the Not-Quite-Good-Enoughs. Everyone had a story. The ex–Major League infielder who couldn't hit the curve consistently. The ex–Major League pitcher whose arm mysteriously went dead. Diamond-in-the-rough kids with dreams of someday being discovered by a kindly scout and signed to a contract spread across the hood of his dusty Dodge. Troubled talents who couldn't escape their darker side. Shining stars trapped in the wrong color skin. The quality of the teams varied from high minor leagues to what you might expect from a literal band of brothers born to the perennially pregnant Mary Stanczak. The semipro champions of Alabama, Arizona, Kansas, Nebraska, and northern California trekked to Wichita. The peach-fuzz team from Poplar Bluff, Missouri, didn't have a single player over age twenty-five. The Halliburton Cementers and United Fuel of Denver, both top-heavy with ex-pros, would have been hard-pressed to produce anybody *under* twenty-five. Some teams paid players a better-than-living wage. Nobody on the Yuma Cubs made a dime.

Jack Crawford, sponsor of the Gadsden, Alabama, team, raved that Jimmy "Lefty" McClure—his nineteen-year-old pitching prodigy, with fourteen shutouts for the season—would machine-gun opposing lineups. "Every big league scout in the south has been trying to sign Jimmy," Crawford drawled. "There's not a pitcher his equal in the National, I'm predicting." Crawford also predicted that a team from the south would win the tournament, since southerners had the benefit of warmer weather and more games under their belts. That came as news to Claude Self, manager of the Chicago Sheridans, a team that coped just fine with crappy weather and had lost only 4 of their last 62 games. Self sent Hap Dumont a pretournament telegram that contained his subjective opinion: ENTERING CHICAGO'S FASTEST TEAM. EXPECT TO WIN NATIONAL CHAMPIONSHIP. Bill Parker, business manager of the Peerless Woolen Mills team from Rossville, Georgia, wouldn't guarantee a championship, but didn't discourage such speculation. "Of course, we came here to win," he admitted, "and I do say that we have a real ball club. All but four of our players come from professional ranks."

The demilitarized zone separating semipro and pro ball drove a news story that broke two days before the tournament opened. The Associated Press reported that three unidentified Western Association players had been suspended for being on the verge of "jumping" their minor league clubs and signing on as ringers in Wichita. The *Wichita Beacon* said rumors were flying that a tournament team from Texas or Oklahoma was prepared to spend $10,000 on pro players. Dumont assured fans that "we have checked our records" and no signs of chicanery were found. "We'll cooperate to the limit in seeing to it that players do not jump their contracts to play in the National," he added. The brouhaha over possible last-minute roster manipulation came in the wake of another flurry of juicy rumors. In late July the San Angelo Sheepherders—who were about to begin play at the National—had traveled from Texas to represent the city of Fort Scott in Dumont's Kansas state tournament. The Sheepherders lost in the finals. It didn't take long for the buzzing to begin about gamblers having paid them to take a dive. A National Baseball Congress source told the *Wichita Eagle* that was groundless innuendo: "There was a strict watch out for gambling in the stands and little was seen, only small bets of a dollar at the most."

With the countdown to the first pitch only days away, Hap Dumont had his own big bet to worry about. He'd rung up $10,000 in pretournament expenses. That necessitated a local radio blackout. Dumont needed fans to come out to the ballpark in sufficiently large numbers for him to turn a profit. The expense money went to hiring part-time ticket sellers, vendors, and support staff. An all-electric scoreboard had been installed, supposedly the finest in the country. In addition, there was at least one hidden expenditure: a hefty appearance fee. Dumont wanted a bankable gate attraction. That imperative had been hammered home the prior October when the St. Louis Cardinals' Dizzy Dean barnstormed in Wichita with his brother Paul. They played the Kansas City Monarchs at Lawrence Stadium and set a sports-attendance record for the city. Nine thousand people clamored to see the Dean brothers, lining up ten deep along the outfield fences. Right before that the Deans had played in Oklahoma City. Twenty thousand spectators had somehow fitted into a stadium there that was built to hold fewer than half that many.

Only one semipro ballplayer came close to generating that kind of excitement: Satchel Paige. Dumont knew it. So did Neil Churchill, and that was why he rarely took his team out of state without the promise of up-front money. One promoter had offered him $250 for an exhibition appearance, but Church wired back: MUST HAVE AT LEAST $500 GUARANTEED. I HAVE TO PAY SATCHEL PAIGE $250 A GAME. Whether $250 really went to Paige is questionable and irrelevant. What mattered was that Churchill used Paige as a bargaining chip and usually got his asking price—or more. Indeed, it cost Hap Dumont $1,000 to get Churchill to bring his team and his crowd-pleasing pitcher to Wichita. Perhaps Dumont was philosophical about that. The money he'd saved by not hiring Alabama Pitts as a celebrity umpire got put to better use buying the services of Satchel Paige.

Dumont and other National watchers believed six teams stood apart from the pack as favorites to win the tournament: Buffalo Blue Coals, Chicago Sheridans, Peerless Mills, United Fuel, the Japanese team from California, and the integrated team from Bismarck. With those clubs in transit to Kansas, Dumont could breathe a sigh of relief and then exhale a cloud of cigar smoke. "We're all ready," he said. "All we need now is 75,000 fans the next two weeks and some clear weather."

The forecast looked good. No rain in sight. Anywhere. The heat wave that fried North Dakota was also cooking Kansas.

16

GUNFIGHT AT
THE COWTOWN CORRAL

Neil Churchill couldn't have picked a worse time to go road tripping. The Midwest melted like an ice cream cone left under a
heat lamp in the summer of 1935. On Sunday, August 11, when
the Bismarck ball team's tiny car caravan left town for Hap Dumont's tournament, the thermometer topped out at a record 105
in Wichita. It was the thirty-second straight day of temperatures at
90 degrees or above. Almost half the Kansas corn crop was gone,
roasted on the stalk. Most semipro teams driving to the National
stopped on the way to play an exhibition game or two, enabling
them to stay sharp and make a little money to defray costs. Just as
important, they needed to escape their four-wheeled sweat boxes for
a spell. Automobiles wouldn't come equipped with air-conditioning
until the 1940s.

Not all managers could get their teams to Wichita in time
for the opening ceremonies that coming Tuesday. Churchill was
one of them. The zigzag ride from Bismarck wound over too many
country roads and gobbled up 1,100 miles. He'd planned ahead
and arranged a practice game late Tuesday afternoon in the town
of McPherson, a few hours' drive from Wichita. McPherson was
home base of the Dickey Oilers, a good semipro team, but not
quite good enough to join the National scrum. For Oilers fans, it
would be their best shot to see this Satchel Paige fellow they'd been

hearing so much about. The teams agreed to play six innings. Three
innings probably were enough to convince the Oilers that they had
no business swimming so far over their heads. Bismarck pounced
on them immediately and kept pouncing. 2–0 . . . 5–0 . . . 11–0 . . .
14–0. Onlookers got restless and irritable. They began ragging
Paige, who hadn't gotten off the bench and seemed quite content
to sit there watching Barney Morris throw darts. In the bottom of
the sixth inning, Paige at last grabbed his mitt and marched to the
mound. What followed, according to an article in the next morning's
McPherson Daily Republican, "was the show staged by the one and
only Satchell [sic] Paige, colored pitcher," a brief but memorable
performance "worth more than the admission price." As Moose
Johnson and the other outfielders trotted to their positions, Paige
shooed them back to the bench. He quickly went to work without
them, striking out the first Oilers batter on three pitches. The
second batter also struck out, also on three pitches. Red Haley
then sauntered over from first base and stood behind the pitcher's
mound as if waiting for a bus.

"Say, now, what's goin' on?" Paige asked him.

"I'm on strike," said Haley, deciding to have a little fun of his
own.

"Well, ain't this somethin'," Paige mumbled. He didn't like to
break concentration while performing surgery on an opposing team.

The next Oilers hitter slapped a line drive though the right
side of the infield exactly where Haley should have been standing.
He legged out a triple before Dan Oberholzer could dash from
second base to the outfield and retrieve the ball. Paige was not
impressed. Just as he'd done with the Twin City Colored Giants,
he doubled down on his dare and told his infielders to go take
a seat too. Only he and Troupe, who was catching and had to
stay put, were left manning the Bismarck defense. A somewhat
startled Oilers batter stepped to the plate, suddenly faced with
all sorts of possibilities to hit 'em where they ain't. Instead, he
hit it right to where they were, banging a hard grounder up the

middle. Paige jabbed at the ball with his spidery left arm, gloved it, and jogged over to first base to record the out. He oozed off the field to waves of applause.

Upon reaching the dugout, Satch silenced his chattering teammates. "Now, lookah heah," he announced with fake indignation, "I don't want *none* of this stuff when we get to Wichita!" Having gotten that out of his system, he grinned broadly and accepted congratulatory slaps on the back. He later insisted that Neil Churchill made the decision to bring in the outfield and also had bet several hundred dollars on the game, obviously with no regrets. The *Daily Republican* said fans thoroughly enjoyed the lonesome-pitcher "stunt." Editors at the *Baltimore Afro-American* did too. They ran a wire-service story about Bismarck's stop in McPherson, adding that Satchel Paige "entered baseball's hall of fame by calling in the infield and outfield in their game with a white Kansas nine." Paige was right, however: There would be "none of that stuff" in Wichita. He'd find another way to put on a show.

More than two dozen teams *did* arrive on time for opening day. A few minutes after noon on Tuesday hundreds of players and coaches lined up outside the Hotel Broadview—tournament headquarters and the redoubt of upper-crust Wichita society—for a tip-of-the-cap march east on Douglas Avenue through downtown. Hap Dumont and assorted city dignitaries were at the head of the parade, but most eyes drifted toward guest of honor Honus Wagner, eight-time National League batting champion during his glory days with the Pittsburgh Pirates. He was the "Flying Dutchman" then. Now sixty-one years old, with a thatch of white hair and a brewmeister's moon face and paunch, "Hans" would have trouble getting airborne. He remained with the Pirates as an elder-statesman coach and was still a competitor at heart. He'd put the squeeze on Dumont. In addition to whatever gratuity Wagner received for coming to Wichita to add some glitter to the occasion, he negotiated exclusive access to one tournament player of his choosing, whom he hoped to sign to a Pirates contract.

In return, Dumont got his money's worth out of Honus Wagner. He had the Dutchman flying all over town. Wagner did an interview with KFH radio before the parade. Afterward there was an extended meet-and-greet with business leaders followed by a banquet at the Broadview. Wagner pumped hands, posed for pictures, talked about the good old days when the St. Louis Cardinals fans used to chuck rocks at the Pirates' team bus, and confessed to being "lukewarm" about Major League baseball's decision to begin experimenting with night games. Shortly after eight o'clock he addressed 6,000 fans at Lawrence Stadium, welcoming them to Hap Dumont's first Little World Series. Wagner walked to the pitcher's mound and lobbed the ceremonial pitch for a tournament-kickoff doubleheader. He sat in the stands and saw the local favorite team, Wichita Water, beat Gadsden, Alabama's supposedly unbeatable young pitcher Lefty McClure, 4–3. In the nightcap, which dragged on till nearly 1 a.m., the Texas Centennials slipped by Stockton, California, 4–2. The *Wichita Eagle* sports department didn't have much experience handling ethnic news, but muddled through. "The colored boys took a lead in the fourth," the paper's story said, but then "the Japs tied it in the sixth" only to watch helplessly as "the Texas colored club went in the fore again in the seventh" after Stockton's center fielder collided with the flagpole, turning a long fly ball into an even longer triple and go-ahead run. Then came the hard part. The editors had to write a headline about a black team winning a ball game in Wichita. They'd never been called on to do that before. Could readers handle it? Was there a way to break the news to them gently? Under pressure, an *Eagle* wordsmith engineered a solution: *Japanese Lose In Pitchers' Battle Against Texans.*

Grappling with issues of race was a Jayhawk tradition. Kansans fought what amounted to a guerrilla war (with wild-eyed John Brown emerging as the most notorious provocateur) over whether to enter the Union in 1861 as a slave or free state. The Free Staters prevailed, but that didn't end discrimination. In 1906 Wichita implemented a segregated school system, adopting a kind of reverse busing policy: black children from majority-white neighborhoods were transported to all-black schools to prevent commingling. Most aspects of civic life were similarly regimented. Dockum Drug Store served as the National Baseball Congress box office. Blacks could buy tickets there for games, but they knew better than to sit down at the lunch counter and expect service. A black team had applied to play in the city's adult baseball league in 1933, but the request was denied. Generally, black teams were confined to their own ball field on Twelfth and Mosely streets, although some were able to arrange pickup games with whites.

The public venue where blacks and whites interacted with the fewest restrictions was Lawrence Stadium. Up in the grandstand, seating was open to everyone. Down on the field, black teams competed in Hap Dumont's Kansas state tournament and, now, the National. This had repercussions beyond the *Wichita Eagle* sports department. The desk clerk at the Hotel Broadview was thrown into a tizzy when Neil Churchill checked in late Tuesday night. Churchill had reserved eight rooms for a party of sixteen people. Only when the team walked through the front door of the hotel together did it become evident that eight of those would-be guests were . . . *black men.* Big black men standing in the lobby waiting for room keys. The desk clerk hemmed and hawed, refusing to register them. Churchill raised hell. The hotel manager came over and apologized, but there was nothing he could do: company policy, sir. For the first time, the Bismarck baseball team had to settle for separate accommodations. The white players, plus Churchill and trainer Roy McLeod, got to sleep in style at the Broadview. The black players went off searching for rooms in a black neighborhood on the northeast side of town.

Double Duty Radcliffe didn't say anything to Churchill, but he actually preferred staying elsewhere. It would be far easier to sneak a lady, especially a white lady, into his room if that room were someplace other than in a snooty downtown hotel. Black ballplayers knew through the grapevine where a bed could be found in most sports towns. Radcliffe and Paige recalled a Miss Jones who ran a Wichita boardinghouse where they could crash for $3 a night, two home-cooked meals included. Radcliffe claimed that the fallback plan worked to perfection. He shacked up for the next two weeks with Juanita Baldinado, a half-Mexican dream girl. Double Duty promised to marry her someday, but of course he didn't mean it and of course she probably knew that. He was an incorrigible hoochie-coochie man. And a flimflammer. "Double Dubious" Radcliffe. It's certainly possible his tournament nights were, indeed, spent wrapped in the warm embrace of lovely Juanita. It's also possible that he killed time reading the *Wichita Eagle*, front to back, alone in his room. One never knew with him. Radcliffe could simply have eaten Tex-Mex for dinner and fed his fantasies: a steak fajita became a sultry señorita.

Hotel snubs aside, it didn't take long for race to become the talk of Dumont's delicately balanced tournament. All of one day. The *Eagle*'s Pete Lightner rode that horse right out of the gate. He covered the National from start to finish and his columns became a running conversation with himself as much as with his readers. Lightner named four teams in attendance from the South—"the old South, Dixie"—as if he were listing bomb-making materials: Gadsden, Alabama; Rossville, Georgia; Shelby, North Carolina; and New Orleans, Louisiana. It looked to him as though Hap Dumont had a big problem in the offing: "To wit: How to run a tournament without having the southern boys clash with the colored teams." Could they be kept at arm's length? If not, could a truce be negotiated? Lightner had his doubts. Blacks and whites competed for the same trophy and the same prize money; there were no parallel separate-but-equal brackets. There could be only one winner.

"Sooner or later there will be reached a spot in the tourney where the color line can't be drawn," he wrote. The implication was clear. Hap Dumont had better know how to mix explosives. If not, his beloved National might blow up in his face.

Lawrence Stadium had more amenities—lights, public address system, clubhouse, that all-electric scoreboard—than a typical small-market ballpark, but it was built in the simple, traditional style that would make a Shaker proud: V-shape grandstand partially enveloped by a roof that curled from first base to third base. No second deck. No ornate facade. No outfield bleachers. Bandbox baseball stadiums were successors to Shakespeare's Globe theater. Players and fans, like Elizabethan actors and audiences, were locked in the slow dance of close quarters. They could smell each other. A lout barely had to raise his voice in order to heckle effectively.

Imagine an NCAA basketball tournament held on a single court with double the number of games because every team had to lose twice to be eliminated. That was the National, an orgy of baseball that ebbed and flowed, heaved and sighed for two weeks; twenty-five day-or-night sessions in all. General admission tickets cost 40 cents, center grandstand 65 cents. A select number of ringside box seats went for $1.09. There was another option. Lawrence Stadium stood alongside the Midland Valley Railroad yard. More often than not, open-box coal cars would be parked on a staging track that hugged the right field wall. Anyone who didn't mind getting dirty could climb aboard and enjoy an unobstructed view of the field. Enough people did so that it became the "Coal Car Grandstand" and, to some, "Tightwad Hill." Most, but not all, of those lurkers were black fans. Hap Dumont didn't take a seat anywhere inside or outside the stadium. He would rather pace and prowl, fidgeting like an expectant father, working his ever-present cigar. If he kept still for a few innings, it was usually in the crow's nest press box that overlooked home plate.

Round-robin play began in earnest on the second day of the tournament with a quadruple-header. As always, some teams talked a good game but couldn't deliver one. They quickly got pegged for an early departure. The New York Union Circulators were among those dead on arrival. Youth and brashness don't go well with eight errors. The Circulators were squished 13–0 by the also young but not so brash team from Poplar Bluffs, Missouri, causing the *Eagle* to remark snidely that they "must have been circulating in poor company in a baseball way" back in old New Yawk. The Duncan Cementers from Duncan, Oklahoma, made quite the opposite impression. They flew into town fashionably late, touching down shortly before their 5:45 p.m. game, but in plenty of time to subdue the Lompoc, California, team, 14–7. Relatively unknown outside their state, the Cementers attracted attention with pristine play and cherry-red uniforms. When they gathered for a team photo it looked like a blood clot forming. The Oklahomans served notice that they were a dark horse and bore watching.

A fifth and final game had been scheduled that second day. It was postponed because the teams from Rossville, Georgia, and Wewoka, Oklahoma, hadn't yet arrived in Wichita. To placate the crowd, Dumont cajoled Bismarck and the San Angelo Sheepherders into playing a five-inning, hit-and-giggle bonus game that started at 10 p.m. Bismarck "won" 3–0 and Neil Churchill managed to get Barney Morris, odd man out in his overstaffed rotation, a little pitching time. Churchill also had a chance to check out some of the competition. He sent a telegram to the sports department at the *Bismarck Tribune* bemoaning that the rosters in Wichita were "loaded" with ringers. Of course, Churchill was as guilty as anybody, with his eleventh-hour additions of Chet Brewer and outfielder Art Hancock.

Tournament top seed was bestowed on the Chicago Sheridans, largely a nod to the Windy City's reputation as a mecca of semipro baseball. The St. Louis Cardinals' scout Jack Ryan preferred the Cleveland Cloth Mills team from Shelby, North Carolina, because of its unflappable defense. Bismarck was no long shot, not with Satchel Paige waiting in the wings. Dumont expected Bismarck to set a Wichita attendance record when they formally entered the fray in Thursday night's featured game. The media were eager to know more about this mixed team from the Dakotas. One unidentified Bismarck player told a reporter that Churchill had promised Paige another new car if they won the tournament. Paige, meanwhile, was busy slicing interview baloney for the *Wichita Beacon*, ad-libbing about being born in Pittsburgh and learning to pitch by osmosis—by attending "every" Pirates home game at Forbes Field. Churchill explained to the press the origins of "Satchel," relaying the hoary tale about floppy feet, but noting, "Moose Johnson has him beat on the total acreage of his dogs." Moose wore size 14 spikes. Churchill was effusive in his praise of Paige, doubting that the sainted Walter Johnson had as lively a fastball: "I have been following major league baseball for 25 years and I think Satchel Paige is the greatest pitcher I've ever seen. If he were eligible to play in the big leagues, I would bet he would win at least 30 games."

Bismarck's opening-round opponent was the Monroe Monarchs, a black team from Louisiana. They had some shared history. In July the Monarchs had traveled to Bismarck and got beaten 7–2. Furthermore, pitchers Hilton Smith and Barney Morris were once Monarchs. Bismarck was the smart pick to win again, but the Monarchs felt they had a fighting chance. "We know Satchel is good, but no human can possibly be as unstoppable as he's supposed to be," the *Eagle* quoted one unnamed player as saying. "We'll give that ball a lambasting if we can only see it."

Hap Dumont didn't get the record crowd on Thursday night that he expected, but came close. Seven thousand Wichitans paid to see what the fuss over Satchel was all about. They almost went home clueless. Paige's stomach had a habit of turning cartwheels without notice. Whether because of the heat wave or, as he surmised, some "strange" water he drank, he felt out of sorts. Churchill contemplated giving Morris the start, but his ace refused to beg off. That day's lineup would be etched in stone for the tournament, with the exception of Churchill's pitching changes:

Dan Oberholzer	second base
Al Leary	shortstop
Quincy Troupe	center field
Vernon Johnson	left field
Red Haley	first base
Art Hancock	right field
Ted Radcliffe	catcher
Joe Desiderato	third base
Satchel Paige	pitcher
Chet Brewer	pitcher
Hilton Smith	pitcher
Barney Morris	pitcher

A rumor might have made Paige forget about his upset stomach. He'd heard that the Monarchs were going to play intimidation ball and bean him when he came to bat. Ol' Satch decided to nip that strategy in the bud by sending a don't-you-dare message. In the first inning he drilled the Monarchs' third baseman Jiggs Maxwell with a rib-seeking fastball. Down he went. Maxwell got up, dusted himself off, and played through the pain, though visibly woozy and wobbly for the rest of the game. It was by no means vintage Paige. He lacked his customary hairsplitting control. His curveball had a mind of its own. He walked the leadoff batter, plunked Maxwell, and walked the third batter. Bases loaded, none out. The cleanup hitter pool-cued a squibbler down the third base line that Joe Desiderato pounced on and threw to Radcliffe for the force at home. Bases loaded, one out. The next man up did the same thing: a weak grounder to the sure-handed Desiderato. But this time he misfired low and wide. The ball skipped past Radcliffe and rolled toward the first base grandstand. One run scored. Another run scored. Paige put away the subsequent two Monarchs, but had dug himself a 2–0 hole.

Highpockets Johnson pitched for Monroe. Bismarck nicked him for a run in the bottom of the first. Al Leary, batting second in the order, reached on an error as the first baseman muffed his ground ball. Troupe, hitting third, lashed a double into the right field corner and Leary scampered home. Johnson elevated his game while Paige tried to adjust his. Satchel relied almost exclusively on fastballs and threw sidearm more than usual, something he liked doing at night because batters seemed to have difficulty seeing balls down low in the zone. It worked. His touch returned. Three times he struck out the side. The teams traded one-run innings; Bismarck's second tally was also unearned: Troupe doubled again to right and scored when the shortstop booted Radcliffe's grounder.

Monroe led 3–2 entering the bottom of the seventh. It was Hap Dumont's turn to feel sick. One of his glamour clubs was on the verge of blowing what should have been a cakewalk game. But Highpockets Johnson blinked. He walked Desiderato, and Paige immediately sacrifice-bunted him over to second. The infield was playing hard and fast, owing to the heat, and Oberholzer took first on another error by the shortstop. Leary took advantage of that miscue, singling sharply to center and knocking in Desiderato. With two runners on and one out, Highpockets chose to intentionally walk Troupe, who had three hits. That brought up Moose Johnson with the bases filled and a chance to bust the game open. Johnson couldn't deliver, but did keep the inning alive. He topped a perfectly slow roller to the second baseman, just slow enough to make a double play impossible and also give Oberholzer time to score from third.

Bismarck now was on top 4–3, but living dangerously. Red Haley provided some breathing room by spanking a low line drive to center field, bringing Leary and Troupe home. Bismarck 6, Monroe 3. Could Paige close the door? He gave up a double and a single with one out in the eighth. Bismarck 6, Monroe 4 and threatening. At times like that pitchers have talks with themselves. *Dig deep, Mr. Be Ball. Wake your sorry butt up.* Paige gunned down the next two batters and then took complete control of the ninth inning. It was an ugly win, but gutsy. In Paige's worst outing of the season, he still managed to strike out seventeen Monarchs.

Satchel went from being a topic of conversation to being the talk of the tournament. Julius Stanczak, one ninth of the Stanczak brothers, was positive he saw Ted Radcliffe stick a slice of steak into his catcher's glove for extra padding. That's the kind of smoke Paige was throwing. *Wichita Beacon* sports columnist Jack Copeland became a true believer. Paige showed him something by not taking the night off when feeling rotten. "He struck out seventeen men. What if the guy was in A-1 condition?" Copeland wrote. "He has everything it takes to be a great pitcher, including coolness under fire and desire to win. Brother Paige certainly cannot be classed with the general run of toilers." Copeland added that many major league scouts already concluded that he would "be a cinch to star in the big show if he were only white."

Cy Slapnicka, a scout for the Cleveland Indians, stopped by the press box during the Bismarck-Monroe game to do a radio interview and shared what could be charitably described as unvarnished opinions. He did not mention any players by name, but clearly a particular pitcher had shone bright. "We wish we could find a chemical to bleach some of those colored boys," said Slapnicka. "We could take some of those players up to the majors and win a pennant with 'em."

The slang expression was "ivory hunters." Clever wordplay, because baseball scouts had a singular and constricted focus: white prospects. They were procurers of the raw human capital that front offices needed to produce a Major League team. A social conscience wasn't part of the job description. The ability to read a map; to drive ninety miles to watch a ball game attended by twenty people; to sit in wooden bleachers for hours, days, months on end: that's what counted. Patience was paramount. Pragmatism carried the day. Can this kid hit or field or throw well enough to be that one in a thousand who makes it? How cheap can I get him? Business was business. If he ain't white, he ain't worth my time.

Scouts were easy to pick out in a baseball crowd: middle-age or older, gray hair, loose tie, sometimes scribbling in a notebook, usually seated alone, always extra attentive; men who'd been around and seen it all and who wished to God they'd been given the kind of arm or batting eye that strangers would drive ninety miles to see. It wasn't glamorous work. Too much bad coffee. Too many nights away from home. Too few Ty Cobbs and Christy Mathewsons waiting to be discovered. The National Baseball Congress answered the prayers of every ivory hunter. It was an open audition with hundreds of players on public display. One-stop shopping. A couple of scouts drifted in and out, but nine of them stayed in Wichita for the whole tournament. Cy Slapnicka of the Indians and Jack Ryan of the Cardinals were joined by Ira Thomas (Philadelphia Athletics), Pat Monahan (St. Louis Browns), Steve O'Rourke (Detroit Tigers), Joe Becker (Brooklyn Dodgers), and Truck Hanna (the minor league Los Angeles Angels). The New York Yankees, always with the deepest pockets, sent two scouts: Joe Devine and Runt Marr.

George Siedhoff, owner of the Hotel Broadview and president of the Wichita Sports Association, invited the scouts and Hap Dumont to lunch on Saturday afternoon. The scouts came bearing compliments. They told Dumont and Siedhoff the tournament was very well organized. They had only good things to say about the crowds and the fans. *But* . . . there was always room for improvement. They'd like to see more young players and fewer ex-pros. (That would better serve their purposes, though not necessarily Dumont's.) As for black players, did they have to be here at all and, if so, couldn't their teams be placed in a separate bracket? The Yankees' Joe Devine pleaded for practicality. Since blacks were banned from organized baseball, it made sense for the National to be "simon-pure" as well. Ira Thomas took things a step further, objecting to the inclusion of all *mixed* teams: that is, Bismarck. To a man, his fellow scouts agreed. Dumont would hear the same suggestions in a meeting he held with team managers: put a cap on the number of players with professional experience and close the door to "colored teams." He promised to take those thoughts into consideration when planning the 1936 National.

The underlying issue of race kept nipping at his heels. On Saturday night, just hours after that "simon-pure" discussion with Major League scouts, the all-white Arkansas City Dubbs—a Kansas team from down south near the Oklahoma border—played the all-black Memphis Red Sox. It turned into the most thrilling game of the tournament thus far, Memphis holding on to the last lead change, 7–6. It also was the most disturbing game. In the fifth inning, a Red Sox runner advanced from first to home on an overthrow. He should have been held to just two extra bases. The umpire corrected himself and sent the runner back to third. That didn't stop tempers from flaring. The Red Sox catcher and the Dubbs second baseman traded words, then punches. The benches cleared. Frank Kice, Dumont's grizzly-bear assistant, lumbered onto the field and wedged himself between the combatants. A brawl was averted. The game continued. However, Hap Dumont must have nearly swallowed his cigar when he saw black and white ballplayers, bats in hand, eyeing each other like opposing armies. At that moment, separate-but-equal tournament brackets might not have seemed such a bad idea to him.

Six teams incurred their two allotted losses by the end of the first weekend of play. Adios, brave hearts from Byron, Nebraska. Peace be with you, Monroe Monarchs, the surprise washout. Three town entries from California—Lompoc, Roseville, and the Japanese contingent from Stockton—reluctantly hit the long road home. The Union Circulators used an ambidextrous pitcher in their second game, but still got clobbered 10–2 and slunk back to New York winless. While those early losers were leaving Wichita, another team arrived unannounced and tried to crash Hap Dumont's semipro party. It was an act of baseball insurrection many years in the making.

Fritz and Lena Deike (rhymes with "hike") came to central Texas in the tidal wave of European immigration. They settled in the wind-whipped town of Hye, about sixty miles straight west of Austin in the hills of Blanco County. Fritz managed a cotton gin. Lena produced babies, eleven in all and only two of them girls. The red-blooded-American Deike boys fell hard for baseball. They scrapped among themselves around the house, but never on the field. During the late 1920s—when seven of the nine Deikes were in their mid-teens to mid-twenties—they formed a sandlot team with some local players. One of them was a tall, garrulous, back-slapping first baseman named Lyndon Johnson, who was fortunate enough to own a baseball in near-pristine condition, an item as rare as the Hope Diamond in that distressed part of Texas. Johnson had exceptional reach at first base; but got it into his stubborn head that he could pitch (which he couldn't), and most times the Deikes wouldn't let him near the mound. Some days this so riled Lyndon that he'd take his precious ball and stomp home.

By 1935 Johnson had given up baseball and landed an entry-level job in politics as head of the Texas National Youth Administration. The Deikes didn't really miss him. By then the two youngest brothers—fourteen-year-old Victor and sixteen-year-old Emil—could hold their own on a ball field. The Deike boys were no longer just a family. They were a *team* and became an attraction in Texas Hill Country. That summer they heard that the organizers of a big semipro tournament in Wichita were looking for teams comprised solely of brothers. The Deikes applied. In addition, they got a local coffee company to donate $600 in travel expenses and uniforms that had "Deike Bros." printed on the front. Their hearts were pumping. Not only had the Deikes never traveled outside Texas before; they'd also never had baseball uniforms. "We all grew about a foot taller the first time we put them on," said Victor.

They felt about two inches small when Dumont notified them by letter that the National had decided to accept only one all-brothers team: the Stanczaks of Illinois. Quite the kick in the pants. The Deikes did what any proud Texan siblings would do who had brand-new uniforms but suddenly no reason to wear them. They jammed themselves into two Model A Fords and set out for Wichita. It took a week of driving and a ferry ride across the Colorado River to get there. Once in town they told anybody who'd listen that the Deike brothers had come all the way from the great state of Texas to challenge the Stanczak gang to a shoot-out. When Hap Dumont got word, he reacted like the smart promoter he was. No need to let this little misunderstanding disrupt the National tournament. No need to lash out at the Deikes. He convened a meeting with the two sets of brothers and proposed a friendly grudge match. They could use Lawrence Stadium at ten o'clock Sunday night. Fans would be welcome to linger on after the regularly scheduled games, no charge. Dumont billed it as a battle royal to settle the "world's 'family' championship title."

It was David versus Goliath. The Deikes had never played before a large crowd in a strange city, and the only baseball money they'd ever made came from passing the hat during games. They also had two teenagers in their lineup and a right fielder (Edwin) who was blind in one eye. Contrast that résumé with the Stanczaks, who ranged in age from twenty to forty and had been together as a unit for six years. They had changed the spelling of their Polish surname from Stanczak to Stanzak for promotional purposes because they thought it looked sleeker on their uniforms without the "c." Three brothers had professional baseball experience. Pitcher Bill Stanczak threw a spitball. (He preferred loading up with Slippery Elm Chewing Tobacco.) Third baseman Mike Stanczak was a priest, so maybe they had God rooting for them too. The Deikes got off to a fairy-tale start. They scored twice in the first inning and added another run in the top of the second. Up 3-0, the bottom dropped out. They got nervous, kicked the ball around, and gave up seven excruciating runs in the third inning, then four more in the next inning. The Stanczaks did not rattle. They took the family baseball crown 11–5.

The next day the Deikes—who wouldn't for a second consider changing the spelling of their name to "Dike," no matter how nice it looked—got into their dirty Fords and drove back to Texas, with no regrets and with everybody feeling at least a foot taller. They had gotten to wear their new wool uniforms and to hit unmarked, bright-white baseballs. That stinking seven-run inning was what did them in. The Stanczaks were good, but the brothers agreed they'd faced tougher teams. They also agreed they'd seen a pitcher in Wichita who would give them something to talk about for years to come. He threw sinfully hard. That boy Satchel Paige could knock a hole in the side of the Alamo.

"If you expect to get a hit off that guy," Herman Deike advised, "you'd better start swinging the bat while he's still in his windup."

Before tangling with the Stanczak brothers on Sunday night, the Deikes relaxed by taking in that afternoon's game between Bismarck and hometown Wichita Water, semipro state champions of Kansas. Five thousand people bought tickets to see Satchel Paige. He had captured the public's fancy. That morning's *Wichita Eagle* had a photo of him nattily attired in a Bismarck warm-up jacket and panama hat; this was believed to be the first time the paper deigned to publish a picture of a black athlete. But Churchill opted to rest Paige and play the odds. Chet Brewer took the ball for Bismarck. He had pitched a dozen times in Wichita for the Kansas City Monarchs and never lost. Paige called him "Dooflackem," a nonsense word Brewer liked to coo when shooting dice. He was six-four, weighed 200 pounds, and had been a Monarch for eleven years, long enough to have honed a sweeping curve, nasty running fastball, and screwball. The Watermen rolled out an equally seasoned veteran: Ed "Lefty" Chambers, who had toiled six years in the minors, going 14–11 in his final stop with the Class A Fort Worth Cats in 1933.

A low-scoring game appeared to be in the offing, but both pitchers wilted in the 100-degree heat. It was oppressive. Catcher Ted Radcliffe sat in the Bismarck dugout between innings with a wet towel draped around his neck. Dooflackem was not his steady self: more like "Don'tflackem." He labored from the third inning on. Brewer benefited from a 6–2 lead only because Chambers gave up so many extra base hits: doubles to Leary and Radcliffe; triples to Oberholzer and Johnson; a majestic home run by Quincy Troupe that dinged a freight car parked in the railyard. By the seventh inning there was nothing left in Brewer's tank. He got clipped for a single and a double that resulted in one run, then issued a base on balls. Churchill signaled for Paige, who extinguished that fire with a grounder and two strikeouts, and pitched a clean eighth inning. In the ninth, he allowed a meaningless run as Bismarck doused the Watermen 8–4. Paige stole the show by whiffing seven batters in three innings of relief. Jack Copeland of the *Beacon*, whose respect for Paige was snowballing into a crush, said skeptics could no longer deny that Satchel Paige was "the wonder man of pitching."

Copeland wouldn't get any argument from Neil Churchill, who had trouble keeping a lid on his confidence. "Don't think for a minute that we're chesty or stuck on ourselves. We simply believe we are the best team here," he said to reporters circling for a comment. "It's a great tournament. There are plenty of splendid teams competing, but I believe at the windup we'll be in the number one spot."

That was not empty talk. The *Denver Post*'s Jack Carberry discussed gambling with Bismarck's manager, who freely admitted to feeling the itch and scratching it. Carberry remarked in his column, "Churchill already has bet heavily, at odds of one to three and one to four, that his team will take the title. And he is seeking to place more money." Those odds indicated that bookies had pegged Bismarck as a prohibitive favorite. For every $100 Churchill slapped down, he stood to net just $30 to $40 if his team won. Betting "heavily" was the only way Churchill could compensate for a low payout.

Give Carberry credit for a scoop. He'd found the one person in Wichita who had more riding on the Little World Series than Hap Dumont.

17

Big Gun

The world did not take an August vacation; it never does. While baseballs flew in Kansas, news stories large and small continued to roll off the assembly line. Papers everywhere warned of gathering "war clouds" in Europe. A quite different threat literally reared its head in North Dakota, where several supposedly reliable sources spotted a lake-dwelling "monster" in Emmons County just south of Bismarck. In Wichita, "William the Walker," age eighty-nine, fell down and was hospitalized with a fractured collarbone. He had no surname and no home. He owned nothing but his clothes, a worn Bible, and a cane. William had been strolling an endless road for thirty-six years; not preaching per se, just casually chatting about scripture with strangers as if he'd found salvation in small talk as much as in the Lord. He rested a few days . . . then walked out of the hospital.

The only news story that really penetrated the bubble surrounding the National was the death of homespun entertainer Will Rogers in a plane crash in Alaska. Millions grieved as if they'd lost a family member. Damon Runyon wrote a column calling Rogers the "unofficial prime minister of the people" and "America's most complete document." Americans cherish genuine characters and outliers. They had one in Rogers and, as tournament attendees in Wichita were learning, perhaps another coming around the bend in the person of Satchel Paige. As human documents go, he was still in the process of being translated, read, and understood, but striking out 24 batters in 12 innings will create a stir at any level of baseball. Two managers were overheard in discussion at Lawrence Stadium. One said that when his team got runners on base against Paige, he'd signal the next batter to call time out and try "to get him worried." The other manager replied, "That's fine, but what I want to know is how to get those runners on base."

As is often the case when pitchers dominate, some suspected that Paige was tampering with the baseball. However, the umpires who called his games in Wichita subscribed to Quincy Troupe's theory: all Paige cheated was gravity, something he accomplished by throwing that anomalous and elusive rising fastball of his. The *Beacon*'s Jack Copeland sought enlightenment from a black Bismarck teammate of Paige's, whom he did the disservice of quoting in *Amos 'n' Andy* dialect: "Folkses, y'all lookin' at de best pitchah in de world. Yasah, dats him, ole Satchel Paige. Your Wichitah Watah boys don't need to be discouraged. He mows de best of de big leaguers down just the same as he's a-mowing you all. That's the kind of pitchah y'all is lookin' at: The best pitchah in de *world*!"

The "Paige effect" could be quantified. On Monday of the second week of play, 2,400 fans sat through an evening triple-header in which the Memphis Red Sox and Yuma (Arizona) Cubs were paired in the eight o'clock featured game. The next night, 6,500 turned out for another three-pack of games. The difference? Bismarck played Denver United Fuel in Tuesday's prime-time billing and Satchel Paige was scheduled to pitch. The interest wasn't exclusively based on race. Legitimate debate and curiosity arose about whether Paige belonged in the tournament by virtue of his ability, not his color. Was he too "professional" and not "semi" enough? Neil Churchill had a ready response. Both the black and the white baseball establishments had shunned Satchel. The man wanted to make a living as a pitcher, and semipro ball was the only avenue currently open to him. Hap Dumont stood firmly in that camp. He had no intention of turning his back on Paige—not after investing $1,000 to get him to come to Wichita, and not with Bismarck's games accounting for about 60 percent of the tournament gate. Dumont was in the business of giving people what they liked—and some people liked Paige enough to take a punch on his behalf. A fistfight broke out in the stands during the Bismarck-Denver game over this burning question: Who's better, Dizzy Dean or Satchel Paige?

Churchill felt frustrated after Paige's start against the Monroe Monarchs. His guy didn't click because of that upset stomach. Church assured reporters they'd "really see something" in his next full outing. Right before the Denver United Fuel game, he went further out on a limb and said Satchel would bounce back with a shutout. Coburn Jones, United Fuel's player-manager, didn't think Paige's spectacular roll could continue. He declared his team would win the ball game and, for that matter, also the National. Jones had reason to be bullish. Right before coming to Wichita, United Fuel had been crowned champion of the always competitive *Denver Post* tournament. Left-hander Maxie Thomas, an eleven-year minor leaguer, pitched the finale in Denver. However, players changed partners promiscuously in semipro baseball. Thomas was at the National pitching for Wichita Water. Jones replaced him as leader of the Denver staff. Jones had played pro ball for three years: two in the Class A Eastern League and one with the Pittsburgh Pirates. All well and good, but his true position was shortstop. Furthermore, he was a five-foot-seven, 155-pound shortstop. A team possibly fatigued from jumping into sequential tournaments was sending a medium-size infielder up against the redoubtable Satchel Paige, whose stomach was now calmed. There was no doubt which of those horses Neil Churchill would bet on.

The 6,500 fans in Lawrence Stadium witnessed a baseball oddity: a low-scoring game that wasn't as close as it sounded. A headline in the *Wichita Eagle* succinctly captured what transpired. "Great Colored Hurler Again Proves Too Good for Opponents." Paige never let up, striking out the first six batters and setting down the first ten in a row while on his way to anesthetizing United Fuel 4–1. He'd gotten into a groove with his fastball in Wichita. Why mess

with success? Keep peppering the strike zone. Moose Johnson—
who had an unorthodox fielding stance, with his upper body bent
forward, arms hanging low by his knees, feet staggered—took to
positioning himself almost on top of the left field line whenever a
left-handed batter came to the plate; this was a good thirty yards
from where he would normally stand. There was room to graze
cattle in left-center field. That's how much Paige's fastball was handcuffing hitters. Moose cut a lonely figure over by that foul line. In
his fielder's crouch, he looked like a sprinter who'd shown up an
hour early for the start of the Hap Dumont Hundred-Yard Dash.

Paige finished the Denver game with twelve strikeouts and no
walks. He handed out five singles: alms for the poor batters. United
Fuel's run came in the eighth inning on two hits and an error by
Haley at first base. Absent that unearned run, Churchill would have
made good on his promise of a shutout. As for Coburn Jones, he
pitched well. For a shortstop. Bismarck scored solo runs in each
of the first four innings, but it was not an overwhelming display of
offense. The only bursts of power came in the third inning, when
Johnson and Haley belted identical-twin doubles to left field that
accounted for one run; and in the fourth, when Desiderato tripled
off the right-field scoreboard. Paige chased Desiderato home with
a single and promptly got cut down trying to stretch his luck into a
double, "legging it for second in a furious manner," said the *Eagle*.
Not since he got caught shoplifting in Mobile as a boy had Satchel
Paige run in anything approximating "a furious manner." Pushing
for that extra base showed how seriously he was taking the National.
When the Major Leagues are hopelessly beyond your reach, you
play for the next sweetest thing: respect. He badly wanted to make
an impression on his white peers in Wichita—and he already had
at least one convert in his corner.

Ira Thomas, the scout who couldn't abide mixed-race teams,
was the Philadelphia Athletics' catcher and team captain during
their glorious run of World Series titles in 1910, 1911, and 1913.
He batted against the best warriors of his era. Near the top of his

list was the Red Sox's Smoky Joe Wood. A sportswriter once said
Wood hurled "great balls of fire from the mound." Pitching god
Walter Johnson opined, "No man alive can throw any harder." After
a few days in Wichita, Ira Thomas begged to differ with Johnson.
The Major Leagues color line was a brick wall. Scouts couldn't give
even a fleeting thought to signing a black player, but they were all
connoisseurs of pure talent. Thomas came to the conclusion that
he'd seen somebody throw a baseball harder than Smoky Joe ever
did. The new king of speed was Satchel Paige.

    Best pitchah in de world?

Bismarck had an off day on Wednesday, so Churchill held a practice.
He borrowed a diamond across town that the Wichita Water team
used. Weather presented no problem (more of the same: sunny and
too hot), but after about half an hour he canceled the session. He'd
brought along two dozen baseballs. Once batting practice got under
way, they quickly disappeared into the hands of neighborhood kids
who'd stationed themselves along the perimeter of the field. When
a ball came within reach, one of the little vultures would scoop it
up and run off. In a furious manner. No market existed for stolen
baseballs. These were petty thefts of the heart. Those kids wanted
a souvenir, some tangible proof that they'd seen the mysterious
stranger, Satchel Paige.

    Baseballs weren't the only things disappearing. The roll call
of fatalities continued to swell as teams accrued their two losses
and vanished from Lawrence Stadium: Wewoka, Oklahoma; Enid,
Oklahoma; Poplar Bluffs, Missouri; Gadsden, Alabama; Holy
Name Baseball Club of New Orleans; Shawnee, Kansas; Ocean-
side, California; those feisty Stanczak brothers; and, yes, the top-
seed Chicago Sheridans. All gone. On Wednesday afternoon the
Memphis Red Sox downed the Buffalo Blue Coals 6–1. The Coals
exited in grand style, leaving the field crooning a tune from the
movie *42nd Street* that Ruby Keeler made famous. "For a little silver

quarter we can have the Pullman porter turn the lights down low!" they sang. "Oh, off we're gonna shuffle! Shuffle off to *Buffalo*!" Back home, the *Buffalo Evening News* tried its best to put an upbeat spin on a downbeat headline: "Blue Coals Win Praise of Fans: Buffalo Nine Highly Regarded Although Losing Again in U.S. Tourney."

A fan of semipro baseball who couldn't spare the time or money to go to Wichita was at the mercy of mass media with dead spots. Hap Dumont had reneged and quietly lifted his self-imposed ban on KFH radio broadcasts, but the station's signal lost oomph outside central Kansas. Listeners had to cup their ears to hear voices fading in and out, getting buffeted about the prairie. Regional papers such as the *Denver Post, Minneapolis Tribune,* and *Omaha World-Herald* sent reporters to Wichita, as did the Associated Press and Continental Press Service. Still, their readers digested day-old box scores. The most timely and reliable source was Western Union. Subscribers to its Teletype service received inning-by-inning game summaries. This was a modern wrinkle on the town crier, but at least the lag time was only a few minutes. Jack Crawford owned the movie theater in Gadsden, Alabama, as well as the semipro baseball team. He read aloud the Western Union game reports from Wichita to fans huddled inside his theater, just as he did for the World Series in October. In Shelby, North Carolina, people gathered on East Main Street as late as eleven o'clock at night to hear updates on how their Cleveland Cloth Mills team was faring. Harry's Brown Derby bar and the Elks lodge were Western Union hangouts for baseball junkies in Duncan, Oklahoma.

At its weekly Monday luncheon the Bismarck Lions Club had voted to send a good-luck telegram to Neil Churchill. The next night his team disposed of United Fuel, and the following morning the front page of the *Tribune* spread the word: "Bismarck Nine Defeats Denver Champions." By then, the win was old news to Wick Corwin, who'd discovered he could, faintly, pick up Wichita's KFH signal on his home radio most evenings if atmospheric conditions were just right and if he fiddled with the dial just so. But the surest bet for game-day coverage was State Recreation Parlor, a billiard hall in the lobby of the Grand Pacific Hotel on Broadway. "State Rec" had a well-scratched bar and some pool tables. It was dark and devoid of ambience, and tobacco smoke thick enough to cure hams hung in the air. The joint had two things that made it popular with Bismarck men. One, a beer license (the town still hadn't totally repudiated Prohibition). Two, Bismarck women avoided it like the plague. The Rec was such an unapologetically male enclave that proprietor Vern Dresbach wouldn't let his own daughter come inside.

Dresbach loved sports. Along with the beer and billiards, he sold tickets to boxing matches and baseball games. When customers asked, "What's the score?" Vern was expected to know, so there was no question he'd have a Western Union line installed for the National Baseball Congress tournament. On the days Bismarck played, Dresbach wisely invited Dayton Shipley to rip and read the Teletype printouts as they came across the wire. Shipley, a state hotel inspector, was blessed with a set of muscular vocal cords that required no amplification. His stentorian voice lent an air of authority to all kinds of events around town. He umpired ball games, emceed Golden Gloves boxing competitions, sang in the Catholic Daughters of America chorus, and served as "ringmaster" at the Bismarck dog show.

On Thursday night, August 22, State Rec was humming. So, too, was Lawrence Stadium: 7,500 people, the largest crowd since Dizzy Dean barnstormed in Wichita, came to see if Cleveland Cloth Mills—the pride of working-class Shelby, North Carolina—could end Bismarck's three-game winning streak. The *Gastonia Daily Gazette* (Gastonia was best known as the most convenient place to stop for gas between Shelby and Charlotte) perfectly framed the task at hand. "The strong point of the Bismarck club is in the pitching department," wrote staff reporter Delbert Lazenby. "The ace hurler of the club is a dusky lad by the name of Satchel Paige, who is a better player than most of the white players on the team. The

Wichita papers have devoted columns to his praise, and the giant Negro had been described as the best colored pitcher in America. Just what Shelby will do against this fellow remains to be seen."

Spot on, Delbert. But Neil Churchill threw everybody a curve. Although he'd talked about using Satchel Paige, he decided at the last minute to rest Paige's arm. Chet Brewer slipped into the pilot's seat. This time the searing heat had no effect on him. If anything, it recharged his batteries. Shelby batted first. Back in Bismarck, Dayton Shipley stepped to the center of the billiard hall. His butterscotch baritone filled the room as he read the play-by-play of the first half inning. "Shelby. Heavner grounded out to Brewer. Oberholzer made hard running catch of Refern's fly ball. Lee struck out. . . ."

Then Shipley delivered those six heavenly words: "No runs, no hits, no errors."

Shelby sent its young ace into battle, the twenty-four-year-old knuckleballer Sam "Porkie" Lankford. Player-manager Mack Arnett had reportedly held Lankford out of action all week so he'd be in peak form. Bismarck greeted him and his knuckler rudely. Dan Oberholzer led off the bottom of the first inning with a double to left field. Al Leary followed with a hard double to center. Bismarck 1, Shelby 0. Chet Brewer had all his pitches working. For five of the next seven innings, Dayton Shipley kept repeating himself, announcing over the yammering of customers when Shelby came to bat, "No runs, no hits, no errors."

Bismarck took a comfortable 7–0 lead into the ninth inning. Brewer had been touched for just one single. Shelby's leadoff man in the ninth reached on a ground-ball error by Oberholzer. The next batter lined a single sharply to left that Johnson misplayed, putting runners on second and third with none out. The crowd inside State Recreation quieted down as Shipley relayed what happened next. "Little flied out to Oberholzer. Arnett grounded out to Oberholzer and Suggs scored." That made the score 7–1 with Shelby down to its last out. Chet Brewer bore down. "Murray grounded out to Oberholzer. One run, one hit, one error."

Drink up, boys! Bismarck sealed its fourth consecutive win. Brewer's two-hitter wasn't the only good news, maybe not even the best news. Moose Johnson got two hits off Porkie Lankford (one of them a thunderous triple to left field) and drove in three runs. After going 0 for 4 against the Monroe Monarchs in round one of the tournament, he'd rebounded with six hits in his last ten at bats. Bismarck needed its slugger to stay locked in for the final rounds.

After Bismarck beat Shelby, the Duncan Cementers took the field for the ten o'clock nightcap at Lawrence Stadium and throttled the Yuma Cubs, 10–2. Eleven teams now remained in contention, two of them undefeated: Bismarck and Duncan. Their bracket paths were due to cross the next night. Through four games, Duncan had outscored its opponents 51 to 23; Bismarck's collective winning margin was 25 to 10. Those numbers implied that the key to the game would be whether Bismarck's strong pitching could neutralize Duncan's strong hitting. Churchill had two pitchers on his bench— Hilton Smith and Barney Morris—who'd yet to see any action. He wanted to get them game time, but this didn't strike him as the right opportunity. That decision was solidified when he learned that the Cementers had tapped Augie Johns for the Bismarck start. He was thirty-four and had pitched parts of two seasons with the Detroit Tigers and fourteen years in the minor leagues. Needless to say, Johns wouldn't be making any youthful mistakes.

Neil Churchill spoke with reporters late Thursday night. "We fear Duncan more than any other club we have played to date," he said, perhaps indulging in a bit of psychological warfare. "They have a hard-hitting club and with Johns on the mound, we're not taking any chances. That's why Paige will draw the assignment."

Paige got not only the assignment but also some extra attention. Hap Dumont designated Friday "Satchel Paige Night," helping to ensure another large, enthusiastic crowd. As Pete Lightner wrote in his column for the *Eagle*, "Satchel is popular with everyone but the opposing hitters." In the black community his popularity was on a par with that of heavyweight boxer Joe Louis. "Satchel is a hero because he is the best in his field," said an editorial in that Friday's *Negro Star*, a weekly newspaper published in Wichita. "The fans are enthralled by his power, his skill and his cunning. There's only one Satchel Paige. The National Base Ball Tournament in Wichita has been a great event. Negro ballplayers are making good showings and it seems there is a great future before them."

Somebody leaked it to Paige that his teammates were going to present him with a wristwatch right before the Duncan Cementers game. Whoever chose that particular gift was either misguided or mischievous. A man notorious for having no regard for time, no concept of time, no *time* for time, had very little use for a watch. Would you give a mime a megaphone for his birthday? As much as Paige appreciated the gesture, he didn't want to offend the baseball gods. He told his teammates there would be no pregame hoopla on Satchel Paige Night. "You boys just wait until this tournament is over and then you can give me anything you like," he said, "but I don't want any presents tonight. It's bad luck."

This was not the night to court bad luck. Churchill expected a cliff-hanger with Duncan and, therefore, managed aggressively. The first inning was uneventful, the teams taking each other's measure. Leading off the top of the second inning for Bismarck, Red Haley singled to right field. Art Hancock did the same, with Haley hustling to third. Churchill then did something uncharacteristic: he called for a double steal. Augie Johns swung into his windup, kicked—and Hancock made a break for second. As Duncan's catcher attempted to peg him out, Haley lowered his head and barreled home. Both runners beat both throws. Radcliffe batted next and struck out, but Desiderato followed with a single that scored Hancock. Paige struck out to end the inning. Dayton Shipley shared the good news with the folks clustered inside State Recreation: "Two runs, three hits, no errors."

Paige wanted to rise to this occasion with special gusto. Johns was a former Major Leaguer while he himself ached to be one. First time through the order the best any Duncan batter could do off him was swat a fly to Troupe in center field. Five others struck out. With Bismarck up 2–0 in the fourth inning, Moose Johnson drove the first pitch he saw to deep center, pulling into third with a triple. Haley grounded hard to Augie Johns, and the ball caromed off his glove for a single. Johnson rumbled home. The Cementers answered in the bottom of the inning with a single and a double off Paige that produced a run. That 3–1 score held into the last inning. Neither pitcher gave ground. Johns posted eleven strikeouts. Paige topped him with fourteen, but opened the door to trouble in the bottom of the ninth. He gave up a single to Joe Hassler, Duncan's star shortstop, who was leading the tournament in hitting. After a ground out, Hassler moved up to third on a passed ball that eluded Radcliffe. With one out and the tying run at the plate, Paige took a deep breath and put his faith in Brother Fastball. A few minutes later, Western Union teletype machines broke their silence. "Gulledge and Brown struck out. No runs, one hit, no errors." Bismarck's fifth win was in the books.

Denver United Fuel and Wichita Water bit the dust in other games, leaving nine teams alive at the National. A wire-service story on the front page of the *Bismarck Tribune* noted that, with five straight wins, "a swashbuckling band of ball players from North Dakota's Capital City" was the only undefeated survivor. Columnist Pete Lightner of the *Eagle* had this to say to his readers: "Surely that Friday game Satchel pitched against Duncan Cementers was as pretty a game as Wichita has ever seen." What a difference twenty-four hours can make. Saturday night brought with it one of the ugliest games Wichita had ever seen. Three more clubs were eliminated: the Yuma Cubs and the last remaining black teams, the Denver Stars and Memphis Red Sox, known in newsprint speak as the "Denver (Colored) Stars" and the "Memphis

(Colored) Red Sox." Unlike the Buffalo Blue Coals, the Red Sox departed the tournament *swinging*, not singing.

They got off to an encouraging 4–0 start in their game with Nebraska's Omaha Ford V-8s . Without warning, things took a nasty turn. In the fourth inning, Omaha batter Roy Luebbe beefed about a called strike. Somebody must have pushed a hot button, because he came to immediate blows with Memphis catcher John "the Brute" Lyles, who just a week earlier had been in the middle of a dustup with the Arkansas City, Kansas team. Teammates bolted from both benches. Dozens of spectators hopped out of the right field stands and joined the melee. Dumont's assistant Frank Kice again interceded as peacemaker, this time with several police officers. Once play resumed, the juiced-up V-8s surged from behind to win 6–5, though they had to do so after replacing their center fielder, who had gotten hurt in the fight. "For a moment it looked like the entire stadium would be plunged into something of a riot," the *Wichita Beacon* reported. "Ill feelings continued throughout the entire game."

The National was a crash course in race relations for players, journalists, and fans. Many of them had a lot to learn. The *Wichita Eagle* published its story about the Memphis-Omaha "near riot" in the Sunday sports section, which also contained a large caricature of Satchel Paige under the heading "Colored Race Produces Another Great Athlete." The accompanying text said that Paige combined the speed of Jesse Owens with the power of Joe Louis, both of whom were depicted as tiny simian-like figures cavorting in the foreground. A footnote explained that Satchel's animated windup was his natural pitching motion, "not an Ethiopian war dance." That crass caricature got picked up in syndication by other newspapers, including the *Bismarck Tribune* and, surprisingly, the black-owned *Kansas City Call*. The *Tribune* exercised its own questionable taste by printing a photo of Paige, the home team hero, with the caption "I'm shoa gonna have that new c-a-a," a reference to the rumor that he'd been promised new wheels if Bismarck won the tournament.

Some days the *Wichita Eagle*'s Pete Lightner gave the impression he lived inside a snow globe, his sensibilities shaped by an insular world of white. In one column he wrote that National officials "praised" the black team from San Angelo, Texas, for its players' sportsmanship and skill, but as an aside added his own opinion that "some of the colored clubs" he'd seen play in Wichita in the past "have had little respect for training rules, or other rules." In another column he passed along the tidbit that scouts attending the National "hand it to the colored players one way and that's in throwing. The fine throwing from the outfield in the tournament has been mostly by colored players. They have a whip the white boys don't seem to get."

Quincy Troupe came to Lawrence Stadium early one night to see part of the game being played before Bismarck's. Two scouts were seated in front of him. He overheard one say that integration of the Major Leagues wouldn't be the traumatic event team owners seemed to fear. The other scout was less sanguine, convinced that players from the South would never accept "colored boys." Troupe didn't know which one to believe. When he went down to the locker room to get dressed, he asked Hilton Smith, the erudite pitcher who'd played college ball in Texas and Negro League ball in Louisiana, if he thought the color line would ever disappear. "Troupe," Smith said, "I've come up playing with white boys. I think some southern people want to hold on to that old tradition, but most are really good at heart."

Al Leary, the shortstop, walked in and started putting on his uniform. He was a Finnish American, from Sand Coulee, Montana. Growing up, Leary had more encounters with bears than with black people. "What do you think, Leary?" Troupe asked. "You think any Negro players will ever get to the majors?"

"That's a pretty hard question. I think *eventually* someone will get up the nerve like Churchill and hire both blacks and whites."

Troupe pressed him: "You think they could play together the same as we do?"

"Why not?" Leary replied. "Quincy, I'm almost sure it will work whenever someone gets the nerve to try it."

Smith told Troupe to look beyond social friction in the South. The Major Leagues were a different landscape: "All those teams are located in cities above the Mason-Dixon Line."

At twenty-two years old Quincy Troupe hadn't given up hope, but he'd seen what cities located above the Mason-Dixon Line had done for Art Hancock, Ted Radcliffe, Satchel Paige, and dozens of other black players. *Nothing.* Men in their athletic prime or past it were still waiting for that phone call, still seeking entry to baseball's sanctum sanctorum. Troupe heard the clock ticking and knew Smith did too. "Smitty," he sighed, "by the time a change does come, I'll be too old to throw the ball back to the pitcher."

Neil Churchill poked his head inside the locker-room door and reminded his players that they had forty-five minutes until first pitch. For a few hours, Troupe could stop worrying about discrimination and growing old. There was baseball to play.

On Sunday the Omaha Ford V-8s were again in a fighting mood, but they wanted to punch themselves. Some of the cognoscenti had a hunch the V-8s could upset Bismarck. They'd won the Nebraska state semipro tournament. Half their players had Major League or minor league credentials. The X factor was that this would be their third tough game in three days. Given the abbreviated rosters of semipro teams, a small pitching staff could crack under such strain. Bill Eissler (16–4 in the Class D minors in 1930) got the call for Omaha. Neil Churchill stayed with his two-man, dynamic-duo rotation and answered with Chet Brewer. "Dooflackem" was delightful through eight innings, rationing four hits that limited the V-8s to just one run.

Eissler caught a break in the first inning when Troupe walloped a ball to right field that looked like a sure inside-the-park home run until he tripped over third base, wrenching his knee. He limped off and Hilton Smith took his place. Haley salvaged the run by slapping a single through the hole just beyond the shortstop's outstretched glove, scoring Smith. The 1–1 tie held until the top of the fifth inning, when Omaha self-destructed. Bismarck's first four batters reached on errors and Smith doubled, making the score 4–1. That brought up a salivating Moose Johnson. Churchill said the only player he'd ever seen who could punish a baseball like Jimmie Foxx, the Philadelphia Athletics' built-like-a-blacksmith power hitter, was Johnson. He promptly put an Eissler pitch into orbit over the right field light tower for a 7–1 lead. Four innings and two Omaha pitchers later, Bismarck was in total command, 15–1. Brewer surrendered five meaningless runs in the bottom of the ninth inning before shutting off the lights. The *Omaha World-Herald* didn't mince words: "Omaha's entry into the national tournament was shelled out of the running here Sunday by the powerful mixed club from Bismarck."

Two other teams were sent packing: Rossville, Georgia; and Shawnee, Kansas. The original field of thirty-two had been whittled down to three. "Satchel can be beaten, but by whom?" Pete Lightner asked. "That's what is drawing thousands to Lawrence field." Those fans would get to see Paige at least once more. By running the table through six rounds, Bismarck assured itself of a spot in the finals. Could Satchel be beaten? It was up to either Shelby, North Carolina, or Duncan, Oklahoma, to figure out how. They played for that opportunity on Monday night, milking every last drop of drama from their semifinal game. Shelby trailed 3–2 in the bottom of the ninth inning. With two outs and the tying run on third, they gambled on a squeeze bunt—and lost. The batter slid into first base a split second after the throw.

Earlier in the day Satchel Paige pronounced himself in the best shape of his career. The Sioux snake oil was working its magic. His arm felt splendid. Long Rifle said he was prepared to "shoot the works" regardless of whether he faced Duncan or Shelby in the championship game. Bismarck fans should consider the National title "in the bag." Confidence is commendable, but his bag had a few potential holes in it. Quincy Troupe was a question mark for the finals because of his swollen knee. The Duncan Cementers, meanwhile, were at full strength and hitting .323 as a team for the tournament, 20 points higher than Bismarck.

Lest Paige forget, this was a corporate team with a big payroll and big expectations. Erle P. Halliburton owned the company. "Mr. Halliburton," as everyone in Duncan, Oklahoma, called him, had fought his way to a position of prominence in the bare-knuckle oil industry. He was rich, smart, hardworking, and accustomed to winning. Only fools bet against him.

18

THE ERLE OF OKLAHOMA

Most people use an outhouse to take care of business. Erle Halliburton used his to start one, which in time transformed the oil industry and made him a multimillionaire.

It took years of personal struggle to get to the point where a privy could be parlayed into a fortune. Erle Halliburton may not have been a humble man, but he came from humble beginnings. His family worked a farm near Henning, Tennessee, just north of Memphis and not far from the Mississippi River. Or did the farm work them? It was cling-to-the-promise-of-a-better-tomorrow rural living. Erle's two sisters never made it to puberty. His father never made it to fifty. When Edwin Halliburton died in 1906, his wife and five of their children moved in with relatives. Erle struck out on his own. He was fourteen. He found employment as a salesman (actually, sales*boy*) and a steam-powered crane operator, but in 1910 enlisted in the navy, where he learned hydraulics and engineering and learned them very well. After his discharge in 1915, Halliburton went to California and found a job with Perkins Oil Well Cementing Company. Before oil can be pumped, a borehole must be drilled and a pipe sunk to line the shaft. Cement gets poured around the pipe in varied thicknesses and depths to hold the casing in place. The Perkins company handled the mixing and making of those cement sheaths. Almond Perkins thought he'd devised a safe, reliable technique for doing that. But Erle Halliburton—a smallish man with an overabundance of opinions—kept suggesting improvements and, after about a year of hectoring, became such a pest that Mr. Perkins suggested he find another job. Erle claimed "the two best things that ever happened to me were being hired and fired by the Perkins Oil Well Cementing Company."

His wife, Vida, stood by her man and they relocated to northern Texas. The oil fields there were booming. Erle picked up spot cementing jobs and, on the side, tinkered with his ideas for streamlining the mixing and pouring process. It was while living in Wichita Falls, Texas—surrounded by wildcatters, roughnecks, stark terrain, and no indoor plumbing—that Halliburton bartered his way into business. A neighbor wanted a better place to answer Nature's calls. Halliburton offered unrestricted access to his own scrupulously tended outhouse in exchange for the use of a wagon and team of horses. He then borrowed a pump and some tools. He then built a cement mixing box that could be transported from oil well to oil well in that wagon. The New Method Oil Well Cementing Company was officially up and running.

The Halliburtons endured the sacrifices that come with getting a business off the ground without financing. Vida hand-washed cement bags and made a little extra money recycling them to manufacturers. Times got tighter and she told Erle to pawn her wedding ring. He did. New Method survived and finally prospered. The Halliburtons were able to get the ring out of hock. By 1920 they had followed the oil boom across the state line into Oklahoma, touching down in the town of Wilson and then Duncan. Erle owned three trucks and had patented a mobile mechanized cement mixer. A few years later he persuaded seven oil company clients to invest in his operation, which he renamed Halliburton Oil Well Cementing. The company went public and Erle Halliburton became rich. In 1926 the Halliburton company went international, branching out into Canada and selling its oil well cementing machines to a British outfit drilling in Burma. Erle Halliburton was on his way to becoming filthy rich. By 1935 he had 1,000 employees and his fingers in an investment firm, a racetrack, a Honduran gold mine—and a semipro baseball team.

His involvement with baseball reflected his allegiance to Duncan. Although Erle and Vida relocated to Los Angeles, they kept the corporate headquarters in Oklahoma. There was mutual affection. Duncan had been good to the Halliburtons. If business had soured during those nascent days, Halliburton Oil Well Cementing might have foundered. Likewise, Duncan's growth and general health would have been stunted without the infusion of those permanent, well-paying jobs. Erle Halliburton proved himself to be one gruff, overbearing son of a bitch. Everybody in Duncan knew that, but nobody in Duncan had a bad word to say about the man. What people did say was: "He built this town." Erle was *their* gruff, overbearing son of a bitch.

The only person to ever match Erle Halliburton's impact was William Duncan, a Scotsman whose wanderlust brought him to Indian Territory in the 1870s. He married a Chickasaw woman and opened a general store at the crossroads formed by the Chisholm Trail and the squiggly line on maps that marked the route to Fort Arbuckle and Fort Sill. A town grew up around Duncan's homestead and store when the Rock Island Railroad pushed through in 1892 on its way to linking Kansas with Texas. Two summers later, and fifteen years before statehood, merchants organized a Duncan baseball team. It remained a town team until Erle Halliburton came to town. Erle loved baseball, although he never had much time to play as a boy. His kid brother John did play, however. John Halliburton joined the company in the mid-1920s and soon afterward joined the baseball team.

Erle's mind was a one-way street and didn't yield to traffic of any kind. He got tired of his luggage getting abused while traveling, so he and some Halliburton staff engineers designed a better mousetrap: an aluminum suitcase. He launched a company just to manufacture it, and damned if those suitcases didn't sell like hotcakes. Erle also was not above threatening to punch out a business competitor. When John Halliburton began playing baseball with the town team, Erle's inclination was to view it as an underperforming municipal asset and a potential takeover target. In 1927 he bought uniforms for the team. Pretty soon the team consisted mostly of Halliburton employees. By the late 1920s, they were *all* Halliburton employees.

In 1931 the team—interchangeably known as the Duncan Cementers and the Halliburton Cementers—went 31–9. That was very good, but not good enough for Erle. In 1933 he decided to step up to the semipro ranks, reasoning that a highly competitive, higher-profile team made sense as "an advertising and good-will venture." Sandlot players like his brother John no longer made the grade, but Erle wasn't casting his lot with sports goons either. Halliburton semipro players were corporate employees who worked at semiskilled jobs for an hourly wage and happened to have some ancillary baseball responsibilities. They received a $25 a month bonus during the summer as compensation for the extra demands of road trips and weekend tournaments. Company mechanics bolted benches to the back of a flatbed and added a canvas roof, turning the truck into a super surrey with a fringe on top that served as the team bus. The Halliburton corporate colors were gray and red—hence the garish tomato-colored uniforms that became the Cementers' calling card.

Oklahoma had a vibrant semipro baseball culture in the 1930s. Many of the best teams were company-based and often oil company–based: the Willburton Miners, El Reno Southwest Utility, Okmulgee Barnsdall Refiners, Enid Eason Oilers, Oklahoma City Wilcox Oilers, Perry Oilers. The Halliburton Cementers took a little longer to work their way up in the pecking order because they refused to hire mercenaries. A core group of player-employees slowly came together, but patience wasn't a hallmark of Erle Halliburton. During the 1934 season he made a decision to reach for higher-hanging fruit and plucked Augie Johns off the Texas League tree. At thirty-four, Johns was a little past his prime, but still had a knee-buckling curveball and the cachet of having pitched two years for the Detroit Tigers during his salad days. He'd also survived fourteen years in the high-level minors, putting up some of the best numbers (134–81 won-lost record and 25 shutouts) in Texas League annals.

Johns was a building block. Halliburton grabbed him from the Fort Worth Cats and in 1935 other Texas Leaguers followed Johns's lead and went corporate: infielder Tom Holley and first baseman Ed Lowell (who had fifteen years' pro experience between them) from the Cats; catcher Alex Coleman from the Tulsa Oilers. Forty-three-year-old "Admiral" John Paul Jones came out of the woodwork to fill the role of spot reliever. He'd pitched for the Boston Braves in 1920 and also six years in the minors. Jones threw submarine style, which was why his arm still had life in it. The best find probably was Joe Hassler, a thirty-year-old shortstop who'd had dalliances with the Philadelphia Athletics and St. Louis Browns in the Major Leagues. He brought stability to the middle infield, plus the right attitude: "I'd rather be playing with this semipro team than a pro team," Hassler once said in a newspaper interview. "I get more of a kick out if it and have a steady job when I'm not playing."

"Steady job" talk tickled the ears of Erle Halliburton. He was one of those self-made millionaires who are perhaps too self-made, who might have to think twice about pulling a drowning man out of the water. Before committing himself to a rescue, Erle would want to know how a chap ever got himself into such a fix and, furthermore, whether he really was kicking as hard as he could to avoid going under. In late June 1935 Halliburton created a firestorm by publicly announcing a change in hiring policy. Henceforth, Halliburton Oil Well Cementing Company wouldn't touch any prospective employee who'd ever accepted a government relief check. "There is not now and never has been any excuse for the dole," Erle Halliburton grumbled. "Certainly, any man who wants to work can take the modern methods of the present day and earn for himself a better living with less effort than the same man could have earned for himself thirty years ago. We continue to tax those who are working for the benefit of those who do not work. As a result we are bound to develop a race of people that can't take it."

Judging by the timing of his announcement, he wanted to give Americans something weighty to ponder over the Fourth of July holiday. But his words sent such a chill that they seemed to be coated with December frost. Halliburton sounded as if he were auditioning early for the part of Ebenezer Scrooge in the Duncan community playhouse production of *A Christmas Carol*. With the country spinning its wheels in the deep mud of the Depression, an oil-industry grandee sermonizing about the evils of "the dole" caused a predictable backlash. Sacks of mail got dumped on Halliburton's office desk. He insisted that letters of support ran "8-to-1 ahead of the squawks." Of course, Erle was doing the counting. So many letters and phone calls contained death threats that the Los Angeles police department assigned a security detail to his house. The protection was lifted in mid-July at Erle's request, coincidentally just as the Halliburton baseball team began to gear up for its end-of-season tournament push.

The Cementers got knocked out midway through the Oklahoma state semipro tournament and then flew to Wichita for Hap Dumont's National, where they gelled at just the right time into a tough, disciplined, businesslike unit. Their appearance in the championship game made for an intriguing backstory: A team owned by a vocal archenemy of New Deal relief programs pitted against a team representing battered-and-bruised North Dakota, where nearly a third of the populace lived on the dole. That political footnote didn't register with baseball fans, who simply looked on this as bracket justice being served: the two teams that played the best baseball for two weeks were going toe-to-toe in a rematch for the national semipro title. Pete Lightner used it as another opportunity to obsess over Satchel Paige's rightful place in the baseball universe. "Just how good is Satchel anyway?" he wrote on the morning of the finals. "The question is often asked. There's no doubt that Satchel's a genius in the semi-pro field. But how would he fare in the major leagues?"

Lightner sought out Joe Hassler, ex-major leaguer, and put that very question to him. Hassler knew better than to denigrate an opposing pitcher right before a big game. No doubt he also knew that in Wichita the Monroe Monarchs' Jiggs Maxwell had felt the wrath of Satchel Paige, as expressed by a special-delivery fastball. Yet Hassler had nothing much to gain by ladling on the superlatives like gravy, but ladle he did. "I never faced a pitcher as fast as he is. I think only Lefty Grove in his prime could come up with Paige in sheer speed," he told Lightner. "Satchel is not only a speed ball pitcher, he's as smart as they make 'em. You never get a good ball to swing at. He places every pitch inside or outside and never does it go over the middle. Paige would certainly make a great pitcher right now in the big leagues."

Hassler was having the finest tournament of any position player, hitting .515 and ranging wide at shortstop. He went 2 for 4 against Paige when Duncan met Bismarck in the fifth round. That day Paige struck out sixteen Cementers. Hassler had to assume he'd be just as sharp the second time around. Duncan's biggest fan no doubt thought the same thing. Minutes after the Cementers beat Shelby, North Carolina, on Monday night to advance to the championship game, a telegram arrived at the Hotel Broadview addressed to "Ed Lowell, manager, Halliburton Cementers." It was sent by someone from Oklahoma who wanted to dole out a little moral support on the eve of Duncan's do-or-die battle with Bismarck and Satchel Paige.

Following the win over Shelby, Ed Lowell had showered at Lawrence Stadium and got back to the Hotel Broadview after 11 o'clock, eager to grab some sleep. Upon his arrival, the desk clerk handed him this sweet-dreams message: CONGRATULATIONS FOR PLAYING A GOOD GAME TONIGHT STOP STAY IN THERE AND HUSTLE WE ARE WITH YOU WIN OR LOSE SIGNED ERLE P. HALLIBURTON.

19

LAST TEAM STANDING

No one needed glasses to read Tuesday morning's headline on the *Bismarck Tribune* sports page. Words marched from the extreme-left column to the extreme-right column in big, look-at-me, boldface type: "Bismarck Battles Duncan for National Crown Tonight." The front page of the paper had a news flash outlined in black. The insatiably curious could relax: Ballgame updates again would be available at State Recreation Parlor starting at 8 p.m. and "D. E. Shipley will be announcing the plays which will be received direct, from Lawrence Stadium [in] Wichita, Kan., over a special leased wire."

That wasn't the only option for fans. A Good Samaritan had agreed to put a microphone in front of his radio in Wichita and relay the KFH broadcast of the ball game via shortwave to Bismarck. The transmission would be picked up and aired locally by station KFYR, much to the delight of those uncomfortable with stepping inside the State Rec lion's den. Helen Churchill, for one, planned to have an ear glued to her radio "listening to the report of Satchel Paige."

The *Wichita Eagle* also ran a reminder about the National tournament at the top of its front page: "North Dakota, Oklahoma in Ball Finals Tonight." The text set the stage in fewer than a hundred words, explaining that this was a must-win situation for Duncan, while Bismarck could afford a loss, in which case there'd be a winner-take-all game on Wednesday. The last paragraph made a blatant appeal to civic pride: "Tonight's game is expected to draw 7,500 fans to the stadium. An overflow crowd will assure financial success for the big tourney and assure its return here in 1936, say sponsors." Hap Dumont apparently had called in a favor.

Dumont's hopes and prayers were answered. Some 10,000 spectators shoehorned into Lawrence Stadium to see Satchel Paige versus Augie Johns, Part II, bringing with them the wonderful bee-hive buzz of a crowded ballpark. Freeloaders packed the Coal Car Grandstand. So many standing room tickets were sold that foul territory along the left and right field lines resembled Times Square on New Year's Eve, minus the pickpockets. Gentlemen surrendered to the heat, loosening their ties and removing jackets. The stands became a sea of bright white shirts, on which bobbed a flotilla of fedoras and straw skimmers. Hollywood tough guy George Raft had a choice box seat, as did J. L. Wilkinson, owner of the Kansas City Monarchs. Erle Halliburton was nowhere in sight. He said he didn't like to attend his team's games, for fear of being a "jinx."

Duncan was averaging nearly ten runs a game for the tournament, almost three more than Bismarck. Nonetheless, Neil Churchill—as always, dressed in black slacks and a white shirt with the sleeves rolled up; the off-duty-undertaker look—liked his team's chances. If Paige lost tonight, Churchill could come right back at Duncan with Chet Brewer. In addition, his other pitchers were beyond well rested. Hilton Smith and Barney Morris hadn't stepped on the mound yet. Bismarck even won the coin toss for the right to be home team. All was well . . . until Moose Johnson walked into the locker room unable to hold a straight line. Churchill's left fielder and power threat was lean-on-a-lamppost hungover.

Troupe had a bum knee and was less than 100 percent. Haley had hurt his groin. Now Johnson showed up good for nothing but cheering on his teammates while propped in a corner of the dugout. Not even one of Double Duty Radcliffe's between-the-legs ice packs could sober him up quickly enough. Whether Moose had fallen off the wagon or jumped, his timing couldn't have been worse. Churchill had bets riding on Bismarck to win the National. He'd invested a decade of his life building this team; taking it from the tragedy of Balzer Klein's beaning to the triumphs of Satchel Paige, from a nearly empty ballpark to 10,000 fans eagerly awaiting an about-to-be-thrown first pitch. Suddenly, on the grand stage of Lawrence Stadium, all that hard work had been reduced to cliché: the show must go on.

Churchill angrily scratched Johnson from his lineup. The easiest fix was to move Art Hancock over to left field and put Hilton Smith in right. Churchill already planned a minor change in the batting order (flipping Hancock, who had a cold bat, with Radcliffe in the six and seven holes), but he didn't want to overreact and overmanage the loss of Johnson. Smith, therefore, would simply take Moose's place as the cleanup hitter. He'd played only one game so far, filling in admirably when Troupe twisted his knee on Sunday by going 2 for 5 with three runs batted in. Churchill trusted his gut: let the quiet man bat fourth and see if he can make some noise.

Shortly after eight o'clock Paige ambled to the mound, bow-legged and heavy-footed. He had a walk made for football: slow and labored, like a halfback returning to the huddle after a long run short of breath and aching head to toe. His oldest baseball friend, Ted Radcliffe, was crouched behind the plate with that silly slab of beef tucked inside his catcher's glove. Paige took his warm-up pitches and then stood still rubbing up the baseball, drinking in the scene. History most often gets made with fuss and fury. It might be Lucky Lindbergh landing a plane in Paris or armies bloodying a battlefield. Smaller moments worthy of attention can steal by on tiptoe. In Wichita a mixed-race team was vying for the honor of being crowned "champion": admittedly, not of the entire sports world, but definitely of a hotly contested semiprofessional piece of it. They'd be performing in front of paying customers with prize money at stake and sportswriters looking on. This was new and different. Satchel Paige, who never overanalyzed anything, sensed an occasion of some import. "Ten thousand people out here to see that game, ten thousand for a couple of semipro clubs," he thought. "But it was the championship and ol' Satch was pitching."

Player-manager Ed Lowell led off for the Duncan Cementers. He batted a pedestrian .278 during seven minor league seasons, but had two of the Cementers' five hits in the last Bismarck game. Paige's first pitch missed the plate. Satchel's Hurry Up ball seemed to be in no particular hurry and oddly unsure of itself. The count stretched to two balls, two strikes. Lowell golfed the fifth pitch into left field for a clean single. The next Duncan batter blooped a pop foul to Desiderato. Joe Hassler came up and became Paige's first strikeout victim. Center fielder Sam Jones, the Cementers' cleanup man, had been stymied by Paige in their first meeting: 0 for 4 with two strikeouts. He exacted immediate revenge by mashing a fastball over Troupe's head in deep center field and hustling to third as Lowell jogged home. Paige got the final out with a ground ball, but Duncan was on the board early, 1–0. In the prior game they didn't get a hit until the fourth inning. On this muggy evening, Ol' Satch looked human.

Teams constantly send and receive messages during ball games. By scoring right away, Duncan delivered one to Bismarck: "Satchel *who*? This isn't last game." Bismarck wanted to reply quickly. Augie Johns wanted to keep the momentum going by setting them down quietly in the bottom of the first inning. He started strong as Dan Oberholzer flied to center for one out and then right fielder John Lowry made a splendid running catch on a line drive, robbing Al Leary of a hit. Quincy Troupe gimped to the plate, batting right-handed against the lefty Johns. He went the opposite way, driving a ball hard into the right field gap. It eluded Lowry and got wedged under the scoreboard for a ground-rule double. That brought up lanky, round-shouldered, bravado-impaired Hilton Smith, who was being asked on short notice to fill Moose Johnson's size 14 shoes. A teammate once said "he looked funny" in a baseball uniform. But Smith was a stealth bomber. He didn't just hit well for a pitcher. He could flat-out hit. In a pressure at bat, he delivered for Churchill and rapped a crisp single to center. Troupe scooted home with the tying run. Johns retired the side by getting Red Haley to line out. In Bismarck, Dayton Shipley finished off his play-by-play accounts of the top and bottom of the first inning with two identical recaps: "One run, two hits, no errors."

Advantage nobody.

For the subsequent five innings Johns and Paige painted the corners like old masters. Bismarck got just two hits off Johns. Paige chalked up seven strikeouts, limiting Duncan to four singles, three of which didn't leave the infield. Both teams played small ball. They sacrificed and stole bases but couldn't move a runner past second. The biggest threat was mounted by the crowd. The umpires had to call time out in the second inning to push back standing-room-only fans who were creeping into fair territory from the sidelines. Duncan squandered the best scoring opportunity. In the third inning Lowell beat out a slow roller (for another hit) and was bunted over to second base. He died there as Paige fanned Hassler and Jones.

In the seventh Bismarck got untracked. Haley led off with a single to center field. After Radcliffe sacrificed him to second, Art Hancock drew a walk. Joe Desiderato hit a laser that Lowry got a glove on as he smacked into the right field wall, but couldn't squeeze for the catch. He then made the questionable decision to throw home. Haley scored easily, with the throw from the outfield allowing Desiderato to take second and get into scoring position while Hancock held at third. That extra base made a difference. With Bismarck leading 2–1 and Satchel Paige coming up, it was manager Ed Lowell's turn to make a questionable decision. He yanked Augie Johns and brought in John Paul Jones, the ancient mariner reliever. Lowell's logic must have been to go with a righty-righty matchup in a key situation. However, as much as Paige enjoyed talking about his hitting, nobody considered him a tough out. What he did have was an uncanny knack for rising to almost every occasion. Sure enough, he lined the second pitch over Jones's head. Hancock scored easily with Desiderato on his heels. Paige, who was becoming a wild man on the base paths, got cut down trying to turn his single into a double. Oberholzer grounded back to the box to end the inning, but Bismarck sent a loud and clear message to Duncan: "You've got six outs to get three runs off Satchel Paige. Good luck."

In the Bismarck dugout, Paige—now riding high with twelve strikeouts—took a few swigs from a bottle of Coke before the start of the eighth inning. He turned toward Radcliffe. "Homey," he said, "there's work to be done. I'm gonna show these sons of bitches it ain't their night." That's what Radcliffe *said* Paige said. One cannot discount the possibility that Satchel took a few swigs from a bottle of Coke and . . . *burped*. Paige probably could count on one hand (one finger?) the number of late-inning 4–1 leads he'd blown in his lifetime. He sashayed to the mound with Lawrence Stadium rocking and with an audibly partisan crowd back in Bismarck tasting victory. Shipley hushed everyone at State Recreation Parlor while he read the latest update as it came over the Western Union wire from Wichita: "Lowell singled to left . . ."

The customers at State Rec didn't like hearing that. It was Lowell's third hit. He might be the only hitter in the world who owned Paige. Or was Satchel tiring?

". . . Holley struck out . . ."

Much better, Shipley. Was there any doubt? Satch never runs out of gas. He was only refuelin'.

"Hassler flied out to Hancock. S. Jones hit to Leary forcing Lowell at second. No runs, one hit, no errors!"

Bismarck added an insurance run in the last of the eighth inning. Hilton Smith singled to right, Red Haley singled to center, and Smith scored on a passed ball that the Duncan catcher failed to hold. Smith and Haley, who between them had five of Bismarck's nine hits, gave Paige a 5–1 lead. The Cementers came to bat in the ninth inning in the kind of dire straits that usually involve a blindfold and a cigarette. Third baseman Joe Gulledge lofted a lazy pop that Leary easily gloved. One down, two outs to go. Ready, aim . . .

George Brown smacked a single to left field. John Lowry singled to center. Catcher Alex Coleman, one of the Texas League crew, cracked another single to left. Brown loped home. Lowry stood on second base, Coleman on first. Score now 5–2, still with two outs to go. This was not going according to script for Bismarck. Could Paige feel it slipping away? Did he try drawing inspiration from some of the strange things written and said during the past two weeks? *We wish we could find a chemical to bleach some of those colored boys. . . . Scouts hand it to the colored players one way and that's in throwing. They have a whip the white boys don't seem to get. . . . I'm shoa gonna have that new c-a-a.* Pitcher John Paul Jones was due up for Duncan, so pinch hitter Dick Adair grabbed a bat from the rack. A home run would tie the game. Standing on deck was Ed Lowell, the man with five hits in eight at bats off Paige.

There was work to be done.

Paige toed the rubber, high-kicked his left leg, cocked his right arm, and fired. Bullets. Radcliffe's glove exploded over and over and over. At State Recreation Parlor it sounded like this: "Adair *struck out!*" Dayton Shipley barked. "Lowell *struck out!* One run, three hits, no errors!" National champions!

Cheers filled the smoky room. Beer glasses clinked. Bismarck celebrated, but Lawrence Stadium went hysterical. Fans vaulted out of the grandstand and flooded the field. Paige took half an hour to wend his way from the pitcher's mound to the dressing room. Kids were clinging to his uniform sleeves like burrs. Adults shouted his name, reached out to shake his hand, and asked for autographs. Paige had seen a lot in baseball, but nothing quite compared to this. Usually when a black man got engulfed by screaming white people someone was carrying a rope.

Neil Churchill, the fussbudget, tried gathering up equipment in the Bismarck dugout as a wave of humanity washed over him. It was futile. Bats, balls, and caps disappeared. Churchill gave up and retreated into the locker room. His players were doing what champions invariably do: laughing, hugging, throwing uniform tops and socks into the air. He got pulled aside by George Siedhoff, owner of the Hotel Broadview. Acting on behalf of the Wichita Sports Association and the business community, Siedhoff presented Churchill with the 1935 National Baseball Congress trophy. Hap Dumont didn't scrimp on hardware. The Honus Wagner Trophy—which looked like an enormous gold-plated champagne flute topped by a winged goddess of victory—stood three feet tall and weighed forty pounds. Flashbulbs popped as Churchill and Siedhoff raised it as high as they could. "It was a great tournament and we're glad it's over," said a drained Churchill. "The pressure is too great to keep up much longer."

Second baseman Dan Oberholzer, who was earning an engineering degree in bits and pieces at the University of Minnesota, kept a tight lid on his emotions. "Just another ball game," he told reporters fishing for a quote. In another corner of the locker room, Paige held court with more enthusiasm. "Just want to say that our boys played a great game and don't go talkin' a lot about *me*," Satch chided the press. "And tell those fans out there that they certainly gave me a thrill the way they came out for the final game tonight."

Reporters slowly drifted back to the press box, where they hunched over boxy typewriters and banged out their stories. The Associated Press went with a simple declarative lead: "A mixed team of negro and white players today were bringing home to Bismarck, North Dakota, the championship of the national semi-pro tournament." The *Wichita Eagle* made no secret of who it thought carried the day: "Bismarck, capital of the state, can build a monument to Leroy 'Satchel' Paige, elongated, skinny, gangling and gawky pride of the colored race. For Satchel last night faced as strong a ball club as was ever organized in independent ranks." Jack Copeland of the *Beacon* paid homage to Paige, but added that he had "a great semi-pro club behind him."

North Dakota was having a rare top-dog experience. For its front-page headline, the *Bismarck Tribune* may have dragged out jumbo typeface that hadn't been used since the signing of the armistice ending World War I, but, then, it's not every day that

"Bismarck Wins National Semi-Pro Pennant." Editorial writers across the state weighed in. The *Mandan Pioneer* asserted that this would "do much to earn for the state and the west slope territory recognition that is too often lacking." The *Grand Forks Herald* felt that "the championship drive of Neil Churchill's squad reflects satisfyingly on every club in the state." The *Valley City Times Record*, which covered one of Bismarck's ardent semipro competitors, commented that an "ordinary small town" always has the baseball odds heavily stacked against it: "We are glad to record the success of the Bismarck semi-pro team. They deserve a pat on the back." The *Jamestown Sun* was conspicuous in its restraint, perhaps reflecting the two cities' well-cultivated enmity. The *Sun* did run a wire story about Bismarck's greatest win ever, but chose to devote its editorial to a circus that was coming to town: "The costumes of the performers are exceptionally well kept and the animals appeared to be very carefully handled." Take that, Mr. Churchill.

George Barton, sports columnist for the *Minneapolis Tribune*, had a cogent take on the National, assigning a dollar value to the Major Leagues' inflexible color line. "Baseball fans, not only of Bismarck, but of the entire state of North Dakota can well feel proud of Bismarck's fine team," he wrote. "Bismarck has in Satchell [sic] Paige, Negro, a pitcher, who, if he were white and eligible to play in organized baseball, would bring around $100,000 in the open market. He possesses everything a great pitcher must have."

Paige won four games in Wichita, piling up 66 strikeouts in 39 innings while allowing just 5 bases on balls. He surrendered only 5 earned runs and 29 hits. His WHIP (walks plus hits per innings pitched, the metric that makes modern baseball statisticians swoon) was .871. A WHIP under 1.00 connotes man-among-boys excellence. Satchel Paige ran away with the most-valuable-player honors. Hap Dumont hastily named a tournament all-star team. Paige was on it, so too Chet Brewer, Quincy Troupe, and Joe Desiderato (and four Duncan Cementers).

Scouts signed fourteen prospects at the National. Paige wasn't on anyone's shopping list, for obvious reasons. Some ivory hunters were thinking of making offers to Desiderato and Al Leary. Of the fourteen players put under contract at the tournament, none ever made a name in the Major Leagues and most vanished without ever being issued a uniform. Back they went to the farm or factory. The ladder was, and still is, hard to climb. Hal Warnock, an outfielder for the Yuma, Arizona, team, signed with the St. Louis Browns. He made it to the big time that September, appearing in six games and roping two doubles in seven at bats. Warnock got sent to the minors for the 1936 season, hit .299, and *poof.* Never heard from again. The Philadelphia Athletics took a shine to pitcher Earl "Pie" Huckleberry, pick of the Shawnee, Kansas, litter at the National. He also proceeded directly to the majors and made his first start September 13, 1935. The kid was shaky, getting banged around for seven runs in six and two-thirds innings. But the A's piled on the Chicago White Sox 19–7 and Huckleberry lucked into his first win, which was his only win—also his only game. The Athletics finished dead last in the American League, 34 games behind the Detroit Tigers, but didn't want another piece of Pie. It was a one-and-done career.

As for Pete Lightner, he hadn't seen anything at the 1935 National that convinced him integrated baseball could work. After the championship game he revealed that "one southern team" (almost certainly Gadsden, Alabama) had arrived in Wichita not knowing black players or black teams would be there. They were incensed and threatened to leave. Dumont persuaded them to stay. But isn't persuasion under those circumstances polite coercion? Would Dumont be able to prevent future walkouts? "By next year some perplexing problems must be taken up and disposed of," Lightner wrote in his tournament postmortem for the *Eagle*. "The separation of white and colored players and teams is the most difficult to solve." The other prickly issue involved overqualified semipros such as Paige tipping the competitive balance.

Dumont grasped those "perplexing problems" and said he'd work hard at finding ways to resolve them. However, he made an immediate decision to stage another National Baseball Congress extravaganza at Lawrence Stadium and announced the dates: August 12–26, 1936. Erle Halliburton marked his calendar. The Cementers planned on coming back to Wichita and, next time, leaving with the trophy.

To the victor went the spoils. "We're ready to cash in now," Churchill confided to reporters during the locker room party. Within hours he received more than twenty telegrams from teams wanting to schedule an exhibition with the National champions. One offer guaranteed him $3,000 for a two-game series. Churchill lined up a week's worth of appearances, which would not be attended by Moose Johnson. As likable as he was, Johnson had committed the unpardonable sin of pulling the rug out from under his teammates and his manager minutes before a big ball game. With regrets and best wishes, Churchill cut the cord and sent him on his way.

The post-tournament tour launched Thursday evening at Lawrence Stadium with the Kansas City Monarchs. It was Churchill's thank-you to J. L. Wilkinson for lending Chet Brewer to Bismarck for the National. They expected a sellout crowd. They badly miscalculated. Only 1,000 tickets were sold. The cool, cloudy weather didn't help, but Wichitans may have seen all they wanted to see of the Bismarck team. Those who did come to the stadium booed. The pregame publicity said Paige would pitch, but he refused to take off his warm-up jacket, telling Churchill his arm was tired and he was worried about getting injured. Left unsaid: Satchel didn't like to pitch for empty seats. The Monarchs drubbed Bismarck 8–0 with Barney Morris losing to Brewer, who just a few days ago had been his teammate.

Bismarck stopped in Burlington, Colorado, to beat its town team and then took two of three games from the House of David in Denver. From there, on to Nebraska. Rain washed out that game, giving Paige plenty of time to play biography ball with a reporter from the *Omaha World-Herald*. Satch said his parents ran a hotel in Phoenix, Arizona. He rarely attended school as a boy because, well, he did so much bell-hopping until he left home at age seventeen. He said he earned $764 a month playing baseball and believed Jim Crow laws would never fall, but had stoically learned to accept that. "I'm making money, more money than if I was hanging paper or diggin' ditches. There's no use feeling sorry for yourself."

The victory lap ended in Kansas City on September 4. Bismarck faced the Monarchs again, only this time Brewer had to go up against Paige, not Barney Morris. Early in the game Paige informed Churchill that he wanted to come out. The umpire's tight strike zone was causing him too much unwarranted pain and suffering. They had a private heart-to-heart. "Satch," Churchill said quietly, "this is my last game as a baseball manager. I'm through after this one. I want you to stay in and win it for me." That touched Satchel, who was genuinely fond of Neil Churchill. But Satchel also had a parking-meter mentality. He pitched his best when you kept feeding him quarters. They conducted a thirty-second negotiation. Whether Churchill felt sentimental or needed to cover a bet (or both), he promised Paige an extra $750 if they won the game. Deal. Chet Brewer had a snowball's chance in Phoenix. Paige struck out fifteen Monarchs and Bismarck finished its dream season with an 8–4 win.

Did Churchill dump $750 just to ice a win over the Kansas City Monarchs? He never said so. And Satchel wasn't always on speaking terms with the truth. Yet Bismarck did beat the Monarchs 8–4. Satchel did strike out fifteen batters. Churchill did step down as manager, although no one else knew it yet. The team parted company in Kansas City. Most players went home. Oberholzer resumed his engineering studies. Troupe and Paige (seemingly in no hurry to go snuggle with wife Janet in Pittsburgh) hooked up with the Monarchs to play some more September baseball. Exhausted by three grueling weeks on the road, Churchill and team trainer Roy McLeod returned to Bismarck, where the *Tribune* extolled him as "the man of the hour" and he got to put that forty-pound Honus Wagner Trophy on display in the Corwin-Churchill showroom. The Association of Commerce and about fifty baseball buffs threw a dinner in his honor at the Rendezvous restaurant. They gave their man of the hour the obligatory wristwatch for thrusting Bismarck baseball into the national spotlight. Mayor Amil Lenhart, former governor Joe Devine, and town umpire Tom Cayou spoke that night. So did Churchill, who said he got a check from Hap Dumont for $2,542, half what the winner of the National was supposed to receive. It seems Hap had underestimated expenses and had also given away too many comp tickets. Thanks to those post-tournament games, Churchill said the team didn't lose money on the Wichita trip and broke "almost even" for the year.

Two days before that dinner Churchill announced in the newspaper what Paige said he'd whispered to him in Kansas City: He was stepping down. "This job is one that requires a full-time manager," he said. "Myself and Babe Mohn, treasurer of the club, have put in more time than we can afford to take away from our businesses and this is the chief reason for relinquishing the management this year." That statement failed to touch a few important bases. There was no mention of how much Neil missed Helen and the children or how much he was looking forward to spending more time with his family. Maybe he didn't want to create the wrong impression that Neil Churchill was about to become a homebody. He'd decided to give up only the small white ball, not the big brown one. The Phantoms' fall-winter season was just gearing up. Church still had basketball responsibilities to fulfill and his chair was getting cold at those late-night Patterson Hotel poker games. Helen shouldn't bother setting a place for him at the dinner table just yet.

The now ex-manager and his meal-ticket pitcher had the same philosophy of life, which Satchel would one day articulate as "Don't look back. Something might be gaining on you." When the calendar turned to October, Paige still didn't rush to Pittsburgh to be with Janet. Instead, he embarked on another barnstorming tour with the Philadelphia Stars and rambunctious Dizzy Dean, dragging Quincy Troupe along as his catcher. When that traveling circus concluded, Troupe hurried home to his mother in Saint Louis and got a job as a store detective. He entered the national Golden Gloves competition in Rhode Island and—bad news for shoplifters—won the heavyweight division. Paige reunited with Janet, until he got antsy around Christmas and assembled the Satchel Paige All-Stars. It was winter ball time in California. Off he flew, free again.

On February 7, the Paige All-Stars took on a patchwork San Francisco–Oakland team that had some top minor league prospects. The blue chipper was a graceful twenty-one-year-old outfielder about to begin his rookie season with the New York Yankees: Joe DiMaggio. Paige lost that game 2–1 in the bottom of the tenth inning when a squib infield single by DiMaggio—an I-got-fooled swing if there ever was one—allowed a runner to prance home from third base. They don't make an uglier run batted in, but a Yankees scout perched in the stands swore he'd glimpsed the future of baseball. He wired the front office a short, ecstatic message: DIMAGGIO ALL WE HOPED HE'D BE: HIT SATCH ONE FOR FOUR.

A black sportswriter at the *Oakland Journal* wrote a piece about that barnstorm game and stirred a familiar pot: why on earth should a talent like Satchel Paige languish on the edge of obscurity? He also spread the annual rumor that some Major League clubs might be ready to grant tryouts to select black players. Another reporter brought that column to Paige's attention, asking if he saw any delicious irony at work: a youngster who'd just cost him a ball game with a Little League base hit was going to The Show while Ol' Satch was going nowhere. Paige wasn't as blasé about Jim Crow as he'd been in Omaha a few months ago. He believed fried foods "angry up the blood." Well, losing does too. "I'm probably drawin' more money right now than any other pitcher in baseball," he snapped. "Even if I did jump, I don't think those white boys from the South'd stand it. They got ahold of somethin' bitter when they were little and they ain't been able to relax and smile at the world since."

It probably wasn't DiMaggio who put him in a foul mood. It probably was the fact that Satchel Paige had gotten a taste of what the Major Leagues would be like without the color line. If only the rest of the baseball world would catch up to Bismarck, North Dakota. If only so many people hadn't got ahold of somethin' bitter.

20

"Plenty of Barn Room"

On July 15, 1936, Rebecca Churchill, pie maker supreme, succumbed to heart disease in Osceola, Wisconsin, at age seventy-five. Her son Neil had been making monthly visits since April, when she began to fail. Her obituary in the *Bismarck Tribune* said she passed away with "daughter" Becky at her side. That was airbrushed family history. Becky, now grown and married, was Rebecca's *grand*daughter and still one of Neil Churchill's best-kept secrets.

On July 24, Nancy Millett died. She was ninety-three years and twenty-one days old. "The faithful colored servant," as she was identified in her *Tribune* obituary, had come to Fort Abraham Lincoln from Kentucky with Lieutenant Colonel George Armstrong Custer in March 1873 and later earned frequent, favorable mention in Elizabeth Custer's best-selling memoir *Boots and Saddles*. Shortly after the Battle of the Little Bighorn she married an enlisted man from Maine. They settled in Bismarck and never left. Per her request, mourners sang "Rock of Ages" at the funeral. Pallbearers included Louis White, the man who rented rooms in his house to ballplayers Quincy Troupe and Red Haley. Such are the ties that bind disparate lives.

Millett had been a direct connection to frontier times, memories of which were fading fast in Bismarck. The summer of 1936 saw another chapter of state history drawing to a close. Though not officially dead, town baseball was terminally ill. On July 6 Valley City canceled a game scheduled the next evening with Bismarck. Citing difficulties in finding enough quality opponents "to keep solvent," the team abruptly disbanded and terminated the contracts of all paid players, black or white. That was only the latest domino to fall. The Cleveland Indians had stopped subsidizing the Devils Lake team, which quickly expired. Jamestown gave up semipro baseball in 1936 and turned its attention toward luring a Northern League franchise away from Grand Forks. The new "Jamestown Jimmies" were the St. Louis Cardinals' Class D affiliate. An expanding list of town teams that had once been competitive either reverted to casual baseball or threw in the towel: Dickinson, Mandan, Turtle Lake, Williston, Beulah, Minot, Washburn, Wilton, and now Valley City.

Rapidly becoming an anomaly in North Dakota, Bismarck took a brief hiatus during early July to consider its own future and viability. Neil Churchill had not been forthright with the Baseball Association in September 1935 when he came back from Wichita and said his team finished the year on an "almost even" financial keel. The team lost money. Exactly how much was hard to say. Churchill never discussed to what degree he was underwriting operations with his gambling winnings. However, that safety net disappeared once he gave up managing. The bottom line suffered accordingly. To help avert a Valley City–type crash, the Bismarck players volunteered to waive twelve days' pay, a noble gesture but not a long-term solution.

No one in uniform saw this coming. The season started on an optimistic note. The WPA had built a new concrete clubhouse at the Bismarck ballpark. A core group of players (Troupe, Morris, Smith, Haley, and Leary) returned for the first year of the post-Churchill era, while Double Duty Radcliffe moved on to try his hand at managing a semipro team in Arkansas and Moose Johnson found new bridges to burn with a minor league team in Albany, New York. Joe Desiderato had a spring tryout with the Chicago White Sox and signed a preliminary contract, but then begged off because Bismarck paid more money and offered more security. The "Cat" didn't want to risk getting cut adrift by the Sox during the Depression and not landing on his feet somewhere else. Dan Oberholzer decided to quit baseball and pursue his civil engineering degree. He was replaced by a familiar face: Harold Massmann, who in 1935 had played minor league ball in Indiana. That didn't work out to his liking, so he rejoined Bismarck. Massmann and his wife rented an apartment with the Desideratos for the 1936 season.

In April, Paige told new manager Babe Mohn that he, too, was back on board. The "Satchel watch" commenced. It ended in early May with the surprise revelation that he and Gus Greenlee had kissed and made up. Paige again would pitch for the Pittsburgh Crawfords; at $600 a month, more than double his old base salary. The *Pittsburgh Courier*, which vilified him for going to North Dakota, cheered Paige's return: "As spectacular as a circus and as colorful as a rainbow . . . He may prove to be the Moses who will help lead Negro baseball into the promised land of economic prosperity."

The Bismarck Baseball Association was searching for that same promised land and taking increasingly desperate measures to get there. In 1936 it sold tickets for seats *inside* the dugout ($25 for forty dates, although that many games never actually made it onto the schedule). The Association raised some capital by selling nonprofit stock in the Bismarck Baseball Club, Incorporated, for $50 a share. There was enough excitement in the air that eighteen merchants showed their support for the national champs by donating prizes to celebrate the new season. Vern Dresbach, owner of smoke-filled State Recreation Parlor, fittingly gave a carton of cigarettes to the first Bismarck batter issued a walk on Memorial Day. Behind the scenes nothing really changed. It was the same sad song that had been playing for half a century: a good baseball team costs money, and Bismarck didn't have enough.

Nothing close to happy days was here again. The *Bismarck Tribune* pointed which way the economy was blowing. Starved for advertising, it got noticeably thinner. Sports coverage was squeezed onto one page, a page that also had to make room for social news, crossword puzzles, and Jesus: for $1.98 plus three coupons clipped from the *Trib*, readers could buy a special leather-bound Bible with "Christ's sayings printed in red for immediate identification." Attendance at the ballpark continued its slide, cutting into revenue and further tightening the noose. The biggest crowd was on Booster Day in June, when only 800 people came out to boost. Fewer than 500 tickets were being sold for most games. The stadium could hold 3,000. The loss of Paige hurt. The weather also was hotter than it had been the previous summer, although that didn't seem possible. In addition, the collegiate-like rivalries waned as town baseball sputtered. Bismarck was forced to book games almost exclusively with traveling clubs, many of them second-rate. Barney Morris and Hilton Smith became a lethal one-two pitching punch and the team played well behind them, but they were beating up on palookas. Instead of Jamestown in its heyday, the Cincinnati Tigers or Detroit Colored Giants were taking the field. On Memorial Day weekend Bismarck played the Cleveland All-Nations, a shadow of its former self. Bismarck won 16–3, 16–0, and 9–1. Morris pitched two of those games and gave up a grand total of 4 hits while striking out 23. Only baseball sadists pay hard-earned cash to watch blowouts like that.

After Bismarck's July break, a group of citizens took out a full-page ad in the *Tribune* to promote an upcoming series with the Boston Royal Giants. They didn't mince words. "A team that will give 12 days' pay to aid in the continuation of baseball has the city's interests at heart and is deserving of a decided increase in attendance. If the town wants baseball to continue until Labor Day . . . your patronage will be the determining factor." Bismarck beaned Boston 4–2, 9–7, and 14–1, extending its season record to 35–7. Yet people didn't flock to see the Royal Giants or the next few victims that staggered into town. Fans, therefore, could forget about baseball on Labor Day. The culmination of the season would be a mid-August road trip. Hap Dumont invited Bismarck back to defend its title at the second National Baseball Congress tournament, and he was guaranteeing a top prize of $5,000. The team accepted his offer. They wanted to win again. They wanted to win so badly that Babe Mohn stepped back into his former role of assistant manager.

Neil Churchill was coming out of retirement to lead the charge in Wichita.

When President Franklin Roosevelt traveled to North Dakota in 1934, Churchill and his ball team missed their chance to see him. He'd stopped at Devils Lake while they were playing a game in Jamestown. The president came back in August 1936 and visited Bismarck. Churchill and his team missed him again. This time they were playing a tournament in Kansas.

Roosevelt arrived on his "Dustbowl Special" train. It being an election year, he felt the urge to press some flesh and spread some empathy, which required a car. His staff wanted to borrow a convertible but had difficulty finding one. Corwin-Churchill Motors rode to the rescue. Company salesman and longtime town ballplayer Bob McCarney, who'd finally hung up his glove, lent the president of the United States his canary-yellow Chrysler convertible. Corwin-Churchill employees washed, waxed, and polished that baby till it gleamed. Roosevelt climbed into the front passenger seat and led a forty-car motorcade through the streets of Bismarck and Mandan. An estimated 20,000 people lined the route to clap and wave or simply stare. At Mandan, the yellow Chrysler and a few trailing vehicles holding reporters and photographers broke off and drove seventeen miles north to inspect a WPA dam under construction at Otter Tail Creek. North Dakota was bone-dry. It would see just 8.8 inches of precipitation in 1936. In June Governor Walter Welford had declared a day of prayer specifically for rain. "Only Providence," he said, could help them now. But the drought dragged on and the federal government did what God couldn't do: it purchased from North Dakota ranchers a million head of cattle at $5 each before they starved or died of thirst.

A thick blanket of dust covered the roads leading to Otter Tail Creek. Nobody thought to put up the top on the president's car. When he got to the dam he looked like he'd been rolling on the ground. A dairyman, Louis Garske, was waiting there and got close enough to make an impassioned plea. "Give us water," he beseeched Roosevelt. "Let us have a little irrigation and we'll get along."

Nearly half the state was on relief now—another reason for those poor turnouts at Bismarck baseball games. On his way back to the Dustbowl Special, the president stopped to check on two embattled farm families. Roosevelt talked with Mike Hellman and his wife. There was no well on their property and the land was too arid to farm anymore. They raised some chickens and turkeys, but depended heavily upon a government check of $16 a month, about one-eighth the salary of the lowest-paid player on the Bismarck team. "It isn't enough," sighed Mrs. Hellman. They had six children to feed. The president sat in the Chrysler convertible making awkward small talk with the couple. "They're good assets," he said, nodding toward the chickens. "Hold on to them. Good luck!"

At the second farm the president asked Jake Boehm how his wheat crop was faring. "Not a grain," Boehm muttered. He and his wife tried planting a patch of vegetables just for their personal use, but the drought sucked the life out of it. "There's the *garden*," he said ruefully, waving a hand. "Full of weeds." A gifted orator, Franklin Roosevelt struggled to find words of comfort, groped for some silver lining that these strained souls could believe in. He came up dry, like the Boehms' garden. "Well, anyway," he finally said, perhaps too cheerily, "you've got plenty of barn room if only you had something to put in it!"

That was a perfectly dumb thing to say, but the president was an easterner and he meant well. He also wasn't too far off the mark in capturing the cruel predicament that bedeviled so many North Dakotans still waiting for better days to come: no rain, but lots of parched, tillable earth to absorb it; no bountiful harvest, but plenty of empty barns in which to store it. As Roosevelt's car pulled away, he called back to the Boehms and their barefoot son, "You'll be all right!"

Once again Wichita offered no escape from the North Dakota heat. In fact, it made Bismarck seem balmy. The city's six hottest days in the last forty-eight years—low, 109 degrees; high, 112—occurred between July 15 and August 10. Weather understandably was a popular topic of conversation. So was the racial climate. The Summer Olympics in Berlin captivated the world as Jesse Owens rained on Adolf Hitler's Aryan superiority parade. Right before the start of the National tournament, Owens captured the last of his four gold medals, in the 4 × 100 relay. In a controversial move, the coach of the U.S. team scratched two white runners (both Jewish) from the race, replacing them with Owens and Ralph Metcalfe, both of whom were black and had finished first and second in the individual 100 meter sprint. That reconstituted relay team burned the rest of the field. They also set a world record, but violated Pete Lightner's strange code of sportsmanship. As he explained in the *Wichita Eagle*, "This column has felt that it is better to give all the boys a chance than to try for records." By "all the boys" he seemed to be implying *white* boys. His mind was still coming to grips with a potentially brave new world of ethnic equality. In another column that August, Lightner mentioned the Brooklyn Dodgers recently drew 14,000 fans on a Sunday afternoon and, on the same day, the semipro Brooklyn Bushwicks attracted a comparable crowd for a doubleheader with Satchel Paige and the Pittsburgh Crawfords. Those numbers prompted New York Giants owner Horace Stoneham to declare that professional baseball would see the light and desegregate within ten years. "Will the majors, through the example set by the Olympic games, drop the colored players ban?" Lightner asked his *Eagle* readers. "Certainly the magnates are doing some thinking."

A few days later he reported that Frank Kice, Hap Dumont's second in command, met for two hours in Saint Louis with Cardinals' vice president, Branch Rickey. The specifics of what they discussed were not made public. However, it would stretch credulity for Rickey not to have inquired about Dumont's hosting a mixed-race baseball tournament or about Bismarck's experience signing Paige and other black players. Rickey was a devout Methodist, so devout that he refused to attend ball games on Sunday. He'd long ago quietly pledged to help end segregation in the big leagues if ever given the power to do so. Just such an opportunity would present itself in 1943, when he took over front-office operations for the Brooklyn Dodgers, whose owners eventually bought into Rickey's heretical idea of offering a contract to Jackie Robinson.

Those developments were still years away when Neil Churchill and his team drove into Wichita seeking to repeat as semipro champions. During the season there had been some lineup changes. Foremost, a new shortstop had been brought in, bumping Al Leary over to first base. This let Red Haley move from first to left field, thereby filling the void created by Moose Johnson's unceremonious departure. Also, just as he'd done in 1935, Churchill beefed up the roster for Wichita by adding four Negro League veterans. Double Duty Radcliffe hustled over from Arkansas to bolster the catching and pitching corps, but the important pickup was Ted Trent, a pitcher for the Chicago American Giants who came with an assortment of breaking balls and a warning label: like Johnson, he'd had battles with booze and lost his share.

Hap Dumont had made some changes, too. Honus Wagner gave them his stamp of approval, saying that the National Baseball Congress was "the greatest step forward baseball has taken in the last 20 years." Dumont had begun putting in place a network of state and regional qualifying tournaments, with the winners graduating to the National in Wichita. That served to expand his semipro empire by mandating the use of NBC-sanctioned equipment and rule books. He was able to require thousands of players and umpires to pay for annual NBC memberships. Wagner toured the country for a month talking up the National. Tris Speaker, another retired ballplayer seemingly beamed down from Mount Olympus (.345 batting average during twenty-two years as a Major League outfielder; reputation slightly soiled by ties to the Ku Klux Klan during his Texas youth) made promotional appearances in Ohio and Kansas. Qualifying tournaments also were a convenient way for Dumont to punt on the race issue. While personally in favor of open baseball, he couldn't expand his business by alienating those who were adamantly opposed. Let the decision regarding whether black and white teams should compete head-on get hashed out at the local level, leaving National officials in Wichita with clean hands. As for the more vexing question of what to do with mixed-race teams, that was a situation unique to Bismarck, North Dakota. No other integrated teams were knocking on the door. Anywhere. How often would Churchill and his merry men want to keep making the trek to Kansas? Stall. Buy time. Wait them out. This too shall pass.

It would take about five years for the effects of Dumont's states'-rights approach to be fully realized and for the National to turn into a whites-only affair. The phasing out began in 1936. Three black entries from Denver, Phoenix, and Mound City, Illinois, managed to make the thirty-two-team draw: three black entries, plus oddball Bismarck. Defending champions usually are a focal point of publicity and hype. Not so with Bismarck. None of the Wichita papers published photos of those players or any quotes from them, although the *Eagle* did review the relevant math: "Bismarck is a mixed team composed of 11 negro and 5 white players." The champs were treated with benign neglect. The pretournament darlings were a couple teams returning from Oklahoma: the Eason Oilers and Erle Halliburton's Duncan Cementers.

Churchill had injuries to worry about. Morris had a swollen knee, Desiderato a leg infection, and Leary was favoring a strained groin. On a positive note, Hilton Smith, the team's Caspar Milquetoast, stepped out of character and told Churchill he was going to win four games, matching Satchel Paige's total from the year before. He got off on the right foot with a two-hitter, stopping the all-black Denver White Elephants cold, 14–0. Bismarck's second game sounded an alarm bell. The Eason Oilers handed Bismarck its first National defeat, an 8–2 smack-down. Bismarck committed an unconscionable eight errors, Trent lasted only five innings, and Radcliffe fractured a finger on a foul tip. The sole redeeming moment came when Quincy Troupe murdered a fat pitch, muscling it deep over the right field wall for what Lawrence Stadium habitués said was one of the longest home runs ever hit in Wichita. But a black man couldn't get his face in the newspaper even if he hit a home run that landed in New Mexico. The photo that appeared the next day showed Troupe's back as he crossed home plate.

What Churchill saw from the dugout was a very capable Bismarck team that looked as if it hadn't been tested all season, which was true. The players weren't tournament-tough and they seemed to be less than the sum of their parts—not too shocking since half the players hadn't made the trip to Wichita in 1935. Hitting and pitching weren't a problem. Base running and fielding were, perhaps a sign that manager Babe Mohn hadn't stressed fundamentals during the season as much as nitpicker Neil Churchill. Yet Troupe and his teammates rebounded nicely from that loss to Eason. They won their next four games by scores of 7–0, 10–0, 10–1, and 8–5. Pete Lightner, applying his uniquely convoluted logic, saw good things ahead for them. "Bismarck is the best fixed club in the tourney right now on pitching," he wrote. "Those colored boys seem to stand the hot weather better." Shortly after the Eason game, Churchill pegged his team's odds of winning the tournament at one in ten, maybe one in five if everything broke their way. He revised his expectations after that four-game winning streak propelled Bismarck into the semifinals. He fired off a telegram to editors at the *Tribune*, asking them to pass a message along to his eight-year-old son, Neil: WE ARE GOING IN TOMORROW NIGHT TO WIN OUT. CALL MY BOY. TELL HIM WE WILL BRING HOME THE BACON FOR HIM.

Their semifinal opponent wanted that bacon too. Bismarck was scheduled to play the Duncan Cementers.

These were the New Look Cementers. They had three different position players and an overhauled pitching staff. Their current ace, another Texas League émigré, needed rest, so left-hander Jimmy Walkup lobbied hard for the Bismarck start and got it. At thirty-nine, Walkup was an old cowhand. He had won 144 minor league games, most of them in the Western Association. Hilton Smith, who'd already won four games as promised, would throw for Bismarck in the finals, if necessary. It was Ted Trent's job to get them there. Bismarckers weren't buying many tickets to baseball games, but they were following the team in force from afar. A second billiard hall had set up a Western Union feed from Wichita. Meanwhile, the crowd at State Recreation Parlor spilled into the lobby of the Grand Pacific Hotel and onto the sidewalk. Dayton Shipley was back reading hot-off-the-wire updates. Fans didn't like what he had to say about the first inning of the Duncan semifinal.

Harold Massmann, who was having a torrid tournament at bat, led off the game on an ominous note. He singled and immediately got picked off first base. That was it for a Bismarck rally. In the bottom of the inning the Cementers nicked Trent for a pair of runs on three soft singles and a walk. Double Duty Radcliffe suspected Trent had taken a few belts of liquor before the game. If so, he should have passed the bottle around. He pitched fine. His teammates played drunk. In the fourth inning, Massmann singled again and Troupe drove him home with a well-placed line drive. Down 2–1 in the fifth inning, Bismarck bungled a golden opportunity. Red Haley and new center fielder Johnnie Lyles lined back-to-back singles with nobody out. New shortstop Steve Slefka fouled off a bunt attempt. He tried bunting a second time and missed, watching in horror as Haley and Lyles attempted a mistimed double steal. *Both* of them got thrown out. Slefka then singled with two strikes, only to get picked off first base. Three hits and no runs to show for it. Churchill, who never bet against his team, must have had visions of winged dollar bills flying out of his wallet. Duncan scored a run in the bottom of the fifth on a walk and a double, extending its lead to 3–1. In the bottom of the seventh inning Duncan got to Ted Trent for three singles, one of which Lyles booted in center field for extra bases. Hilton Smith dropped a fly ball in deep right field. It was death-watch quiet at State Recreation when Shipley spoke the painful words "Three runs, three hits, two errors."

Bismarck went down swinging, scoring once in the ninth inning. The final score was 6–2, a bitter loss, since the Cementers benefited from four unearned runs. The next night they beat Buford, Georgia, 4–1 and were crowned 1936 National Baseball Congress champions. Erle Halliburton and the town of Duncan rejoiced. When the team got back to company headquarters from Wichita, the local paper reported, work was halted for an hour "while employees oohed and aahed at the trophy."

Hap Dumont had wanted the third- and fourth-place finishers to meet in a consolation game right before the Duncan-Buford finale. Bismarck declined and left Wichita that morning. Neil Churchill talked to a *Tribune* reporter a few days after arriving home. He was not "making alibis," he said, but proceeded to vent his frustration. The National struck him as too much of a one-man show, especially with regard to scheduling. Instead of devising a master bracket and sticking to it, Dumont reseeded surviving teams after each round of play, guided by instinct or whim. That jiggering might have served the arguably constructive purpose of keeping black teams and southern teams apart, thus avoiding potentially sticky confrontations. However, some of the manipulation seemed less well intentioned. It was odd, for instance, to have the returning champion, Bismarck, paired in the second round with the favored Eason Oilers. Why? Because brackets generally are designed to keep the better teams from meeting too early in tournament play. Churchill also questioned the umpiring in Bismarck's semifinal game against the Duncan Cementers. That was unlike him, but he felt his players had been confused on the base paths by Jimmy Walkup's pitching motion, "a semi-balk delivery that I know wouldn't be allowed in league games."

Churchill did not allege any impropriety, but his comments had the whiff of suspicion. Had Hap Dumont conspired behind the scenes to try to get Bismarck knocked out of the National? Would it have been a public relations disaster to have an integrated team win the championship twice in a row? Dumont continued to get blowback for staging a tournament that jumped the racial divide. The 1936 National was marred by an incident that came close to spinning out of control. It occurred in a game between a white team from Franklin, Massachusetts, and the black Phoenix Broncos. Franklin's second baseman thought he'd been deliberately spiked by a Broncos runner. Those two players got into a fight. Fans charged out of the stands, as they had during an equally tense moment at the 1935 tournament. Another near-riot was quelled, but this time a *Wichita Eagle* photographer took what was described in the next morning's paper as "a hot action photo" of black men and white men squaring off on the infield grass.

Such doings had Pete Lightner fretting (again) about "the perplexing problem of mixed races." Although he seemed to occasionally beat the drum for what could be construed as those good ol' plantation days, to his credit Lightner printed verbatim a long letter he'd received from a baseball fan. He considered it "worth reading" by a mass audience. D. M. Osborne wrote to say he'd been impressed during the National by Quincy Troupe's comportment as much as his ability. Osborne saw Troupe come to bat during the Bismarck-Duncan game in a key situation and work the count to two balls, two strikes. On the next pitch he was guessing fastball. Jimmy Walkup fooled him with a curve that caught a sliver of the plate. The ump called strike three. Troupe grimaced and walked back to the dugout. No lip. No theatrics. Sitting in the stands at another game, Osborne watched Troupe get "beaned accidentally" and trot to first base with a smile on his face. "Troupe is a good enough ball player that one might expect him to be a bit temperamental," his letter concluded. "But he isn't and when a man is a credit to the game, whether he is black, white, green, pink or what have you, we just can't resist speaking up for him."

Most likely Quincy Troupe never saw that letter. It was published after he left town. He had been more than just a good sport, though. He hit .400 (landing in the top five for tournament batting average, along with Leary and Massmann) and made the all-star team for the second consecutive year. On the day of their departure from Wichita, Troupe and Hilton Smith swung by the Hotel Broadview, where the white coaches and white players were staying. They needed to drop off their Bismarck uniforms and collect their final paychecks from Churchill. In the posh lobby—lit by crystal chandeliers that looked like large inverted umbrellas—they bumped into Hap Dumont. He pulled them aside. "Boys," he half-whispered, "I was talking to a couple of scouts yesterday at the park. What do you suppose one of them said to me?"

Tight-lipped Hilton Smith certainly wasn't going to play along, but Troupe did. "What, Mr. Dumont? Are they interested in signing someone off our club?"

Dumont lowered his voice even further. Matter of fact, yes, he said. One scout was very interested and very willing to pay big money. "For you two boys—if you were *white!*"

"Well, sir," Troupe replied, "we're available right now." A long pause followed. They all knew availability wasn't the issue.

"Sorry, fellows," Dumont said softly. "I just thought you might like to know what the scouts think of you as ballplayers." That was his way of saying Troupe and Smith had plenty of barn room, but nothing to put in it. The little man turned and walked away, heels clicking on the hotel's marble floor, straw hat bobbing on his head. The sound of footsteps quickly died away and the white hat disappeared from view. Hope was gone too.

Three years earlier, at the Crawford Grill in Pittsburgh, Satchel Paige had told a young, moonfaced catcher "You can go a long way in this game." Now Troupe understood in his bones that you can go a long way, but get only so far. He could hit, he could catch, and he could throw. Better than most. But he couldn't be white. Al Leary and Bismarck's new shortstop Steve Slefka got signed to professional contracts in Wichita, by the Boston Red Sox and St. Louis Browns. Troupe went home to Saint Louis and got a job as a salesman for a milk distributor.

When winter melted into spring, he didn't pick up his glove and bat. The love of his life kept breaking his heart. So he decided to stop pursuing her. At the tender age of twenty-five, Quincy Troupe turned his back on baseball and walked away.

21

ENDINGS

"There's hell and there's Dakota. If I owned them both, I'd live in hell and rent out Dakota." So said Lieutenant Colonel Daniel Huston, who in 1872 supervised construction of Fort Lincoln, the military post that sat downriver from Bismarck. The winter of 1936 lent credence to his jaundiced opinion. Months of record heat were followed by months of record cold. The temperature dropped below zero and remained there for forty-two straight days. When at last spring unfolded, town baseball did not bloom in full color and glory. The Bismarck Baseball Association dropped the hammer for good, deciding that the only way to address a large, accelerating deficit was to get back to keep-it-simple basics and stay there. Every semipro got pink-slipped except Red Haley, who was retained as player-manager of the all-new, all-amateur Bismarck Independents. He had the unenviable task of molding a bunch of untested unknowns (one of them a second baseman right out of high school) into a credible team.

The molding did not go well. By the end of July 1937 the Independents had disappeared from the sports pages. In 1938 Haley drifted north to manage the Acme Colored Giants, a black touring team that had been planted for years in Shreveport, Louisiana, but—in another sign of the upheaval in semipro baseball—had recently taken up summer residence in Dunseith, a Dakota town of less than 700 people near the Canadian border. Glenn Vantine, owner of a paint store in downtown Bismarck, picked up the sputtering torch and organized a do-it-yourself town team. The Vantine Cubs opened the season against Fort Lincoln on a Sunday in May. The result (Cubbies romped, 15–3) appeared in Thursday's paper, testimony of the depths to which public indifference had sunk. The Cubs dissolved in 1939, and a team sponsored by the Fraternal Order of the Eagles (Neil Churchill, charter member) took their place. A season ticket to Eagles' home games cost just $1, but there weren't many buyers. A *Tribune* editorial remarked with gracious understatement, "Baseball—amateur baseball, at least—hasn't proved much of a drawing card here of late."

The drawing card known as Satchel Paige was out of sight, but not out of mind or out of print. The Bismarck press covered all his loop-the-loop peregrinations. He began 1936 with the Pittsburgh Crawfords, wandered off with a team of northern California all-stars for a month, came back to the Crawfords, and afterward did a black-versus-white winter barnstorming tour with some Negro League and Major League players. When spring 1937 dawned, Gus Greenlee once again was in money trouble. Paige didn't hang around waiting for a pay cut. The *Bismarck Tribune* reported that he dashed off "to Cuba" for a few extra pesos. Not quite. He was bound for the Dominican Republic.

Baseball and politics made strange bedfellows in the Dominican Republic. Rafael Trujillo, the dictatorial *presidente*, was titular head of Los Dragones, a ball club in the capital city, Santo Domingo. There were only two other professional teams in the country, but dictators don't like to lose at anything. An intermediary for Trujillo traveled to New Orleans, where the Crawfords were holding spring training. He carried a suitcase stuffed with $30,000 in cash, which he offered to Paige in exchange for packing the Dragones with ballplayer buddies. Deal! Satchel sold a dozen Negro League veterans on the idea of going to the Caribbean. For leading that jail break, the Negro National League banned Paige a second time. He pitched Los Dragones to the 1937 Dominican national championship, but Trujillo ran into the same problem that stymied Gus

Greenlee and the Bismarck Baseball Association. He overspent himself into a hole. So did the Dragones' competitors. Hiring expat players broke the bank. There would be no organized baseball in the Dominican Republic for the next twelve years.

Paige returned to the United States. The Negro National League made peace with him, mainly because cash-strapped Gus Greenlee wanted to hold a Crawfords fire sale and his biggest asset was his headline-grabbing pitcher, whom he shipped off to the Brooklyn Eagles for the 1938 season. Paige stayed a few months, but the Eagles made the mistake of not confiscating his passport. A representative of a team in Mexico City called and whispered "$2,000 a month" in his ear. Satchel immediately headed south of the border. The Negro National League took umbrage again and banned him "for life." Maybe Paige ran out of rejuvenating Sioux snake oil in Mexico. The unthinkable happened: his right arm gave out. Mexican fans booed him and his pathetic fastballs unmercifully. Some screamed racial slurs. He pitched until the pain got so bad he couldn't lift his arm. Then he hightailed it back to Pittsburgh in despair and disgrace.

Rather than go home to Janet, where he belonged, Paige hunkered down in a rooming house. Word soon got around that Satch was done, invincible no more. *Finito!* Low on money and with no pitching prospects on the horizon, he pawned clothes and fishing rods to pay the bills. He sat in that flophouse for days, sickened by the thought of his ignominious fall to earth. "Ten years of gravy," Paige would later write, "and then nothing but an aching arm and aching stomach."

Neil Churchill gave up managing, but not baseball. When the curtain came down on Bismarck's semipro days, he kept his hand in the game by doing a little sports promoting on the side. He teamed up with Abe Saperstein and with J. L. Wilkinson about half a dozen times, bringing black touring teams to town to play each

other. The Kansas City Monarchs, Chicago American Giants, Atlantic City Bacharachs, and Zulu Cannibal Giants (dressed in grass
skirts) made exhibition appearances. Saperstein urged Churchill
to switch careers and come work with him in Chicago. Helen
vetoed that idea.

Why uproot? Despite the Depression, Corwin-Churchill
Motors cemented its standing as the largest Chrysler-Plymouth
dealer west of Minneapolis and east of Spokane. Business was
healthy enough to justify an expansion to Fargo. Wick Corwin
relocated there while Churchill stayed behind. He had everything
he wanted in Bismarck, most of the time at his fingertips. When the
Fraternal Order of the Eagles formed in 1936 (with golden-throated
Dayton Shipley as president), they rented a building on 2nd Street
directly across from Churchill's office. According to the talk around
town, that was no accident. Church supposedly helped launch the
Eagles so he'd have a convenient place to court Lady Luck. Bismarck
authorities turned a blind eye to service organizations when it came to
gaming laws. The lower level of the Eagles club had a false wall, behind which could be found slot machines, gambling tables, and, on occasion, the chief of police relaxing in his off-hours. The Eagles called
their hidden casino "Glitter Gulch." Churchill's appetite for risk was
such that he patronized the Eagles club and still regularly attended
those marathon poker sessions at the Patterson Hotel. The latter
venue wasn't as secretive or secure as Glitter Gulch, but that didn't
make him any more cautious in his betting. Late one night, Churchill
mumbled to his tablemates at the Patterson, "I have everything in
this pot but my house. If I threw that in, my wife would kill me."

The extent of his poker habit wasn't all he kept from Helen.
On the morning of February 17, 1939, she glanced at the front page
of the *Tribune* and promptly telephoned her husband at work. "Are
you crazy?" she exclaimed. "I just read in the paper you're going
to run for *mayor*?"

"If you read it in the paper," he replied sheepishly, "it must
be true."

It was. Six months earlier Mayor Obert Olson had died of heart failure. Friends spent hours leaning on Neil Churchill to enter the race to fill Olson's unexpired term. He acquiesced. Although a registered Republican, he campaigned without party affiliation under the apolitical slogan "I am going to bat for Bismarck," vowing that the city "must ever remain the metropolis of Western North Dakota." Apparently lots of people had fond memories of that 1935 championship baseball team. Church won in a landslide, doubling the vote total of his two mayoral opponents put together. About the only concession he made upon stepping into public life was to do more gambling at home. When the Churchills moved into a larger house on the west side of town (with room for *two* live-in maids), they had part of the basement converted into a "whoopee room" outfitted with a pool table and jukebox; the perfect hideaway for poker bums. When Neil and the boys commandeered the whoopee room for a long night of card playing, Helen did what any good midwestern wife would do: plied them with tuna casserole.

Being mayor of Bismarck wasn't a purely ceremonial position, but, on the other hand, nobody ever cracked under the pressure of holding that office. Neil Churchill presided over the installation of the first traffic light in town in November 1939. He issued proclamations designating carnation sales day for the United Spanish War Veterans Auxiliary. In October 1941 he was everywhere during the State Corn Festival. Mayor Churchill crowned Mabel Stockhand "Maize Princess," participated in the hog-calling contest, and helped calm fears after the popcorn giveaway backfired. The *Tribune* reported a "near-riot" on Wednesday night when "the city's juvenile population stormed the free popcorn stand and prevented the distribution of popcorn to adults." The Bismarck police were called in. The festival continued without further mayhem, thanks to a one-bag-per-child limit imposed by officers stationed at the popcorn machine.

Two months later Churchill gave the signal to illuminate the downtown Christmas display. The next day Japanese airplanes bombed and strafed Pearl Harbor. "U.S. AT WAR" the *Tribune* headline shouted. Volunteers from American Legion posts in Bismarck and Mandan shouldered rifles and patrolled the twin bridges spanning the Missouri River, eyes peeled for saboteurs or submarines. Churchill would remain mayor for the duration of the war, reelected in 1942 and serving through 1946. He chaired bond drives and expressed condolences to the families of Bismarck men who went off to fight and came back in flag-draped coffins.

World War II ignited the economy and dragged most of the country out of hard times. The *Bismarck Tribune* won a Pulitzer Prize in 1938 for a series of articles about citizens and bureaucrats coping with the Depression, but North Dakota would never completely rebound. The federal government pumped hundreds of millions of dollars into relief programs (voters still turned their backs on Franklin Roosevelt, going solidly Republican in the 1940 and 1944 presidential elections), yet one third of family farms went into foreclosure between 1930 and 1944. Town baseball and semi-pro baseball were cultural casualties of the war. Returning veterans got seduced by television, softball, and the restlessness of a newly mobile society. They left their hometowns and their home state, following the tire tracks of farm refugees who'd gone elsewhere to start over and plant anew. North Dakota got permanently stuck in neutral; any subsequent growth was offset by the steady drip of out-migration. In 2011 the estimated population of 683,000 was virtually unchanged from the 1930 Census.

Helen and Neil Churchill were part of that exodus. In September 1952, Church cashed out and sold his interest in Corwin-Churchill Motors. He was sixty-one years old and precariously overweight, no match for the Great Plains' wicked winters. The Churchills retired to Los Angeles. The *Tribune* waved good-bye with an editorial entitled "Neil Churchill Leaves Town." At the peak of his civic involvement, Churchill had sat on thirty-one committees and attended as many as eighteen nighttime meetings a week. "Men who will devote their time and energy to public activities are vitally important to a community's progress," said the *Tribune*. "What he has today he won for himself, in the time-honored American tradition of the poor-boy-makes-good."

Wick Corwin didn't want to see his partner gamble away a nest egg and wind up dirt-poor again. The buyout was structured in such a way that Churchill received a monthly stipend rather than a lump-sum payment. That was prudent planning, but it's impossible to completely protect a man from himself. Two powerful forces were pulling Neil Churchill west to California: mild weather and year-round horse racing.

22

DEEP SMOKE WINDING

The Chicago chapter of the Baseball Writers Association of America held its tenth annual "Diamond Dinner" on January 22, 1950, at the tony Palmer House hotel. Ray Dumont was among the 800 people in attendance, there to present an award to Major League Commissioner Albert "Happy" Chandler in appreciation of his support for amateur baseball. By coincidence, in the early 1940s the Palmer House employees' team had been one of the last all-black entries in Dumont's National semipro tournament.

Some observant sportswriters at the dinner spotted vaguely familiar faces across the room, not seated at tables, but hovering over them. Five waiters in starched shirts and ties turned out to be veterans of the Negro Leagues, among them Roosevelt Davis, the first black player brought to Bismarck by Neil Churchill in 1933, the scuffed-ball maestro who treated his thinning hair with mange medicine. Davis last pitched for the Negro National League's Philadelphia Stars in 1945. Now in his mid-forties (and balding), he carried serving trays for a living. Ballplayers die twice: when they leave this mortal coil and when they retire from competitive sports. The latter tends to be the more agonizing transition, but eventually every athlete must cross the river and stand blinking and unsteady on that strange opposite shore known as The Rest of Your Life. Roosevelt Davis had plenty of company.

Affable and versatile Granville "Red" Haley probably played integrated baseball in North Dakota longer than any black man.

He arrived in 1932 and stayed until 1938, based in Bismarck five of those years. After that, he ducked across the Canadian border and put in two more seasons of semipro ball with the Southwest Saskatchewan League. That was it. At forty he moved in with his mother in Sandusky, Ohio, and got a job operating a crane for Farrell-Cheek Steel. He managed the company's black baseball team. When his legs could no longer dance around second base, he gave up hardball and managed a black softball team. "Very sociable," says his sister-in-law Dorothy Farrar. "Everybody in town knew Gran." Everybody but the sports editor of the *Sandusky-Register*. Satchel Paige was spotted in town in September 1948 and the paper pinned him down for an interview, reporting that he'd come to Sandusky to visit "his long-time friend, Randall Haley."

Like Red Haley, Barney Morris, that hard-to-come-by pitcher who combined a good knuckler with a crisp fastball, stayed in North Dakota after the team disintegrated. His wife, Betty, worked as a cook at the Elgin Cafe in Bismarck while he ricocheted among teams in the United States and abroad: the Pittsburgh Crawfords; Cienfuegos of the Cuban Winter League; two teams in Monterrey, Mexico. When last heard from, Morris was driving a cab in Queens, New York.

His baseball travels paled in comparison with Chet Brewer's. "Dooflackem" was the postseason insurance policy addition to Neil Churchill's 1935 roster who nicely complemented Satchel Paige by winning three games in Wichita. Brewer spent the bulk of a twenty-four-year pitching career with the Kansas City Monarchs. His 87–63 win-loss record in the Negro Leagues would have been much better had he not had such itchy feet. In 1937 Brewer was part of the invasion that Paige led in the Dominican Republic. In 1938 he broke the color line in Mexico. He also pitched in the Philippines, Panama, Hawaii, Cuba, Puerto Rico, Canada, Japan, and China, plus forty-four of what were then the forty-eight states. In 1945 the still segregated Major Leagues remained off-limits to Brewer, who reacted with appropriate consternation when the St. Louis

Browns signed one-armed white outfielder Pete Gray. "Shoot," he said, "the only thing a one-armed man could do as good as a two-armed man is scratch the side that itches!" Chet Brewer made it across the American baseball color line in 1952, but only at the minor league level. At the ripe old age of forty-five, he pitched a few games as player-manager of the Porterville, California, Comets of the Southwest International League. He later scouted nearly twenty years for the Pittsburgh Pirates. As part of that job Brewer developed a youth baseball program in the Watts section of Los Angeles, where today a ball field bears his name.

Joe Desiderato had trouble crossing a different kind of line. His was the last name you'd expect to pop up on a blacklist. Yet he firmly believed Baseball Commissioner Kenesaw Mountain Landis banned him in 1936 for renegging on a contract with the Chicago White Sox and returning to Bismarck. That allegation was impossible to prove, but four months after Landis died in November 1944, the Cleveland Indians signed Desiderato as a free agent. The lightning-fast reflexes were gone. He turned thirty-five during spring training and got dumped by the Indians in May without appearing in a major or minor league game. His cup wasn't empty, though. He continued as a semipro third baseman until he was forty, playing mostly with the Lafayette Red Sox of the Michigan-Indiana League.

"The Cat" never left Cabrini-Green, his childhood neighborhood in Chicago, not even when the streets got too mean to walk at night. He and his wife, Marie, raised two daughters on his machinist's salary at Chicago Screw Company, a job made for an unassuming, nuts-and-bolts man. One of the girls married Joe DiMaggio: not the Yankees' center fielder but Joe DiMaggio the fireman who was stationed at the engine house on Waveland Avenue just beyond the left field wall at Wrigley Field. Desiderato came from an extended family of warring White Sox and Cubs fans. He bled Cubs' blue. Terry Sullivan, a retired high school coach who scouts for the Boston Red Sox, learned a lot of baseball from his uncle Joe. "He loved sitting in the outfield bleachers, watching guys who couldn't shine his shoes," says Sullivan. "He would often critique Cubs players as guys who 'couldn't have played' when *he* was playing. Even though that sounds like a generational complaint, I'm sure it was accurate."

Whereas Joe Desiderato was the simplest of men, nobody ever solved the riddle of Moose Johnson, least of all Moose Johnson. But he sidestepped the tragic ending that appeared to be his destiny. After getting the heave-ho by Neil Churchill for showing up hungover at the National, he tested the patience of three minor league teams in 1936 and then slid back to semipro ball in Mount Pleasant, Texas, in 1937. That team went to the National tournament and Johnson scorched the ball in Wichita that summer, leading all batters with a .571 average. A scout commented that he was one of the best hitters in all of baseball: majors, minors, semipro, sandlot, parking lot. Anywhere. "If he would just behave himself and take the game a little seriously," Pete Lightner wrote in the *Wichita Eagle*. Moose Johnson probably couldn't take hand-to-hand combat seriously, but the next year he worked his way back to the minor leagues and had cups of coffee with four different teams.

In all, he flopped around the minors for eleven seasons and 911 games with some twenty teams from D to A level, hitting .311 in 3,368 at bats despite serial hangovers. Through those ups and downs, he had his first marriage annulled; married his second wife, Lizzy (whom he met during a fling with the Anniston, Alabama, Rams); divorced Lizzy, remarried her, and found what for Moose constituted a kind of impure bliss. He never stopped drinking to extremes. Never stopped gambling to excess. Never wore the straitjacket of a nine-to-five routine after leaving baseball. He put down his bat in 1944 and picked up an ax. From early spring to late fall he'd swing at trees in the quiet, uncomplicated forests of Yellowstone, Montana. The laughing lumberjack. "He was his own worst enemy. My dad was a genius with unfulfilled potential," says his daughter, Hilma Jones. "He never bragged on himself. He loved the game and stayed a baseball fan his whole life. He tried to be sober, but I guess he never got any help like they have now for alcoholics. He had good intentions and a good heart, but just made poor choices."

Family and friends still talk about how Moose sent Lizzy flowers almost every day after their divorce until she took him back; about his paychecks that vaporized in Las Vegas; about those click-of-the-ivories, pool-shooting exhibitions he'd put on at the Smoke House bar in Anniston; about the time he got drunk in Minneapolis and took a taxi three hundred miles home to Crystal Falls, Michigan. "A happy, happy guy. He could hit the ball and drink," says his nephew Donald Johnson. "He was our Mickey Mantle."

Two players from the 1935 Bismarck team went to war. Bob McCarney, who lent his Chrysler convertible to President Roosevelt, entered the army in 1942 and saw action in North Africa and Italy. Captain McCarney came home and opened a Ford dealership that made him a friendly competitor of his ex-boss and ex-manager, Neil Churchill. "Mac" served as president of the Bismarck Chamber of Commerce and fashioned himself into one of North Dakota's most colorful political gadflies. A fiscal hawk, he was responsible for some fifteen statewide tax or spending referenda. McCarney didn't stop there. He ran unsuccessfully for governor three times and the U.S. Senate twice.

Al Leary went from Bismarck to the minor leagues and no further. He hit well, but couldn't progress beyond Class B, the equivalent of AA ball today. After the 1940 season he got married and moved back to his native Montana, content to play semipro ball and drive a truck for Great Falls Brewery. In October 1943 he enlisted in the marines. Leary was thirty-four and had a ninth-grade education. Asked on his induction papers to describe "the jobs or enterprises in which you exercised the greatest authority or leadership," he wrote "manager baseball teams."

They stuck him in a tank.

On June 15, 1944, American forces invaded Japanese-held Saipan. They gained control of the island after three weeks of vicious fighting, but at an awful price: 3,100 dead, more than 13,000 wounded. Private Leary's tank took heavy fire the first day. One tank mate was killed, another's legs were blown off. Shrapnel bit into Leary's left shoulder and left flank. Those wounds healed, but depression, insomnia, and fits of stuttering lingered. Military doctors diagnosed "combat fatigue" and transferred him to light duty stateside. Upon being discharged in April 1945, he sought comfort in the familiar. Al Leary became player-manager of the semipro Great Falls Selectmen. His nerves were frayed, but he could still hit. "One of the strongest sluggers in Montana," the *Helena Independent-Record* said in 1946. "Leary has been known to break up more than one game with his clutch clouting." He also returned to his old job, driving a beer truck for Great Falls Brewery until it closed in 1968.

Ted Trent, the rent-a-pitcher who had a rocky Wichita tournament for Bismarck in 1936, was an early casualty of hard living. The four-time Negro League all-star threw his final pitch in 1939 and died five years later at age forty, ravaged by tuberculosis and a long-running battle with alcohol. The more privileged in society are not immune to calamity. Pete Lightner, the *Wichita Eagle* sports columnist who grappled with the complexities of integration at Hap Dumont's tournament, perished in a plane crash on the Fourth of July 1960. He was returning from the U.S. Summer Olympic trials in Palo Alto, California. The topic of race had stuck with him. In a column that ran the day before he died—as fate would have it, his parting words to *Eagle* readers—Lightner considered the composition of the Olympic team, just as he had done with semipro baseball teams twenty-five years earlier: "The Negro boys hold pretty much to winning medals in the hurdles and are great jumpers, broad as well as high. Another event the colored boys are going to go after for their own is the hop, skip, and jump. Of the total Olympic team, the Caucasians predominated, with about two-thirds of the total, due to their high superiority in weights, vault and longer runs."

In an ironic coda to the Depression, Lorena Hickok, the brassy newspaperwoman who went to work for the Roosevelt administration and filed heart-wrenching reports from the front lines of North Dakota, fell victim to hard times herself. Broke, severely diabetic, and partially blind, she became a ward of the Roosevelts, staying rent-free in a cottage on their Hyde Park, New York, estate. There she wrote a biography of Eleanor Roosevelt, *Reluctant First Lady*, and wondered what went wrong. "I was just about the top gal reporter in the country," she said in a letter to a friend. "God knows, I've had the conceit taken out of me plenty in the years since."

Carl Sandburg, who as a boy daydreamed about playing for the Chicago Cubs, released his last original book of poetry, *Honey and Salt*, in 1963. He was eighty-five. The title poem is a lengthy rumination on the conundrum of love. The last lines—Sandburg's bottom-of-the-ninth, closing metaphor—equate love with "a deep smoke winding over one hump of a mountain and the smoke becomes a smoke known to your own twisted individual garments: the winding of it gets into your walk, your hands, your face and eyes." He was writing about romantic love, but his description applies to any passion that mightily stirs heart and soul: jazz, the sea, religion, van Gogh's paintings, double-fudge ice cream sundaes . . . baseball.

Raymond "Hap" Dumont got married again—fittingly, to a woman he'd met at a drugstore cigar counter—but that deep smoke wound around him and his National Baseball Congress. He nurtured it into a semipro command-and-control center, active at its peak in forty-nine states and twenty-nine countries. He outgrew his desk at Goldsmith's mini department store. He had an office built at Lawrence Stadium and hired a few underlings. All year long Hap was the first to arrive at work and the last to leave, consumed with fine-tuning his creation. Some ideas deservedly went nowhere, such as his cockamamie experiment with letting batters run the bases in the direction of their choice, either first-to-third or third-to-first. Putting an extra umpire in the bucket of a movable crane in order to get a bird's-eye view of the field proved ridiculously impractical. The pneumatic duster that popped out of the ground next to home plate wasn't worth the engineering effort. His proposed "Sandlot Baseball Museum" fell flat. But some other ideas were crystal-ball prescient. In 1940 Dumont tested protective helmets for batters and had four "electric eyes" installed to assist umps in calling balls and strikes. (Back to the drawing board for those electric eyes: The sensors kept getting triggered by batters' swings between pitches.) Two years later he used a designated pinch hitter for pitchers in practice games, a full three decades before the American League adopted its DH rule. He hired a woman umpire for the National tournament in 1943 (then gently canned her after players complained that "they couldn't carry on their regular chatter") and, in 1962, introduced a twenty-second clock between pitches to speed up games.

Dumont and his National survived by adapting to changing times. During World War II as many as half the slots were reserved for service teams such as the Las Vegas Army Horned Toads and Camp Wheeler Spokes. Dumont forbade any states to hold segregated qualifying tournaments in 1959 and, when faced with the demise of semipro ball, went completely amateur, positioning the National as a showcase for top collegiate talent. The tournament is still going strong. Hap Dumont is not. He died with his boots on, keeling over at his desk of a heart attack in July 1971. An umpire found the body, but the medical examiner officially called Hap out. His spirit didn't leave the building. In 1972 the ballpark in Wichita was renamed Lawrence-Dumont Stadium.

Hilton Smith could have benefited from some of Dumont's self-promotional zaniness. Reporters avoided him after games because he'd say painfully drab things like "Just throwing that old apple on up in there where they can't hit it has always been a great thrill to me." A comatose Satchel Paige could give better interviews. Fortunately for Smith, sometimes actions don't just speak louder than words. They can scream. He inherited the mantle of Bismarck's pitching ace from Paige in 1936 and his career took off. He moved on to the Kansas City Monarchs in 1937, throwing a no-hitter and being named to the Negro League all-star team, the first of six consecutive appearances. Smith said he learned to pitch in Kansas City from wise owls like Bullet Rogan. His fastball, curve, and screwball got junkyard-dog nasty. In twelve years with the Monarchs he won 20 or more games every season. From 1939 through 1942 his record was an ungodly 93–11. He didn't make a fuss about that. "He just played baseball because he loved it so much," his wife, Louise, said.

During a West Coast winter barnstorming swing in the mid-1940s, Smith checked out a young infielder from the Los Angeles area. The kid made such a favorable impression that Smith urged Monarchs' owner J. L. Wilkinson to sign him as soon as possible. That infielder was Jackie Robinson. When the Brooklyn Dodgers purchased Robinson's contract in 1947, they tried to land Hilton Smith too. At forty, he no longer had his best stuff, and knew it. Smith elected to stay a Monarch and watch from afar as his young friend made baseball history. Three years later he was done with baseball. He became a supervisor for a Kansas City steel company and, after retiring, worked part-time as a scout for the Chicago Cubs. Looking back upon his career, Smith matter-of-factly told a sportswriter, "I won 161 games and lost 22, but most people have never heard of me." (Actually, Negro League records show he may have lost all of . . . 32 ballgames.) That remark would come back to haunt him. In his mid-seventies Hilton Smith did something shockingly out of character: he wrote a letter to the National Baseball Hall of Fame committee in Cooperstown and tooted his own horn, politely stating his qualifications for admission.

He never received a reply.

After getting injured in Mexico, Satchel Paige did something equally out of character for him: he quietly begged for work. J. L. Wilkinson, the softhearted boss of the Kansas City Monarchs, threw him a bone. He hired Paige in 1939 to front the Monarchs B-team barnstormers, rebranded as the "Satchel Paige All-Stars." The plan was to exploit his name, mostly sticking him at first base, where he could do minimal damage. During a game in Canada a ball rolled out of the bullpen and Paige tossed it back. Without pain! As he rather biblically described it, "The miracle was passed." And lo, unto him a pitching career was born anew in the city of Winnipeg. Whatever the ailment (probably a partially torn rotator cuff), it had healed with rest. By 1941 Paige was fully recovered and reunited with ex–Bismarck teammate Hilton Smith on the Monarchs' parent team. For seven years they functioned as an odd but effective tag team. Paige was the honey that attracted ticket buyers. To avoid overtaxing his arm, the Monarchs usually had him pitch the opening three innings of a game and relied upon Smith or another reliever to carry the heavy load for the last six. On days when Satchel didn't show up—and he got easily waylaid fishing, tossing dice, or shooting at deer from the window of his car—Smith would sometimes serve as his body double, pretending to be the great Satchel Paige so fans wouldn't feel disappointed.

After the Dodgers tapped Jackie Robinson to step over the color line, Paige dropped his guard (once) for an instant and conceded that it "hurt me down deep." What about the guy who had lit the way to integration? Why no quid pro quo? "I'd been the one who'd opened up the major league parks to the colored teams. I'd been the one who the white boys wanted to go barnstorming against." His time came a year later. In 1948 Paige finally crossed the threshold when the Cleveland Indians offered him a contract. The *Bismarck Tribune* put that news on its front page, along with *New York Times* columnist Arthur Daley's observation, "For almost twenty years the belief has been rather general that the best pitcher in baseball was

Leroy (Satchel) Paige." More than 200,000 people came to see his first three Major League starts. Paige appeared in the 1948 World Series with the victorious Indians, but subsequently got dealt to the woeful St. Louis Browns, who in 1953 told him his services were no longer required. At forty-seven (baseball scholars having come to the conclusion that his birth date was July 7, 1906), Paige picked up right where he'd left off, barnstorming and playing ball for whoever would still have him: the minor league Miami Marlins, Portland Beavers, and Peninsula Grays; the Kansas City Monarchs; the baseball Harlem Globetrotters; the semipro Salina (Kansas) Etherington Blue Jays; and the "Caribbean Seas" Cuban all-start team that for some reason pitched its tent in Beloit, Wisconsin.

No player, with the possible exception of Babe Ruth, cut a broader swath. A *Collier's* magazine writer nailed it, saying that Paige "is one of the last surviving totally unregimented souls." He was Satchel. He did as he did and transcended statistics. What to make of a man served divorce papers at Wrigley Field (representatives of long-suffering Janet Paige tracked him down July 17, 1943 on Satchel Paige Day), whom both Ted Williams and Joe DiMaggio rated the best pitcher they'd seen, and yet who pinballed among a minimum of 100 teams? His Negro League pitching record was 117–77, but who knows how many off-the-books games and exhibitions took place outside the country or outside organized baseball?

In 1960, Paige made a sentimental journey back to the National Baseball Congress tournament with the Wichita Weller Indians. Hap Dumont squeezed every drop of publicity out of that twenty-fifth-anniversary return. During the opening ceremonies he had the head football coach of Wichita State University present Satchel, resplendent in cap and gown, with an honorary diploma as NBC's most distinguished alumnus. (The 66 strikeouts he rang up in 1935 have yet to be matched, although the roll call of NBC tournament pitchers includes the likes of Tom Seaver, Roger Clemens, and Tim Lincecum.) Paige didn't embarrass himself or the

Weller Indians. He pitched four games and was charged with five runs in fourteen innings. Not bad numbers for a fifty-four-year old.

Five years later, the Kansas City Athletics activated Paige for a one-day publicity stunt. They plopped him in a rocking chair out in the bullpen before a home game with the Boston Red Sox. Funny stuff. Then Satch walked ketchup-slow to the mound and shut down the Sox for three innings. He was then fifty-nine and got touched for only a single hit, by a Hall of Famer in the making, Carl Yastrzemski. There was still more baseball in him. He earned $50 a game in 1967 and 1968 chucking for the Indianapolis Clowns, onetime Negro American League champions who had turned into a barnstorming comedy act. One of Paige's teammates was a contortionist; another stood thirty-one inches tall. Satchel kept his figurative distance by refusing to wear a Clowns uniform, opting for a Cleveland Indians jersey. It was a sad epilogue to his career, but a perfect twist of fate. As schlocky as they'd become, the Indianapolis Clowns were the sole surviving Negro League team.

In 1971 Leroy Paige became the first full-fledged Negro Leaguer inducted into the National Baseball Hall of Fame. Jackie Robinson had gained entry earlier, but he'd played only a half season of black baseball. The Major League lords nearly bungled the induction by announcing that Paige would be enshrined in a separate "Negro wing," which smacked of a servants' entrance to immortality. Ultimately he was welcomed into the Cooperstown brotherhood proper. Hilton Smith joined him there in 2001, but, typically, his moment in the sun was cloaked in shadow: he'd died in 1983. Furthermore, the Hall of Fame's press release that broke the good news referred to him as "Milton Smith."

Through all the games and all those teams and tens of thousands of artful pitches, Satchel Paige fondly remembered Bismarck. True to form, he gilded the lily of that 1935 championship season, asserting in various forums that the team had gone 106–1, 104–1, 100–1, 102–5, and 96–8. He told a *Chicago Daily Tribune* reporter, "That was the best team I ever saw. The best players I ever played

with. But who ever heard of them?" Was that straight talk or a
Two-Hoop Blooper? Could it have been his eliptical way of saying, "Bismarck was very, very good. But don't ask me to name my
teammates."

Paige also said, "Bases on balls is the curse on the nation"
and lots of other things. As wedded as he was to overstatement
and puffery, he did utter one absolutely irrefutable fact: "There
never was a man on earth who pitched as much as me." Quincy
Troupe caught some of those innings and many more. He spent
1937 in self-imposed exile selling milk, but soon soured on that
vocation. He followed his heart and returned to baseball in 1938
with the Indianapolis ABCs of the Negro National League. The
next spring he gave sunny Mexico a try and enjoyed it so much he
stayed six years. Troupe added an extra "p" to his surname to match
the pronunciation "Señor *Tru-pay*," which he fancied. He never
dropped that alternative spelling. Troupe—now Trouppe—felt so
comfortable in Latin America that he returned like clockwork for
more than a decade, playing winter ball in Puerto Rico, Venezuela,
Cuba, and Colombia.

The Cleveland Buckeyes drew him home for the 1945 baseball
season with an offer to be their player-manager. The Buckeyes upset
the vaunted Pittsburgh Crawfords in the Negro National League
World Series that year. Quincy Trouppe had an outstanding play-
offs, hitting .400. In 1946 he signed the first white player in the
Negro Leagues. Pitcher Eddie Klepp lasted only a few months with
the Buckeyes because segregation laws blocked him from taking
the field in so many southern towns. Trouppe soon was gone from
Cleveland as well: to the Chicago American Giants, New York Cu-
bans, Canada's Provincial League, and back to Mexico, where fans
called the boyish catcher *El Rorro* ("The Baby") at age thirty-seven.

"He was terrific," Joe Desiderato said of Trouppe. "How they
kept him out of the Major Leagues, I never could understand."
Technically, they didn't keep him out. Trouppe got the long-awaited
tap on the shoulder in 1952 from the Cleveland Indians. He was

thirty-nine, Methuselah in shin guards. The Indians let him go after just two and a half months in uniform and the skimpiest of stat lines: 6 games played, 1 hit in 11 at bats. Trouppe had much more to show for his ten years in the Negro Leagues: a .311 lifetime average and five all-star selections. He also batted over .300 during his time in Mexico. However, his enduring legacy may be as an accidental sports archivist. Trouppe became an avid amateur photographer and accumulated boxes of still pictures and film footage. There's no comparable visual record of Negro League history. Ken Burns dipped heavily into that trove for his multipart documentary *Baseball*.

During twenty-three years as a player and ten more devoted to beating the bushes as a scout for his hometown St. Louis Cardinals, Trouppe burned through two marriages. When he ventured down the aisle a third time, he left baseball behind. He moved to Los Angeles and opened a storefront restaurant called Trouppe's Dugout a few miles from Dodger Stadium. His Major League dream had been cut cruelly short, but he professed to be at peace despite all that time lost on the wrong side of the color line. "The happiness and the sadness always blended into something that made my life more complete."

Nobody remains boyish forever. Alzheimer's disease corroded Trouppe's brain and brawn. "I watched a man who could turn on a fastball as quick as anyone become a man unable to turn a spade of dirt," Larry Lester, a cofounder of the Negro Leagues Baseball Museum in Kansas City, wrote in the introduction to a posthumous edition of Trouppe's autobiography. "I watched a man who could remember the batting lineup of every team in the league become a man sometimes unable to remember the security access code to his apartment building."

When the grill was sizzling at Trouppe's Dugout, a customer with a major league appetite occasionally stopped in. Neil Churchill always said his favorite player to manage had been Quincy Troupe. Most likely he dropped by the restaurant on his way to or from a racetrack. That was about as physically demanding as his California retirement got. He wasn't the type to take up surfing in his golden years. Churchill loved sinking into an armchair to enjoy a baseball, football, or basketball game on television while simultaneously listening to a baseball, football, or basketball game on the radio as he thumbed through the *Daily Racing Form*. The Couch Potato Trifecta. Sometimes he'd take a sports break and sit down in that chair to watch a John Wayne movie or read a Louis L'Amour shoot-'em-up novel about the old West.

Church kept playing cards, but wore a path to Santa Anita, Del Mar, and Hollywood Park racetracks with almost daily trips. Horse fever led him and a North Dakota friend to invest in a few thoroughbreds. One filly was sired by Seabiscuit but didn't inherit those million-dollar legs. Sea Novice won 8 of 41 races in a brief, also-ran career. Ownership didn't dissuade Churchill from wagering. He never mastered his addiction; merely transferred it from the poker table to the pari-mutuel window. He once gave Helen $100 for Christmas and the next day borrowed the money back to go to Santa Anita. Another time he dropped $10,000 on a can't-miss nag that faded in the stretch. "Right down to the end he was involved with gambling," says Randy Churchill, his surviving son.

The end was prostate cancer. Even that didn't mend his fractured family circle. Becky Churchill, Neil's seldom-seen daughter, lived in San Diego. He used to visit her on the sly. Helen could never bring herself to accept a stepdaughter, and her husband could never bring himself to force her. Becky had to sneak into the hospital to see him on his deathbed. There was no inheritance to fight over. Neil Churchill lived the high life in California—membership in the ritzy Turf Club at Hollywood Park; giving his kids new cars as wedding presents—but he lived it on the razor's edge. Gambling losses drained his bank account dry. Randy Churchill says his father made a lot of money, but it was Neil's to blow, which he did. Why be bitter? Churchill chuckles, remarking that both he and his late brother Neil C. battled (and beat) prostate cancer. "So he did leave us *something*."

There were no baseball souvenirs to pass on, not so much as an autographed photo stashed in a desk drawer. Nothing. That waist-high trophy from the 1935 National tournament didn't get repurposed as a lamp or a doorstop. It disappeared. Neil Churchill was not a nostalgic man. However, he did take one stroll down memory lane. In July 1954 he flew back to Bismarck to see Satchel Paige pitch for Abe Saperstein's not-so-famous Harlem Globetrotters baseball team. They came to town to help celebrate the opening of Corwin-Churchill Motors' new used-car lot. Wick Corwin never had the heart to change the company name after his longtime partner left the business.

Right before his move to California, Churchill told the *Bismarck Tribune*, "If Paige had been a white man at the time I sponsored him and the team in 1935, there is no doubt in my mind he would have been recognized as the greatest pitcher of all time." Nineteen years later, Paige returned to a hero's welcome. A sellout crowd of 3,400 fans strained the ballpark grandstand. A military guard raised the American flag. Satchel lobbed a ceremonial pitch to Mayor Evan Lips, who graciously swung and missed so that ceremonial catcher Neil Churchill could fire the ball around the horn to ceremonial infielders Babe Mohn and Bob McCarney. The Globetrotters then took over and toyed with a group of Bismarck sandlot stars, gently clubbing them 9–0.

You *can* go home again as long as your fastball still sings. Neil Churchill sat behind home plate and watched his choice for the greatest pitcher of all time stand storklike on the mound and kick his left leg high enough to block the North Dakota sun. Just like old times. Satchel Paige threw fire. In the first inning he struck out the side on eleven pitches.

On a frigid Saturday in February 2007, a throng of 8,962 bundled-up men, women, and children gathered on the long landing strip of ground that sprawls in front of the State Capitol Building in

Bismarck. It wasn't a political rally. On cue, all 8,962 of them flopped onto their backs and began doing horizontal jumping jacks, arms and legs swishing like windshield wipers. Those few seconds of silliness were enough to earn a spot in the *Guinness Book of World Records* for "Most People Making Snow Angels." The State Historical Society of North Dakota had organized the event, which suited eighty-four-year-old angel Edna Arvidson just fine. "It's fun and puts us on the map," she said. "People think there's nothing going on up here."

Dennis Boyd believes plenty of things have gone on in North Dakota. He'd like North Dakotans to dust off their past and make more of a fuss about it; there's no need to stoop to orchestrating goofy world records. Boyd is volunteer president of the Bismarck Historical Society. He says that somewhere on the public-awareness continuum that stretches from Sakakawea to synchronized snow angels, room should be made for Neil Churchill and his ahead-of-their-time semipro team. It's always tempting to romanticize baseball days of yore. Yet if the romantics hung a plaque at Bismarck's municipal ball field that read "Birthplace of Integrated Sports in America," would they be wildly off the mark? Boyd thinks not. He sees parallels between George Armstrong Custer and Leroy "Satchel" Paige. "Both men spent a relatively short amount of time in Bismarck yet both men made national history during their stay here."

In 1909 the city dedicated Custer Park, a pleasant swatch of greenery just off Main Street. Boyd and the Bismarck Historical Society are pushing to have the nearby ballpark named "Satchel Paige Field," a nice gesture but one that gives short shrift to Neil Churchill, who happens to be buried just across the river in Mandan. Grand plans are on the table to renovate the field and to construct a North Dakota baseball museum. The Bismarck Board of Park Commissioners hopes to find a corporate angel willing to write a check that will make everything possible. To drum up support for Satchel Paige Field, Boyd constantly speaks up on behalf of that

1935 team and the ground they broke. "Being the first integrated baseball team to win a national championship? It was extremely improbable," he says, "for a dusty little town like Bismarck, North Dakota, to be able to pull in talent like that."

The task of renaming the ball field is burdened somewhat by the fact that Churchill and his players fell between the cracks of the Depression, World War II, and the civil rights movement. Time marched on. People forgot. Bismarck of the 1930s succumbed to wrecking balls and redevelopment. It now exists mostly in the mind's eye. The Princess Hotel, home away from home for many Bismarck ballplayers, has been recycled as an apartment building. Jack Lyons's hamburgers are no more. That site is now a garage serving up parking spaces. The Northern Pacific train station became a Mexican restaurant. State Recreation Parlor, where Dayton Shipley ripped and read the Western Union feeds from Wichita, made way for a Wells Fargo bank. Another bland bank stands where rows of Chryslers once titillated customers at Corwin-Churchill Motors. The dealership left downtown for a spacious west-end location in 1998 and was sold in 2010. The new owners retired the Corwin-Churchill name after an eighty-five-year run.

Jamestown's ballpark has been painstakingly repaired and restored; its wooden grandstand looks virtually untouched since the Depression. Bismarck wasn't so fortunate. The town ball field occupies the same plot of land, but has been reconfigured. Deep center field is where home plate used to be and vice versa. The grandstand burned down decades ago. Fans today sit on aluminum bleachers that clank when struck by foul balls. Ghosts flit about, however, as they're wont to do at old battlefields and ballparks. On a sultry summer's night it's not difficult to envision Joe Desiderato sucking up a hard grounder or Satchel Paige windmilling fastballs. To walk the infield is to wish that dirt could talk, really cut loose, gossip to a fare-thee-well: about moonshiners and wee-hours card games at the Patterson Hotel, about the secret of Hilton Smith's twelve-to-six curveball.

You wish dirt could talk because most people who saw the team play have died off and because so little tangible evidence remains of what Neil Churchill wrought. Nobody squirreled away scorecards. No windbreakers or caps with the diamond B insignia are known to be in storage; no bats or gloves on display anywhere. Rumors—but only rumors—persist that some 35-mm film clips of the team are in the possession of a Bismarck resident who won't let go of them. Dennis Boyd would be ecstatic just to learn that someone had saved a crushed beer can discarded by Moose Johnson.

The memorabilia pickings are slim. A Bismarck uniform worn by an unknown player at the 1936 National tournament, an original 1935 team photo, and a ball autographed by Satchel Paige at the 1935 National have surfaced at auctions. They sold for $2,300, $5,100, and $6,000, respectively. Ballboy Bob Myhre, now an octogenarian, donated a ball signed by thirteen members of the 1933 team to the Negro Leagues Baseball Museum.

The most interesting item is another baseball that's in private hands in Cincinnati. It's kept in a Lucite cube for protection, like the bones of a saint. The cube sits on a desk in a bedroom inside a single-family house on a tree-shrouded street a couple of miles from Great American Ballpark, the Reds' throwback stadium. That ball—aged to the color of tobacco spit—belongs to Patrick Hammond, an outfielder on the Xavier University varsity team. It was a gift from his grandmother, Sharon Spaedy, the daughter of Bismarck utility player Bob McCarney. "Not just any ball," says Patrick's father, Tim, "but a ball from *The Game*." He's referring to August 13, 1933. That's the Sunday Satchel Paige toed the pitching rubber in Bismarck for the first time. He was king of the hill that afternoon, striking out 18 batters in a nip-and-tuck 3–2 win over Jamestown. The circus had arrived in town.

McCarney played first base that day and went 0 for 4. Normally, when somebody goes hitless they don't want keepsakes, but McCarney not only filched a game ball, he also joyously scribbled all over it. He'd invited Elizabeth Huttner, a vivacious lawyer soon to be his wife, to the game. Afterward he drew a large heart on that ball and inside the heart jotted "Mac & Betty." He also wrote "Prettiest Girl I Ever Met" . . . and "Jamestown 2 vs. Bismarck 3" . . . and "3,000 people attended the game." . . . and "Paige & Troupe" and "Hancock & Brown." Those last four names refer to the all-black pitcher-catcher batteries, something never before seen on a North Dakota diamond: Paige and Troupe for Bismarck, Charlie Hancock and Barney Brown for Jamestown.

Bob McCarney was a down-to-earth, glad-handing, back-slapping car salesman. It's a mystery why he felt compelled to turn a smudged baseball into a mash note, but good thing he did. The ball has a tangled tale to tell of intersecting lives and commingled passions. Boy meets girl. Town embraces team. Blacks play with whites. Winning beats losing. Wick Corwin once chided Neil Churchill for wasting too much time "chasin' that goddamn little, white ball around." McCarney apparently sensed something bigger afoot: a deep smoke winding that can get into a man's walk, his hands, his face, and eyes. Maybe he intuitively understood that Churchill wasn't just chasing a goddamn little, white ball around. He was making history. He was putting Bismarck on the map.

Joe Desiderato died in Chicago in January 1994, sixty-one years after that city threw a World's Fair celebrating the "Century of Progress." He was eighty-three, blessed with grandchildren and great-grandchildren, and had been rooted like an oak in the same neighborhood for a lifetime. The viewing was held at Cumberland Chapels Funeral Home on the North Side. Cubs turf. An already-hushed room of family and friends fell completely silent when a tall, corpulent black man entered, wearing a dark blazer and an open plaid shirt, topped by a porkpie hat. He huffed and leaned hard on a cane. Oblivious of any queue, he proceeded directly to the casket and bowed his head, laying his meaty right hand on the arm of the deceased. He then turned and, without introduction, addressed the mourners in a booming stadium voice. "Joe was my friend," the old man announced. "When they was callin' us 'niggers,' he stood by me. And I want you to know he could play. Otherwise he wouldn'ta been with us."

The coffin-line crasher was Ted Radcliffe, ninety-one years old and still able to bend the ears of an audience. Double Duty's moonface seemed to be fashioned from worn leather. He'd come to look like his catcher's mitt, much the way some dog owners resemble their dogs. His train had stayed on the track a long time. In 1943 he'd been chosen most valuable player of the Negro National League. He chugged along for thirty years' worth of baseball with at least thirty teams in five countries before running out of steam in 1954 with the Winnipeg Elmwood Giants. The knees finally went. Radcliffe was then fifty-two. He would live to be 103, the last man standing from Bismarck's 1935 championship team and still spinning yarns about exploits gone by, real and imagined. "I remember it because I love baseball," Duty would say, professing total recall even while mangling details of his own biography. "Anything you love, you can keep in your mind."

He and Joe "The Cat" were teammates for parts of only two seasons: six weeks in 1935 and three weeks in 1936. That's all. But they were young and strong during those golden summers and played on a team like none other they would ever know and played under big skies in places they would never again see. Fifty years later that bond kept them yakking on the telephone at least once a week. After Radcliffe delivered his mini eulogy, he continued talking from the comfort of a couch in the foyer of Cumberland Chapels. He talked about Satchel Paige and traveling to North Dakota and Kansas, about blacks and whites together whipping the best of the best semipros. "Joe was a vacuum cleaner at third base. Like a Hoover." Desiderato's relatives and friends huddled around the doddering stranger, enthralled.

Double Duty became lost in the memories and in the moment. His baseball reflexes remained sharp. He reached into a jacket pocket, pulled out a pack of five-by-seven photos of his younger self, and began signing autographs.

ACKNOWLEDGMENTS

This book was a dredging operation. For the most part, these are unknown men who played for a team that few people alive today can remember. The era of town baseball long ago faded into oblivion. Fortunately, events sink to the bottom of collective memory but rust away slowly. Bit by bit, fragment of information by fragment of information, the submerged saga of Neil Churchill and semipro baseball rose to the surface.

I am grateful that Quincy Trouppe and Satchel Paige made mention of the Bismarck, North Dakota, years in their respective autobiographies and that Ted Radcliffe cooperated on a biography that is oral-history based. Ballplayers generally are unreliable sources, but imperfect recollections can be cross-checked and distilled until hard facts get rendered. I'm indebted to those three men for the historical record they left behind.

My research likely would have stalled without the cooperation of Neil O. Churchill's family. His late son Neil C. (whom I much regret did not live to see my note taking make it to the printed page) and Neil C.'s wife Margie opened that door for me. Neil Churchill's youngest son, Randy, and Randy's wife, Jennifer, also welcomed my inquiries; as did Churchill's daughter, Diane Churchill Rapf and his granddaughter, Karen Gunderson. Thank you all.

I also would like to express my gratitude to the families of Vernon Johnson (his daughter Hilma Jones, nephews Donald and Duane Johnson, and grand nephew Rick Johnson); of Joe Desiderato (daughter Marie Desiderato DiMaggio and nephew Terry Sullivan); of Bob McCarney (daughter Sharon and her husband Jerry Spaedy, and grandson-in-law Tim Hammond), and Granville Haley (sister-in-law Dorothy Farrar, niece Claudia Randleman, and nephew Ronald Craig). In addition, Floyd Fuller, who saw the Churchill teams as a boy and whose father played for Bismarck in the 1920s, was a vital and amiable source.

Wick Corwin did not pick up a bat for the Bismarck team, but he was Churchill's empathetic business partner and key off-field operative. His son, Charlie, recalled Neil Churchill and the early days of the car dealership for me. I tapped that memory bank multiple times. Hap Dumont's stepson, Ray Eden, assisted me on the National Baseball Congress end of this story.

Book writing is an individual pursuit, but not a solitary one. My agent, Deborah Grosvenor, gave this idea wings to fly in the marketplace. Jamison Stoltz, my editor at Grove/Atlantic, proved himself a most valuable player with his sound editorial judgment and patient resolve through some unexpected circumstances. My thanks to Morgan Entrekin and the entire Grove/Atlantic lineup, consummate professionals all. A tip of the cap also to Jofie Ferrari-Adler, formerly of Grove and now pitching for Simon & Schuster, and Nick Trautwein, Bloomsbury Publishing's ace editor now with *The New Yorker*. Both were early advocates of this book.

Writers invariably lean on colleagues for advice and moral support. Chris Hunt, Neil Cohen, Robin McMillan, and Carl Cannon offered feedback in the earliest stages of this project. I owe them. Barbara and Bob Dreyfuss were both sounding boards and steadfast friends. David Rowell (my unflappable editor at the *Washington Post Magazine*), Jeff Shear, Susan Shipp, Dale Willman, Steve Kemper, and Robin Marantz Henig read parts of the manuscript and offered insightful comments. My appreciation to Linda Robinson at the *Washington Post* and Vera Titunik at the *New York Times Magazine* for helping me pay some bills during the time spent laboring on this book. My thanks to fellow journalists Nell Minow, Kristie Miller,

Steve Brookes, Bill Whalen, Susanne Sternthal, Gene Weingarten, Keith Bellows, Bill Heavey, Skip Kaltenheuser, Rick Kozak, Kathy Mangan, Jon Salant, Megan Cogswell, Marguerite Kelly, and others for answering a critical S.O.S.

Members of the Society of American Baseball Research (SABR) saved me from myself on numerous occasions. Scott Simkus, who edits the wonderful *Outsider Baseball Bulletin*, provided important leads and game details, particularly in regard to the Pittsburgh Crawfords. SABRites Brian Carroll, Phil Dixon, Timothy M. Gay, Leslie Heaphy, Bob Hector, John Holway, Larry Lester, Jay-Del Mah, Ray Nemec, Royse Parr, Rob Rives, Bill Staples, and Lynn Womack graciously shared their knowledge.

A small army of strangers came to my aid on the North Dakota leg of this book. I must single out Scott Caya in Mandan for unearthing an essential phone number at just the right time. I pestered members of the Bismarck Historical Society for several years and they kept answering my calls and questions. Thank you Myron Atkinson, Jim Christianson, and Dennis Boyd. John Sakariassen and Chuck Eastgate served as able guides during my Bismarck reporting visit. Bruce Whittey helped me with Corwin-Churchill Motors history. Kevin Carvell and Clay Jenkinson schooled me on North Dakota history. The following people helped bring to life Bismarck and North Dakota during the Depression, some through personal remembrances of those difficult times: Jim Bankes, Spencer Boise, Marc Conrad, Muriel Dresbach Copeland, Tom Johnson, Charlie Krahler, Ed and Erna Lahr, Rufus Lumry, Bill Melech, Bob Myhre, Gil Olson, Lyle Porter, Robert Ritterbush, Ray Shaefer, Ed Schumacher, Jack Schwartz, Gene Severson, Stan Sharkey, Jim Thompson, Robert Watts, Harry Valdie, and Frank Vyzralek. Apologies to anyone I've unwittingly overlooked.

Kelly Morgan and John Morse confirmed details about Satchel Paige and Standing Rock Indian Reservation. Bruce Berg took me on a tour of Jamestown, North Dakota, and its lovely ball field. Mary Young and Al Wiest relived their younger days in town for me. Keith Norman of the *Jamestown Sun* carved time out of his workday on the spur of the moment. Charlie Cookson, Bill Kentling, Paul Roberts, Steve Shaad, and Casey Stewart filled in some of the blanks related to Wichita, Hap Dumont, and the National Baseball Congress tournament. Brian Corn of *The Wichita Eagle* offered a helping hand with photos. Buddy Campbell, Pee Wee Carey of the Stephens County (Oklahoma) Museum, Gail Davis, and Susie McMichael expanded my understanding of the Duncan Cementers and oil baron Erle P. Halliburton.

The late Hall of Famer Bob Feller, the late "Mr. Red Sox" Johnny Pesky, former Negro Leaguers Stanley Glenn and Mahlon Duckett, and Texas League President Tom Kayser provided me with valuable views from the baseball trenches.

My praises go to the following librarians, curators, and educators, without whom I'd have been lost: Greg Wyck and Jim Davis, State Historical Society of North Dakota in Bismarck; Raymond Doswell, Negro Leagues Baseball Museum in Kansas City; the research staffs at the Library Congress in Washington, D.C., and National Baseball Hall of Fame in Cooperstown, New York; Karen Billman and Doreen Paul, Sandusky, Ohio, Public Library; Karen O'Connor, Davenport, Iowa, Public Library; Janis Granthwol Burke, Erie County Chapter of the Ohio Genealogical Society; Shirlene Newman, District of Columbia Public Library; Chris Siriano, House of David Museum; Kathye Spilman, Mandan Public Library; Lawrence Hogan, senior professor of history at Union County College of New Jersey; Thomas Aiello, assistant professor of history and African American studies, Valdosta State University.

A big hug to my old amigos Karen Lee, Maggie Davis, and Caren and John Sellers for their hospitality during my California research trip. Sharon Baker and Rosa Benn were key parts of my Washington, D.C., support crew. Nonwriter friends Elfego Gomez, Tom and Louise Boyton, Rod McKenzie, and Bruce Reitz plowed through rough drafts from afar without complaint.

Blood is thicker than water, but not childhood Whiffle Ball games. Nonetheless, I extend my hand in affection, respect, and deep appreciation to my older brother Bill, even though he refused to teach me how to hit to right field. My love and thanks to Bill's wife Chris, their children Kate and Bryan, and spouses Steve and Charlotte. I promise to find something else to talk about at holiday dinners besides Bismarck, North Dakota.

Lastly, Jessica Lefevre read every word of this manuscript multiple times and offered her boundless encouragement with each page and each travail. Love, kisses, and a fist bump, Jess. You're a true team player. Quincy and Satchel would be proud.

Tom Dunkel
Washington, D.C.
January 2013

A Note on Sources

I was up late one night in the summer of 2007 writing a freelance magazine article when a Google search led me to an off-topic, two-year-old *Chicago Tribune* obituary with the headline: "Ted 'Double Duty' Radcliffe, 103; Star Catcher in Negro League Also Pitched."

After reading that obit, I wanted to know more about Radcliffe. I found a 2003 *Los Angeles Times* profile that referred to his "leaving the Negro Leagues in 1935 to play for wealthy auto dealer Neil Churchill, who owned the semipro Bismarck Churchills in North Dakota." A black man playing baseball in white-as-snow North Dakota in 1935? There had to be a story behind that. I soon learned sports history is often flawed history. Misinformation abounds. To begin with, the Bismarck ball team was never called the "Churchills." Neil Churchill would never have stood for that. He was far too modest a man. It took several years to untangle the spaghetti of conflicting facts, half truths, and rumors surrounding the Bismarck team and the lost world of semipro baseball. Ted Radcliffe became just a small piece of that larger puzzle.

In trying to reconstruct a full and fair account of events that took place in relative obscurity more than seventy-five years ago, I did more than two hundred interviews and dipped into dozens of books. But the old bones of this story were mostly found buried in newspaper and magazine archives, patiently waiting to be unearthed.

Books

Satchel Paige was the only protagonist who left a large media footprint, thus I had the pleasure of reading *Satchel: The Life and Times of an American Legend* by Larry Tye; *Satchel, Dizzy & Robert* by Timothy M. Gay; *Don't*

Look Back: Satchel Paige in the Shadows of Baseball by Mark Ribowsky; *Pitchin'*
Man by Leroy "Satchel" Paige as told to Hal Lebovitz; and *Maybe I'll Pitch*
Forever by Leroy "Satchel" Paige as told to David Lipman.

For others in this cast of characters, I relied upon *20 Years Too Soon: Prelude*
to Major-League Integrated Baseball by Quincy Trouppe; *Ted "Double Duty"*
Radcliffe: 36 Years of Pitching & Catching in Baseball's Negro Leagues by Kyle
M. McNary; *Baseball's Barnum: Ray "Hap" Dumont* by Bob Broeg; and Ben
Green's biography of Abe Saperstein entitled *Spinning the Globe: The Rise,*
Fall, and Return to Greatness of the Harlem Globetrotters. Seabiscuit: The Rest of
the Story by William H. Nichols provided a few tidbits on Neil Churchill's
foray into horse racing ownership.

I found the following books helpful for various facets of professional and
semiprofessional baseball: *Baseball in the Garden of Eden: The Secret History*
of the Early Game by John Thorn; *Complete Armchair Book of Baseball* edited
by John Thorn; *Baseball, the People's Game* by Harold Seymour; *Baseball in*
Wichita by Bob Rives; *Oh, Brother How They Played the Game: The Story of*
Texas' Greatest All-Brothers Baseball Team by Carlton Stowers; *Baseball and*
Richmond: A History of the Professional Game, 1884-2000 by W. Harrison
Daniel and Scott P. Mayer; *Biographical Encyclopedia of the Negro Baseball*
Leagues edited by James Riley; *Only The Ball Was White* by Robert Peterson;
Diamonds in the Rough: The Untold History of Baseball by Joel Ross and John
Bowman; *The Forgotten Players: The Story of Black Baseball in America* by
Robert Gardner and Dennis Shortelle; *The Glory of Their Times* by Law-
rence S. Ritter; *Wilber "Bullet" Rogan and the Kansas City Monarchs* by Phil
S. Dixon; *History of Colored Baseball With Other Documents on the Early Black*
Game, 1886-1936 by Sol White; *Voices from the Great Black Baseball Leagues*
by John Holway; *Swinging for the Fences: Black Baseball in Minnesota* edited
by Stephen R. Hoffbeck; *The Negro League Book,* edited by Dick Clark and
Larry Lester; *The House of David* by Christopher Siriano; *The House of David*
Baseball Team by Joel Hawkins and Terry Bertolino; *Tris Speaker: The Rough*
and Tumble Times of a Baseball Legend by Timothy M. Gay; *The California*
Winter Leagues by William McNeil; *The Boys of Summer* by Roger Kahn;
Always the Young Strangers by Carl Sandburg.

For historical background on certain states, cities, and the Great Depression,
I drew from: *History of North Dakota* by Elwyn B. Robinson; *WPA Guide to*
1930s North Dakota compiled and written by the Federal Writers' Project;
History of Bismarck, North Dakota: The First 100 Years, 1872-1972 by George F.
Bird and Edwin J. Taylor, Jr.; *African-Americans in North Dakota* by Thomas
Newgard, William Sherman and John Guerrero; *Images of America: Bismarck,*

North Dakota by Cathy A. Langemo; *Historic Downtown Bismarck* by the Bismarck Historical Society; Bismarck, North Dakota, City Directory for 1908, 1924, 1928, 1932, 1934, 1938, and 1940; *Mantini: A History of Mandan-Morton County* by Sarah Tostevin; *Main Street in Crisis: The Great Depression and the Old Middle Class on the Northern Plains* by Catherine McNicol Stock; *Common Ground: McElroy Park's Jack Brown Stadium* by Bruce Berg; *Kansas: A Guide to the Sunflower State*, Federal Writers' Project; *One Third of a Nation: Lorena Hickok Reports on the Great Depression* edited by Richard Lowitt and Maurine Beasley; *WPA Guide to 1930s Alabama* compiled and written by Federal Writers' Project; *A Collection of Recollections: Crystal Falls 1880-1980* edited by Lynn Mille; *Images of America: Northwest Airlines, the First 80 Years* by Geoff Jones; *Showdown at Little Big Horn* by Dee Alexander Brown; 1890, 1900, 1910, 1920, 1930 U.S. Census data.

NEWSPAPERS AND PERIODICALS

I relied upon the *Bismarck Tribune* as a primary source for nearly a century of local news and the *Wichita Eagle* for several decades. Their newspaper competition, the *Bismarck Capital* and *Wichita Beacon*, were secondary sources. In addition to that Top Four I made use of these other newspapers and periodicals: *Ada (Oklahoma) News; Anderson (Indiana) Herald; Arkansas Historical Quarterly; Arizona Independent Republic; Atlanta Daily World; Baseball Digest; Benton Harbor(Michigan) News-Palladium; Baseball Research Journal; Beulah (North Dakota) Independent; Brooklyn Eagle; Buffalo Evening News; Carroll (Iowa) Daily Herald; Charleston (West Virginia) Daily Mail; Chattanooga Times; Chicago Daily Tribune; Chicago Reader; Cleveland Plain Dealer; Collier's* magazine; *Danville (Virginia) Bee; Denver Post; Des Moines Register; Duncan (Oklahoma) Banner; East Texas Historical Journal; Elyria (Ohio) Chronicle Telegram; Emporia (Kansas) Gazette; Farm Collector; Farmers Advocate; Hartford Courant; Helena (Montana) Independent-Record; Honolulu Record; Galveston (Texas) Daily News; Gastonia (North Carolina) Daily Gazette; Grand Forks (North Dakota) Herald; Great Falls (Montana) Tribune; Hampton (Virginia) Daily Press; Hutchinson (Kansas) News; Indiana Evening Gazette; Jamestown (North Dakota) Sun; Jefferson City (Missouri) Post Tribune; Joplin (Missouri) Globe; Kansas City Call; Kansas City Star; Kansas History Quarterly; Lawrence (Kansas) Journal World; Lethbridge (Saskatchewan) Herald; Los Angeles Times; Lowell (Massachusetts) Sun; Mandan (North Dakota) Pioneer; Mantiwoc (Wisconsin) Herald-Times; McPherson (Kansas) Daily Republican; Minneapolis Tribune; Monessen (Pennsylvania) Daily Independent; Montana: The Magazine of Western History; (Wichita) Negro Star; New Amsterdam (New York) News; New York Age; New York Daily News; New York Times; NINE: A Journal of Baseball History and Culture; Oakland Tribune; Omaha World-Herald; Paris (Texas) News; Philadelphia Tribune; Pittsburgh Courier; Pittsburgh Press; Reading (Pennsylvania) Eagle; Salina (Kansas) Journal; San Antonio Light; San Diego City Beat; Sandusky (Ohio)-Register; Saturday Evening Post; Silverton (Oregon) Appeal; The Sporting News; Steubenville (Ohio) Herald; TIME; Tulsa Tribune; USA Today; Valley City (North Dakota) Times; Washington Post; Wilton (North Dakota) News; Winnipeg Free-Press; Zanesville (Ohio) Signal.*

UNPUBLISHED WORKS

"Amateur and Semi-Professional Baseball in North Dakota Communities" by Kyle Robert Johnson, Arizona State University master's thesis, 1994; "The Denver Post Tournament and Pre-Organized Baseball Integration" by Eric Mark Stoneberg, Arizona State University master's thesis, 2009; *A Journal for Katherine* by Bismarck, North Dakota, native John F. Holloran; Robert P. McCarney papers at the University of North Dakota's Chester Fritz Library; Eleanor Roosevelt Papers Project at George Washington University.

WEB SITES

ballparksofthepast.com; baseball-almanac.com; baseballlink.com; baseball-reference.com; baseballfever.com; bismarckpride.com; peppergame.com; pitchblackbaseball.com; seamheads.com; Society of American Baseball Research Biography Project (sabr.org/bioproj); ESPN.com; House of David Museum (hodmuseum.com); i70baseball.com; legendsofamerica.com; littlebighorn.com; Negro Leagues Baseball Players Association (nlbpa.com); Minor League Baseball (milb.com); National Baseball Congress (nbcbaseball.com); Oklahoma Historical Society (http://digital.library.okstate.edu); Economics History Association (eh.net) Society of Professional Engineering (spegcs.org); cherokee-strip-museum.org; city of Crystal Falls, Michigan (crystalfalls.org); custerwest.org; Duncan, Oklahoma Convention and Visitors Bureau (duncanok.org); guinnessworldrecords.com.

NOTES

PREFACE

"burned with a dark fire": Roger Kahn, *The Boys of Summer*, p xix.

President Reagan's Medal of Freedom remarks about Jackie Robinson are available at www.reagan.utexas.edu/archives/speeches/1984/32684a.htm.

CHAPTER 1

48 million people: *Chicago Sun Times*, May 11, 2008.

A Televisor contraption: It was designed by Chicagoans M. L. Hayes and V. A. Sanabria. To see a photo of Hayes at the machine, go to www.earlytele-vision.org/chicago_1933_worlds_fair.html. The Web site www.cityclicker.net/chicfair has photos and descriptions of other world's fair exhibits.

Miracle Whip dressing: Charles Chapman invented it. See www.mentalfloss.com/difference/miracle-whip-vs-mayonnaise/.

Willie the Robot: He also sang. A picture of Willie is posted at: http://blog.modernmechanix.com/scientific-highlights-of-chicagos-world-fair/1/#mmGal.

47,595 people purchased tickets: www.booksonbaseball.com/2010/07/july-6-1933 has details on the game and the Ruth baseball sale. Lew Freedman wrote a book about the 1933 all-star game: *The Day All the Stars Came Out*.

The Orion was a puddle jumper: *Images of America: Northwest Airlines, the First 80 Years* by Geoff Jones, p. 10 makes reference to early Northwest planes. For photos of the six-seat Orion, see www.fiddlersgreen.net/models/aircraft/Lockheed-Orion.html.

He had never been on a plane: *20 Years Too Soon* by Quincy Trouppe, p. 42. Note: In the 1940s Quincy Troupe added an extra "p" to his surname.

Purely white enterprises: *Baseball, the People's Game* by Harold Seymour, pp. 546–7.

Good head for the game: Former Troupe teammate Stanley Glenn described him to me as "brainy" and a good manager in a 2009 phone interview.

"catching a bullet": *Ted "Double Duty" Radcliffe* by Kyle McNary, p. 24.

Pulverized a knee-high fastball: Troupe's home run and the Crawford Grill scene is described in *20 Years Too Soon*, pp. 37–38. Troupe's account appears to commingle games played on June 3 and June 5, 1933. Thanks to Scott Simkus of SABR for digging up those box scores. Troupe, indeed, homered off Paige. It happened on June 3, but he had only two at bats in that game with only one hit. Details and ballpark photos provided to me by Simkus in e-mails on November 3 and 4, 2011.

All-purpose pleasure palace: *Satchel* by Larry Tye, p. 71.

Troupe tapped on Kent's office door: *20 Years Too Soon*, pp. 29–30.

Complimentary transportation: *Bismarck Tribune*, July 27, 1933.

He offered Troupe $175: *20 Years Too Soon*, p. 39.

One of the whitest, poorest states: *History of North Dakota* by Elwyn Robinson, p. 400. In 1935 per capita income was $145 for North Dakota; $375 for the United States.

CHAPTER 2

Chicago's Comiskey Park: the stadium held 52,000 in 1926, see www.ballpark sofbaseball.com/past/ComiskeyPark.htm.

Dour Norwegian ancestry: Author phone interview with North Dakota writer-historian Kevin Carvell, June 6, 2010.

Elizabeth Preston Anderson: "Battle with the Bottle" by Jack Sullivan, undated *Fargo Forum* clip posted at http://legacy.inforum.com/specials/century/jan3/week27.html.

3.2 percent alcohol: e-mail interview with Bismarck Historical Society member Jim Christianson, February 22, 2012.

"Some counties stayed dry": "1933 Beer Legal in North Dakota": Mandan Historical Society Web site, www.mandanhistory.org/areahistory/prohibitioninmandan.html.

Little Chicago: "Minot History 1920–1940" by Professor Charles Dickson, Minot State University; http://www.minotlibrary.org/minot_history1920-1940.htm.

Run by the police commissioner: Mandan Historical Society, http://www.mandanhistory.org/areahistory/prohibitioninmandan.html.

30 gallons of bliss: "Battle with the Bottle" by Jack Sullivan, *Fargo Forum*.

Federal agents: Author phone interview with Bismarck native Ray Shaefer, Sept. 28, 2009.

It would happen: phone interview with John Sakaraissen, Feb. 18, 2010.

Less than 9 inches: *History of North Dakota* by Elwyn Robinson, p. 398; in 1936 only 8.8 inches of rainfall, p. 10.

"Too-Much Mistake": ibid, p. vii.

foreclosure epidemic: *Main Street in Crisis: The Great Depression and the Old Middle Class on the Northern Plains* by Catherine McNicol Stock, pp. 18–19.

Airborne swarms: *History of North Dakota*, p. 398. Grasshoppers arrive in 1931 and wreaked havoc for nearly a decade.

"hoppers" covered more: ibid and *Main Street in Crisis* by Catherine McNicol Stock, pp. 21–22.

"more Cold than I thought": From Fort Mandan National Historic site Web site, http://lewisandclarktrail.com/section2/ndcities/BismarckMandan/fortmandan.htm. Fort Mandan is near the current city of Washburn, North Dakota.

"a hundred drums": *Images of America: Bismarck, North Dakota*, p. 7 and p. 54.

traverse 833 miles: *History of the City of Bismarck* by the Bismarck Centennial Commission, p. 27.

"I have on my table": http://www.legendsofamerica.com/nd-fortabrahamlincoln.html. Per Army Regulation (AR) 600–20, the title of address for a Lieutenant Colonel is "Colonel," which I've employed for most references to George Armstrong Custer.

Headline writers: *Bismarck Tribune*, August 12 and August 26, 1874.

A physical inventory: ibid, May 26, 1975, p. 1.

"the character of Bismarck changed": ibid, November 3, 1920, p. 4.

Colonel Custer and 1,200 troops: Author's on-site notes taken at Fort Lincoln, September 2009.

Regimental band played: *WPA Guide to North Dakota*, p. 45. The word "Me" is sometimes added to the end of the song title "The Girl I Left Behind."

Astride a mule: *Showdown at Little Big Horn* by Dee Alexander Brown, p. 161.

268 fatalities: This is the most common figure for the total killed. http://www.bookrags.com/wiki/Battle_of_the_Little_Bighorn and http://custer.over-blog.com/categorie-10044479.html; also see the introduction to the 1879 Court of Inquiry report: http://www.loc.gov/rr/frd/Military_Law/Reno_court_inquiry.html.

Missing only one ear: Wyoming Tales and Trails Web site, www.wyomingtalesandtrails.com/custer4a.html. For a list of Little Big Horn casualties see http://www.littlebighorn.info/Cavalry/NameM.htm.

"Benteen Base Ball Club": *Montana: The Magazine of Western History*, Summer 1970, pp. 82–87.

Possibly putting his arm to work: For the McCurry accusation, see www.custerwest.org/coverup2.htm.

A copy of 678-page inquiry is posted on the Library of Congress Web site: www.loc.gov/rr/frd/Military_Law/Reno_court_inquiry.html.

Bat-and-ball games: *Baseball in the Garden of Eden* by John Thorn, p. 18, p. 56.

Nine innings weren't the norm: ibid, p. 72.

Overhand pitches: "The Prehistory of Baseball" by Bruce Weber, *New York Times*, April 8, 2011.

His fantasy: *Always the Young Strangers* by Carl Sandburg, p. 186.

"What is this fascination": ibid, pp. 183–184.

"House of Baseball": *Baseball, the People's Game*, p. 3.

Young Mr. Eisenhower: ibid, p. 262; also *Eisenhower: A Soldier's Life* by Carlo D'Este, p. 53.

When Nashville, Alabama hosted Dierks: "Baseball Calls," *The Arkansas Historical Quarterly*, Winter 1992, p. 423.

Family owned Bona Allen: Team details from "The Bona Allen Shoemakers" by J. P Alexander, baseballink.com, June 1, 2000.

246 minor league teams: From www.milb.com, the official Web site of minor league baseball.

102 teams and 14 leagues: ibid.

At the "light" end: Use of light and heavy semipro jargon, *Baseball: The People's Game*, p. 260.

read the newspaper: ibid, p. 245.

Hopscotch bars: Phone interview with former semipro player Al Wiest, October 7, 2009.

Earned about $65 a month: *Baseball, The People's Game*, p. 252.

Lefty Grove: ibid, p. 241.

Less than $30 a week: U.S. Department of Labor says the average worker made $24.94 a week after deductions for unemployment.

"Shoeless Joe" Jackson: "Baseball Calls," *The Arkansas Historical Quarterly*, Winter 1992, p. 415.

Charles "Swede" Risberg: Signs with Jamestown, North Dakota team, *Bismarck Tribune*, March 19, 1930; Risberg playing in Montana, *Montana: The Magazine of Western History*, Summer 1970, p. 89.

Recruited by Silver Falls Lumber: Phone interview with Johnny Pesky, April 10, 2009. Some details come from "Yawkey's Other Red Sox," *Silverton Appeal*, August 27, 2005.

"I used to get $100": Interviews with Bob Feller, June 20–21, 2009.

In the spring of 1909: Joe Cutting's quote and biography details come from photo captions in the State Historical Society of North Dakota's digital archives collection. Additional details from *Football in Minnesota: The Story of Thirty Years' Contests on the Gridiron*, p. 155.

All future ghost towns: Team references in *Bismarck Tribune*, February 2, 1928, p. 9 (Sanger); April 4, 1911, p. 2 (Russell); August 30, 1926, p. 6 (Omemee); January 22, 1915, p. 1 (Ambrose); May 3, 1926, p. 3 (Mercer); February 13, 1915, p. 6 (Van Hook). The towns of Omemee, Russell, and Sanger are gone. The 2000 population of Ambrose was 23, of Van Hook, 42, and of Russell, 52.

Challenge Fort Abraham Lincoln: *Bismarck Tribune*, July 1, 1881, p. 4.

"a number of bets": ibid, June 28, 1889, p. 8.

Sitting Bull brandishing a banner: ibid, Sept 7, 1930, p. 5; also July 5, 1889, p. 5.

Cut the heart out: http//custerlives.com/custer9.htm.

Hawk autographed photos: See collections of Mrs. J. A. Burgum, *Bismarck Tribune*, Sept. 7, 1929, p. 5.

Camp for the summer: Author phone interview with Bismarck native Robert Ritterbush, August 29, 2009. Numerous Bismarck people I interviewed remember the Sioux dancers, including Randy Churchill, Chuck Eastgate, John Sakariassen, and Ritterbush.

Shooed them away: *History of the City of Bismarck: The First 100 Years*, p. 135.

Reuben Stevens duck hunting accident: *Bismarck Tribune*, May 21, 1890, p. 1.

"baseball teams are draining the towns": *Bismarck Tribune*, Aug. 3, 1907, p. 4.

Salary cap of $600: ibid, April 13, 1907, p. 8.

Reins turned over to Chick Kirk: ibid, May 14, 1917, p. 6; May 28, 1917, p. 3.

Convict players bolted: ibid, April 13, 1921, p. 8.

Voters approved only Sunday baseball: "Amateur and Semi-Professional Baseball in North Dakota Communities," master's thesis by Kyle Robert Jansson, 1994, Arizona State University; pp. 38–39.

Sunday ritual: Interview with Bismarck resident Erna Lahr, August 8, 2009.

park along the foul lines: Kyle Robert Jansson thesis, p. 36; interviews with Gil Olson, John Sakariassen, and Chuck Eastgate.

a budget gap of nearly $5,000: *Bismarck Tribune*, May 8, 1922, p. 8. The team was $1,600 in debt and $1,200 remained on the note for the ball field. They also needed $2,500 for 1922 operating expenses.

Negro mammies and old darkies: ibid, May 20, 1922, p. 2 and May 27, 1922, p. 2.

A touring team from Scobey: "Scobey's Touring Pros" by Gary Lucht, *Montana: The Magazine of Western Culture*, summer 1970.

"Is Bismarck a baseball town?": *Bismarck Capital*, March 18, 1926, n.p.

CHAPTER 3

She sold cakes and pies: Biographical details come from Rebecca Churchill's untitled obit in the family scrapbook dated July 16, 1936 and interviews with family members Margie Churchill and Karen Gunderson.

"If there was another side": *Bismarck Tribune*, Sept. 31, 1969, p. 2.

Two years of semipro catching: ibid, June 7, 1928, p. 11.

Neil borrowed $800: Churchill's early work history is a combination of 1910 Census data and a *Bismarck Tribune* article, Sept. 3, 1952, p. 2.

Tribune editorial: *Bismarck Tribune*, May 18, 1911, p. 2. The top speed of a 1911 Ford was 45 mph.

North Dakotans gobbled up motor vehicles: *History of North Dakota*, pp. 378–379.

On their honeymoon: Wedding and honeymoon details come from *Bismarck Tribune*, September 20, 1924 and interviews with Randy, Jennifer, and Margie Churchill, July 15, 2009.

"the best retail salesman": Phone interview with Wick Corwin's son Charlie, January 2008. Wick's early biography details come from an interview with Charlie Corwin, August 17, 2009.

"You smoke, don't you?": Charlie Corwin gave his recollection of a typical Churchill sales pitch in a phone interview, February 19, 2010. The $1,670 price of a Chrysler is taken from a Corwin-Churchill ad in the *Bismarck Tribune*, September 24, 1925.

Assuming control of the Bismarck Phantoms: Churchill's role with the Phantoms comes from phone interviews with former player Gil Olson, September 9 and September 25, 2009.

Got hired in 1926: *Spanning the Globe: The Rise, Fall and Return to Greatness of the Harlem Globetrotters* by Ben Green, p. 24.

New York Harlem Globetrotters: ibid, p. 50. They launched in the winter of 1929–1930. Saperstein obituaries and news clips are often inaccurate. Ben Green's biography is considered a definitive source.

"The Great White Father": *Ogden (Utah) Standard-Examiner*, August 8, 1947.

"Abe, how are you?": The Saperstein-Churchill conversation and the winter blizzard anecdote come from a phone interview with Gil Olson, September 25, 2009.

"has taken a leading interest": *Bismarck Capital*, April 29, 1926, p. 14.

Dumped all the semipros: ibid.

"Church looked like a trained walrus": *Bismarck Capital*, August 19, 1926, p. 2.

Each player wore: *Bismarck Tribune*, April 27, 1926, p. 6.

Players who didn't show up: ibid, May 1, 1926, n.p.

Bismarck papers praised him: "The Bismarck team has set an enviable record this year," *Bismarck Tribune*, August 30, 1926, p. 6; "This team brought baseball back," *Bismarck Capital*, August 26, 1926, p. 4.

season-high crowd: *Bismarck Capital*, July 15, 1926, p. 4.

Broom-maker preacher and prophesy: *The House of David* by Christopher Siriano, p. 11 and p. 16.

Colony became a tourist attraction: House of David history and amenities, see House of David Web site: www.hodmuseum.tripod.com.

His case heading to court: Benjamin Purnell was found guilty of fraud November 20, 1927, but the sex charges were never resolved. He died in December 1927. "The Last Days of the House of David," by Adam Langer, *Chicago Reader,* June 30, 1994.

Held a parade: Details of the Ku Klux Klan "Klonclave" come from Klan ads in the *Bismarck Tribune,* June 2, June 24, and June 25, 1926.

150 fans and "literally made monkeys": *Bismarck Capital,* July 1, 1926, n.p.

100 degrees: *Bismarck Tribune,* June 28, 1926, p. 1.

Mock fashion show: ibid, April 13, 1928, p. 6.

Elks Band and "give 'im the dark one!": *Bismarck Capital,* Sept. 1, 1927.

Danced with glee: *Bismarck Capital,* Sept. 1, 1927.

"most startling feat" and heavyweight race: *Bismarck Tribune,* August 29, 1927, p. 6. Arthur Fred Ziegenhagel's full name confirmed by 1920 Census data, 1917 draft registration, and 1954 death certificate.

"developed civic pride": *Bismarck Tribune,* September 3, 1927, p. 8.

How many sandwiches to eat: *Bismarck Capital,* June 23, 1927, n.p.

"filthy, insulting fan element": ibid, July 12, 1928, p. 16.

"Few men have done more": *Bismarck Tribune,* July 10, 1928, p. 6.

"Churchill named manager": ibid, April 2, 1929, p. 8.

broadcast from New York City: ibid, January 14, 1926, p. 2.

"training healthy manly boys": ibid, January 18, 1930, p. 4.

A bizarre compensation plan: ibid, May 16, 1931, p. 6.

A fractured skull and accounts of Balzer Klein's death: ibid, July 14, 1932, p. 1; July 15, 1932, p. 3; July 14, 1932, p. 5. *Bismarck Capital,* Sept. 12, 1935, n.p.; *Wilton (North Dakota) News,* July 15, 1932, n.p.

CHAPTER 4

"a world I did not know": *20 Years Too Soon,* p. xiv.

26 in 1933: Tuskegee Institute lynching statistics, www.law.umkc.edu/faculty/projects/ftrials/shipp/lynchingyear.html.

"I have no comment to make": *New York Times,* November 29, 1933, n.p.

"collective murder . . . pagan ethics": ibid, December 7, 1933, n.p.

Efforts to move a bill: The Dyer Act passed the House of Representatives in 1922, but was filibustered to death in the U.S. Senate; the Costigan-Wagner bill was introduced in 1934, and again filibustered. See *New York Times*, December 3, 1933 and November 4, 1934, n.p.

Ethnicity and achievement: *New York Times*, June 29, 1933, p. 3; editorial on "pure race," Nov. 12, 1933, section VII, p. 6.

Taught their ten children and details on Troup's youth: *20 Years Too Soon*, pp. 9–17.

Just 269 feet: www.stlmag.com/St-Louis-Magazine/April-2008/Our-Hallowed-Ground/.

Died of heart failure: *20 Years Too Soon*, p. 22. Quincy Troupe says he was 16 when his father died. However, Charles Troupe's death certificate is dated 1930, when Quincy was 18 and a high school senior.

$80 a month contract and Troupe's early career details: ibid, pp. 23–28, pp. 34–35.

At least fifty-five blacks: According to Merl Kleinknecht for *SABR Journal Archive* and also *Baseball, The People's Game*, p. 546. Some say seventy are possible: *Satchel* by Larry Tye, p. 31.

Inventing the shin guard anecdote: William White, *Satchel*, p. 30 and Negro League Baseball Players Association's Web site profile of Bud Fowler.

tragic flaw was pigmentation: www.JockBio.com. This is a good resource for Fleetwood Walker biographical details.

He would go on to bat: www.bioproj.sabr.org. SABR's Baseball Biography Project is a good resource for Cap Anson details, including his aversion to baseball gloves.

played in 42 and batted: Fleet Walker's career statistics from www.baseball-reference.com.

Argyle Hotel: *Satch, Dizzy & Rapid Robert* by Timothy M. Gay, p. 21.

"esteemed Bible of Baseball": www.sportingnews.com/archives/history/1920a.html.

"A new trouble": "Cap, Jackie, and Ted" by Mark Harnischfeger and Mary E. Corey, Organization of American Historians, *Magazine of History* (2010) 24 (2), pp. 29–36.

"Get that nigger": Cap Chronicled Web site, www.capanson.com/chapter4. html.

In order to keep the peace: Baseball-reference.com bio of George Stovey, which includes an excerpt from the *Newark Sunday Call* of July 1887 that mentions the White Stockings game was, indeed, played that day.

"no more contracts with colored men": *The Complete Armchair Book of Baseball*, p. 677.

Bert Jones, banished: *The Negro League Book*, edited by Dick Clark and Larry Lester, n.p.

"almost criminal to attempt": *The Complete Armchair Book of Baseball*, p. 682.

About noon: *Bismarck Tribune*, July 25, 1933, p. 6.

"Bismarck Drubs Fort Lincoln": ibid, June 26, 1933, p. 6.

The Princess had been built: Hotel details from National Register of Historic Places application.

"This is mange medicine": Troupe and Davis hotel room scene, *20 Years too Soon*, p. 43.

Millett married and stayed: details from her obituary, *Bismarck Tribune*, July 27, 1936, p. 3.

That son was grown now: Phone interview with Bismarck resident Floyd Fuller, January 26, 2011. Fuller's mother told him the story about the tinsmith, who lived next door to the Fullers.

CHAPTER 5

North Dakotans decided overwhelmingly: Prairie Public Broadcasting, March 16, 2011. www.prairiepublic.org/radio/dakota-datebook?post=30639.

Makeshift hobo camp: Location of that camp and Jaszkowiak farm, plus spring flooding details come from phone interviews with Bismarck resident Myron Atkinson, August 3 and August 31, 2009 and July 30, 2012.

The spinster sisters: John Halloran's private memoir *A Journal for Katharine*, pp. 26–27.

Jack Lyons's Ideal Irish Lunch Stand: ibid, pp. 18–22.

Quickly excused himself: Phone interviews with Bismarck resident Marc Conrad, May 6, 2009 and July 26, 2012.

Dolan's barbershop: from *City of Bismarck: The First 100 Years*, p. 183.

Will Company details: "George Will Helped Tell the State's History," *Bismarck Tribune*, July 5, 2009, and "Seed Corn to Shelterbelts," by Oscar H. Will III, undated clip from *Farm Collector*.

"Bismarck's pioneer garage": Advertisement in 1940 Bismarck City Directory. Also called the oldest garage in North Dakota, *Bismarck Tribune*, November 27, 1937, p. 14.

Shipped autos by train: Interviews with Corwin-Churchill Motors then-executive Bruce Whittey, February 1, 2010 and local historian Frank Vyzralek, August 3, 2009.

provided ambulance service: Interview with Bruce Whittey, August 26, 2009.

Shortwave radios, etc.: Interview with Bruce Whittey, February 11, 2010. Ads in *Bismarck Tribune*, May 27, 1933, p. 8; September 14, 1932, p. 6; April 10, 1933, p. 5; November 27, 1937, p. 8.

Cars that reeked of whiskey: Interview with Bruce Whittey, August 26, 2009 and other sources.

Low-slung, two-story building: Descriptions of the Corwin-Churchill dealership and Churchill's office come from articles and photos in the *Bismarck Tribune*, February 27, 1926, p. 22 and November 27, 1937, p. 8.; also interview with Bruce Whittey, February 11, 2010.

Ladies Aid Society, bridge club, Study Club: *Bismarck Tribune*, February 3, 1933, p. 5; September 30, 1937, p. 4; March 13, 1935, p. 5 (Carlyle); September 14, 1932, p. 5 (Scandinavia).

he always was served last: Neil C. Churchill undated letter to author, summer 2009.

"Minstrel Frolic": *Bismarck Tribune*, March 27, 1928, p. 3.

All-night poker session: Interview with Stan Sharkey, September 23, 2009. As a teenager Sharkey served as a gopher during those poker games.

"I don't have any reason to smoke": Author interview with Bismarck resident Chuck Eastgate, August 13, 2009.

buying a judge: Interview with Jim Christianson, August 28, 2009. Patterson and Alexander McKenzie "were wheeling and dealing, buying the judges." Christianson is a member of the Bismarck Historical Society and his company now owns the Patterson Hotel.

Waiver from paying property taxes: Details on the tax loophole are contained in the National Register of Historic Places application for the Patterson Hotel. Anecdote of the workers and mule come from interviews with Jim Christianson, August 28, 2009 and with Robert Ritterbush, August 29, 2009. According to the *Bismarck Tribune* of January 2, 1936, the hotel ultimately settled its tax bill for $58,807.

free typewriter: Interview with Chuck Eastgate, August 30, 2009.

bovine stench: Interview with Myron Atkinson, August 3, 2009.

"bumped him for fifteen hits": *Bismarck Tribune*, July 5, 1904, p. 2.

quietly tapped into the Negro Leagues: Pitcher Wilber "Bullet" Rogan and catcher Charlie Hancock join the Jamestown team, *Jamestown Sun*, April 21, 1932, p. 5.

"Bismarck's biggest weakness": *Bismarck Tribune*, July 18, 1933, p. 6.

"giant Negro catcher": ibid, August 12, 18, 19, and 30, 1933.

"one of the niftiest baseball games": ibid, August 3, 1933, p. 8.

everyone called her "Blondie": Interview with Red Haley's nephew, Ronald Craig, April 29, 2011. His light skin and "Red" nickname: interview with Haley's niece, Claudia Randleman, May 3, 2011.

Tendency to golf low pitches: Interview with former Bismarck ballboy Bob Mhyre, April 3, 2012.

 bashed 41 home runs: *Bismarck Tribune*, June 4, 1930, p. 8; *Lethbridge* (*Saskatchewan*) *Herald*, August 5, 1930.

"Satchel Paige leading right-handed flinger": *Bismarck Tribune*, August 10, 1933, p. 8.

CHAPTER 6

"like the sun just came out": *Satchel* by Larry Tye, p. 46.

a goat had gobbled: *New York Times*, June 8, 1982.

"let us ramble!": "The Fabulous Satchel Paige" by Richard Donovan, *Colliers*, May 30, June 6, June 13, 1953.

"spake in diverse tongues": www.baseball-almanac.com/legendary/libr6.shtml.

"looks like a fish egg": *New York Daily News*, February 12, 1971.

"He threw fire": *Maybe I'll Pitch Forever* by Satchel Paige and David Lipman, p. vi.

A favorite trick: "Was Satchel Paige as Great as They Say He Was?," *Baseball Digest*, June 1996, p. 68.

Finish hammering the heads: *Mansfield (Ohio) News Journal*, August 17, 1998.

"Satchel was a comedian": Buck O'Neil quote is from Ken Burns' documentary *Baseball*, www.pbs.org/kenburns/baseball/shadowball/oneil.html.

"He rather play baseball": *Satchel*, p. 12.

"Unless you've gone around with nothing": *Maybe I'll Pitch Forever*, p. 22.

Alabama Reform School: Details on Paige's stint, *Satchel*, pp. 14–17.

"I traded five years of freedom": ibid, p. 20.

"I do it all the time": *Maybe I'll Pitch Forever*, p. 29.

$250 a month contract: *Pitchin' Man*, p. 38 and *Satchel*, p. 25.

"The Crawfords might possibly be interested": *Collier's*, May–June 1953.

"It burned me": *Satchel*, p. 52.

Sportswriter Damon Runyon: Radcliffe biography entry, www.baseballreference.com.

"I began to feel paralyzed": *Collier's*, May–June 1953.

As low as $250, as high as $550: *Satchel*, p. 312, footnote 57.

About $170 a month: *The Forgotten Players: The Story of Black Baseball in America* by Robert Gardner and Dennis Shortelle, p. 45.

Equivalent of $1,100 a month: The average Major Leaguer made $7,700 a year in 1930, the equivalent of about $1,100 a month during the baseball season. See "The Economic History of Major League Baseball" by Michael J. Haupert, a study posted on the Web site of the Economics History Association (www.eh.net), December 3, 2007; see also "Babe Ruth is Better than Dow Jones" by Michael Haupert, in *Outside the Lines*, SABR magazine, June 8, 2008.

"We want the greatest colored pitcher": *Bismarck Tribune*, June 21, 1939, p. 6.

"wouldn't throw ice cubes": Wendell Smith's column, "Smitty's Sports Spurts," *The Pittsburgh Courier*, April 16, 1938.

"It wasn't until after": *Maybe I'll Pitch Forever*, p. 88.

CHAPTER 7

"He'd gamble on what time": Interview with former ball boy Lyle Porter, February 2, 2011.

Churchill raced Harry Potter: Interviews with Chuck Eastgate, August 13, 2009 and Ray Shaefer, September 28, 2009.

he raced sprinter Jesse Owens: Interviews with Chuck Eastgate, August 30, 2009 and Bill Melech, February 8, 2011.

He lost an apartment building: Interview with Charlie Corwin, August 1, 2009.

keys to a shiny Chrysler: Interview with Bismarck resident Stan Sharkey, February 2, 2011.

Some Bismarckers took umbrage: Interview with Bismarck resident Marc Conrad, May 6, 2009.

$500 side bet: *Bismarck Tribune*, March 25, 1926, p. 6.

The Tribune story reiterated; "in their reply offered": *Bismarck Tribune*, August 12, 1933.

Paige detained by Pittsburgh police: *Bismarck Tribune*, June 21, 1939, p. 6.

"I do as I do": *Colliers*, May–June 1953.

Pulled into Bismarck late Saturday afternoon: *20 Years Too Soon*, p. 48. The *Bismarck Tribune*, Aug 12, 1933 says Paige "was expected here Saturday." *Bismarck Tribune*, June 21, 1939 says Paige arrived in town Saturday. A June 15, 1948 article in the *Tribune* says Paige arrived a few hours before the game, which seems highly unlikely.

Princess Hotel: Charlie Whittey, who worked for Neil Churchill at the car dealership, told his son that ballplayers stayed at "the hotel by the Patterson," meaning the Soo Hotel, later called the Princess Hotel. Interview with his son Bruce Whittey, August 26, 2009.

"givin' Bismarck the hee-haw": *Pitchin' Man*, p. 51.

"It is so cheap": *Jamestown Sun*, August 12, 1933, p. 5.

Painted dark green: Bismarck residents Floyd Fuller, Bill Melech, Harry Valdie all said in interviews that the ballpark was painted green. Fuller said his father and mother installed the wire screen. Locker room details come from Valdie.

estimated 3,000 people: *Jamestown Sun*, August 14, 1933 and *Bismarck Capital*, August 14, 1933 say 3,000. *Bismarck Tribune*, August 13, 1933 says 2,200, but the paper likely was referring only to tickets sold and not counting onlookers on the hill outside the park.

"balls that were so fast": *Jamestown Sun*, August 14, 1933, p. 5.

"a masterpiece . . . ," ibid.

"darkies who were well dressed": Phone interview with a Bismarck resident, September 23, 2009.

He strummed a guitar: *Bismarck Tribune*, March 14, 1899, p. 3.

A new black suit, "good friend" and "brave to the last": ibid, March 24, 1899, p. 3.

Doomed vocalist Jim Cole: ibid, February 21, 1899, p. 3.

"Nigger Baker": *A Journal for Katherine*, p. 10; "Nigger Betty": Phone interview with a former Bismarck resident, April 3, 2012.

two spring minstrel shows: *Bismarck Tribune*, April 29, 1933, p. 5 and May 3, 1933, p. 5.

Corwin fired him: Interview with Charlie Corwin, Aug. 17, 2009.

"If you did that": *Maybe I'll Pitch Forever*, pp. 89–90.

Using his spitball: *Bismarck Tribune*, August 25, 1933, p. 9.

He'd get even with Stewart: Interview with McCarney's daughter, Sharon Spaedy, June 5, 2008. She didn't know the injured player by name, but Frank Stewart is identified in the game-day account.

"equal to any big league game": *Jamestown Sun*, Aug 28, 1933, p. 5.

Stewart was carted off: ibid, p. 6.

Found his way to the Dome, cab driver delivered moonshine: Interview with Bismarck native Bob Myhre, April 3, 2012. He heard the Paige story directly from the cab driver.

Raised the awkward topic: *20 Years Too Soon*, p. 50.

Quincy Troupe Night: *Bismarck Tribune*, August 31, 1933, p. 8.

"something of farce": ibid, September 7, 1933.

"It will be interesting to see": ibid, September 11, 1933, p. 6.

"'Mahatma' Satchell [sic] Paige": *Bismarck Capital*, September 14, 1933, p. 4.

"I was never so let down": Troupe attends Cardinals game, *20 Years Too Soon*, p. xiii.

CHAPTER 8

"The games this past summer": *Bismarck Capital*, Aug. 24, 1933, n.p.

two thousand miles: *One Third of a Nation: Lorena Hickok Reports on the Great Depression*, p. 70. Details from Hickock's trip, pp. 56–68.

$5,000 renovation: *Bismarck Tribune*, March 28, 1934, p. 8.

stole Roosevelt Davis away: ibid, March 29, 1934, p. 8.

talk with Saperstein: ibid, January 26, 1934, n.p.

CHAPTER 9

via Pittsburgh and Nashville; with Matlock or Cornelius: *Bismarck Tribune*, May 5, 1934, p. 6; *Bismarck Capital*, May 15, 1934, p. 5.

"a million miles": *Bismarck Tribune*, May 9, 1934, p. 6.

"momentarily": ibid, May 7, 1934, n.p.; "later this week": May 15, 1934, p. 5; "whereabouts unknown": May 21, 1934, p. 6.

Greenlee laid down law: ibid, May 17, 1934; court injunction: May 21, 1934, p. 6.

"Indian hurler": ibid, September 4, 1934.

Loved to dress up players' biographies: *Spinning the Globe* by Ben Green, p. 64. Throughout his career Saperstein planted false information in the press.

Whacked his son: That anecdote and other details come from a series of e-mails with Desiderato's nephew, Terry Sullivan, February 2010 and August 2011.

Churchill offered him $140 a month: Interview with Terry Sullivan, September 12, 2009.

"Big League park": *Bismarck Tribune*, September 29, 1934. That's one of many references.

Only Philadelphia's Shibe Park: ibid, May 22, 1934, p. 6.

Half the community and imposter baseball teams: House of David Baseball Team Research Project, www.peppergame.com.

The same bearded look: The House of David Baseball Team Research Project says the Spring Valley House of David team sported beards. That's a reliable source. There's conflicting evidence regarding the Colored House of David having beards. I found an undated photo of the team without beards.

The pitchblackbaseball Web site says they were beardless. In a March 23, 1981 letter to *Sports Illustrated*, a former Colored HOD player says they did have beards. Two 1930s newspaper clips confirm that, but those are pre-game stories likely based on team publicity, not eyewitness accounts. I opted to go with beards primarily on the basis of that former player's letter.

"the athletic phenomenon of all time": *New York Times*, November 24, 1996 and *Life* Magazine, June 23, 1947, p. 90.

good curve and mediocre fastball: Interview with former semipro player Al Wiest, October 7, 2009. He saw Didrikson pitch.

Never attended another Bismarck ball game: Interview with Floyd Fuller, Jr., April 18, 2011.

A straw hat for hitting the first home run: *Bismarck Tribune*, May 25, 1934, p. 3; free haircuts: ibid, May 28, 1934, p. 6; Vincent's straw hat: ibid, May 30, 1934, p 6; shaving kits: ibid, May 29, 1934, p. 3.

Chucking baseballs over the left field fence: Interview with Bismarck resident Tom Johnson, August 31, 2009. Johnson used to frequent the park as a boy.

Deliberately walked the bases loaded: *Bismarck Tribune*, June 18, 1934.

Marveled at her palms: Mandan Historical Society profile of Era Bell Thompson, www.mandanhistory.org/biographieslz/erabellthompson.

You couldn't safely assume: Interview with Floyd Fuller, Jr., August 4, 2009. Blacks in Bismarck knew to stick to the South Side of town.

Takeout meals at the back door: Interview with Bismarck native Bill Melech, February 8, 2011.

"Moose got scared": The Moose Kay story comes from *McLeod, 1886–1986*, p. 56, as cited in "African Americans in North Dakota: Sources and Assessments" by Thomas P. Newgard and William C. Sherman, University of Mary Press, 1994.

"We always stayed as a family": *Ted "Double Duty" Radcliffe*, p.107.

one of those black players who crossed the color line: Interview with Al Wiest, October 7, 2009. Wiest was a semipro player who lived in Jamestown at that time and interacted with Radcliffe.

Miscegenation was a taboo: The Troupe-and-Jackie story is from *20 Years Too Soon*, pp. 31–32.

He knelt down: Troupe's encounter with red-haired girl, ibid, pp. 51–52.

CHAPTER 10

"Black Sunday" and message to Senator Nye: *Main Street in Crisis*, p. 24.

"curtain of flying earth": *Saturday Evening Post*, July 21, 1934.

Correct figure was 3 percent: *Jamestown Sun*, Aug. 3, 1934, p. 1.

"confused to the point": *Saturday Evening Post*, August 4, 1934.

"They spent a broiling Tuesday": *Bismarck Tribune*, August 7, 1934, pp. 1, 3.

"the 17-inch average": The U.S. Geological Survey's 30-year average annual rainfall for North Dakota (1961 to 1990) is 17.17 inches: http://www.nationalatlas.gov/printable/images/pdf/precip/pageprecip_nd3.pdf.

"We have lived here 28 years": *Bismarck Capital*, September 6, 1934, p. 2.

He'd acquired a lakefront house: Interview with Randy Churchill, July 1, 2008. The house was on Lake Melissa in Minnesota. Randy described taking a long-awaited father-son vacation there as a boy. They planned to go fishing one morning, but Neil Churchill got some spots of oil on his white shirt while struggling to start the boat engine. He immediately stomped back inside the house. "That was the end of my fishing outing with my father," said Randy.

called Neil Churchill "yellow": *Beulah Independent*, July 26, 1934, p. 1.

"singing its swan song": *Bismarck Tribune*, September 4, 1934, p. 6.

retreating to "other climes": *Beulah Independent*, September 6, 1934, p 1.

61 wins, 19 losses, and 3 ties, and $600 debt: *Bismarck Tribune*, September 13, 1934, p. 10.

Minimum of $1,700 a month: That conservative estimate is based on an average of $140 pay per player for 12 players.

"wipe out the remaining deficit": *Bismarck Tribune*, September 13, 1934, p. 10.

Paige sent a letter to Red Haley: *Bismarck Tribune*, September 26, 1934, n.p.

A miserly 2.16 runs per game: The Negro Leagues didn't distinguish between earned and unearned runs. They used an aggregate statistic for combined runs allowed.

"they *all* gonna jump": *Satchel* by Larry Tye, pp. 65–66.

Nearly 30,000 people: There are conflicting accounts of this game. I opted to rely heavily on *Satchel* by Larry Tye, pp. 66–69, presuming it was more thoroughly fact-checked. I also used details from baseballfever.com, baseball-reference.com, and *Don't Look Back* by Mark Ribowsky, pp. 108–110.

"the House of Satchell [sic]": *Satchel*, p. 69.

"Bismarck will be mecca": *Bismarck Tribune*, September 29, 1934, p. 8.

"I knew there were a lot of good Negroes": "A Paige in Bismarck's History," by Marc Conrad, *Bismarck By The River* (a *Bismarck Tribune* special inset), June 1997.

Jamestown dumped all its black semipros: *Jamestown Sun*, April 23, 1935, p. 2; May 5, 1935, p. 6; July 20, 1935, p. 1.

A 38–15 season: pitchblackbaseball.com, p. 10.

"Jamestown's latest diamond venture": *Jamestown Sun*, April 23, 1935, p. 2.

CHAPTER 11

"Trouble" nickname: Interview with Bob McCarney's daughter, Sharon Spaedy, June 5, 2008. "Toadalo" nickname: Interview with Bismarck resident Jim Bankes, August 27, 2009.

Greenlee made the Crawford Grill available and other wedding details: *Don't Look Back*, p. 119.

$250 plus bonuses: ibid.

"Satchel won't be leaving us": *Maybe I'll Pitch Forever*, p. 86.

"Knowing how good he could hit": *Don't Look Back* by Mark Ribowsky, p. 120.

As much as $5,000: *Satch, Dizzy & Rapid Robert* by Timothy M. Gay, p. 98. Note: This book was the source for most Dean-Paige barnstorming details, pp. 72–105.

"Mistah Satchel Paige": James E. Doyle column, *Cleveland Plain Dealer*, October 23, 1934.

Baseball salaries beaten down: According to Baseball Almanac, Major League salaries declined 25 percent between 1929 and 1933. http://www. baseball-almanac.com/dugout0c.shtml.

Paying him about $20,000: *Chicago Daily Tribune*, December 6, 1934 says Dizzy Dean signed a new contract paying him "$20,000 plus" for the 1935 season and quotes Dean as saying he'd just made $14,000 barnstorming that fall. Baseball Almanac says Dean's salary was $18,500 in 1935.

"the peanut circuit": *Don't Look Back*, p. 120.

let black teams participate: *(Wichita) Negro Star,* July 27, 1934; record crowd: ibid, August 24, 1934.

Seated in a chair: ibid (but a separate news story from above).

Prize of $5,964: *Negro Star,* August 31, 1934; $5,389 bonus: www.baseball-almanac.com/ws/wsshares.shtml.

No more race mixing: *New York Age*, May 11, 1935, p. 5; *Mandan Pioneer,* August 18, 1935.

"After that honeymoon": *Satchel* by Larry Tye, p. 75.

Study group topics: *Bismarck Tribune,* January 29, 1935 (Civil War), March 13, 1935 (Thomas Carlyle), and March 27, 1935 (philosophy of life).

Whose grandmother was Nancy Millett: *African-Americans in North Dakota*, p. 243.

Carnival and minstrel show: *Bismarck Tribune*, November 30, 1934, p.1 and October 20, p. 2.

"Hambones": For role of end men, see www.english.illinois.edu/maps/poets/a_f/berryman/minstrel.htm.

"Liza Jane": *Bismarck Tribune*, November 27, 1934, p. 1.

Gazing through a telescope: ibid, November 30, 1934, p. 1.

Chicago American Giants wanted him: *Negro Star,* March 15, 1935; Monarchs locked him up: *20 Years Too Soon*, p. 52.

Only 1,500 tickets sold: *Bismarck Tribune*, October 8, 1934, p. 6.

Alma Sundquist, team's prospects: ibid, March 1, 1935, n.p.

CHAPTER 12

the filibustering opposition: *New York Times*, April 30, 1935.

None of the twenty victims: ibid, December 27, 1935.

Before order could be restored: ibid, March 31, 1935; *New York Age*, March 23, 1935.

$2 million in property damage: *Africana, Civil Rights: An A-to-Z Reference of the Movement that Changed America* by Kwame Anthony Appiah and Henry Louis Gates, p. 202.

first "modern" race riot: George Mason University professor Jeffrey Stewart,

PBS Online Newshour Forum, February 20, 1998; *Racial Violence in the United States* by Allen Grimshaw.

Claimed to have lost $30,000: *New York Age*, September 14, 1935, p. 8.

Churchill met his pitcher's demands: *Bismarck Tribune*, June 21, 1939, p. 6. *Chattanooga Times*, September 3, 1935, p. 8, reported "the rumors" that Paige "draws down about $450 a month," but that would have been exclusive of his other perks.

snazzy Red Chrysler convertible: Interview with Neil C. Churchill, July 1, 2008.

drove directly to Bismarck: "Paige Arrives in Bismarck": *Bismarck Tribune*, March 25, 1935, p. 6.

Greenlee warned Churchill: "A Paige in Bismarck's History," *Bismarck by the River*, June 1997.

Paige made it to Bismarck: *Bismarck Tribune*, March 25, 1935.

Passed their swimming-pool test: *Bismarck Capital*, August 13, 1935.

students who had perfect attendance: *Bismarck Tribune*, February 20, 1935, p. 3.

"Satchel Paige Arrives": ibid, March 25, 1935.

Opened up a shoeshine parlor: *Wichita Beacon*, August 21, 1936, p. 20.

Desiderato never showed emotion, shrank from spotlight: Interview with his daughter Marie, November 16, 2009.

"Joe, you've got to speak up": Interview with Desiderato's nephew, Terry Sullivan, Sept. 12, 2009.

Moved into converted box car: *Maybe I'll Pitch Forever*, p. 88. It's rumored that Wick Corwin's cabin on the west side of town housed Satchel Paige, according to current owner, Jack Schwartz. Interview with Schwartz, October 17, 2009 and July 13–14, 2011. In an August 3, 2012 interview, former ballboy Bob Myhre said cab driver Veral Speaks told him Paige lived in a converted box car by South 9th and Front streets. Speaks said he delivered liquor to Paige at that site.

Little Marie got to sit in dugout: Interview with Marie Desiderato, Nov. 16, 2009. "Coo 'Uncle Satchel,'" interview with Terry Sullivan, Sept. 12, 2009.

"hats full of money": *Chicago Daily News*, June 9, 1943, n.p.

Welfare rolls approached 70 percent: *History of North Dakota*, p. 407.

The all white Jamestown baseball team: *Jamestown Sun*, May 6, 1935, p. 6.

"All the club needs": *Bismarck Tribune*, May 9, 1935, n.p.

Tossing one pitch underhanded: ibid, May 20, 1935, n.p.

The Mansfield Iron Mine collapsed: For details, see the Web sites www. crystalfalls.org/mining.htm; www.3gendisasters.com/michigan/1971/crystal -falls; http://my/net-link.net/~prostock/mansfield.html.

the next to last person: Interview with Moose Johnson's grand-nephew, Rick Johnson, February 27, 2011.

"tippling houses": Interview with Moose Johnson's nephew, Donald Johnson, March 17, 2010.

"a binge drinker": Interview with Moose Johnson's nephew, Duane Johnson, March 16, 2010.

Herculean home run and other feats: Interviews with Donald and Duane Johnson, March, 2010.

"a million-dollar arm": Interview with Donald Johnson, March 17, 2010.

Manager Jack Shemky and protective custody: *A Collection of Recollections: Crystal Falls 1880-1980*, p. 206.

"emulated Babe Ruth last summer": *Ironwood [Michigan] Daily Globe*, March 8, 1929, n.p.

"Swatting Swede": undated story from *The Tulsa Tribune* provided by the Johnson family, likely published in spring 1932.

"They can't throw fastballs by me": ibid.

"broken training": *Emporia (Kansas) Daily Gazette*, August 8, 1933 and an un-identified August 1933 clip provided to me by baseball historian Ray Nemec.

Red Sox and Reds came sniffing: *Ted "Double Duty" Radcliffe*, p. 103.

Reverted to rambunctious ways: *Omaha World Herald*, September 3, 1935, n.p.

pressed a gold telegraph key: See Web sites www.crosley-field.com/FNG/index.html and www.baseball-almanac.com/firsts/first10.shtml.

one of the longest home runs ever seen: *Bismarck Tribune*, May 29 and May 30, 1935, n.p.

CHAPTER 13

Brewer highest-paid black player and Troupe as backup catcher: *(Wichita) Negro Star*, April 19, 1935, n.p.

the school's debating team: "Wiley College's Great Debaters" by Gail Beil, *East Texas Historical Journal*, February 2008. The team became the subject of the 2007 film, *The Great Debaters*, starring Denzel Washington.

Found themselves in a running argument: *20 Years Too Soon*, pp. 52–53. Troupe misremembered the chronology of his quitting the team, implying it was in early April during spring training. The *Emporia Gazette* reported on April 24 that he was still with the Monarchs when they left training camp. According to the *Bismarck Tribune* of May 29, 1935, he arrived in town that day from Kansas City. Researchers at the Kansas City Public Library and St. Louis County Library confirmed Troupe's likely driving route to North Dakota in 1935 would have been Route 71 north, a two-day trip to Bismarck.

Memorial Day doubleheader: *Bismarck Tribune* and *Mandan Pioneer*, May 31, 1935 game accounts.

"more smoke than a burning oil well": *Winnipeg Free Press*, June 1, 1935, n.p.; "finest mound duel": ibid, June 7, 1935, n.p.

Brewer needled his counterpart: *Bismarck Tribune*, June 14, 1935, n.p.

Gopher Day cash prizes: *Bismarck Tribune*, June 23, 1938, p. 11 and May 26, 1921, p. 3; 100,000 gopher tails: ibid, May 26, 1921, p. 3.

speculated about "a jinx": ibid, June 26, 1935, n.p.; Morris hospitalized: ibid, June 28, 1935, p. 8.

Desiderato banged up hand: *Ted "Double Duty" Radcliffe*, p. 125.

A Canadian journalist got snookered: *Lethbridge Herald*, June 7, 1935, n.p.

Driving at "a fast clip": *Bismarck Capital*, May 23, 1935, n.p. Conrad describes Paige's car as a Chrysler Airflow in his article. Neil C. Churchill described Paige's car as a "red convertible" in a July 1, 2008 phone interview with me. I believe they are both correct.

The Sioux called him *Mila Mazawakan*: Interview with Kelly Morgan, June 18, 2010. Morgan lives on Standing Rock Indian Reservation and recalls her mother and uncle talking about Paige's visits. She provided me the Sioux translation of "Long Rifle."

Bismarck had 29 games: My examination of news clips combined with author Kyle McNary's statistics culled from June 5, 1935.

Flyspeck towns like Heaton and $5 combat pay: Interview with Charlie Krahler, September 24, 2009. He had a North Dakota friend who caught Paige during that Heaton game.

A friendship with Dorothy Running-Deer: "The Fabulous Satchel Paige," *Collier's*, May 30, 1953, n.p.

"It's a wonder my arm": ibid.

Refused to divulge: *Maybe I'll Pitch Forever*, p. 98; possible ingredients: *Collier's*, May 30, 1953, n.p.

All the swagger of a librarian: *Wilber "Bullet" Rogan and the Kansas City Monarchs* by Phil S. Dixon, p. 208, mentions Smith's unatheletic demeanor. Smith's life: *Biographical Dictionary of American Sports*, edited by David L. Porter; tutoring: undated 2001 *Bismarck Tribune* article by Lou Babiarz and author interview with Phil Dixon, March 1, 2011.

$150 a month: Hilton Smith's biography on baseball-reference.com.

"greatest ball team on the road": *Bismarck Tribune*, July 2, 1935, p. 8.

2,000 fans. *Bismarck Tribune*, July 13, 1935, p. 6 and *Mandan Pioneer*, July 14, 1935. *Tribune* estimates the crowd at 1,500 (second biggest of season); *Pioneer* says 2,000 (biggest of season). I used the *Mandan Pioneer* figure, which likely takes into account fans watching from outside the ballpark.

Moose Johnson couldn't hide: He misses the Devils Lake game, *Mandan Pioneer* and *Bismarck Tribune*, July 15, 1935, n.p.

Bob McCarney hopped a freight: Interview with McCarney's daughter, Sharon Spaedy, June 5, 2008. Speady says her father rode the rails into town. A biography on file at the Chester Fitz Library at the University of North Dakota (the repository of McCarney's papers) says he hitchhiked. His daughter was emphatic he hopped a train.

A schoolteacher in the western Badlands: Interview with Charlie Corwin, January 2008.

McCarney enjoyed a liquid lunch: ibid.

Haley a practical joker: *20 Years Too Soon*, p. 55.

teammates gleefully reminded him: Undated 1935 clip of Jack Carberry's column in the *Denver Post* provided to me by Neil Churchill's family.

Played pinochle and poker: *Ted "Double Duty" Radcliffe*, p. 108; also liked Conquin or "Coon Can": *Satchel*, p. 103.

"Come down to the palace of broken hearts": E-mail interview with Johnson family friend Peyton Lacy, August 18, 2012; Moose and Inkspots: interview with Johnson's daughter Hilma Jones, April 23, 2010.

Paige and Mills Brothers: *Satchel*, p. 72.

"I will always do anything I can": *Pitchin' Man*, p. 54; Rearview mirror and rifle: ibid, pp. 52–53.

Shooting rabbits: *20 Years Too Soon*, p. 49; Paige fancied himself a boxer: *Satchel*, p. 104.

"He could clown one moment": *20 Years Too Soon*, p. 55; Driving back to Bismarck: ibid, pp. 53–54.

CHAPTER 14

the conflicted farmer: Interview with Randy Churchill, July 1, 2008.

"Another step in their great experiment of all white baseball": *Jamestown Sun*, July 20, 1935, n.p.

A reporter for the *Mandan Pioneer* took note: *Mandan Pioneer*, July 24, 1935, p. 6.

Hendee arrested for violating blue laws: *Baseball and Richmond: A History of the Professional Game, 1884–2000* by W. Harrison Daniel and Scott P. Mayer, p.103. Also *Danville (Virginia) Bee*, May 9, 1934, n.p.

Crowds topped 2,000 only a few times: The *Mandan Pioneer*, July 14, 1935, says the crowd of 2,000 on July 12 was the biggest of year. The *Bismarck Tribune*, July 13, 1935 estimated that same crowd at 1,500 and said it was second biggest of season. Regardless, the team failed to achieve its Booster Day goal of 3,000 fans.

Hustle side wagers in the grandstand: *Bismarck Tribune*, September 18, 2005 interview with Neil C. Churchill and *Satchel*, p. 80.

Chrysler executive came to Bismarck: Interview with former ballboy Bob Myhre, August 3, 2012.

Bismarck awarded a birth in tournament: *Bismarck Capital*, July 23, 1935, p. 8.

"Satchel was wild as a March hare": *Ted "Double Duty" Radcliffe* by Kyle McNary, p. 10. McNary quoted Radcliffe as saying simply "wild as marsh." I believe he misunderstood Radcliffe. "As wild as a March hare" is a common Southern expression and Radcliffe was from Alabama.

"We used to make a rag ball": ibid, p.11; use wisps of smoke to communicate: ibid, p. 14.

Radcliffe posted career numbers in 1932: *New York Times* obituary, August 12, 2005.

"Here comes my fastball!": *Ted "Double Duty" Radcliffe*, p. 105; Why insult my pitcher: ibid, p. 109; "The two best talkers": p. 107; KKK threatens Churchill, Radcliffe carries gun: p. 99; Paige goes to Mayo Clinic: p. 109; "A different girl every day": p. 93.

His foot got caught under the bag: *Bismarck Tribune*, July 30, 1935, p. 6.

July heat wave: ibid, July 27, 1935, p. 4.

"You son of a bitch!": *Ted "Double Duty" Radcliffe*, p. 105. Interview with Marc Conrad, May 6, 2009. Conrad originally reported that anecdote in the 1980s.

"The balance was thrown catawampus": Interview with semipro player Al Wiest, October 7, 2009.

"Shoot the banker": *Main Street in Crisis* by Catherine McNicol Stock, p. 140; One-third of family farms would go under: ibid, p. 17; almost 6 percent of population leaves: ibid, p. 401.

hail stones as plump as baseballs: *Bismarck Tribune*, August 7, 1935, p. 1.

The Giants were a second-tier traveling club: Team details from *Swinging for the Fences: Black Baseball in Minnesota*, edited by Steven R. Hoffbeck, pp. 112–119.

A fund-raising booster game: *Bismarck Tribune*, July 25, 1935, p. 6; other plans: ibid, July 29, 1935, p. 1; July 31, 1935, p. 1; August 8, 1935, p. 3.

Pom-pom waving editorial: *Bismarck Capital*, July 30, 1935, n.p.

entered the weekend at 63-14-4: *Bismarck Tribune*, August 12, 1935, p. 6. The *Tribune* had the team's record at 66-14-4 following a three-game sweep of the Twin City Colored Giants. "Belting base hits almost at will"; bat from un-natural side of the plate; "the staccato-like explosions": ibid.

Johnson jacked 26 home runs: On July 13, 1935 the *Bismarck Tribune* reported Johnson had 17 home runs. He hit nine more between then and August 12. On July 6 the *Tribune* reported Johnson was hitting .444. Johnson hit .432 for the season: *Ted "Double Duty" Radcliffe*, p. 258. Paige's pitching record is a synthesis of author's game research, *Bismarck Tribune* statistics reported on July 6, 1935, and statistics in *Satchel*, p. 102.

He negotiated a deal with Wilkinson: *Bismarck Tribune*, August 12, 1935, p. 6.

Churchill left for Kansas: ibid. A number of sources say the team drove to Wichita in two cars provided by Corwin-Churchill Motors. However, the *Bismarck Tribune* of Sept 9, 1935 quotes Churchill as saying tournament expenses wound up being high because of train fare. A possible explanation for that discrepancy is that the team trainer and injured players took the train to Wichita with surplus gear that couldn't fit into those cars. There would have been a lot of extra luggage since the players were going home for the off-season after the tournament and, therefore, took along all their belongings. Also, Paige and Troupe kept cars in Bismarck and almost certainly drove them to Wichita. Neither of them returned to North Dakota after the National tournament.

CHAPTER 15

Soon Wyatt Earp blew into town: He lasted a year, from 1875–76. See Earp's bio on history.com and www.wyattearp.net.wichita.html.

"Our callow youths": *Baseball in Wichita,* by Bob Rives, p. 11 and *Wichita Beacon,* June 21, 1925, n.p.

Paige said Wichita was baseball crazy: *Maybe I'll Pitch Forever,* p. 98.

an estimated 6,000 Klan members: "Kansas Battles the Invisible Empire," by Charles William Sloan, Jr., *Kansas History Quarterly,* Fall 1974. The population of Wichita was 72,000 in the 1920 Census.

No incidents of violence, 10–8 score: "Beating the Klan: Baseball Coverage in Wichita Before Integration, 1920-1930," *Baseball Research Journal,* Winter 2008, pp. 51–61.

Raymond Dumont: Biographical details from his obituary, *Wichita Beacon,* July 4, 1971, p. 1; and *Baseball's Barnum* by Bob Broeg, pp. 1, 7, 29.

Theater packed with native Greeks: Interview with former NBC employee Bill Kentling, February 4, 2010.

Ate ice cream for breakfast, leaving clothes in hotels: *Baseball's Barnum,* pp.178, 53; slobber on shirts, forgot stop signs: interview with former NBC employee Charlie Cookson, January 15, 2010; afraid to fly: interview with Dumont's stepson Ray Eden, January 15, 2010; sat on his hats: Bob Considine column, *Washington Post,* December 30, 1940; books Swedish wrestling champ: *Lawrence (Kansas) Journal World,* November 11, 1926, n.p.

the circus came to town, the game grossed $1,600: *Baseball's Barnum,* p. 32. Dumont's biography on nbcbaseball.com says clowns played in that ball game.

"I had to comb the state": *Wichita Eagle,* February 16, 1959, n.p.; none of them could afford socks: ibid.

Baseball and equipment were purchased from Goldsmith's: *Baseball's Barnum,* p. 32.

Dumont met with city manager Bert Wells: *Wichita Eagle*, February 16, 1959, n.p.

An industrial tract called Payne's pasture: Interview with former NBC employee Steve Shaad, February 15, 2010.

"If that city'll put up a good baseball park": *Wichita Eagle*, February 16, 1959, n.p.

Some $60,000 in Civil Works Administration funds: *Wichita Eagle*, February 6, 1934, n.p.

Goldsmith had access to Wells: Interview with Charlie Cookson, January 15, 2010.

Plans call for $125,000 stadium: *Kansas: A Guide to the Sunflower State*, Federal Writers' Project, p. 304.

Gladys found a small pimple: *Wichita Eagle*, January 29, 1934, p. 1; to hospital on Friday: ibid, January 30, 1934, p. 2; Erysipelas diagnosis: *Baseball's Barnum*, p. 36.

broadcast emergency messages: *Wichita Eagle*, January 30, 1934, p. 2; train delayed for Dumont: ibid, p. 8.

Associated Press news brief: *The Kansas City Star*, January 29, 1934, p. 10.

pallbearers: (I believe Pete Lightner was mistakenly identified as "Paul Lighter") and Lightner's column: *Wichita Eagle*, January 30, 1934, pp. 2, 8.

stadium dimensions: *Wichita Eagle*, February 8, 1934; seating capacity increases: *Wichita Eagle*, July 22, September 17, and November 22, 1934.

previous attempts: *Baseball: The People's Game*, p. 268.

1935 NBF tournament and 1934 Kansas tournament: *Elyria (Ohio) Chronicle Telegram*, September 5, 1935; *Steubenville (Ohio) Herald*, September 12, 1936 (which notes that Petrolia, Pensylvania, won the 1936 NBF tourney), p. 283.

Denver Post Tournament: baseball-reference.com and "The Denver Post Tournament and Pre-Organized Baseball Integration" by Eric Mark Stoneberg, Arizona State University master's thesis, August 2009, pp. 44–45, 50–51, 55.

predicted payout: *The Sporting News*, July 18, 1935, p. 2.

"Mr. Spink, if you carry me": *Baseball's Barnum*, p. 53.

"Most promising jailbird": Edwin Pitt's biography entry at bioproj.sabr.org, Philadelphia Athletics Historical Society, and www.baseball-reference.com.

More than 300 teams: *Wichita Eagle*, August 8, 1935, n.p.

Inquiries from ten brothers teams: Associated Press, July 18, 1935, n.p.

"world championship family team": *Wichita Eagle*, August 16, 1935. Other details: ibid, see Pete Lightner column.

Ten teams travel more than 1,000 miles: *Wichita Beacon*, August 8, 1935.

Pinch hitter named Ball: *Wichita Eagle*, August 25, 1935.

Nushida: *Carroll (Iowa) Daily Herald*, August 31, 1935 and *Honolulu Record*, August 3, 1956.

"Every big league scout in the south" and McClure's 14 shutouts: *Wichita Eagle*, August 11, 1935.

"We came here to win": *Wichita Eagle*, August 13, 1935.

The Associated Press reported: *Wichita Beacon*, August 10, 1935, p. 5; "There was a strict watch out for gambling": *Wichita Eagle*, June 27, 1935, Lightner column.

$10,000 in pre-tournament expenses: *Wichita Eagle*, August 13, 1935, Lightner column.

Churchill wired back: *Wichita Eagle*, July 18, 1935, Lightner column.

it cost Hap Dumont $1,000: Payment confirmed in interview with Paul Roberts, February 1, 2012. Roberts worked for Dumont and saw him write a $1,000 check and hand it directly to Satchel Paige.

"We're all ready": *Wichita Eagle*, August 13, 1935, Lightner column.

CHAPTER 16

Record 105 degrees: *Wichita Eagle*, August 12, 1935; half corn crop gone: ibid, August 12, 1935, n.p.

gobbled up 1,100 miles: *Wichita Beacon*, August 8, 1935, n.p. Precise distance from Bismarck: 1,134 miles.

Agreed to play six innings: "The Fabulous Satchel Paige," *Collier's*, May 30–June 13, 1953, p. 86; "the show staged by Satchell[sic] Paige": *McPherson (Kansas) Daily Republican*, August 14, 1935, p. 7.

Haley sauntered over: There are multiple, sometimes conflicting, versions of the McPherson game. I relied most heavily on the *Daily Republican*'s. There also was a wire service story that ran on August 28 in the *Winnipeg Free Press* and other papers. In addition, there are accounts in Quincy Troupe's

autobiography, *Twenty Years Too Soon;* Mark Ribowsky's biography of Satchel
Paige, *Don't Look Back;* the 1953 *Collier's* article on Paige; and *Pitchin' Man.*
I used some details from those conflicting accounts. Haley walking behind
the mound is from *Twenty Years Too Soon,* p. 56, although I had to slightly
amend the dialogue to make it compatible with events as described in the
Daily Republican. Troupe's version had the infield standing idly and sitting
down. The *Daily Republican* has Haley first stepping behind the mound, then
Paige waving off the infield. Troupe seems to have confused the McPherson
game with one played a few weeks before in Pierre, South Dakota. The box
score indicates no clowning took place in Pierre.

Legged out a triple; hard grounder up the middle: *McPherson Daily Republican,* August 14, 1935, n.p.

"Now, lookah, heah": *Twenty Years Too Soon,* p. 56.

Churchill made the decision to call in the outfield and also bet on the game:
Pitchin' Man, p. 53.

Paige "entered baseball's hall of fame": *Don't Look Back,* p. 129. Author
Mark Ribowsky doesn't say what date the McPherson wire story ran in
the *Baltimore Afro-American.* However, that same wire story appeared in
the *Winnipeg Free Press* on August 28, 1935.

Lined up outside Hotel Broadview for parade: *Wichita Eagle,* August 13,
1935, n.p. Former NBC employee Charlie Cookson confirmed in a January 15, 2010 interview that the hotel was NBC tournament headquarters.
Wichita native and baseball historian Bob Rives confirmed the Douglas
Avenue parade route in a January 18, 2012 interview.

Wagner negotiated access to one tournament player: *Emporia (Kansas) Gazette,*
June 28, 1935; Wagner's hectic schedule: *Wichita Eagle,* August 14, 1935, n.p.

Wichita segregated school system and reverse busing: "School Desegregation in Wichita, Kansas," a staff report by the U.S. Commission on Civil
Rights, August 1977, p. 3. Dockum lunch counter remained segregated
until 1958: civil rights leader Ronald Walters's obituary, *New York Times,*
September 14, 2010.

A black team applied to play: "Jim Crow Strikes Out" by Jason Pendleton,
Kansas History, Summer 1997, p. 95; black teams confined to ball field: ibid,
p. 91 and interview with Bob Rives, January 19, 2012.

Fewest restrictions: Interviews with former NBC employee Paul Roberts,
February 1, 2012 and Wichita resident Bob Rives, December 8, 2011 confirmed the integrated seating policy at Lawrence Stadium.

Miss Jones ran a boardinghouse: *Ted "Double Duty" Radcliffe*, p. 115; $3 a night and two meals: *Don't Look Back*, p. 130; Radcliffe and Juanita: *Ted "Double Duty" Radcliffe*, p. 115.

"How to run a tournament": *Wichita Eagle*, August 13, 1935, Lightner column.

general admission tickets: *Wichita Beacon*, August 9, 1935; Midland Valley Railroad yard: interview with Paul Roberts, February 1, 2012; "Coal Car Grandstand" name: interview with Bob Rives, December 8, 2011; "Tightwad Hill" name: *Wichita Eagle*, August 29, 1947, p. 15 and Lightner column.

If he kept still: Dumont's stepson Ray Eden said in January 14, 2010 interview that Hap only sat in the press box.

"circulating in poor company": *Wichita Eagle*, August 15, 1935; Cementers red uniforms: *Wichita Beacon*, August 27, 1935, p. 13.

He sent a telegram to the sports department: *Bismarck Tribune*, August 15, 1935, n.p.

Churchill promised Paige another car: *Wichita Beacon*, August 15, 1935, p. 3; *Bismarck Tribune*, August 29, 1935, p. 1.

Paige interview baloney: *Wichita Beacon*, August 15, 1935, n.p.

"Moose Johnson has him beat": *Wichita Eagle*, August 16, 1935, Lightner column; Moose wore size 14 spikes: *San Antonio Express*, March 22, 1938, n.p.

"I've been following major league baseball": Undated 1935 column by Jack Carberry of the *Denver Post*.

"We know Satchel is good": *Wichita Eagle*, August 13, 1935, n.p.

"strange" water Paige drank: *Wichita Eagle*, August 16, 1935, n.p.

A rumor might have made Paige forget: *Pitchin' Man*, p. 54.

Visibly woozy and wobbly: *Wichita Eagle*, August 16, 1935. Jiggs Maxwell first name confirmed by Tom Aiello in a January 29, 2012 e-mail interview.

Highpockets Johnson pitched for Monroe: Game accounts from *Wichita Eagle*, *Wichita Beacon*, and *Bismarck Tribune*, August 16, 1935. Box scores credited Paige with 16 strikeouts. A few days later the total was revised to 17: see *Wichita Beacon*, August 19, Jack Copeland's column. I changed the word "sixteen" to "seventeen" in one Copeland quote to reflect that strike out correction.

Radcliffe stuck a slice of steak into glove: *Ted "Double Duty" Radcliffe*, p. 113.

"He struck out seventeen men": *Wichita Beacon*, August 16, 1935, p. 15.

"wish we could find a chemical bleach": ibid, Lightner column; Slapnicka's full name and other scouts at the tournament: *Wichita Eagle*, August 17, 1935, Lightner column.

Siedhoff invited scouts and Dumont to lunch: *Wichita Beacon*, August 17, 1935, p. 12A; "simon-pure" comment: *Arizona Independent Republic*, August 24, 1935, p 12; Ira Thomas objects to mixed-race teams: *Wichita Eagle*, August 18, 1935, Lightner column; Dumont meeting with managers: *Arizona Independent Republic*, August 24, 1935, p.12 and *Wichita Eagle*, August 21, 1935, Lightner column.

Fritz and Lena Deike: Unless otherwise noted, Deike family details come from *Oh, Brother How They Played the Game: The Story of Texas' Greatest All-Brothers Baseball Team*, by Carlton Stowers.

They were a team: *Paris (Texas) News*, August 19, 1935, p. 6.

"We all grew about a foot taller": *Oh, Brother How They Played the Game*, p. 57. Names of all the Deike brothers: *Wichita Eagle*, August 18, 1935.

Contrast that résumé with the Stanczaks: *Wichita Eagle*, August 18, 1935, n.p.; they changed the spelling of their surname: *Oh, Brother How They Played the Game*, p. 57.

"If you expect to get a hit:" ibid, p. 51.

He had pitched a dozen times in Wichita: *Wichita Eagle*, August 18, 1935, n.p.; Paige called him Dooflackem: *Satchel*, p. 85.

Radcliffe sat in dugout: *Ted "Double Duty" Radcliffe*, p. 116.

"the wonder man of pitching": *Wichita Beacon*, August 19, 1935, n.p.

"Don't think for a minute" and Churchill's bets in Wichita: Undated August 1935 column by Jack Carberry of the *Denver Post*.

CHAPTER 17

a quite different threat: *Bismarck Capital*, September 5, 1935, n.p.

"William the Walker": *Wichita Eagle*, August 25, 1935, n.p.

"America's most complete document": *Buffalo Evening News*, August 17, 1935, n.p.

"That's fine, but": *Wichita Eagle*, August 23, 1935, Lightner column.

"Folkses, y'all lookin'": *Wichita Beacon*, August 20, 1935, Jack Copeland column.

Bismarck's games accounting for: *Wichita Eagle*, August 25, 1935, Lightner column.

"really see something": August 1935 undated Jack Carberry column from the *Denver Post;* Satchel will bounce back: *Wichita Eagle*, August 20, 1935, n.p.; Coburn Jones prediction: ibid.

Unorthodox: *Galveston Daily News*, May 3, 1933, n.p.; lonely figure near foul line: *Wichita Eagle*, August 22, 1935, Lightner column.

Thomas came to the conclusion: *Wichita Eagle*, August 17, 1935, Lightner column.

kids wanted a souvenir: ibid, August 23, 1935, Lightner column.

Coals exited in high style: *Wichita Eagle*, August 22, 1935, n.p.; headline: *Buffalo Evening News*, August 23, 1935, Section 2, p. 23.

Wick Corwin, who'd discovered: *Bismarck Tribune*, August 24, 1935, p. 1.

State Recreation Parlor: Description comes, in part, from comments by Frank Vyzralek of the Bismarck Historical Society in a letter to the author dated April 13, 2011. He grew up in Minot, which had similar pool halls/sports bars. State Rec issued beer license: *Bismarck Tribune*, November 21, 1933. State Rec off-limits to women: interview with Vern Dresbach's daughter, Muriel Dresbach Copeland, April 14, 2011. Sold boxing and baseball tickets: *Bismarck Tribune*, March 31, 1936; May 21 and September 26, 1934.

He umpired ball games: *Bismarck Tribune*, July 8, 1933; boxing competitions: November 11, 1934 and June 10, 1938; sang in chorus: November 23, 1935; ringmaster at dog show: May 4, 1936.

"The strong point": *Gastonia (North Carolina) Daily Gazette*, August 22, 1935, n.p.

"Heavner grounded out to Brewer": *Bismarck Tribune*, August 23, 1935, p. 10. The paper printed a complete transcript of the Western Union play-by-play.

Eleven teams now remained: "Ark City Loses Out," *Wichita Eagle*, August 23, 1935, n.p.; "We fear Duncan": ibid.

"Satchel is popular": *Wichita Eagle*, August 24, 1935, Lightner column.

"Satchel Paige is a hero": *(Wichita) Negro Star,* August 24, 1935, n.p.

"You boys just wait": Unmarked, unidentified clip in the Churchill family scrapbook. It's likely from the *Wichita Beacon* or *Eagle.* Teammates to present him a wristwatch: *Wichita Eagle*, August 23, 1935, p. 8.

"Surely that Friday game": *Wichita Eagle*, August 25, 1935, Lightner column.

Kice again interceded: *Wichita Eagle*, August 25, 1935; outfielder hurt: *Ted "Double Duty" Radcliffe*, p. 118; "For a moment it looked": *Wichita Beacon*, August 25, 1935, n.p.

"not an Ethiopian war dance": *Wichita Eagle*, August 25, 1935; Paige caricature appears in September 6 *Kansas City Call* and August 28 *Bismarck Tribune*.

"I'm shoa gonna have": *Bismarck Tribune*, August 24, 1935, n.p.

"Some of the colored clubs": *Wichita Eagle*, July 23, 1935, Lightner column; "hand it to the colored players": ibid, August 22, 1935.

Two scouts were seated in front of him and locker-room scene that followed: *20 Years Too Soon*, p. 57.

punish a baseball like Jimmie Foxx: *Wichita Eagle*, August 15, 1936, Lightner column; Johnson put Eissler's pitch into orbit: *Bismarck Tribune*, August 27, 1935, n.p.

"Omaha's entry": *Omaha World-Herald*, August 25, 1935, n.p.

"Satchel can be beaten": *Wichita Eagle*, August 25, 1935, Lightner column.

Paige pronounced himself: *Wichita Beacon*, August 27, 1935, p. 13; Paige to "shoot the works" and title "in the bag": *Bismarck Tribune*, August 26, 1935, n.p.

"Mr. Halliburton," as everyone called him: Interview with Pee Wee Carey, former Halliburton employee and director of Stephens County Historical Society, October 20, 2011.

CHAPTER 18

He came from humble beginnings: Parts of Halliburton's early biography come from 1900 and 1910 U.S. Census data and the Oklahoma Historical Society Web site: http://digital.library.okstate.edu/encyclopedia/entries.

"the two best things": Oklahoma Historical Society Web site.

Relocated to northern Texas: Society of Professional Engineering Web site; www.spegcs.org/en/art/19/

branching out into Canada and selling cementing machines: halliburton.com corporate Web site.

By 1935 he had: *Washington Post*, July 4, 1935, n.p.

Duncan's homestead and store: Duncan Convention and Visitors bureau Web site, www.duncanok.org and Duncan DAR Web site, www.oklahomadar.org.

Merchants organized a baseball team: "A Tale of Two Cities" by Royse Parr, *NINE: A Journal of Baseball History and Culture,* Fall 2006; his kid brother John did play: *Duncan (Oklahoma) Banner,* June 21, 1992.

He launched a company: "Halliburton-by-the-Sea" by David Sheff, *New York Times,* May 2, 2004, n.p.

Went 31-9: *Duncan Banner,* June 21, 1992, n.p.; see also *Baseball: The People's Game,* pp. 252–253.

"An advertising and good-will venture" and other details: ibid.

"I'd rather be playing": Associated Press story in *Hartford Courant,* September 1, 1939, n.p.

"8-to-1 ahead of the squawks": Associated Press story in *Washington Post,* July 4, 1935, n.p.

"Just how good is Satchel?": *Wichita Eagle,* August 27, 1935, Lightner column.

"I never faced a pitcher as fast": ibid.

"Congratulations for playing a good game": *Wichita Eagle,* August 27, 1935, n.p.

CHAPTER 19

"listening to the report of Satchel Paige": *Wichita Eagle,* August 30, 1935, n.p.

George Raft had box seat: *Ted "Double Duty" Radcliffe,* p. 120; J. L. Wilkinson: *Wichita Beacon,* August 25, 1935, n.p.

for fear of being a "jinx": *Duncan Banner,* August 31, 1936, n.p.

lean-on-a-lamppost hung over: *Wichita Eagle,* August 15, 1936, Lightner column on Neil Churchill's recollection of the 1935 finale. *Ted "Double Duty" Radcliffe,* p. 119; many years later Joe Desiderato recalled Johnson never coming to the game and being found the next day passed out in the street. Churchill's recollection was fresher and seems more plausible.

"Ten thousand people out here": *Maybe I'll Pitch Forever,* p. 99.

"he looked funny": *Wilber "Bullet" Rogan and the Kansas City Monarchs* by Phil S. Dixon, p. 208. Teammate Connie Johnson made that comment about Hilton Smith.

Umpires had to call time out: *Bismarck Tribune,* August 28, 1935; see inning-by-inning recap.

Paige enjoyed talking about his hitting: *Twenty Years Too Soon*, p. 56.

Lined the second pitch: *Daily Oklahoman*, August 28, 1935; over Jones' head: *Wichita Eagle*, August 28, 1935, n.p.

"Homey, there's work to be done": *Ted "Double Duty" Radcliffe*, p. 120.

Paige took half an hour: *Wichita Eagle*, August 28, 1935, p. 4; Churchill in dugout and locker room: ibid.

Jack Copeland paid homage: *Wichita Beacon*, August 28, 1935, p. 1.

Editorial writers across the state: *Mandan Pioneer*, August 29, 1935, p. 5; *Grand Forks Herald*, August 30, 1935, p. 10; *Valley City Times*, September 3, 1935, p. 2; *Jamestown Sun*, August 28, 1935, n.p.

"Baseball fans, not only of Bismarck": *Minneapolis Tribune*, August 29, 1935, p. 21.

piling up 66 strikeouts and other statistics: *Bismarck Tribune*, August 28, 1935, see Paige cartoon, p. 6.

tournament all-star team: *Wichita Eagle*, August 29, 1935, Lightner column.

Scouts signed fourteen prospects: NBC ad, *The Sporting News*, April 30, 1936, p. 12; thinking of making offers to Desiderato and Leary: *Bismarck Tribune*, September 11, 1935, n.p.

"Some perplexing problems": *Wichita Eagle*, August 29, 1935, Lightner column.

more than 20 telegrams: *Wichita Beacon*, August 28, 1935, p.10; guaranteed him $3,000: *Wichita Eagle*, August 29, 1935, n.p.

Churchill cuts the cord: Multiple sources. *Wichita Eagle*, August 29, 1935, J. L. Wilkinson objected to Johnson playing in Bismarck's post-tournament games with the Monarchs because Moose technically was still on the suspended list from the Western League and Wilkinson didn't want any problems with organized baseball. Johnson's name doesn't appear in any post-tournament box scores I found. *Wichita Eagle*, August 15, 1936, Churchill told Pete Lightner he "severed connections" when Moose showed up hungover for the 1935 championship game.

Only 1,000 tickets sold and crowd booed: *Wichita Beacon*, August 29, 1935, n.p. Churchill and Wilkinson had hoped to sell 8,000 tickets. Monarchs drubbed Bismarck 8-0: *Bismarck Tribune*, August 31, 1935, p. 6.

stopped in Burlington, Colorado: ibid, September 3, 1935, n.p.; Paige plays biography ball: *Omaha World-Herald*, September 4, 1935, n.p.

Paige struck out fifteen Monarchs: *Kansas City Call*, September 6, 1935, p. 12. *Bismarck Tribune*, September 5, 1935, p. 8, has a wire story that says Paige struck out sixteen. I gave preference to the local paper's account.

"my last game as a baseball manager": *Pitchin' Man*, p. 54. Paige says Churchill offered him $750 to win that game, which sounds preposterously high. But if Churchill had put a large bet down, who knows?

Troupe and Paige hooked up with the Monarchs: *Bismarck Tribune*, September 11, 1935, n.p.; *20 Years Too Soon*, p. 58; "the man of the hour": *Bismarck Tribune*, September 11, 1935.

check from Dumont for $2,542 and team broke "almost even": *Bismarck Tribune*, September 13, 1935. The *Tribune* reported on August 29 that the winner's share was $2,551.87.

"This job is one that requires": *Bismarck Tribune*, September 11, 1935, n.p.

Job as a store detective: *Bismarck Tribune*, April 9, 1936, n.p.; entered Golden Gloves: *20 Years Too Soon*, p. 65.

"DiMaggio all we hoped for": *Don't Look Back*, p. 137; "I'm probably drawin' more money": ibid, p. 138.

CHAPTER 20

Rebecca Churchill succumbed: *Bismarck Tribune* obituary, July 16, 1936, n.p.

"the faithful colored servant": Nancy Millett obituary, *Boots and Saddles* mention and other details, *Bismarck Tribune*, July 25, 1936, n.p.

"team abruptly disbanded": *Bismarck Tribune*, July 7, 1936, n.p.; difficulties in finding opponents: ibid and *Bismarck Tribune*, August 5, 1936, n.p.

Bismarck players waive pay: *Bismarck Tribune*, July 16, 1936, n.p.

WPA had built new clubhouse: *Bismarck Tribune*, April 9, 1936, n.p.

Paige back on board: ibid; Paige again would pitch for Crawfords: *Don't Look Back*, p.141; "as spectacular as a circus": *Pittsburgh Courier*, May 9, 1936, n.p.

seats inside the dugout: *Bismarck Capital*, April 28, 1936, n.p.; selling non-profit stock: *Bismarck Tribune*, April 14, 1936, p. 4 and April 27, 1936.

merchants showed their support: *Bismarck Tribune*, May 28, 1936 article and advertisement; special leather-bound Bible: *Bismarck Tribune*, June 23, 1936, n.p.

only 800 people came out: *Bismarck Tribune,* June 8, 1936, n.p.; fewer than 500 tickets: *Bismarck Tribune,* August 12, 1936. The *Tribune* says crowd of 500 for that game was second-biggest of the season. On August 11 the paper mistakenly says that the crowd of 600 was the largest of the season.

Full-page ad and "a team that will give": *Bismarck Tribune,* July 16, 1936, n.p.

guaranteeing a top prize of $5,000: *The Sporting News,* March 5, 1936, n.p.

Dustbowl Special train: "The Case of the Inappropriate Alarm Clock," *New York Times,* October 18, 2009, n.p.

Bob McCarney lent his convertible and other details: *Bismarck Tribune,* August 28, pp. 1–2. A photo in the paper shows President Roosevelt seated in his car chatting with farmer Mike Hellman and his son.

8.8 inches of precipitation: *History of North Dakota,* p. 10.

Declared a day of prayer; purchase cattle: "The Case of the Inappropriate Alarm Clock," *New York Times,* Oct. 18, 2009.

"Give us water": *Bismarck Tribune,* August 29, 1936, p. 4 editorial.

Nearly half the state on relief now: *History of North Dakota,* p. 10.

The city's six hottest days: *Wichita Eagle,* August 11, 1936, n.p.

"This column has felt": *Wichita Eagle,* August 11, 1936, Lightner column.

In another column: *Wichita Eagle,* August 7, 1936. Lightner did not identify the particular Paige game in New York. Most likely it was July 26, when the Crawfords played the Brooklyn Bushwicks in front of 12,000 fans. That was the Bushwicks' largest crowd of the year, according to the *Brooklyn Eagle* of August 27. Lightner, however, mentions a crowd of 19,000. That probably was an error on his part.

Frank Kice met for two hours: *Wichita Eagle,* August 12, 1936, n.p.

He'd long ago quietly pledged: It's well known that when Rickey coached baseball at Ohio Weslyan University in 1903 he was appalled at the prejudice directed against Charles Thomas, the only black on the team. Rickey said that experience motivated him to integrate the Dodgers in 1947.

New shortstop brought in: *Bismarck Tribune,* May 15, 1936, n.p; adding Negro League veterans: *Bismarck Tribune,* August 27, 1936 and *Ted "Double Duty" Radcliffe,* p. 134.

"the greatest step forward": *Wichita Beacon*, August 9, 1936, n.p.

Wagner and Tris Speaker: ibid; reputation soiled by Klan ties: among other sources see *Tris Speaker: The Rough and Tumble Times of a Baseball Legend* by Timothy M. Gay.

He couldn't expand his business by alienating: *Atlanta Daily World*, July 26, 1937. Dumont acknowledged "there has been some agitating" regarding his inclusion of mixed teams.

It would take about five years: *Wichita Eagle*, August 17 and August 21, 1936. Three black teams competed at Wichita in 1936, one in 1937, one in 1938, one in 1939, two in 1940, and none in 1941: from author's reading of the *Wichita Eagle*.

"Eleven negro and 5 white players": *Wichita Eagle*, August 16, 1936, n.p.

Churchill had injuries to worry about: *Bismarck Tribune*, August 27 and August 28, 1936, p. 10; Desiderato leg infection: *Bismarck Tribune*, August 11, 1936, n.p.

Hilton Smith stepped out of character: "Smith's Talent Began to Blossom" by Lou Babiarz, *Bismarck Tribune*, August 5, 2001, n.p.

"Bismarck is the best fixed club": *Wichita Eagle*, August 27, 1936, Lightner column; Churchill pegged his team's odds: ibid, August 22, 1936, Lightner column.

"Call my boy" telegram: *Bismarck Tribune*, August 28, 1936, n.p.

Radcliffe suspected Trent: *Ted "Double Duty" Radcliffe*, p. 135.

"while employees oohed and ahhed": *Baseball: The People's Game*, p. 285.

Bismarck declined consolation game: *Wichita Eagle*, August 31, 1936, Lightner column.

He was not "making alibis" and "semi-balk delivery": *Bismarck Tribune*, September 4, 1936, n.p.

"hot-action photo": *Wichita Eagle*, August 21, 1936, n.p.

Lightner fretting: *Wichita Eagle*, August 30, 1936, Lightner column; letter "worth reading": ibid, September 1, 1936, n.p.

they bumped into Dumont: *20 Years Too Soon*, pp. 66–67.

Leary and Slefka got signed: *Bismarck Tribune*, September 4, 1936, n.p.; Troupe went home: *20 Years Too Soon*, p. 67.

CHAPTER 21

Lieutenant Colonel Huston: Fort Lincoln Web site. "There's hell and there's Dakota": E-mail interview with Kim Fundingsland, North Dakota journalist and historian, March 10, 2012. General Philip Sheridan used the same words to describe Texas. Fundingsland believes Huston said it first.

42 days below zero: Pioneer Trails Regional Museum radio interview with North Dakotans Josie Andrews and Kelly Oien, March 19, 1942.

Dropped the hammer for good: *Bismarck Tribune*, May 21, 1937, n.p.; all-amateur Bismarck Independents: ibid, June 7, 1937, n.p.; Haley retained as player-manager: ibid, June 17, 1937; second baseman was "just up from junior [American] Legion ranks": ibid, July 3, 1937. Last mention of 1937 team in the *Tribune* was July 24, 1937.

Haley drifted north: "Red Haley's Acme Giants," *Winnipeg Free Press*, July 9, 1938, p. 23.

Vantine Cubs open season: *Bismarck Tribune*, May 19, 1937; $1 season tickets: ibid, May 20 , 1937.

"hasn't proved much of a drawing card": ibid, April 22, 1937, n.p.

Press covered peregrinations; Paige not out of mind: *Don't Look Back*, pp. 143–145; "to Cuba": *Bismarck Tribune*, June 11, 1937, n.p.

Trujillo's team: *Don't Look Back*, p. 157; *Satchel*, p. 109; banned Paige a second time: *New Amsterdam News*, May 8, 1937, n.p.; expat players broke the bank: *Don't Look Back*, p. 157.

Satchel headed south of the border: ibid, pp. 165–170; "Ten years of gravy": ibid, p. 171.

Bringing black teams to town: *Bismarck Tribune*, July 14, 1938, July 2 and July 20, 1939; Saperstein urged Churchill: Interview with Randy Churchill, October 3, 2011.

Fraternal Order of Eagles formed: 118 2nd Street listing in 1938 Bismarck City Directory; Shipley president: *Bismarck Tribune*, September 21, 1936, p. 1 and October 6, 1936, p. 2.

a false wall and Glitter Gulch: Interview with Stan Sharkey, former gopher at the Patterson Hotel poker games, February 2, 2011; "I have everything in this pot . . . ," ibid. Sharkey was present when Churchill said that.

"Are you crazy?": *Bismarck Tribune*, September 3, 1952, n.p.

"I am going to bat for Bismarck": *Bismarck Tribune*, April 3, 1939, p. 3; keep Bismarck "the metropolis of Western North Dakota,": ibid, April 1, 1939; Churchill won in a landslide: ibid, April 5, 1939. Churchill got 3,125 votes, his two opponents a combined 1,516.

Whoopee Room and casserole: Interview with Randy Churchill, July 16, 2009.

"stormed the free popcorn stand": *Bismarck Tribune*, October 9, 1941, p. 1.

Volunteers from the American Legion: ibid, December 8, 1941.

One-third of family farms, population migration: *History of North Dakota*, pp. 400–401.

"Neil Churchill Leaves Town": *Bismarck Tribune*, September 4, 1952; committees and meetings: ibid, September 3, 1952, n.p.

Received a monthly stipend: Interview with Sam Corwin's son, Charlie, August 17, 2009. "His attorney and my dad knew he'd spend it [a lump payment] in a week."

CHAPTER 22

"Diamond Dinner": *Chicago Daily Tribune*, January 22, 1950, n.p.; Roosevelt Davis a waiter: ibid, January 27, 1950, n.p.

Managed the company's black team: *Sandusky-Register*, April 29 and August 10, 1941, n.p.

"Very sociable": Interview with Dorothy Farrar, April 26, 2011.

Everybody but the sports editor: *Sandusky-Register*, September 16, 1948, n.p.

Good knuckler, crisp fastball: Morris entry on www.pitchblackbaseball.com. He reportedly threw 90 mph.

He ricocheted among teams: baseball-reference.com and *Monessen (Pennsylvania) Daily Independent*, February 7, 1941, p. 5. Morris was with Monterrey Industriales and Carta Blanca in Mexico; driving a cab in Queens: pitchblackbaseball.com.

His 87–63 win-loss record and broke the color line in Mexico: baseball-reference.com; pitched in foreign countries and forty-four states: Brewer's Negro Leagues Baseball Museum online biography, www.nlbm.com.

"The only thing a one-armed man": *Des Moines Register*, April 1, 1984, n.p.

Player-manager of California Comets, Watts ball field bears his name: Negro Leagues Baseball Museum online biography of Brewer.

Believed Commissioner Landis banned him: Interview with Desiderato's nephew, Terry Sullivan, September 12, 2009.

Indians signed Desiderato: *Zanesville (Ohio) Signal*, March 3, 1945, p. 9; dumped by Indians: *Charleston (West Virginia) Daily Mail*, May 22, 1945, p. 8; with Lafayette Red Sox: *Benton Harbor (Michigan) News-Palladium*, May 13 and Sept. 20, 1949, and August 8, 1950.

.571 average: *Wichita Eagle*, August 31, 1937, n.p.

"If he would just behave himself": *Wichita Eagle*, August 31, 1937, Lightner column.

Johnson's marriages, lumberjacking and other details: Interviews with his daughter, Hilma Jones, February 28 and April 23, 2010, and June 29, 2012.

Took a taxi 300 miles: Interview with Johnson's nephew Duane Johnson, March 16, 2010.

"A happy, happy guy": Interview with Johnson's nephew Donald Johnson, March 17, 2010.

Bob McCarney details from his biography on file at the University of North Dakota's Chester Fritz Library, repository of his personal papers.

All Leary's military experience and combat fatigue diagnosis come from his file at the National Personnel Records Center. Statistics for the battle of Saipan are the most conservative numbers available.

"One of the strongest sluggers": *Helena Independent-Record*, May 25, 1946, n.p.

returned to his old job: Leary obituary, *Great Falls Tribune*, March 1, 1985; Great Falls Brewery closed 1968: ibid, November 11, 2007.

Ted Trent biography details: baseball-reference.com.

Lightner perished in plane crash: *Indiana Evening Gazette*, July 5, 1960, n.p.

"The Negro boys": *Wichita Eagle*, July 3, 1960, p. 6B, Lightner's last column.

Lorena Hickok fell victim to hard times: *One Third of a Nation*, pp. xxxiv–xxxv and George Washington University's Eleanor Roosevelt Papers Project; www.gwu.edu/~erpapers/teachinger/glossary/hickok-lorena.cfm.

"I was just about the top gal reporter": Hickok letter to James Thompson, July 23, 1949.

Hap Dumont met a woman at a cigar counter: *Baseball's Barnum*, p. 66.

Forty-nine states and twenty-nine countries: *Wichita Eagle*, February 16, 1959, n.p.

first to arrive at work, last to leave: Interview with former NBC employee Bill Kentling, February 4, 2010.

letting batters run the bases: *Baseball's Barnum*, p. 13; *Time*, January 24, 1944, n.p.

extra umpire in bucket of crane: *Time*, March 16, 1942, n.p.

pneumatic duster: *Wichita Eagle*, August 12, 1984, p. 8D.

Sandlot Baseball Museum: Associated Press, December 24, 1953, n.p.

tests batting helmets: *Pittsburgh Press*, June 26, 1940, n.p.

electric eyes: *Washington Post*, December 30, 1940, Bob Considine column; also *New York Times*, July 5, 1971, p. 22.

Woman umpire: *Wichita Eagle*, August 5, 1943. Dumont also used a woman umpire for the Wisconsin state tournament that summer: *Farmers Advocate*, April 9, 1943.

Designated hitter experiment: Wire story in *Joplin (Missouri) Globe*, January 30, 1941; twenty-second clock: *Baseball's Barnum*, p. 14.

Las Vegas Army Horned Toads and Camp Wheeler Spokes: *Wichita Eagle*, August 16, 1943; all-military tournament: ibid, August 15, 1945, p. 15.

Died with boots on, found by umpire: *Wichita Eagle*, July 4, 1971, p. 1; also *Sporting News*, July 12, 1971, p. B1. Name changed to Lawrence-Dumont Stadium: Interview with Casey Stewart, National Baseball Congress account executive and clubhouse manager, March 26, 2012.

"Just throwing that old apple": Unidentified clip in Baseball Hall of Fame files from the 1940s with Hugh S. Gardner byline.

learned to pitch in Kansas City: *Voices from the Great Black Baseball Leagues* by John Holway, p. 287.

"He just played baseball": *Kansas City Star*, March 6, 2001, n.p.

Smith checked out young infielder: *Voices from the Great Black Baseball Leagues*, pp. 283–284.

Elected to stay with Monarchs: *Voices from the Great Black Baseball Leagues*, p. 292 and baseball-reference.com.

"I won 161 games": *Voices from the Great Black Baseball Leagues*, p. 281.

Wrote a letter to the Hall of Fame: Smith's entry on baseball-reference.com and the SABR Biography Project, http://sabr.org/bioproj/person/a4c98932.

He hired Paige in 1939: *Satchel* by Larry Tye, p. 122.

"the miracle was passed": *Pitchin' Man*, p. 61.

Easily got waylaid: *Satchel*, pp. 152–153.

Smith served as body double: Smith's entry on baseball-reference.com and SABR Biography Project.

"hurt me down deep": *Don't Look Back* by Mark Ribowsky, p. 231 and *Anderson (Indiana) Herald*, November 23, 1955, n.p.

Put the news on front page: *Bismarck Tribune*, July 16, 1948, p. 1. Arthur Daley's quote originally appeared in *The New York Times*, July 8, 1948.

More than 200,000 people: *Maybe I'll Pitch Forever*, p. 12.

"one of the last surviving": *Collier's*, May 30, 1953, n.p.

served divorce papers at Wrigley Field: *Satchel*, pp. 158–160 and *Don't Look Back*, p. 221. He was served on Satchel Paige Day, July 17, 1943: *Oakland Tribune*, July 17, 1943.

both Ted Williams and Joe DiMaggio rated him the best: Williams called Paige "the greatest pitcher in baseball," www.baseballalmanac.com; DiMaggio called him "the best I've ever faced," *New York Times*, June 9, 1982, n.p.

a minimum of 100 teams: *Pitchin' Man*, p. 44; Paige biographer Larry Tye says the total could be as high as 250, *Satchel*, p. 81.

Charged with five runs in fourteen innings: Author's review of box scores from Paige's 1960 NBC games.

got touched only for a hit by Yastrzemski: *Satchel*, p. 239.

chucking for the Indianapolis Clowns: ibid, pp. 273–274.

Referred to him as Milton Smith: *Kansas City Star*, March 6, 2001, n.p.

Paige gilded the lily: *Philadelphia Tribune*, February 14, 1950; *Pitchin' Man*, p. 53; *Chicago Daily Tribune*, June 8, 1943; *Bismarck Tribune* (quoting *Ebony* magazine), July 16, 1952.

"The best team I ever saw": *Chicago Daily Tribune*, June 8, 1943, n.p.

"There never was a man on earth": *New York Times*, June 9, 1982, n.p.

Gave sunny Mexico a try: Baseball details from Troupe's Negro Leagues Baseball Museum online profile, which relies on James A. Riley's *Biographical Encyclopedia of the Negro Baseball Leagues*.

He added an extra "p" to surname: *20 Years Too Soon*, p. 2.

"He was terrific": Quincy Troupe entry on www.pitchblackbaseball.com Web site.

Indians let him go: *20 Years Too Soon*, p. 135; Trouppe's Indian statistics from baseball-reference.com; Negro League statistics from his Negro Leagues Baseball Museum online biography.

Ken Burns dipped heavily: *20 Years Too Soon*, p. 6 and e-mail interview with Burns's producer Mike Welt, May 30, 2012.

Trouppe's Dugout: *20 Years Too Soon*, p. 126. The Dugout was located off Wilshire Boulevard near South Vermont Ave: Interview with Randy Churchill, July 15, 2009. According to Google Maps that is 4.8 miles from Dodgers Stadium at Chavez Ravine. *San Diego City Beat*, August 21, 2002 says the Dugout was on Pico Boulevard, which runs parallel to Wilshire and intersects with South Vermont Ave. Trouppe's son, Quincy Jr., says it was just called The Dugout.

"The happiness and sadness always blended": *20 Years Too Soon*, p. xiv.

"I watched a man who could turn on a fastball": ibid, p. 7. Quote confirmed in interview with Larry Lester, June 10, 2012.

Churchill loves sinking into armchair to watch sports on TV and read *Daily Racing Form*: interviews with Randy Churchill, July 1, 2008 and October 3, 2011; John Wayne movies and Louis L'Amour books: interview with Churchill family, July 16, 2009; went to the racetrack "daily for decades": interview with granddaughter Karen Gunderson, December 21, 2009.

Invest in a few thoroughbreds: Interview with Churchill family, July 1, 2008. Sea Novice was a 1947 foal of Seabiscuit and Dark Convent, www.allbreedpedigree.com. The horse won 8 of 41 races: *Seabiscuit: The Rest of the Story* by William H. Nichols, p. 116.

Gave Helen $100 for Christmas: Interview with daughter-in-law Jennifer Churchill, July 15, 2009; once lost $10,000: interview with daughter-in-law Margie Churchill, October 3, 2011. Gambled "right down to the end": Interview with Randy Churchill, July 1, 2008.

Membership in Turf Club: Interview with granddaughter Karen Gunderson, December 21, 2009.

"He wound up broke": Interview with daughter-in-law Margie Churchill, October 3, 2011.

"So he did leave us something": Interview with Churchill family, July 1, 2008.

No baseball souvenirs: Interview with daughter-in-law Margie Churchill, October 3, 2011.

Harlem Globetrotters game: *Bismarck Tribune*, July 29, 1954, n.p.

"If Paige had been a white man": ibid, September 3, 1952, n.p.

Struck out side on eleven pitches: *Bismarck Tribune*, July 29, 1954, n.p.

State Historical Society of North Dakota organized: Snow angels entry at www.guinnessworldrecords.com.

"It's fun and puts us on the map": *USA Today*, February 19, 2007, n.p.

"Both men spent": E-mail interview with Dennis Boyd, Bismarck Historical Society, March 31, 2012; confirmed in phone interview June 6, 2012.

Custer Park dedicated 1909: www.bismarckpride.com.

pushing to have ballpark named Satchel Paige Field: Interview with Dennis Boyd, president of Bismarck Historical Society, April 1, 2012. "Being the first integrated baseball team": Interview with Dennis Boyd, June 6, 2012.

Time marched on: E-mail interviews March 28, 2012 with Myron Atkinson and Jim Christianson of the Bismarck Historical Society about modern use of downtown buildings. Corwin-Churchill sold to owners from Minot: www. bismarckpride.com and confirmed by former Corwin-Churchill executive Bruce Whittey.

An original 1935 team photo and Bismarck uniform: Author confirmed sales prices with representatives of Hake's Americana & Collectibles, August 2012. Auction was held March 21, 2012.

Ball autographed by Satchel Paige: Sales price from May 3, 2008 auction posted on Heritage Auctions Web site, http://www.icollector.com/The -Earliest-Known-Satchel-Paige-Single-Signed-B_i8019064.

Bob Myhre donated a ball: Interview with Bob Myhre, April 3, 2012.

"Not just any ball": Interview with Tim Hammond, January 13, 2012. Inscriptions confirmed in e-mails from Hammond, February 19, 2012 and interview July 24, 2012.

Joe Desiderato died: *Chicago Sun-Times*, January 4, 1994, p. 61.

"Joe was my friend": Details of Joe Desiderato's viewing come from e-mail interviews with Terry Sullivan on March 25 and June 11, 2012 and a September 12, 2009 phone interview.

Thirty years worth of baseball: Details of Radcliffe's last team and his career statistics come from *Ted "Double Duty" Radcliffe*, pp. 231–235, 252.

"I remember it because I love baseball": "The Recall of Duty," *Los Angeles Times*, June 15, 2003, n.p.

INDEX